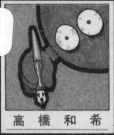

高橋和希

THIS MANGA'S BEEN RUNNING FOR OVER TWO YEARS NOW.
YU-GI-OH! CARDS AND VIDEO GAMES AND ALL SORTS OF
THINGS HAVE BEEN RELEASED, BUT STUCK HERE SITTING
BEHIND MY DESK, I CAN'T WATCH PEOPLE PLAYING THEM. I
WISH I COULD SEE YOU GUYS ENJOYING THEM. BUT IF YOU'VE
MADE A FRIEND THROUGH SHARED INTEREST IN YU-GI-OH!,
THEN I'M HAPPY THAT I MADE THIS MANGA. THAT'S WHAT
BRINGS ME THE MOST JOY.
                    —KAZUKI TAKAHASHI, 1999

Artist/author Kazuki Takahashi first tried to break into
the manga business in 1982, but success eluded him
until **Yu-Gi-Oh!** debuted in the Japanese **Weekly
Shonen Jump** magazine in 1996. **Yu-Gi-Oh!**'s themes
of friendship and fighting, together with Takahashi's
weird and wonderful art, soon became enormously
successful, spawning a real-world card game, video
games, and two anime series. A lifelong gamer,
Takahashi enjoys Shogi (Japanese chess), Mahjong,
card games, and tabletop RPGs, among other games.

YU-GI-OH!: DUELIST VOL. 6
The SHONEN JUMP Graphic Novel Edition

STORY AND ART BY
KAZUKI TAKAHASHI

Translation & English Adaptation/Joe Yamazaki
Touch-up Art & Lettering/Rina Mapa
Design/Andrea Rice
Cover Design/Sean Lee
Editor/Jason Thompson

Managing Editor/Elizabeth Kawasaki
Director of Production/Noboru Watanabe
Vice President of Publishing/Alvin Lu
Vice President & Editor in Chief/Yumi Hoashi
Sr. Director of Acquisitions/Rika Inouye
Vice President of Sales & Marketing/Liza Coppola
Publisher/Hyoe Narita

In the original Japanese edition, YU-GI-OH! and YU-GI-OH!: DUELIST are known collectively as YU-GI-OH!. The English YU-GI-OH!: DUELIST was originally volumes 8–31 of the Japanese YU-GI-OH!.

Printed in the U.S.A.

Published by VIZ, LLC
P.O. Box 77010
San Francisco, CA 94107

SHONEN JUMP Graphic Novel Edition
10 9 8 7 6 5 4 3 2 1
First printing, June 2005

THE WORLD'S
MOST POPULAR MANGA

SHONEN JUMP
GRAPHIC NOVEL
www.shonenjump.com

www.viz.com

SHONEN JUMP GRAPHIC NOVEL

Vol. 6

THE TERROR OF TOON WORLD

STORY AND ART BY
KAZUKI TAKAHASHI

⟨MAIN CAST⟩

YUGI MUTOU/YU-GI-OH
武藤遊戯

Using the power of his Millennium Eye, Pegasus stole the soul of Yugi's grandpa and forced Yugi to enter a "Duel Monsters" tournament on his private island, Duelist Kingdom. Little did Yugi realize that the tournament was all part of a plot by Pegasus to beat Yugi and gain control of Kaiba Corporation! Kaiba rushed to the island to defend his fortune and rescue his little brother Mokuba from Pegasus. But despite their common enemy, Kaiba is still no friend of Yugi's. On the parapets of Pegasus Castle, the two arch-rivals dueled over the right to fight Pegasus. And the ending of that duel was a shock to everyone involved...

SUGOROKU MUTOU
武藤双六
SETO KAIBA
海馬瀬人
MAXIMILLION J. PEGASUS
ペガサス・J・クロフォード
MAI KUJAKU
孔雀 舞
RYO BAKURA
獏良 了
KATSUYA JONOUCHI
城之内克也
ANZU MAZAKI
真崎杏子
HIROTO HONDA
本田ヒロト

THE STORY SO FAR...

When 10th-grader Yugi solved the Millennium Puzzle, he became Yu-Gi-Oh, the King of Games, a dark avenger who challenged evildoers to "Shadow Games" of life and death. Using his gaming skills, he faced deadly adversaries like Seto Kaiba, obsessive gamer and teenage corporate president, and Ryo Bakura, whose friendly personality turned evil when he was possessed by the spirit of the Millennium Ring. But Yugi's toughest opponent was Maximillion Pegasus, bearer of the Millennium Eye and super-rich creator of "Duel Monsters," the world's most popular collectible card game.

YU-GI-OH!™ DUELIST

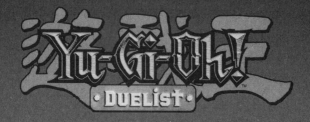

Vol. 6

CONTENTS

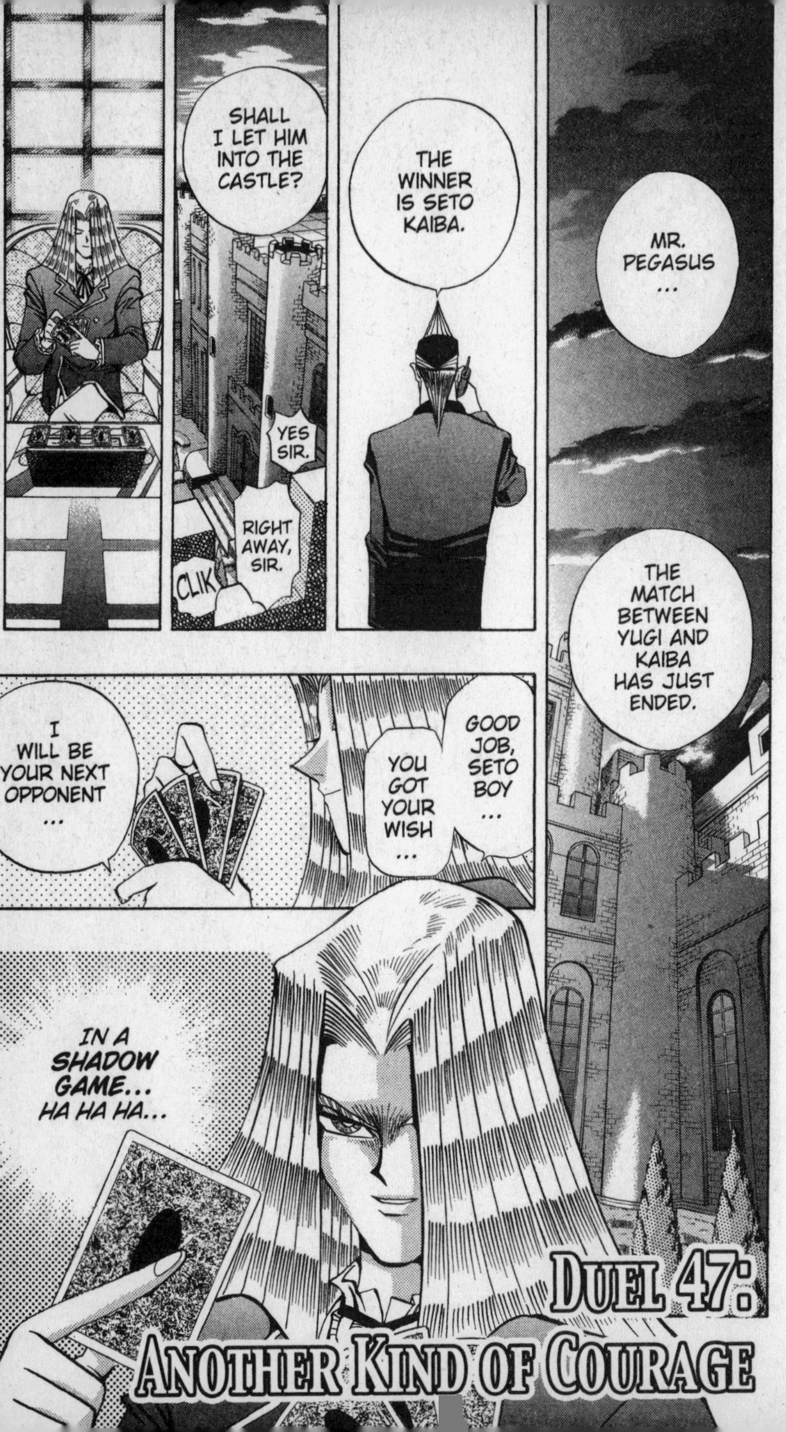
MR. PEGASUS ...
THE MATCH BETWEEN YUGI AND KAIBA HAS JUST ENDED.
THE WINNER IS SETO KAIBA.
SHALL I LET HIM INTO THE CASTLE?
YES SIR.
RIGHT AWAY, SIR.
CLIK
GOOD JOB, SETO BOY ...
YOU GOT YOUR WISH ...
I WILL BE YOUR NEXT OPPONENT ...
IN A SHADOW GAME... HA HA HA...
DUEL 47:
ANOTHER KIND OF COURAGE

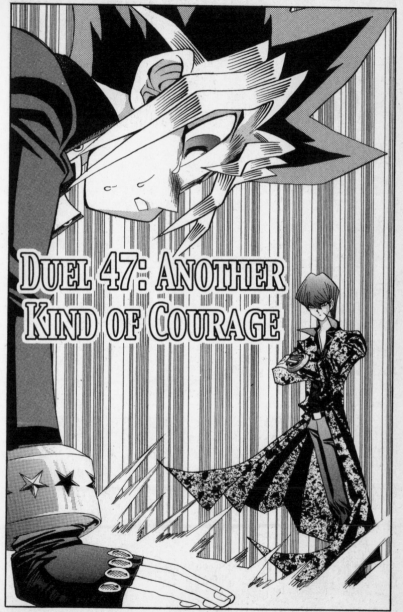

DUEL 47: ANOTHER KIND OF COURAGE

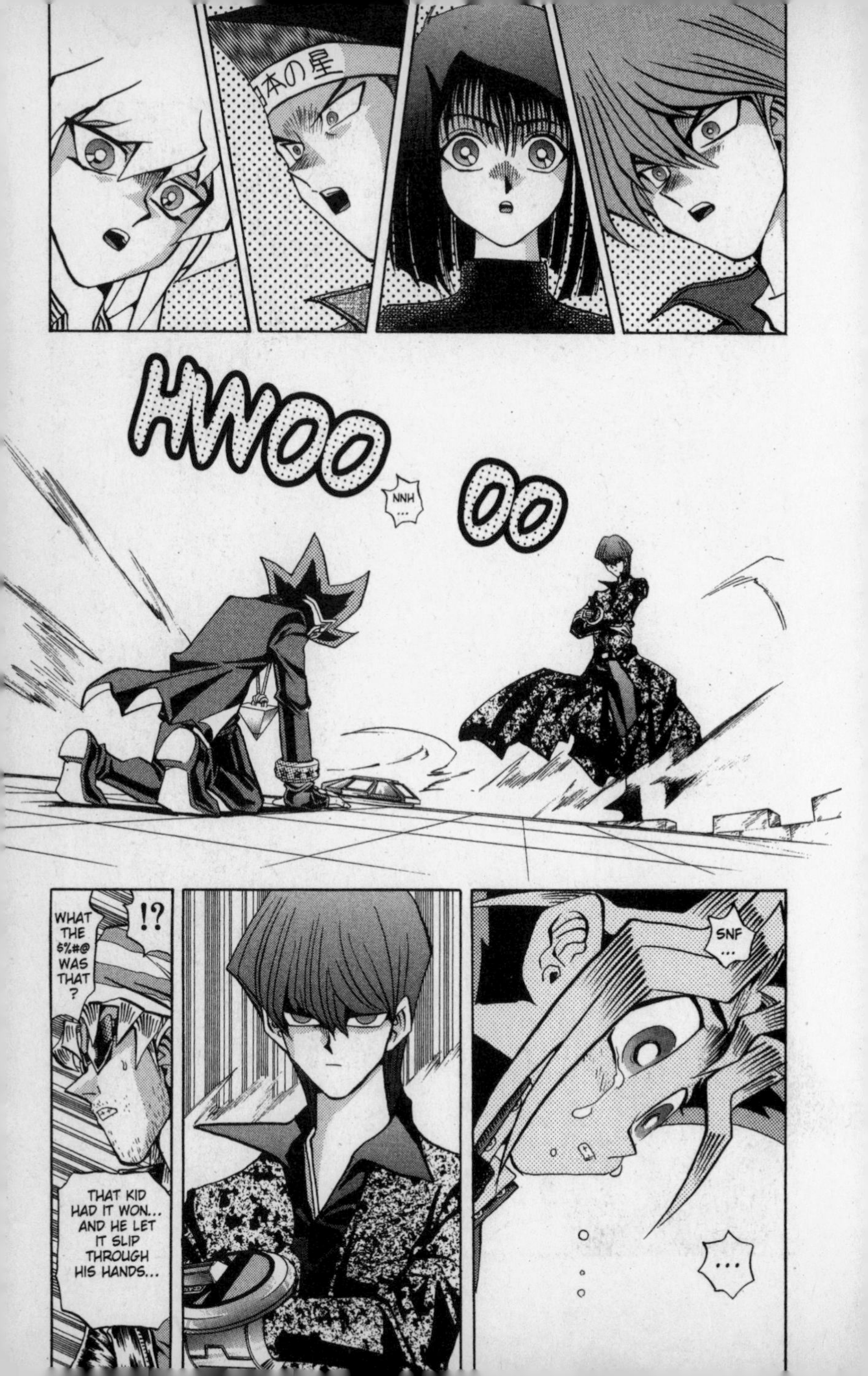
本の星
HWOO
OO
NNH...
SNF...
...
!?
WHAT THE $%#@ WAS THAT?
THAT KID HAD IT WON... AND HE LET IT SLIP THROUGH HIS HANDS...

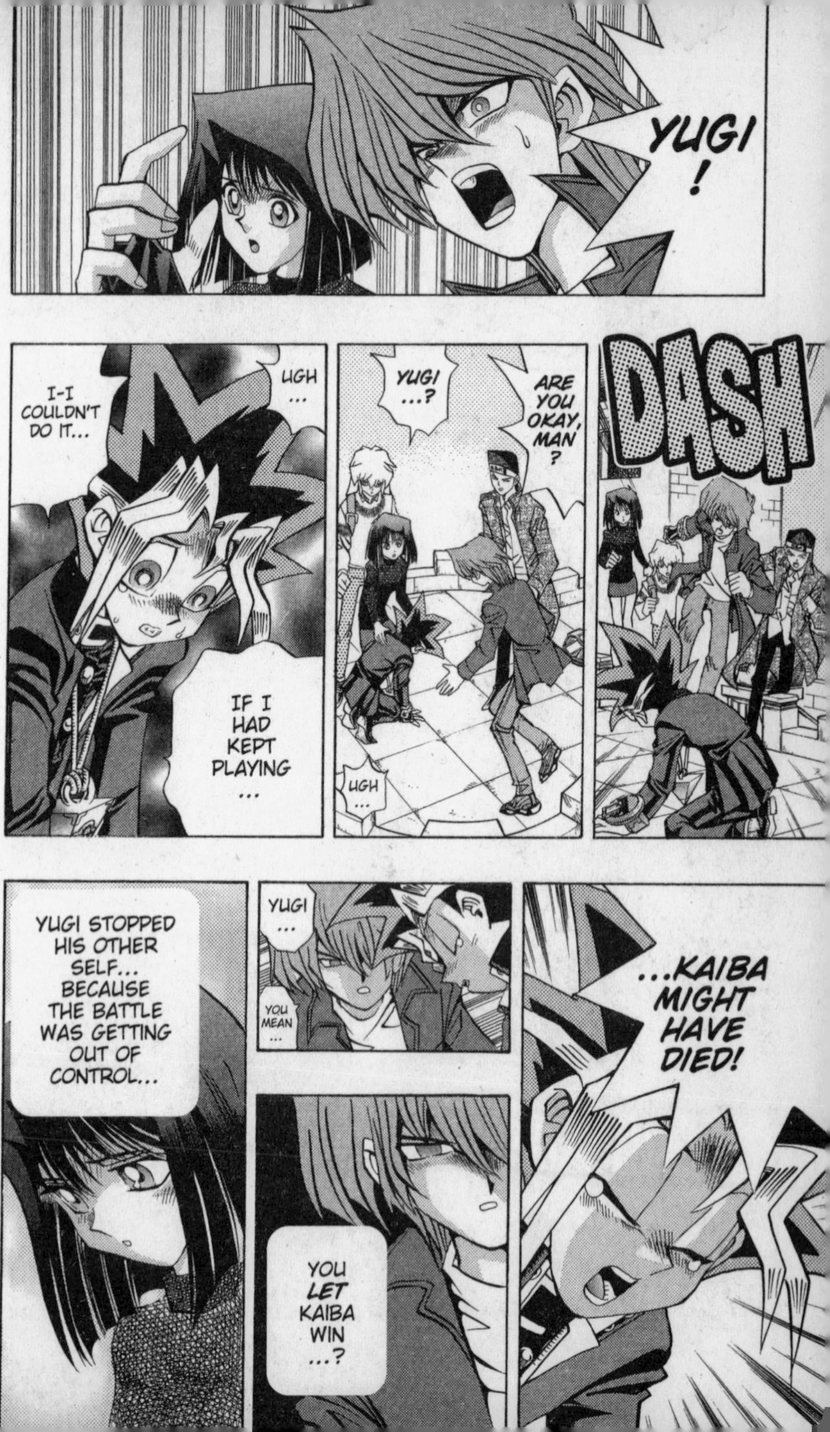
YUGI !
DASH
YUGI …?
ARE YOU OKAY, MAN?
UGH …
UGH …
I-I COULDN'T DO IT…
IF I HAD KEPT PLAYING …
…KAIBA MIGHT HAVE DIED!
YUGI …
YOU MEAN …
YOU LET KAIBA WIN …?
YUGI STOPPED HIS OTHER SELF… BECAUSE THE BATTLE WAS GETTING OUT OF CONTROL…

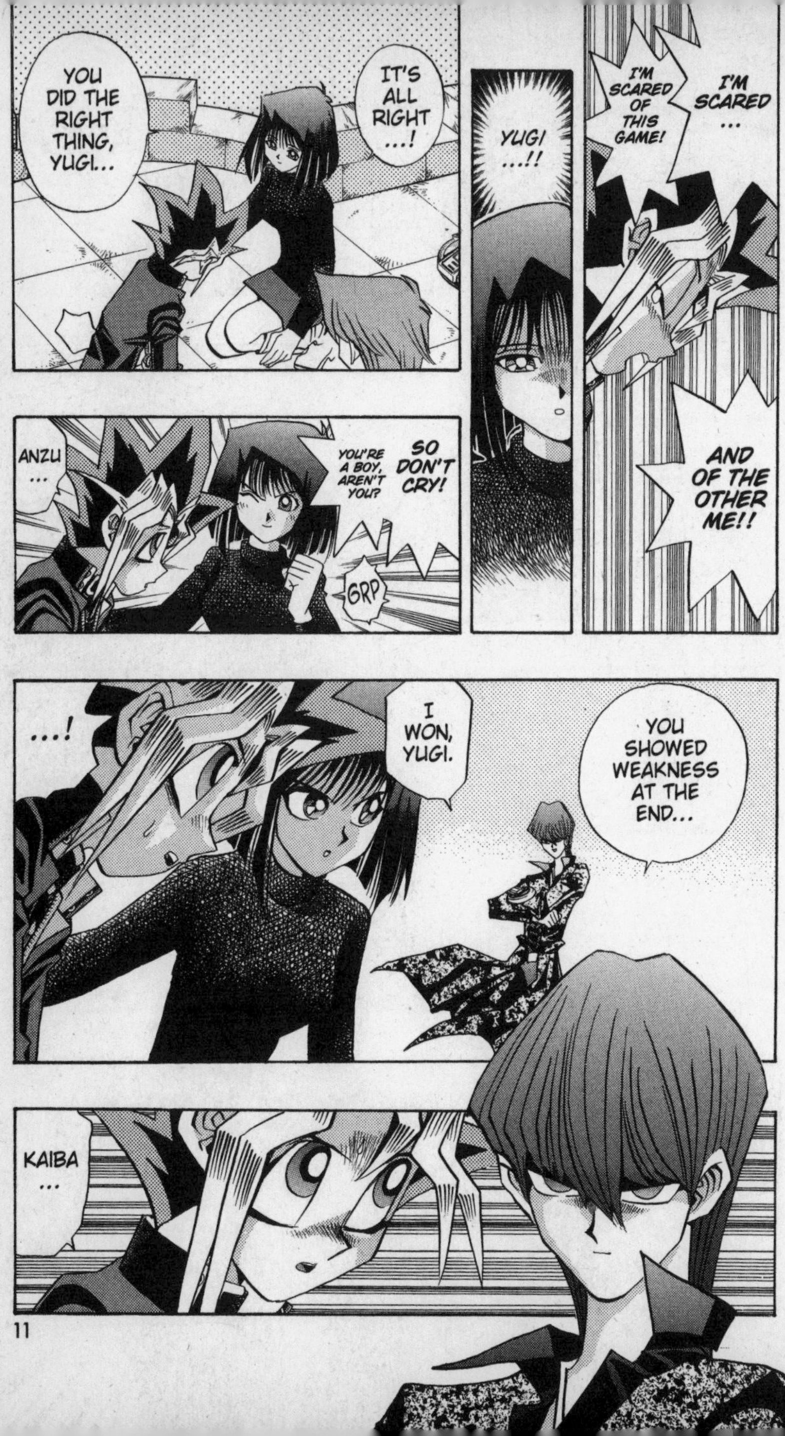
I'M SCARED...
I'M SCARED OF THIS GAME!
AND OF THE OTHER ME!!
YUGI...!!
IT'S ALL RIGHT...!
YOU DID THE RIGHT THING, YUGI...
SO DON'T CRY!
YOU'RE A BOY, AREN'T YOU?
GRP
ANZU...
YOU SHOWED WEAKNESS AT THE END...
I WON, YUGI.
...!
KAIBA...

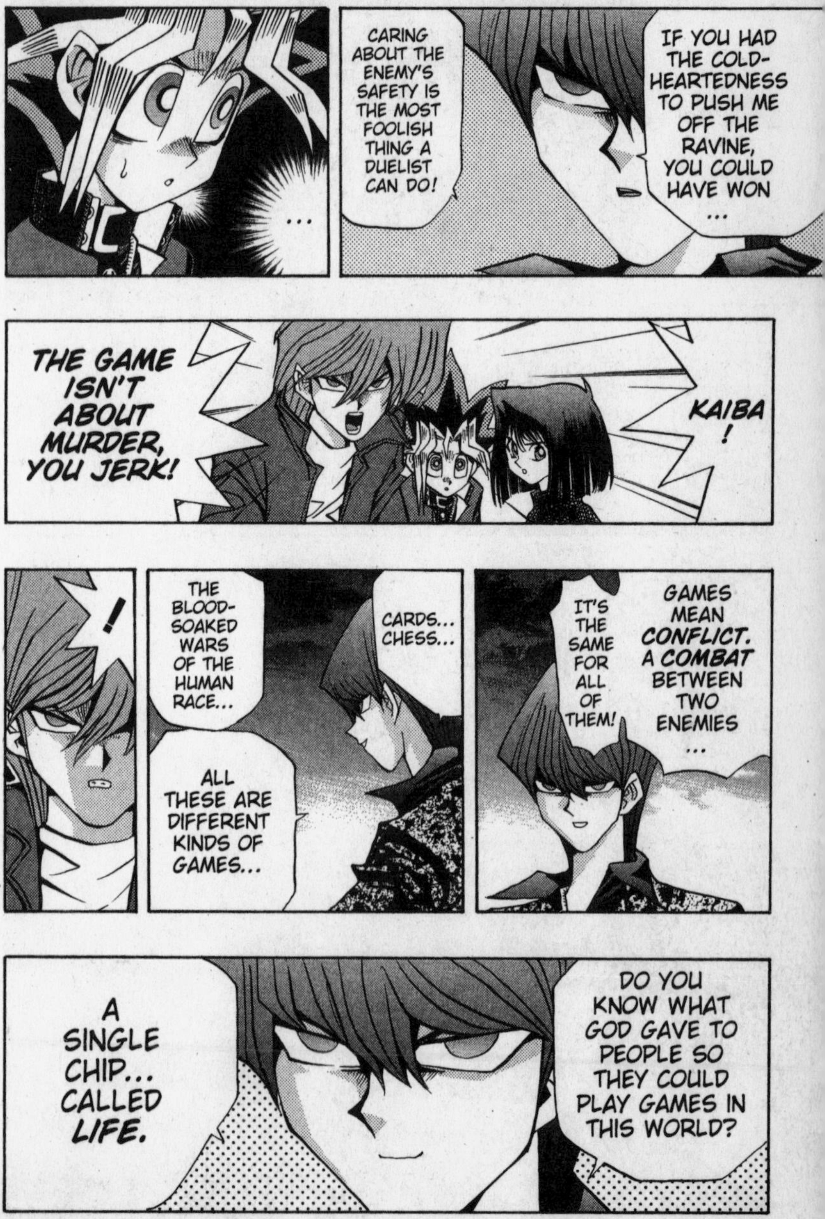
IF YOU HAD THE COLD-HEARTEDNESS TO PUSH ME OFF THE RAVINE, YOU COULD HAVE WON ...
CARING ABOUT THE ENEMY'S SAFETY IS THE MOST FOOLISH THING A DUELIST CAN DO!
...
KAIBA!
THE GAME ISN'T ABOUT MURDER, YOU JERK!
GAMES MEAN CONFLICT. A COMBAT BETWEEN TWO ENEMIES ...
IT'S THE SAME FOR ALL OF THEM!
CARDS... CHESS...
THE BLOOD-SOAKED WARS OF THE HUMAN RACE...
ALL THESE ARE DIFFERENT KINDS OF GAMES...
!
DO YOU KNOW WHAT GOD GAVE TO PEOPLE SO THEY COULD PLAY GAMES IN THIS WORLD?
A SINGLE CHIP... CALLED LIFE.

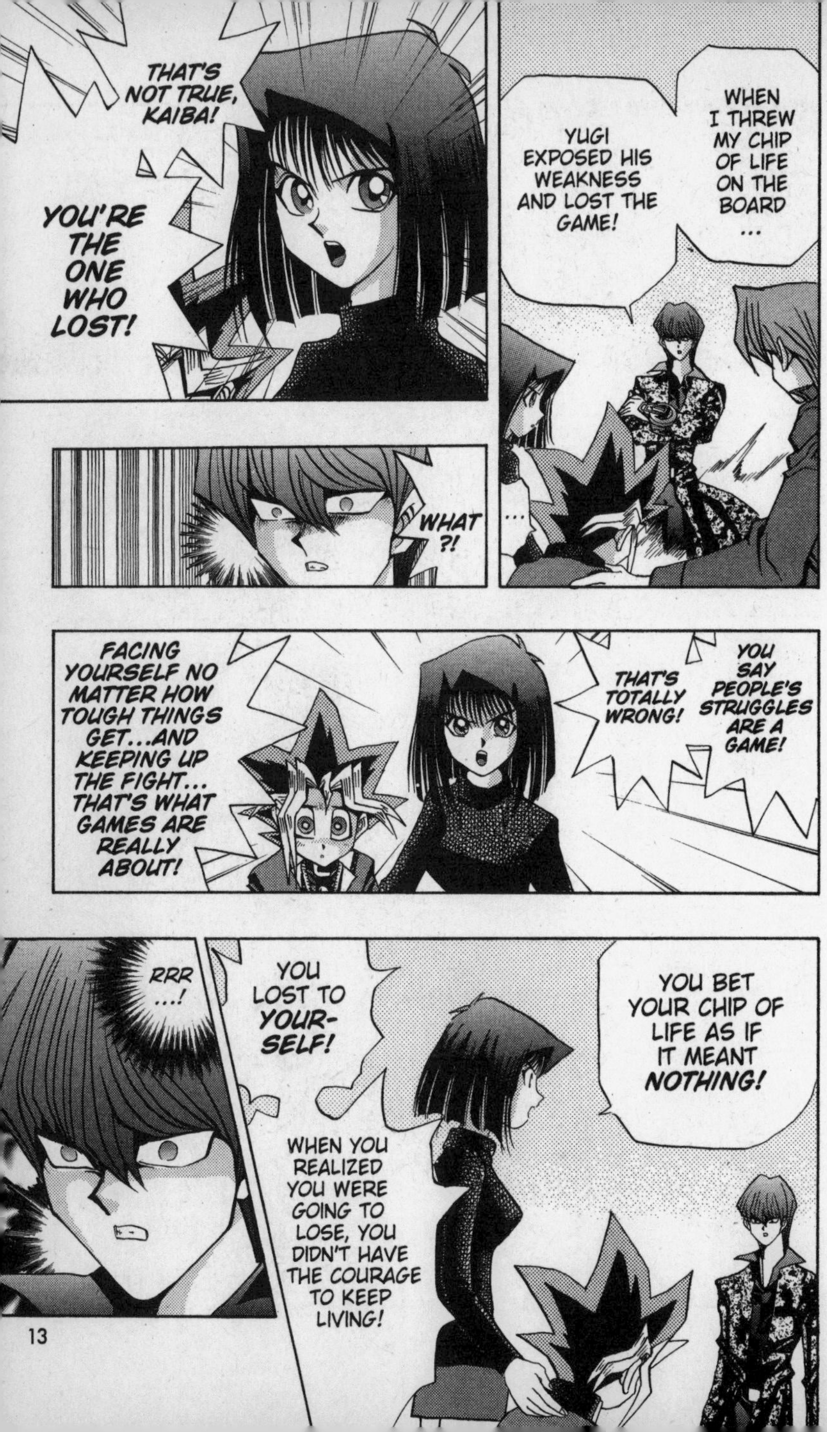
WHEN I THREW MY CHIP OF LIFE ON THE BOARD ...
YUGI EXPOSED HIS WEAKNESS AND LOST THE GAME!
...
THAT'S NOT TRUE, KAIBA!
YOU'RE THE ONE WHO LOST!
WHAT ?!
YOU SAY PEOPLE'S STRUGGLES ARE A GAME!
THAT'S TOTALLY WRONG!
FACING YOURSELF NO MATTER HOW TOUGH THINGS GET...AND KEEPING UP THE FIGHT... THAT'S WHAT GAMES ARE REALLY ABOUT!
YOU BET YOUR CHIP OF LIFE AS IF IT MEANT NOTHING!
WHEN YOU REALIZED YOU WERE GOING TO LOSE, YOU DIDN'T HAVE THE COURAGE TO KEEP LIVING!
YOU LOST TO YOURSELF!
RRR ...!

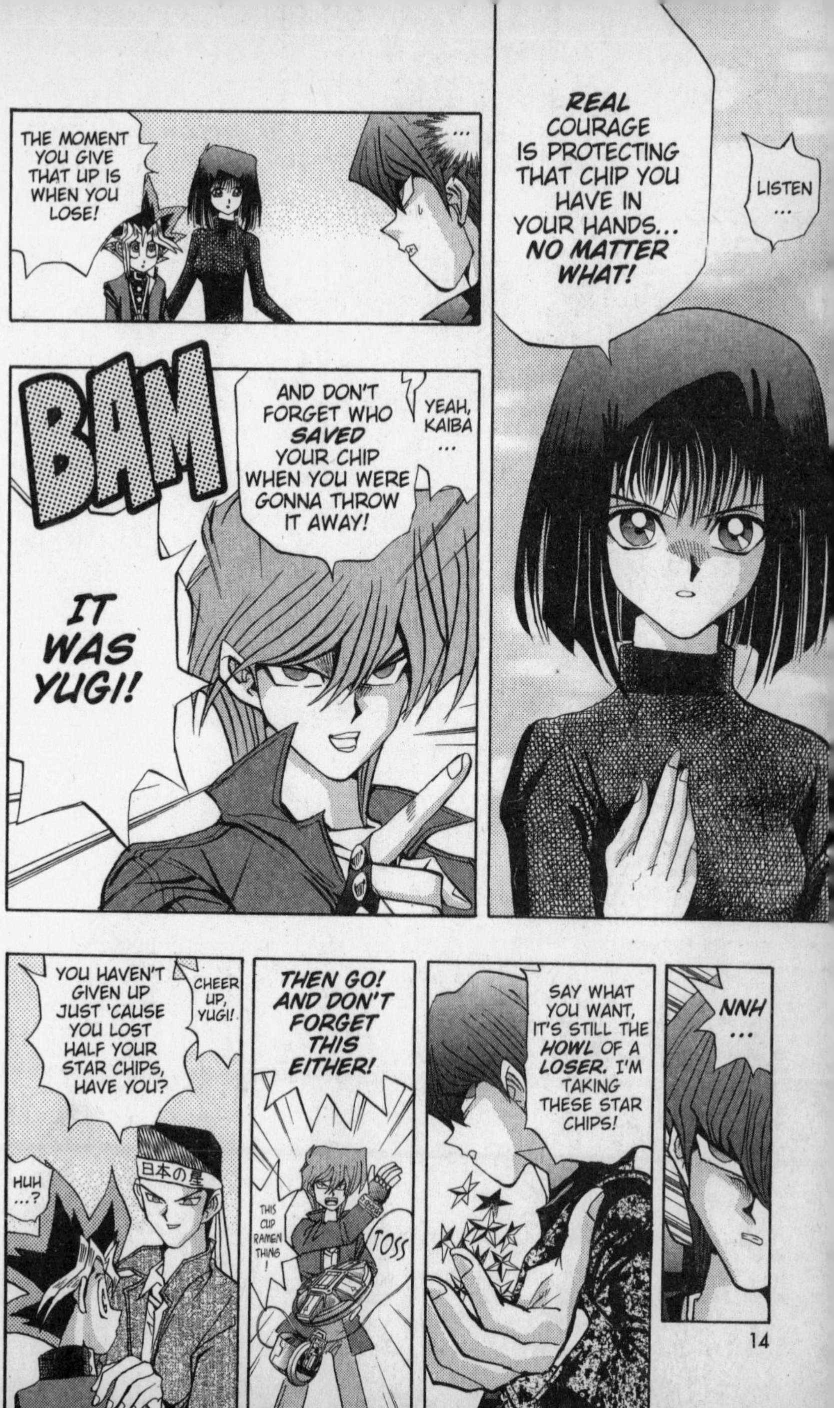
LISTEN ...
REAL COURAGE IS PROTECTING THAT CHIP YOU HAVE IN YOUR HANDS... NO MATTER WHAT!
...
THE MOMENT YOU GIVE THAT UP IS WHEN YOU LOSE!
YEAH, KAIBA ...
AND DON'T FORGET WHO SAVED YOUR CHIP WHEN YOU WERE GONNA THROW IT AWAY!
BAM
IT WAS YUGI!
NNH ...
SAY WHAT YOU WANT, IT'S STILL THE HOWL OF A LOSER. I'M TAKING THESE STAR CHIPS!
THEN GO! AND DON'T FORGET THIS EITHER!
TOSS
THIS CUP RAMEN THING!
CHEER UP, YUGI!
YOU HAVEN'T GIVEN UP JUST 'CAUSE YOU LOST HALF YOUR STAR CHIPS, HAVE YOU?
日本の星
HUH ...?

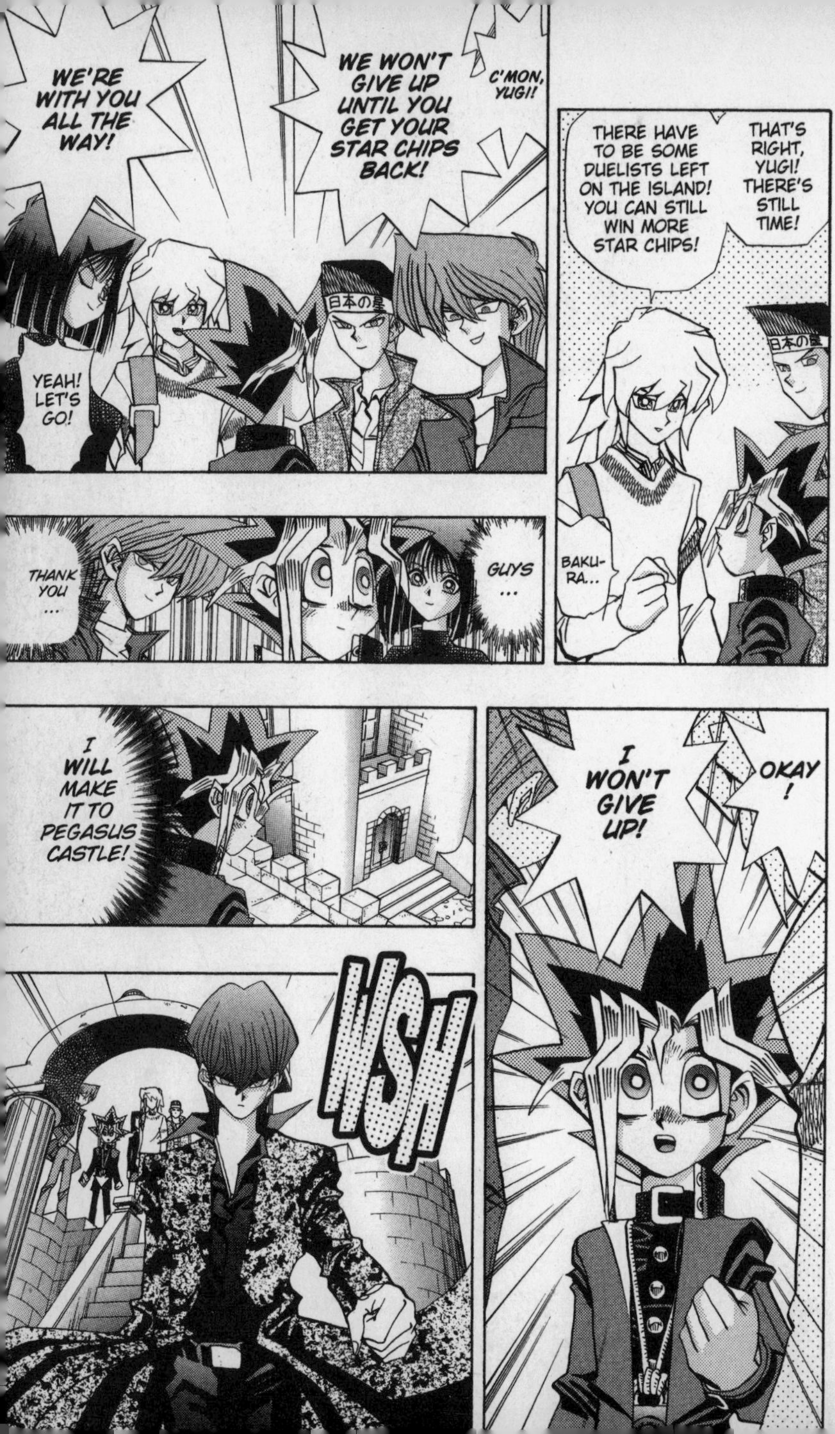
THAT'S RIGHT, YUGI! THERE'S STILL TIME!
THERE HAVE TO BE SOME DUELISTS LEFT ON THE ISLAND! YOU CAN STILL WIN MORE STAR CHIPS!
BAKU-RA...
C'MON, YUGI!
WE WON'T GIVE UP UNTIL YOU GET YOUR STAR CHIPS BACK!
WE'RE WITH YOU ALL THE WAY!
YEAH! LET'S GO!
GUYS ...
THANK YOU ...
OKAY!
I WON'T GIVE UP!
I WILL MAKE IT TO PEGASUS CASTLE!
WSH

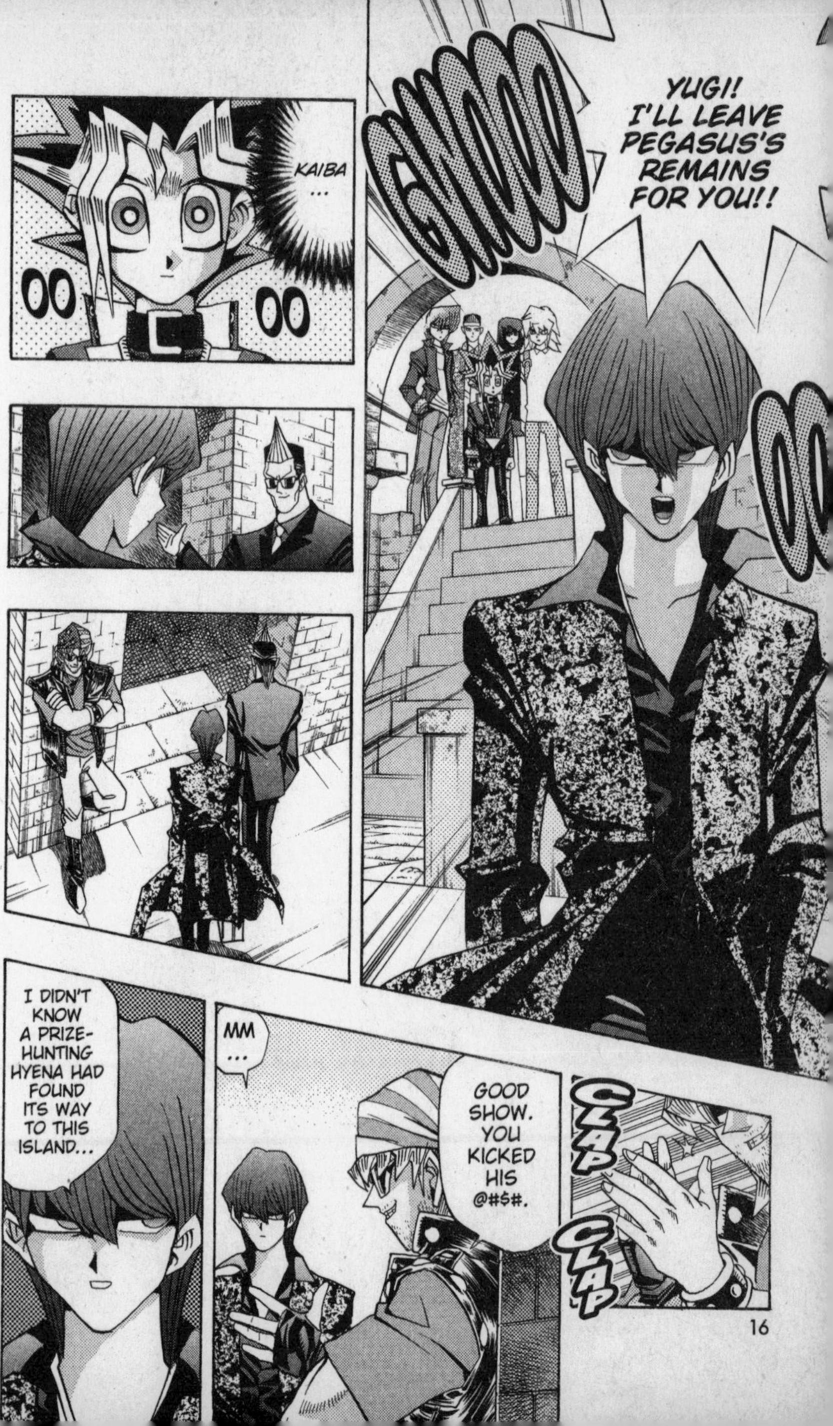
GHOOO
YUGI!! I'LL LEAVE PEGASUS'S REMAINS FOR YOU!!
KAIBA ...
OO
OO
CLAP
CLAP
GOOD SHOW. YOU KICKED HIS @#$#.
MM ...
I DIDN'T KNOW A PRIZE-HUNTING HYENA HAD FOUND ITS WAY TO THIS ISLAND...

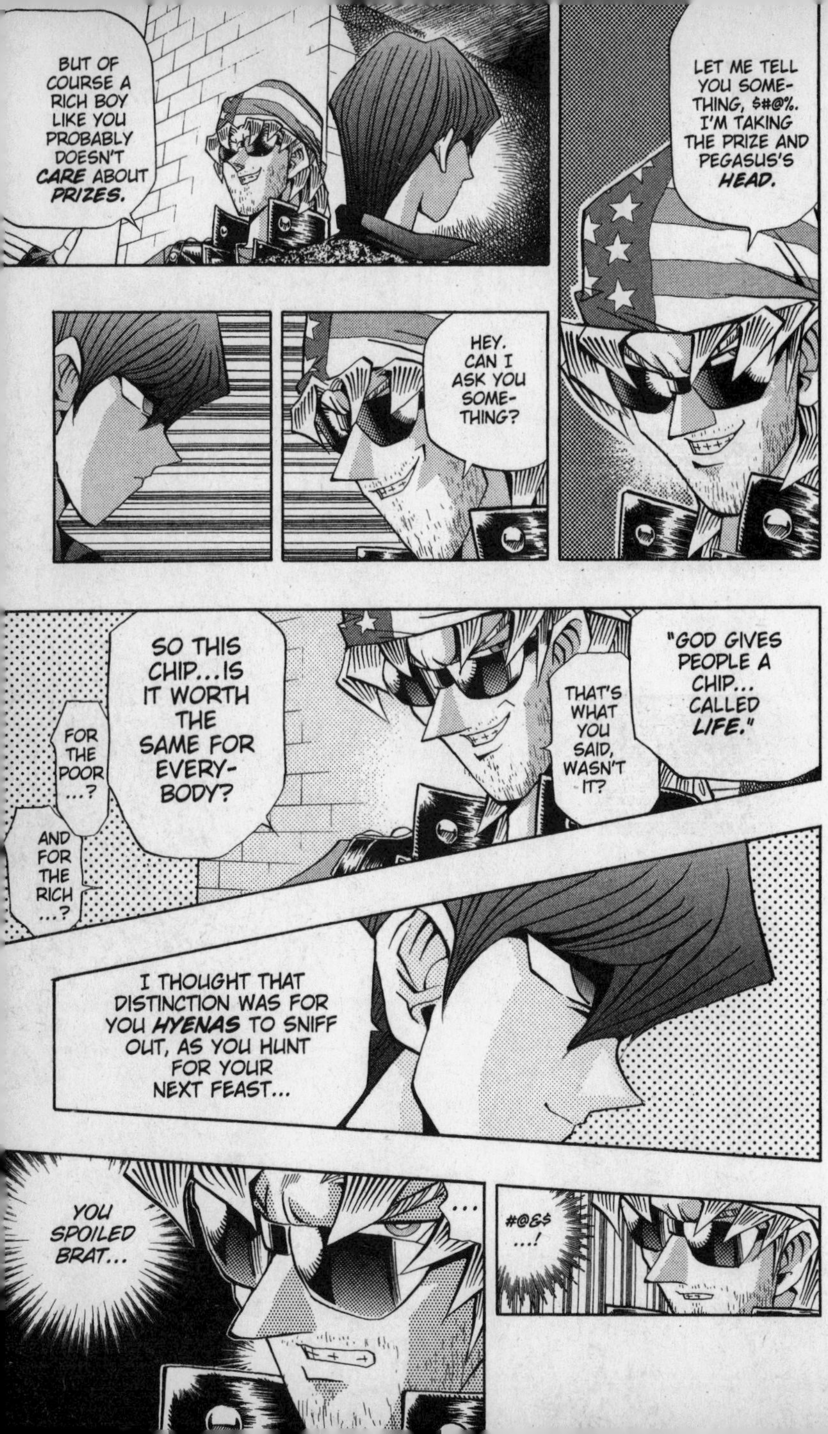
LET ME TELL YOU SOME-THING, $#@%. I'M TAKING THE PRIZE AND PEGASUS'S **HEAD.**
BUT OF COURSE A RICH BOY LIKE YOU PROBABLY DOESN'T **CARE** ABOUT **PRIZES.**
HEY. CAN I ASK YOU SOME-THING?
"GOD GIVES PEOPLE A CHIP... CALLED **LIFE.**"
THAT'S WHAT YOU SAID, WASN'T IT?
SO THIS CHIP...IS IT WORTH THE SAME FOR EVERY-BODY?
FOR THE POOR ...?
AND FOR THE RICH ...?
I THOUGHT THAT DISTINCTION WAS FOR YOU **HYENAS** TO SNIFF OUT, AS YOU HUNT FOR YOUR NEXT FEAST...
#@&$ ...!
...
YOU SPOILED BRAT...

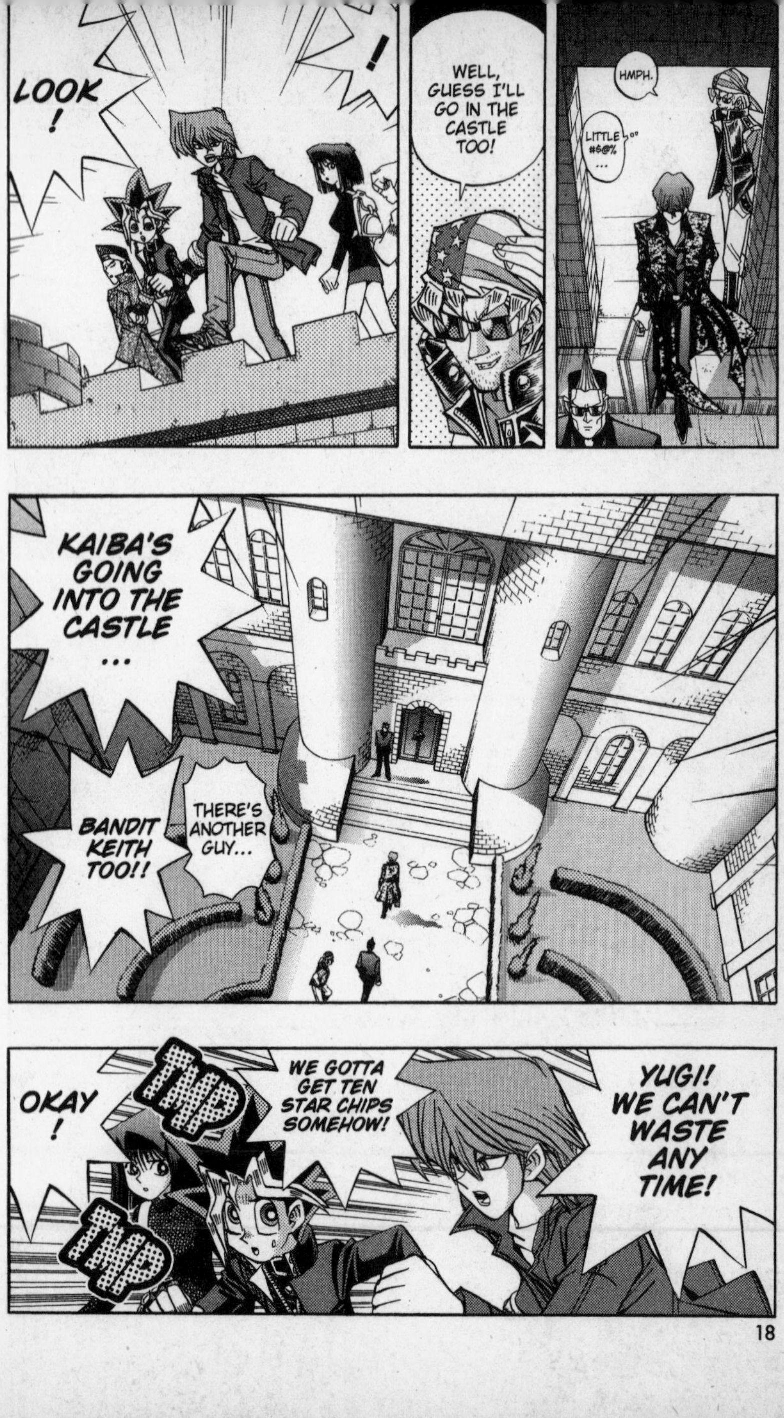
HMPH.
LITTLE #$@% ...
WELL, GUESS I'LL GO IN THE CASTLE TOO!
!
LOOK!
KAIBA'S GOING INTO THE CASTLE ...
BANDIT KEITH TOO!!
THERE'S ANOTHER GUY...
YUGI! WE CAN'T WASTE ANY TIME!
WE GOTTA GET TEN STAR CHIPS SOMEHOW!
TMP
TMP
OKAY!

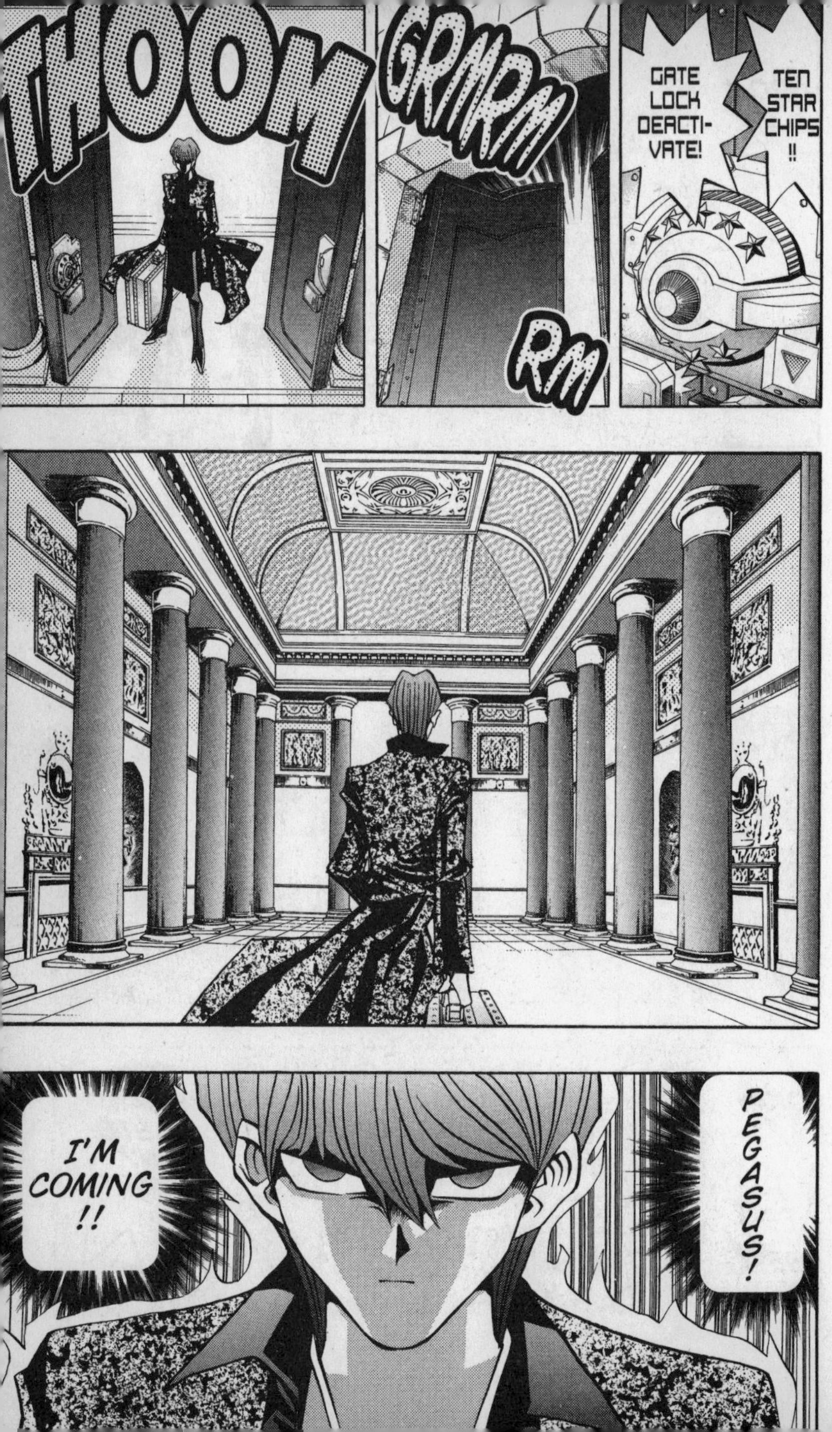
TEN STAR CHIPS !!
GATE LOCK DEACTI- VATE!
GRRRM
RM
THOOM
PEGASUS!
I'M COMING !!

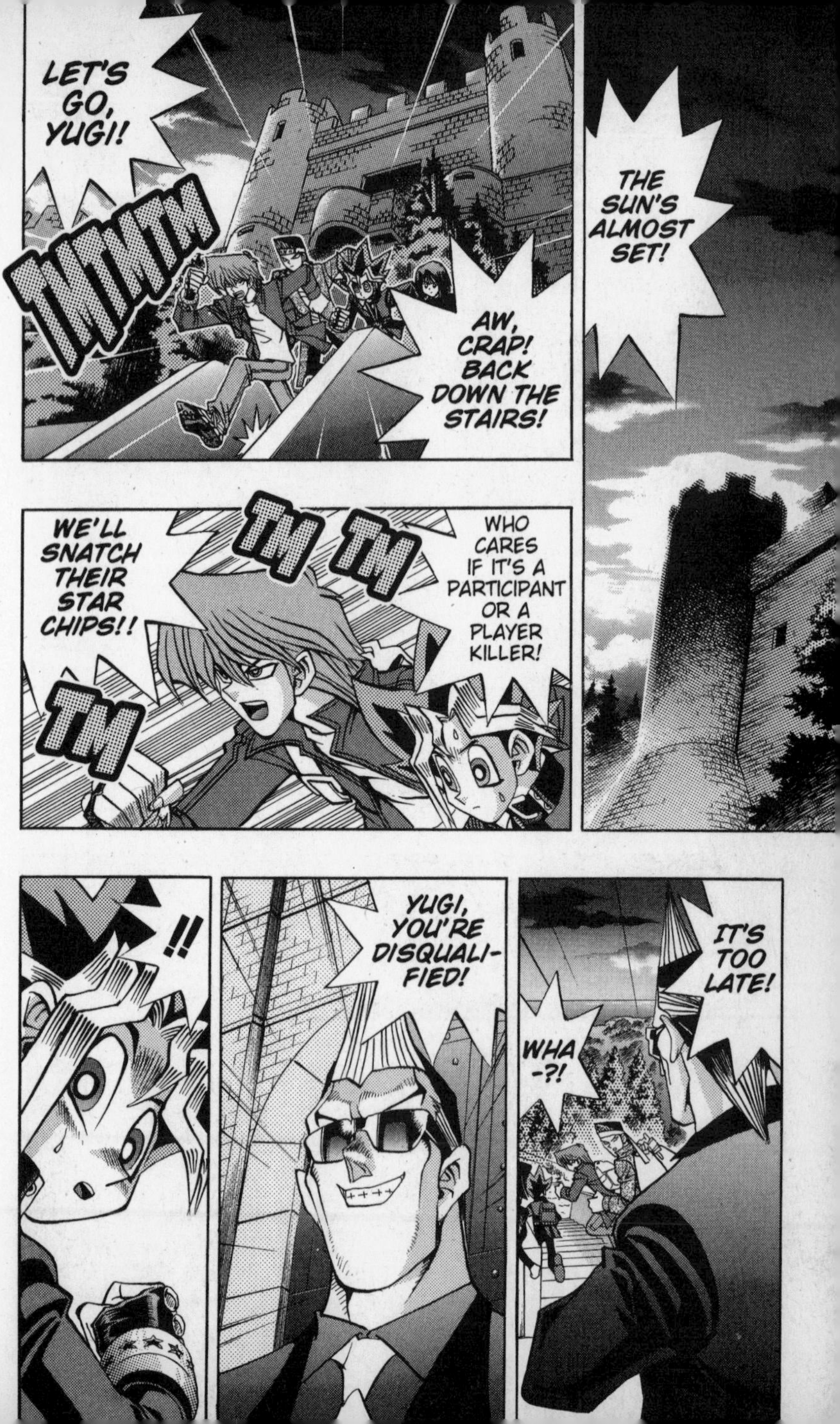
THE SUN'S ALMOST SET!
LET'S GO, YUGI!
TMTMTM
AW, CRAP! BACK DOWN THE STAIRS!
TM TM
WHO CARES IF IT'S A PARTICIPANT OR A PLAYER KILLER!
WE'LL SNATCH THEIR STAR CHIPS!!
TM
IT'S TOO LATE!
WHA-?!
YUGI, YOU'RE DISQUALI-FIED!
!!

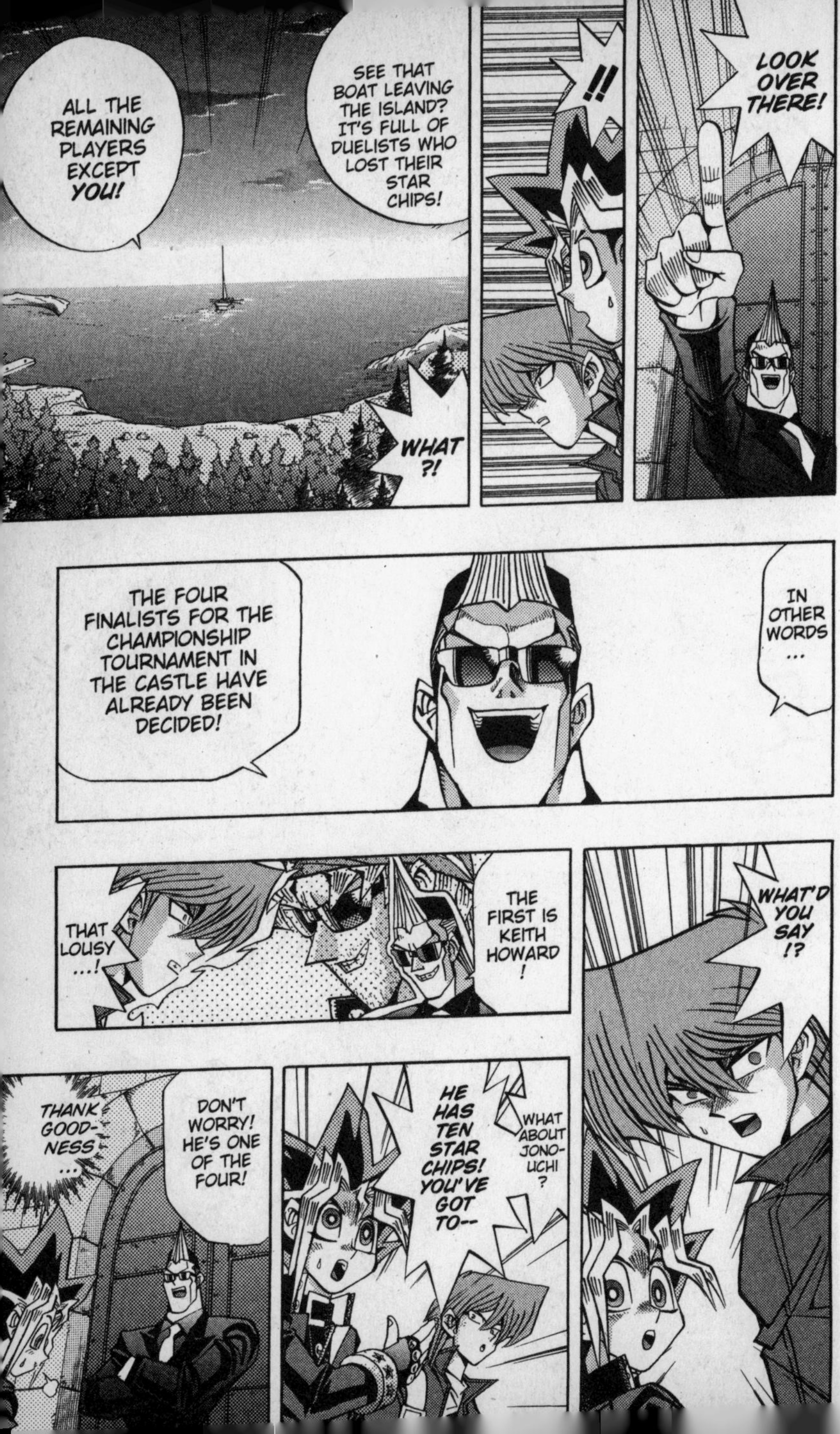
LOOK OVER THERE!
!!
SEE THAT BOAT LEAVING THE ISLAND? IT'S FULL OF DUELISTS WHO LOST THEIR STAR CHIPS!
ALL THE REMAINING PLAYERS EXCEPT YOU!
WHAT ?!
IN OTHER WORDS ...
THE FOUR FINALISTS FOR THE CHAMPIONSHIP TOURNAMENT IN THE CASTLE HAVE ALREADY BEEN DECIDED!
WHAT'D YOU SAY !?
THE FIRST IS KEITH HOWARD !
THAT LOUSY ...!
WHAT ABOUT JONO-UCHI ?
HE HAS TEN STAR CHIPS! YOU'VE GOT TO--
DON'T WORRY! HE'S ONE OF THE FOUR!
THANK GOOD-NESS ...

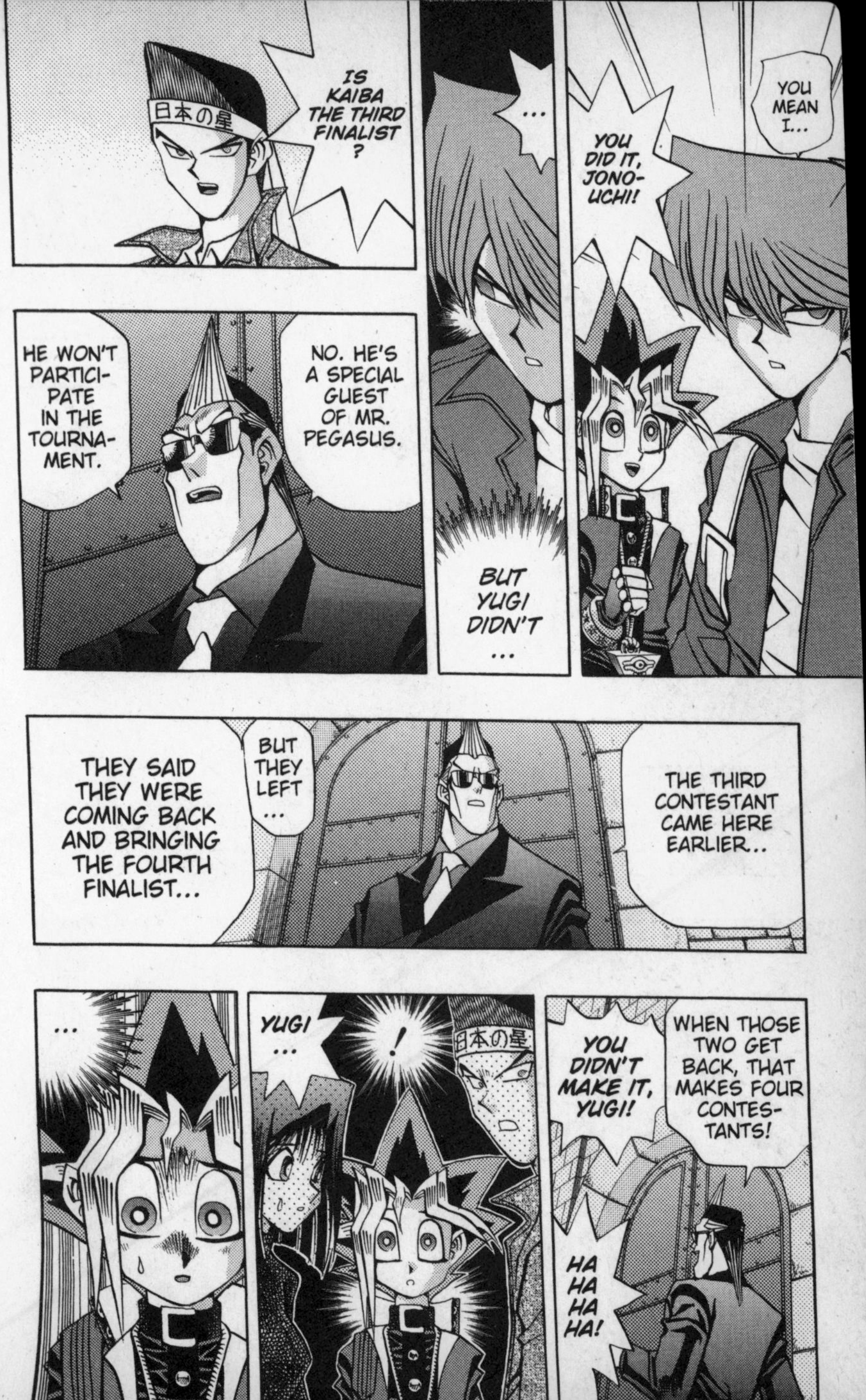
YOU MEAN I...
YOU DID IT, JONOUCHI!
...
BUT YUGI DIDN'T ...
IS KAIBA THE THIRD FINALIST ?
NO. HE'S A SPECIAL GUEST OF MR. PEGASUS.
HE WON'T PARTICI-PATE IN THE TOURNA-MENT.
THE THIRD CONTESTANT CAME HERE EARLIER...
BUT THEY LEFT ...
THEY SAID THEY WERE COMING BACK AND BRINGING THE FOURTH FINALIST...
WHEN THOSE TWO GET BACK, THAT MAKES FOUR CONTES-TANTS!
YOU DIDN'T MAKE IT, YUGI!
HA HA HA HA HA!
!
YUGI ...
...

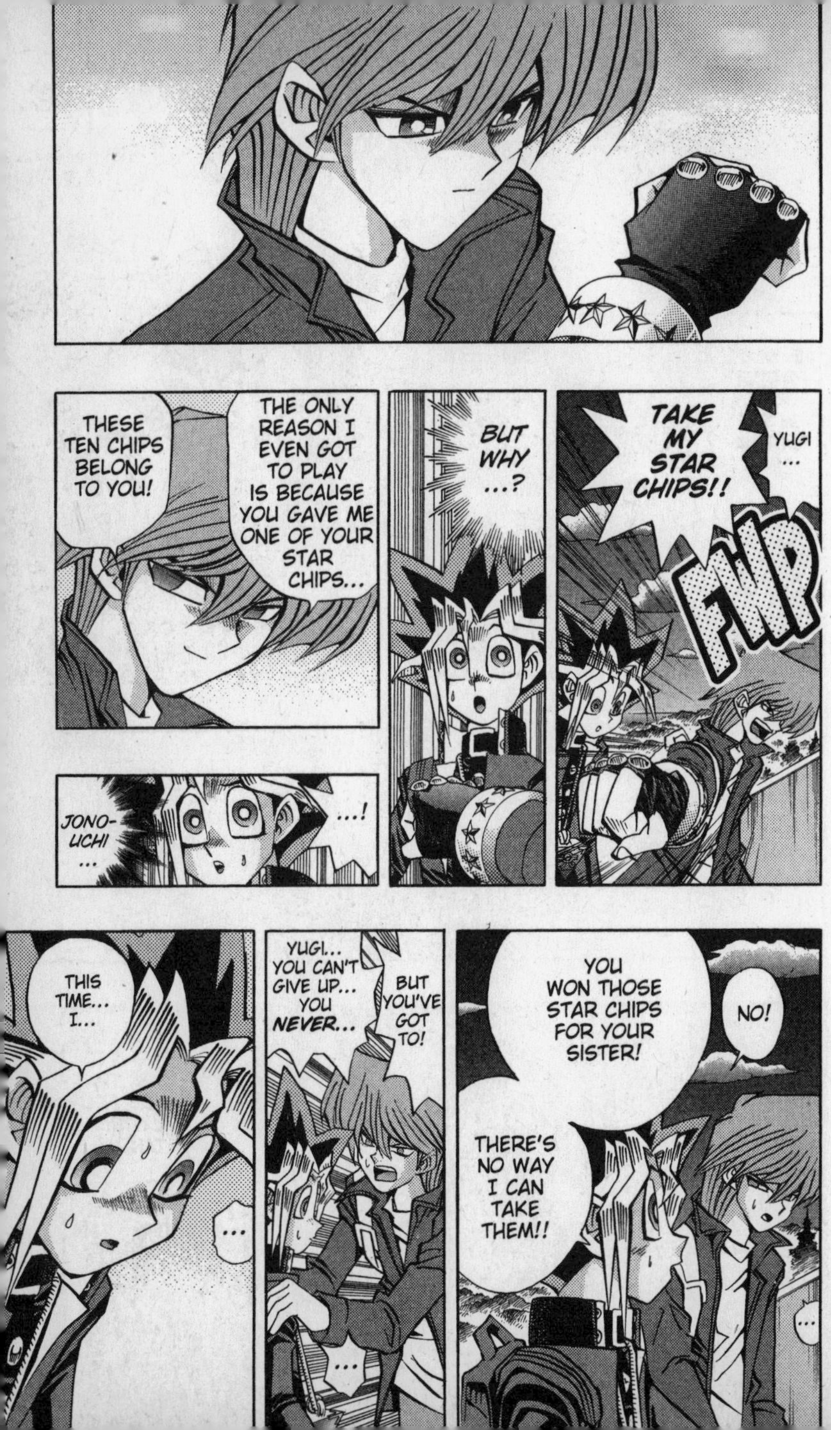
YUGI ...
TAKE MY STAR CHIPS!!
FWP
BUT WHY ...?
THE ONLY REASON I EVEN GOT TO PLAY IS BECAUSE YOU GAVE ME ONE OF YOUR STAR CHIPS...
THESE TEN CHIPS BELONG TO YOU!
...!
JONO-UCHI ...
NO!
YOU WON THOSE STAR CHIPS FOR YOUR SISTER!
THERE'S NO WAY I CAN TAKE THEM!!
...
BUT YOU'VE GOT TO!
YUGI... YOU CAN'T GIVE UP... YOU ***NEVER***...
...
THIS TIME... I...
...

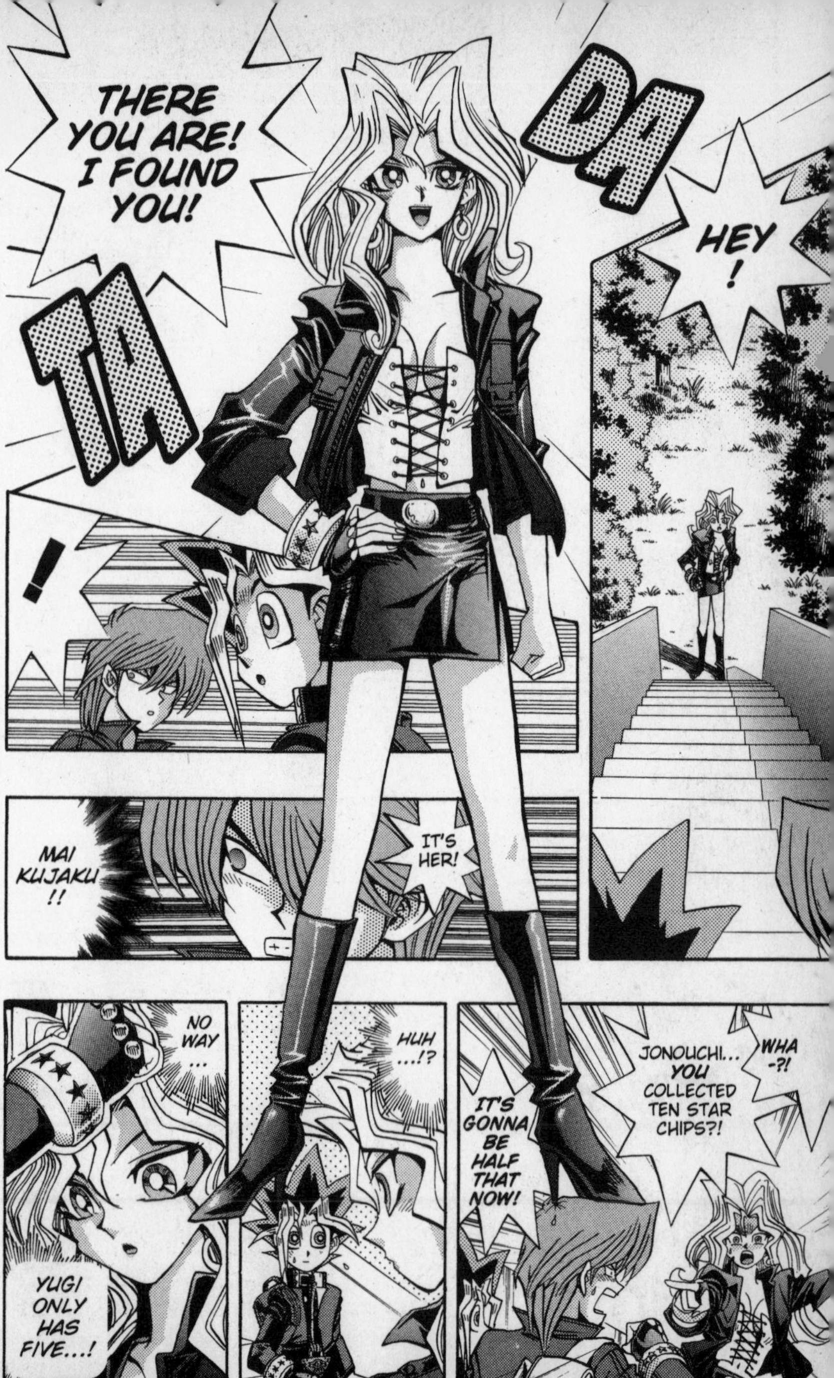
HEY!
DA
THERE YOU ARE! I FOUND YOU!
TA
!
IT'S HER!
MAI KUJAKU!!
WHA-?!
JONOUCHI... YOU COLLECTED TEN STAR CHIPS?!
IT'S GONNA BE HALF THAT NOW!
HUH...!?
NO WAY...
YUGI ONLY HAS FIVE...!

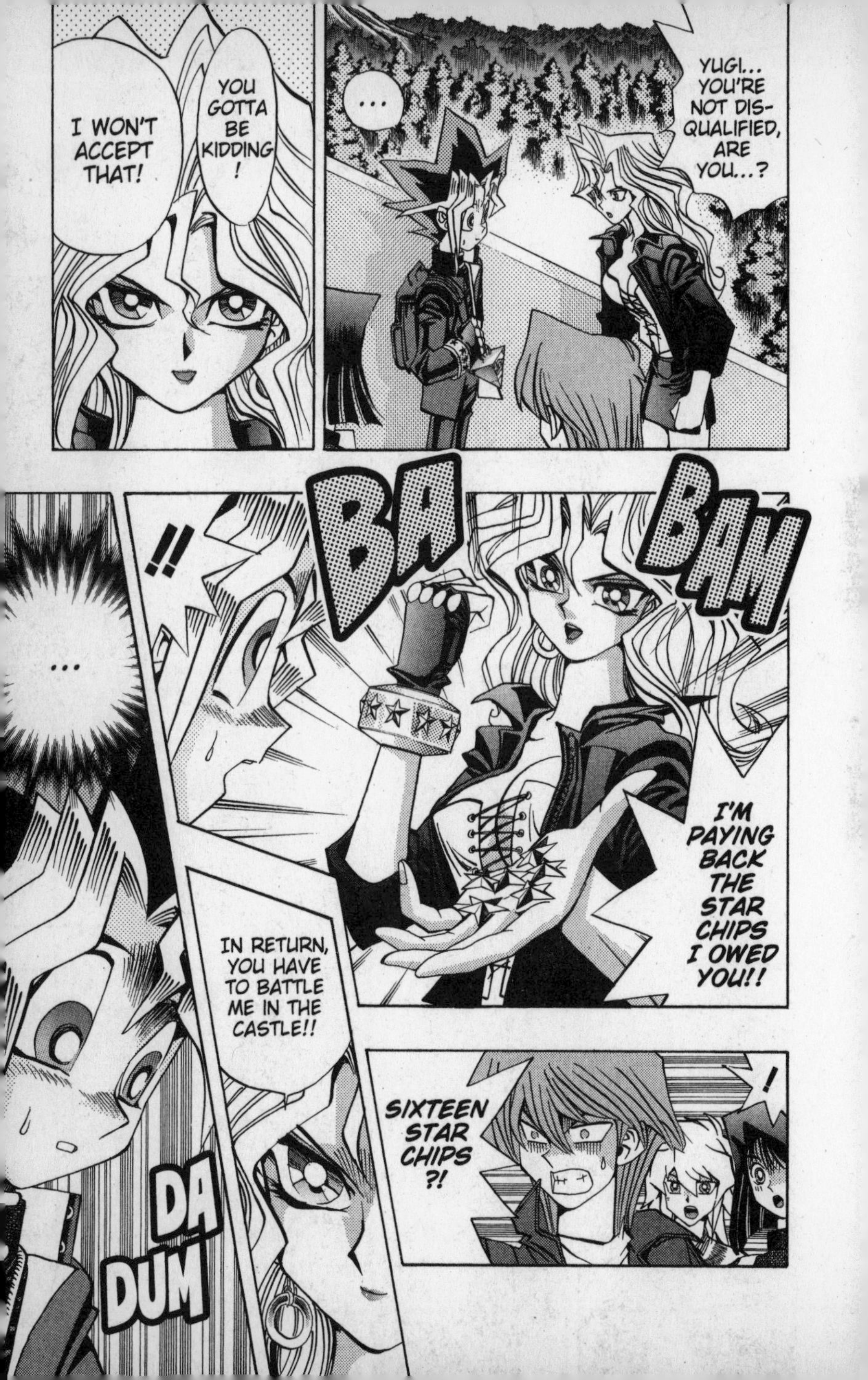
YUGI... YOU'RE NOT DIS-QUALIFIED, ARE YOU...?
...
YOU GOTTA BE KIDDING!
I WON'T ACCEPT THAT!
BA BAM
I'M PAYING BACK THE STAR CHIPS I OWED YOU!!
!!
!
SIXTEEN STAR CHIPS?!
IN RETURN, YOU HAVE TO BATTLE ME IN THE CASTLE!!
DA DUM
...

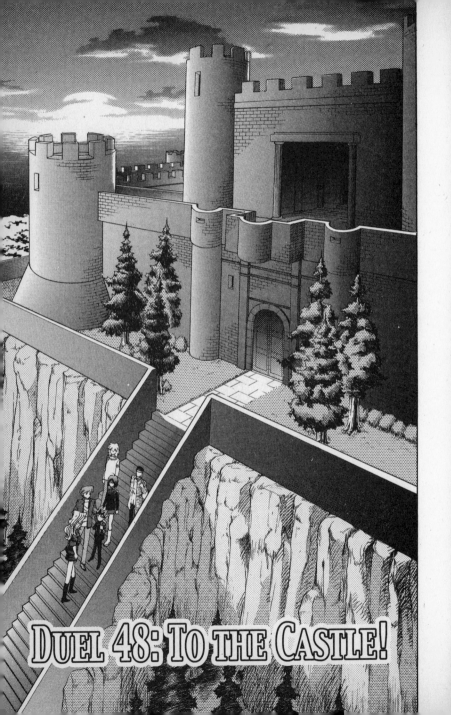

DUEL 48: TO THE CASTLE!

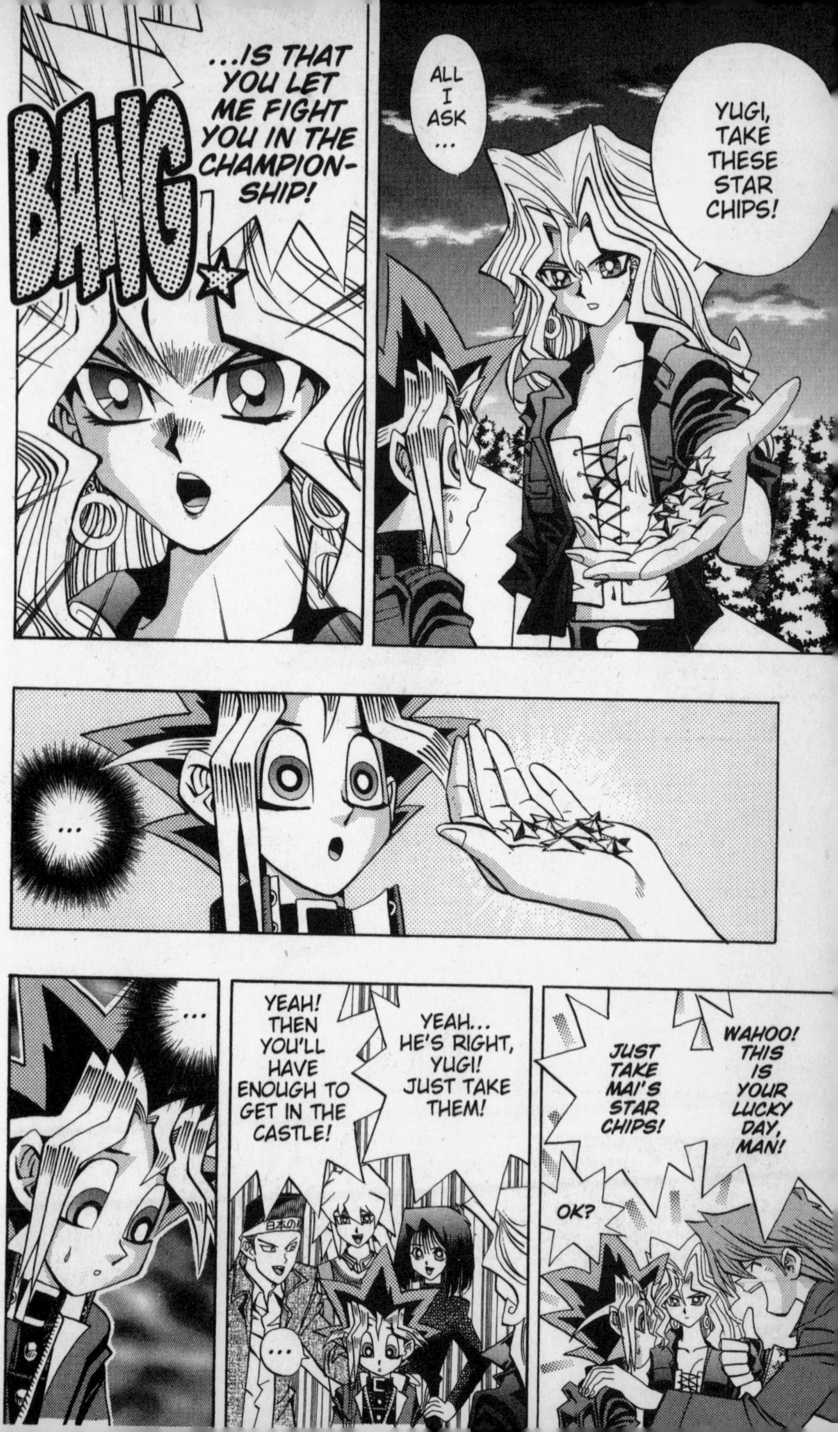
YUGI, TAKE THESE STAR CHIPS!
ALL I ASK ...
...IS THAT YOU LET ME FIGHT YOU IN THE CHAMPIONSHIP!
BANG
...
WAHOO! THIS IS YOUR LUCKY DAY, MAN!
JUST TAKE MAI'S STAR CHIPS!
OK?
YEAH... HE'S RIGHT, YUGI! JUST TAKE THEM!
YEAH! THEN YOU'LL HAVE ENOUGH TO GET IN THE CASTLE!
...
...

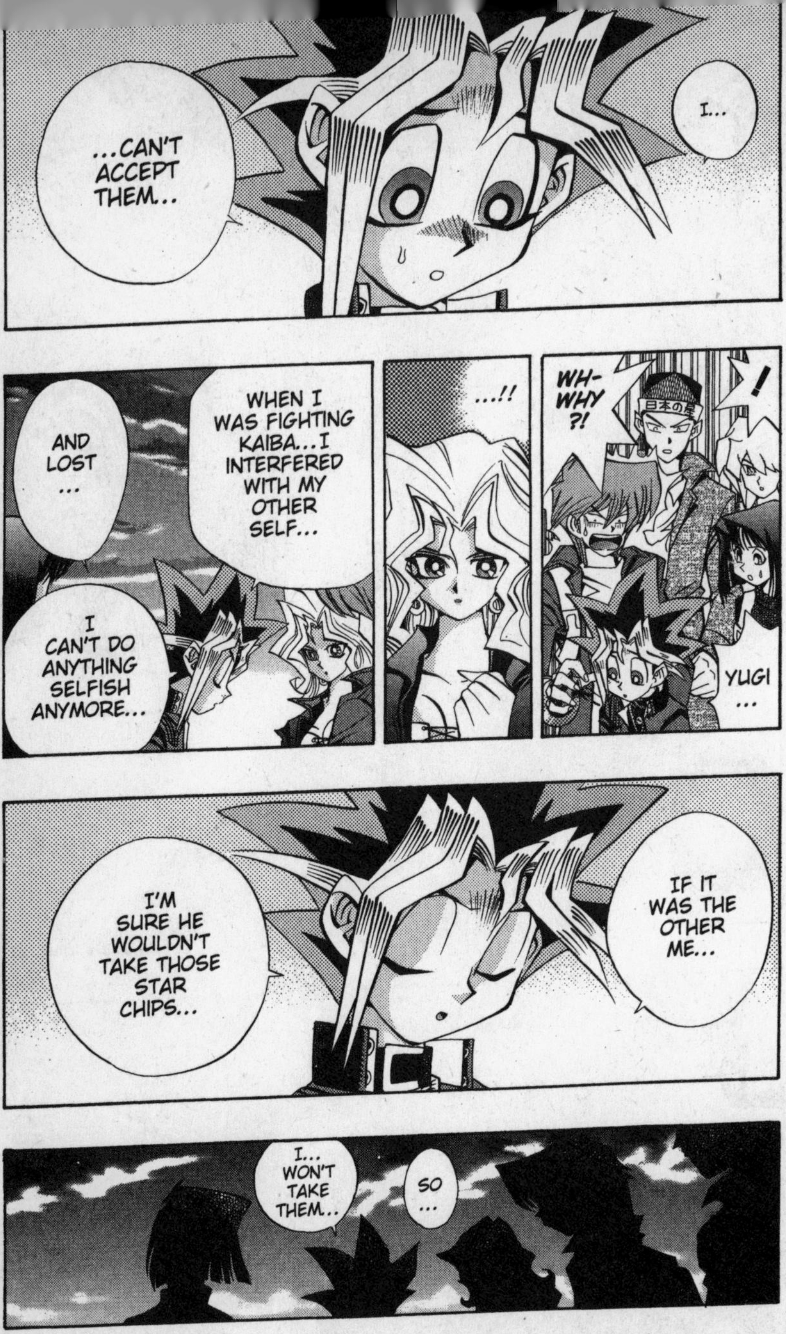
I...
...CAN'T ACCEPT THEM...
!
WH-WHY?!
YUGI...
...!!
WHEN I WAS FIGHTING KAIBA...I INTERFERED WITH MY OTHER SELF...
AND LOST...
I CAN'T DO ANYTHING SELFISH ANYMORE...
IF IT WAS THE OTHER ME...
I'M SURE HE WOULDN'T TAKE THOSE STAR CHIPS...
I... WON'T TAKE THEM...
SO...

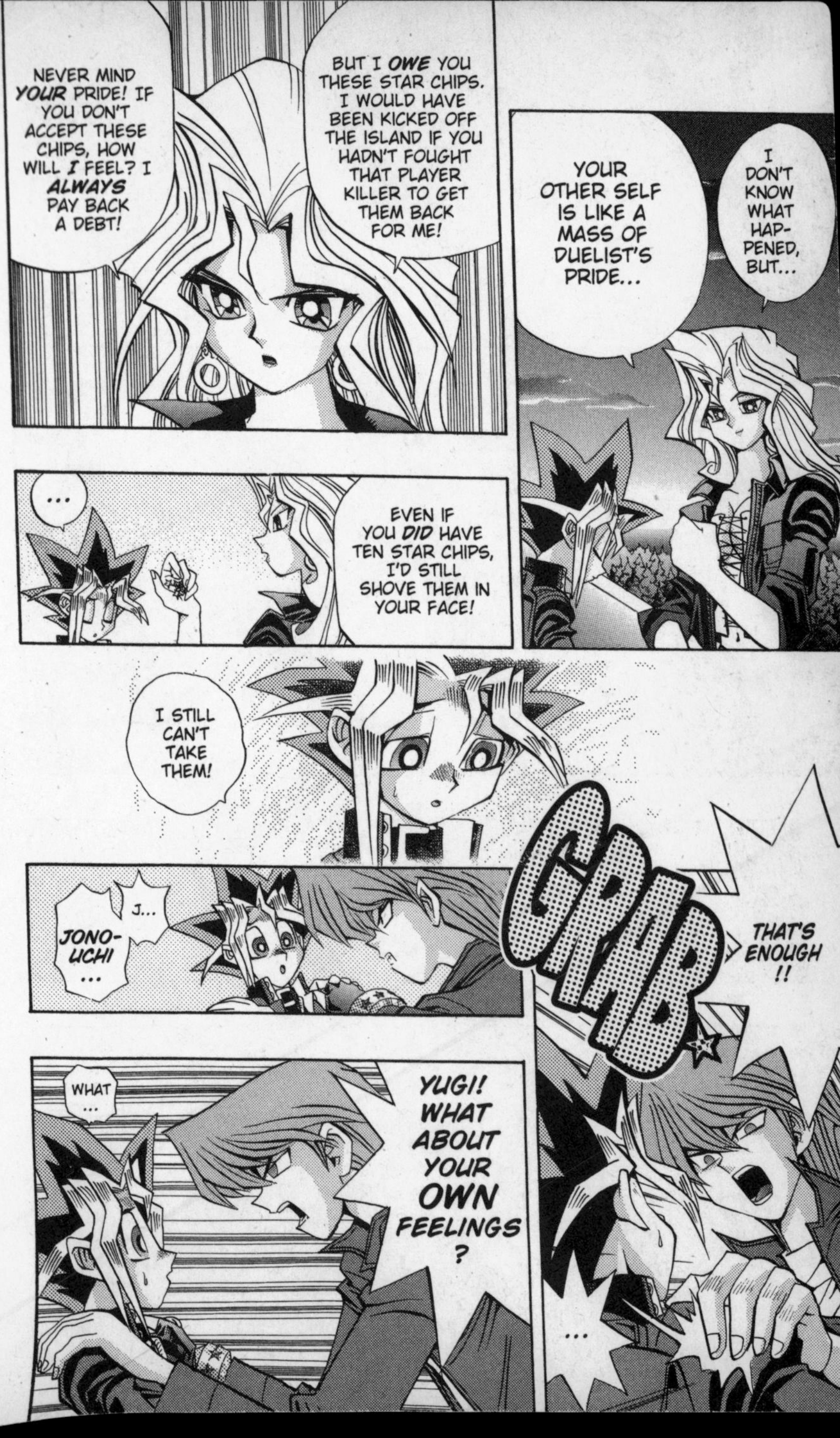
I DON'T KNOW WHAT HAP-PENED, BUT...
YOUR OTHER SELF IS LIKE A MASS OF DUELIST'S PRIDE...
BUT I *OWE* YOU THESE STAR CHIPS. I WOULD HAVE BEEN KICKED OFF THE ISLAND IF YOU HADN'T FOUGHT THAT PLAYER KILLER TO GET THEM BACK FOR ME!
NEVER MIND ***YOUR*** PRIDE! IF YOU DON'T ACCEPT THESE CHIPS, HOW WILL *I* FEEL? I ***ALWAYS*** PAY BACK A DEBT!
EVEN IF YOU *DID* HAVE TEN STAR CHIPS, I'D STILL SHOVE THEM IN YOUR FACE!
...
I STILL CAN'T TAKE THEM!
GRAB
THAT'S ENOUGH!!
J...
JONO-UCHI...
...
WHAT...
YUGI! WHAT ABOUT YOUR OWN FEELINGS?

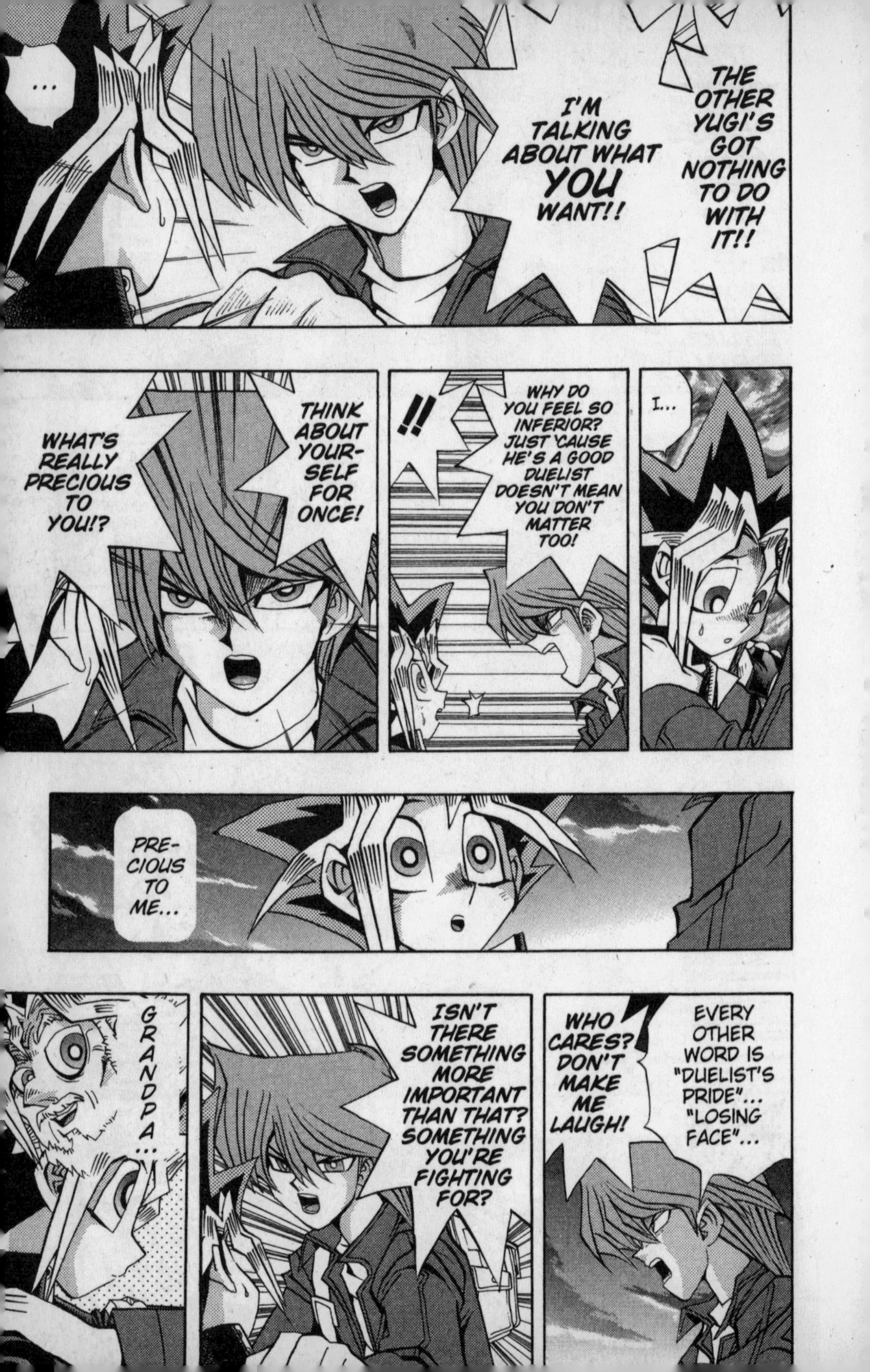
THE OTHER YUGI'S GOT NOTHING TO DO WITH IT!!
I'M TALKING ABOUT WHAT YOU WANT!!
...
I...
WHY DO YOU FEEL SO INFERIOR? JUST 'CAUSE HE'S A GOOD DUELIST DOESN'T MEAN YOU DON'T MATTER TOO!
!!
THINK ABOUT YOURSELF FOR ONCE!
WHAT'S REALLY PRECIOUS TO YOU!?
PRECIOUS TO ME...
EVERY OTHER WORD IS "DUELIST'S PRIDE"... "LOSING FACE"...
WHO CARES? DON'T MAKE ME LAUGH!
ISN'T THERE SOMETHING MORE IMPORTANT THAN THAT? SOMETHING YOU'RE FIGHTING FOR?
GRANDPA...

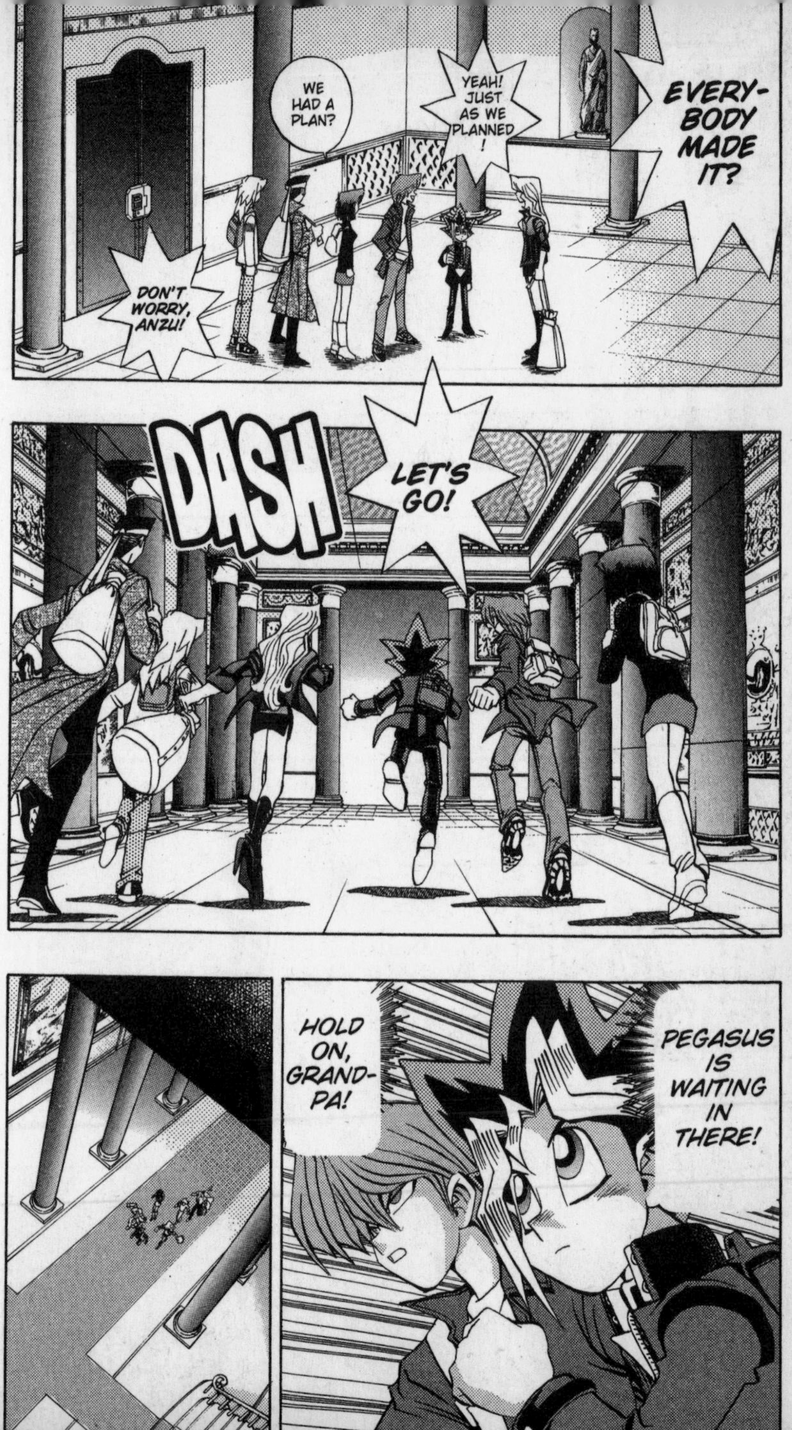
EVERY-BODY MADE IT?
YEAH! JUST AS WE PLANNED!
WE HAD A PLAN?
DON'T WORRY, ANZU!
LET'S GO!
DASH
PEGASUS IS WAITING IN THERE!
HOLD ON, GRAND-PA!

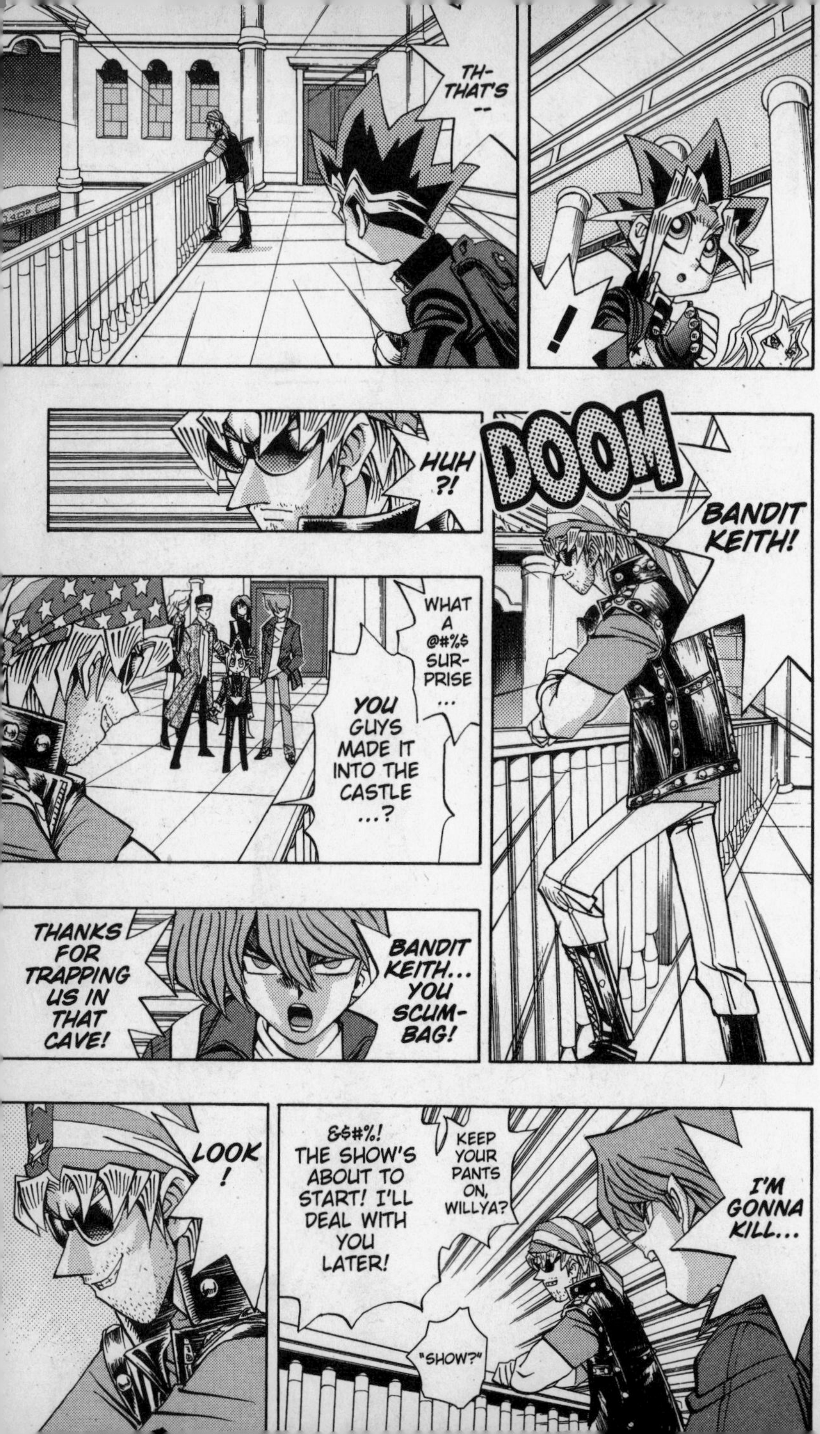
!
TH-THAT'S --
DOOM
BANDIT KEITH!
HUH ?!
WHAT A @#%$ SURPRISE ...
YOU GUYS MADE IT INTO THE CASTLE ...?
BANDIT KEITH... YOU SCUM-BAG!
THANKS FOR TRAPPING US IN THAT CAVE!
I'M GONNA KILL...
KEEP YOUR PANTS ON, WILLYA?
&$#%! THE SHOW'S ABOUT TO START! I'LL DEAL WITH YOU LATER!
"SHOW?"
LOOK !

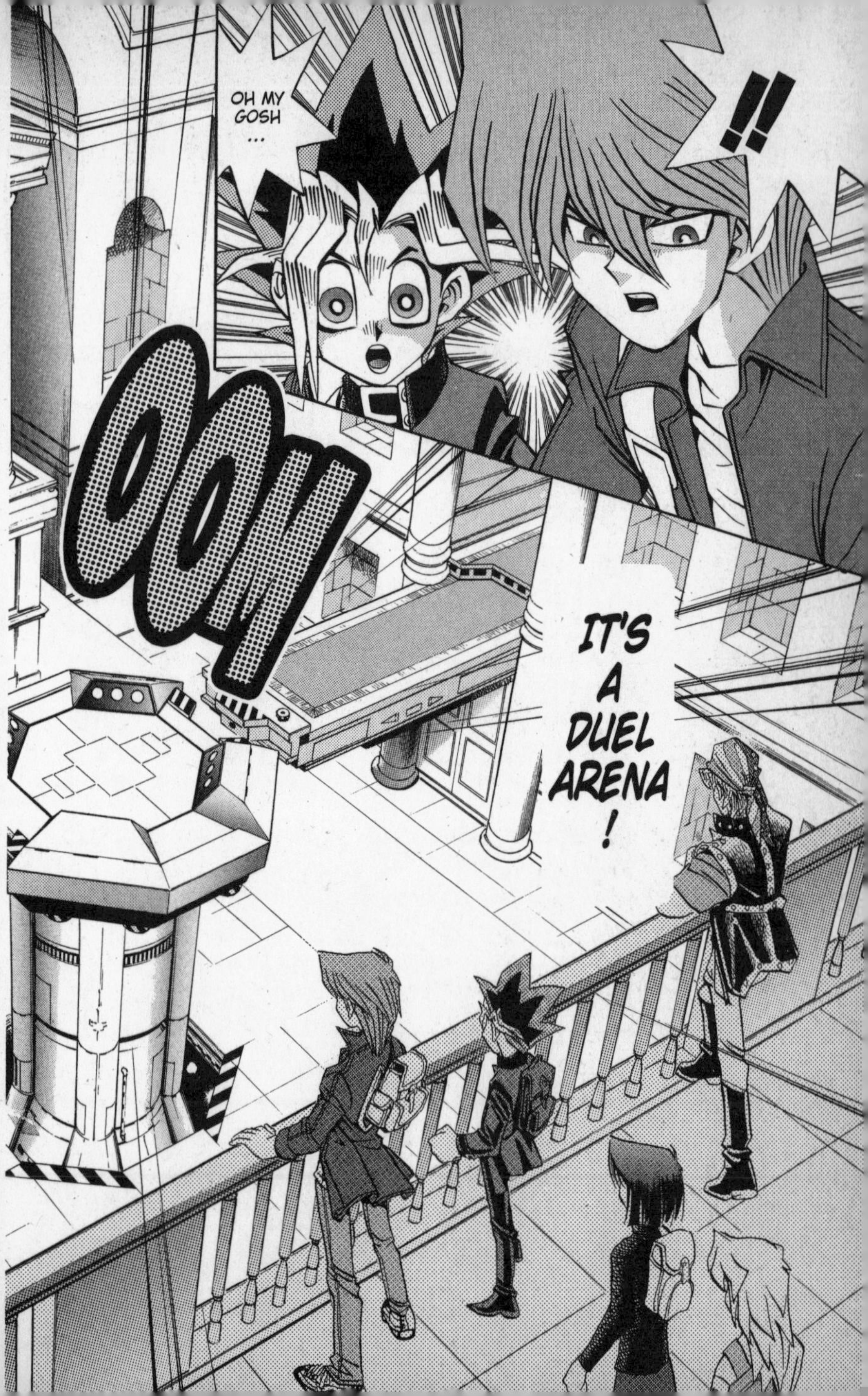
!!
OH MY GOSH ...
IT'S A DUEL ARENA!

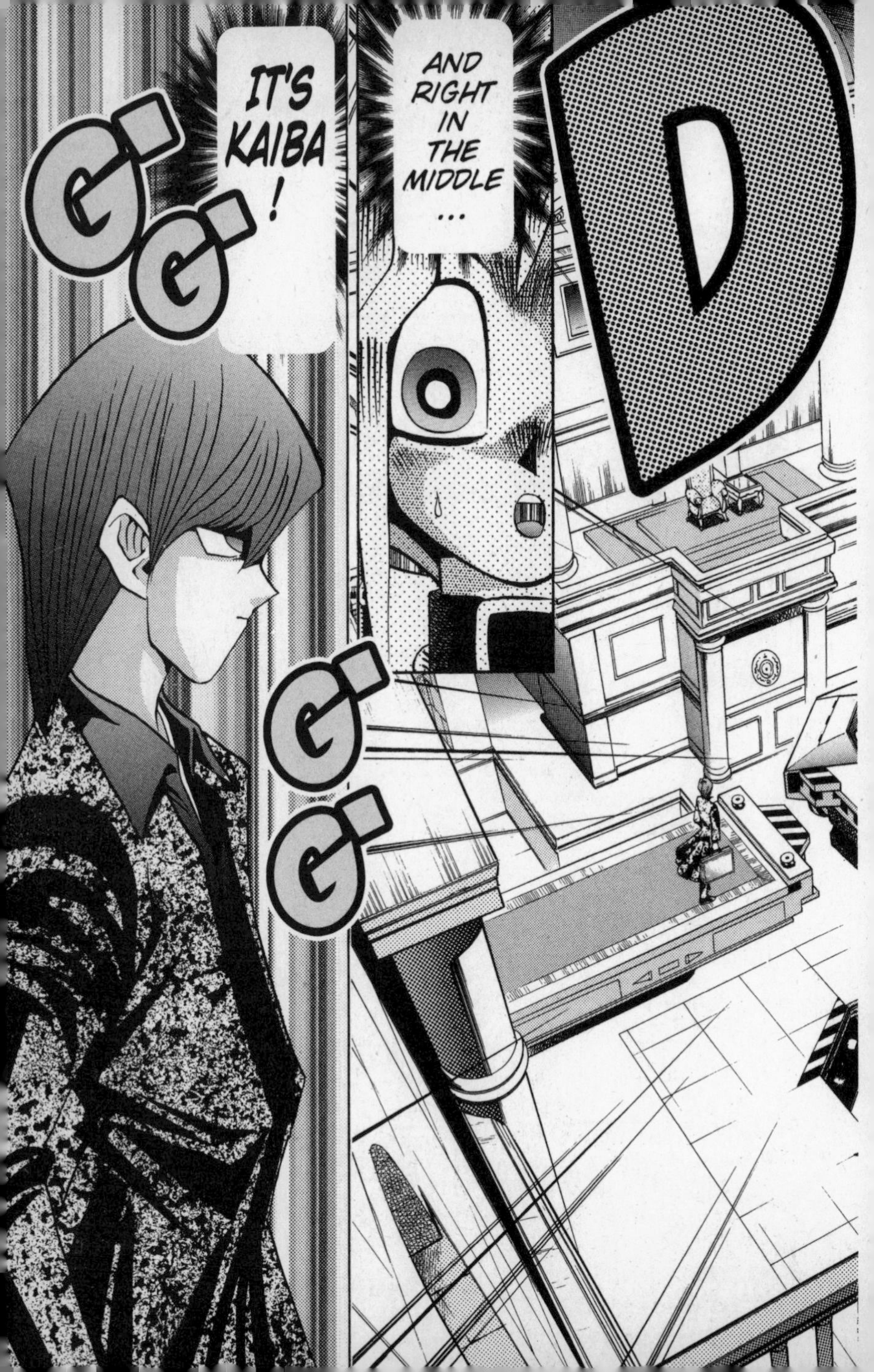
D
AND RIGHT IN THE MIDDLE ...
IT'S KAIBA !
G G
G G

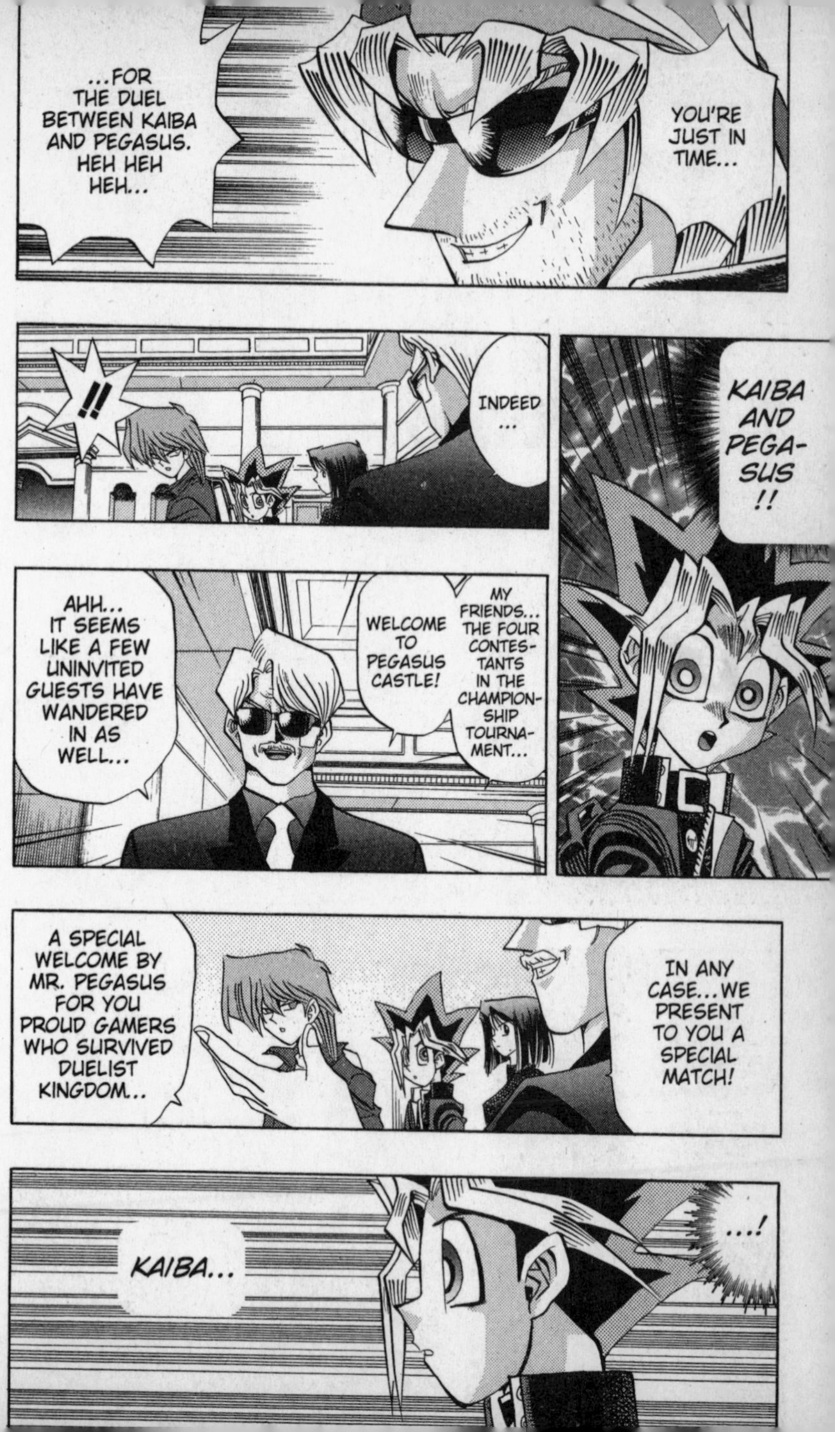
YOU'RE JUST IN TIME...
...FOR THE DUEL BETWEEN KAIBA AND PEGASUS. HEH HEH HEH...
KAIBA AND PEGA-SUS !!
INDEED...
!!
MY FRIENDS... THE FOUR CONTES-TANTS IN THE CHAMPION-SHIP TOURNA-MENT...
WELCOME TO PEGASUS CASTLE!
AHH... IT SEEMS LIKE A FEW UNINVITED GUESTS HAVE WANDERED IN AS WELL...
IN ANY CASE...WE PRESENT TO YOU A SPECIAL MATCH!
A SPECIAL WELCOME BY MR. PEGASUS FOR YOU PROUD GAMERS WHO SURVIVED DUELIST KINGDOM...
...!
KAIBA...

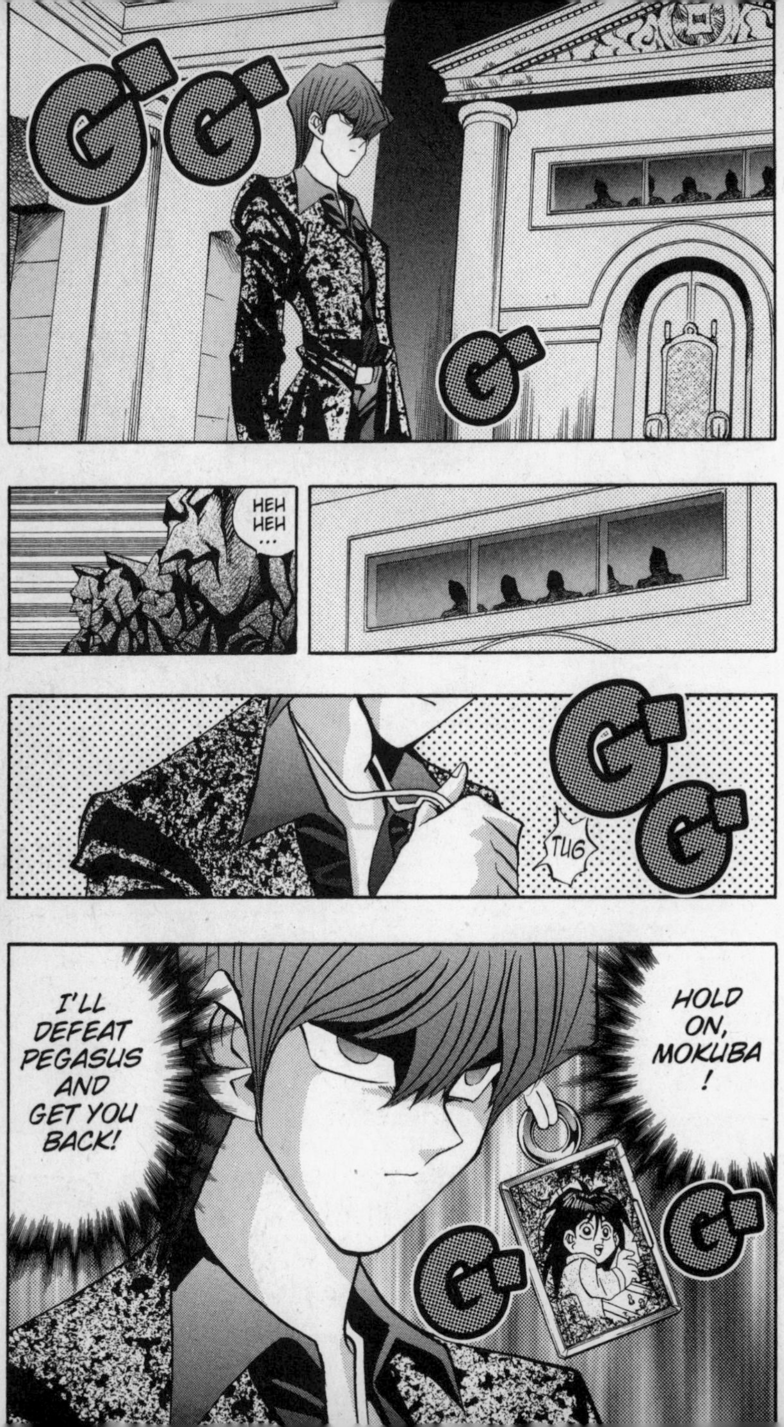
HEH HEH ...
TUG
HOLD ON, MOKUBA!
I'LL DEFEAT PEGASUS AND GET YOU BACK!

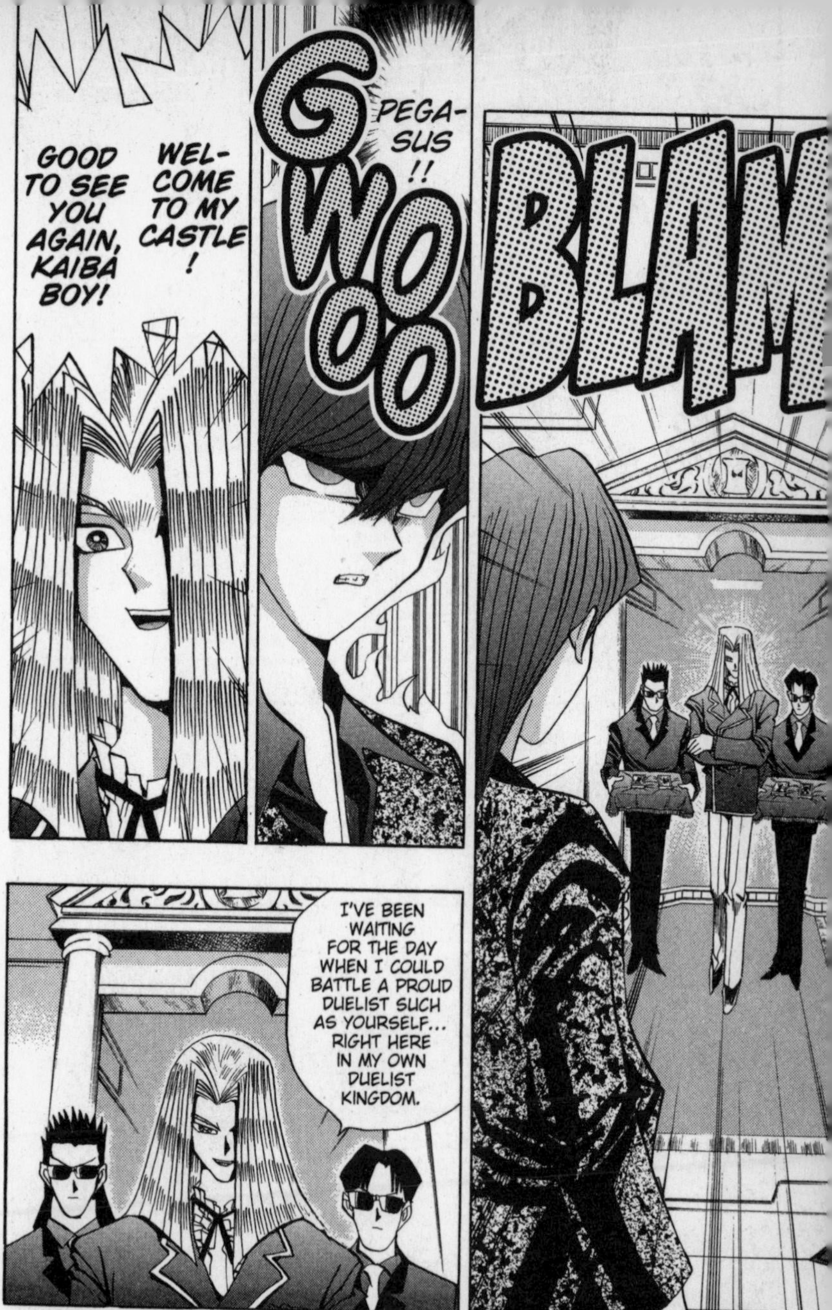
BLAM
PEGA-SUS!!
GWOOOO
WEL-COME TO MY CASTLE!
GOOD TO SEE YOU AGAIN, KAIBA BOY!
I'VE BEEN WAITING FOR THE DAY WHEN I COULD BATTLE A PROUD DUELIST SUCH AS YOURSELF... RIGHT HERE IN MY OWN DUELIST KINGDOM.

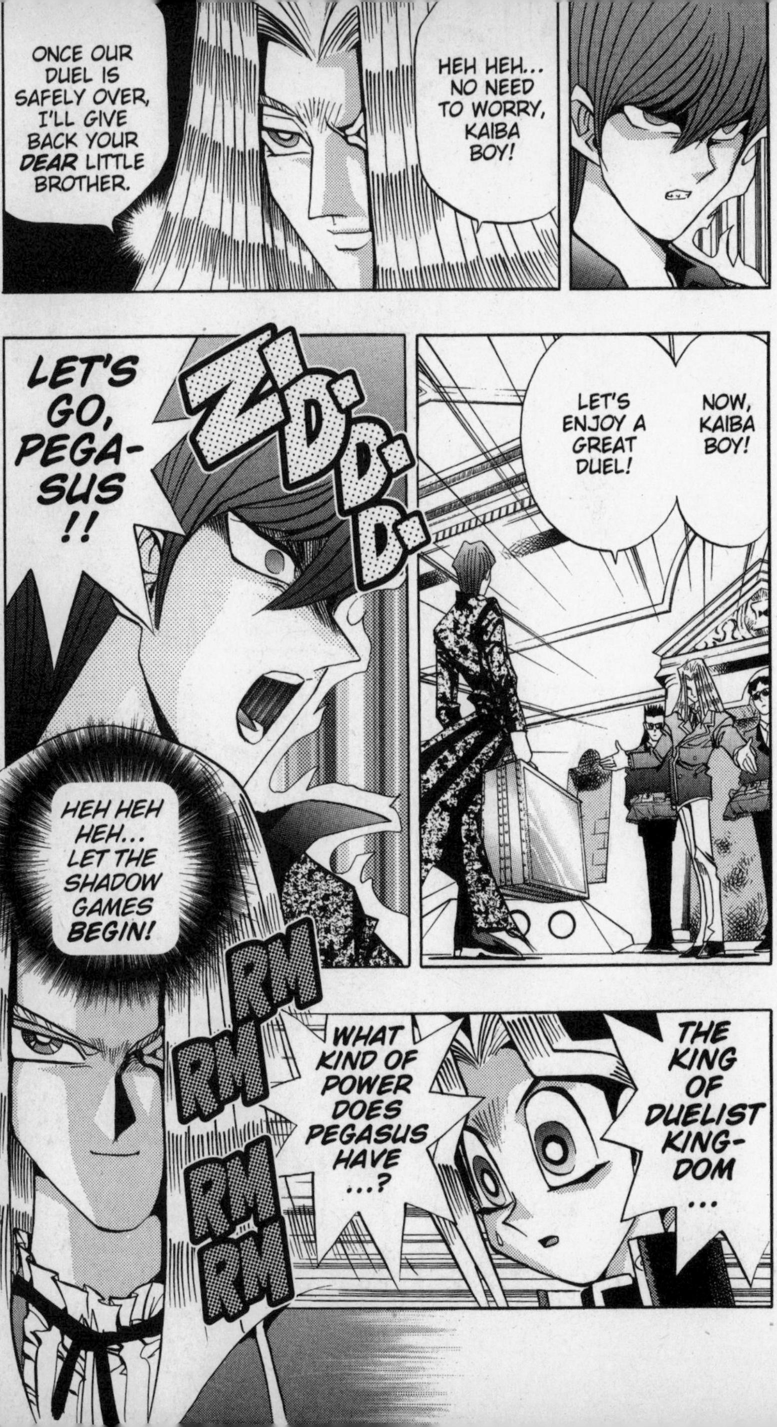
HEH HEH... NO NEED TO WORRY, KAIBA BOY!
ONCE OUR DUEL IS SAFELY OVER, I'LL GIVE BACK YOUR DEAR LITTLE BROTHER.
NOW, KAIBA BOY!
LET'S ENJOY A GREAT DUEL!
ZDDD
LET'S GO, PEGASUS!!
THE KING OF DUELIST KINGDOM...
WHAT KIND OF POWER DOES PEGASUS HAVE...?
HEH HEH HEH... LET THE SHADOW GAMES BEGIN!
RM RM RM RM

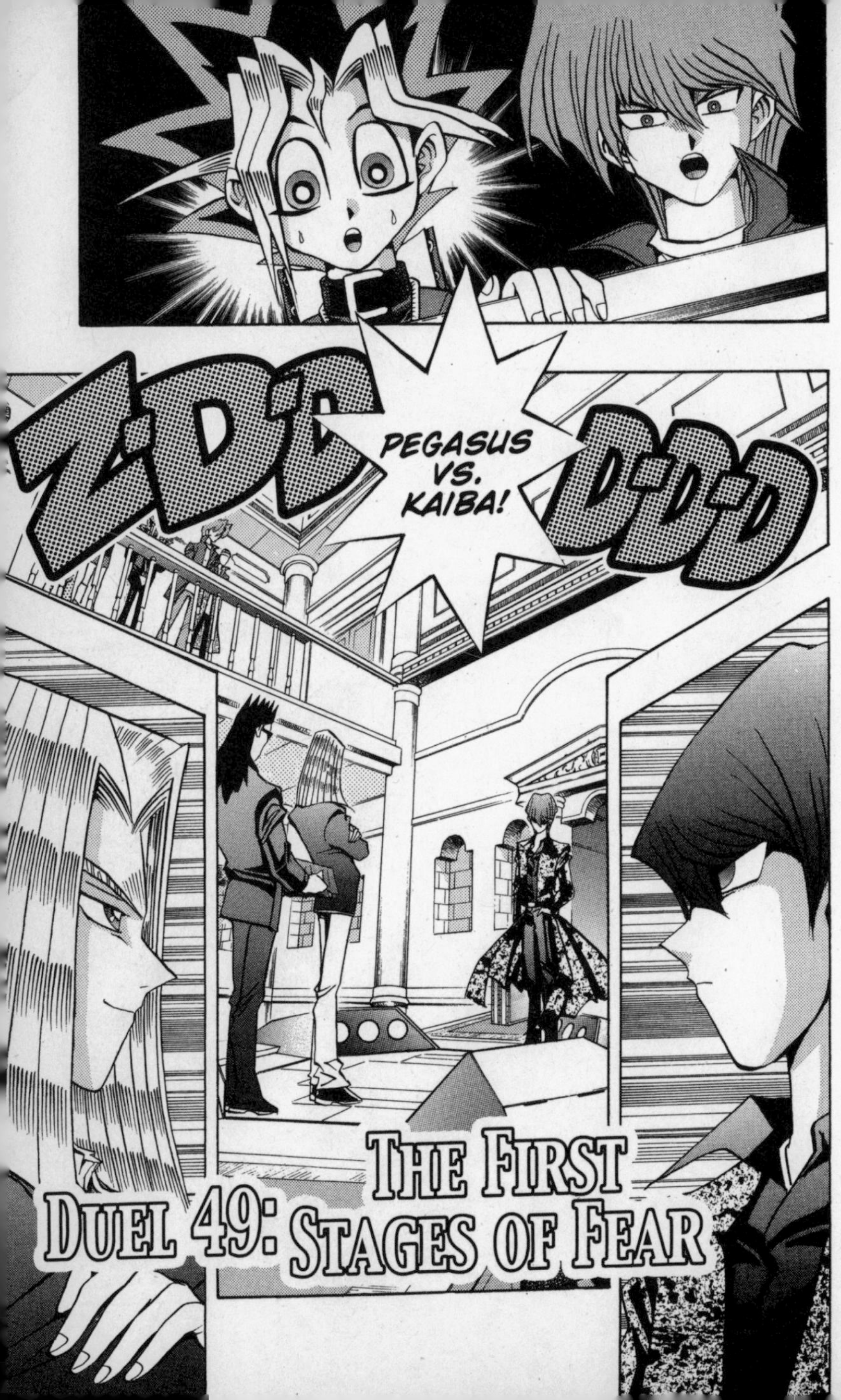
Z-D-D-D-D-D
PEGASUS VS. KAIBA!
DUEL 49: THE FIRST STAGES OF FEAR

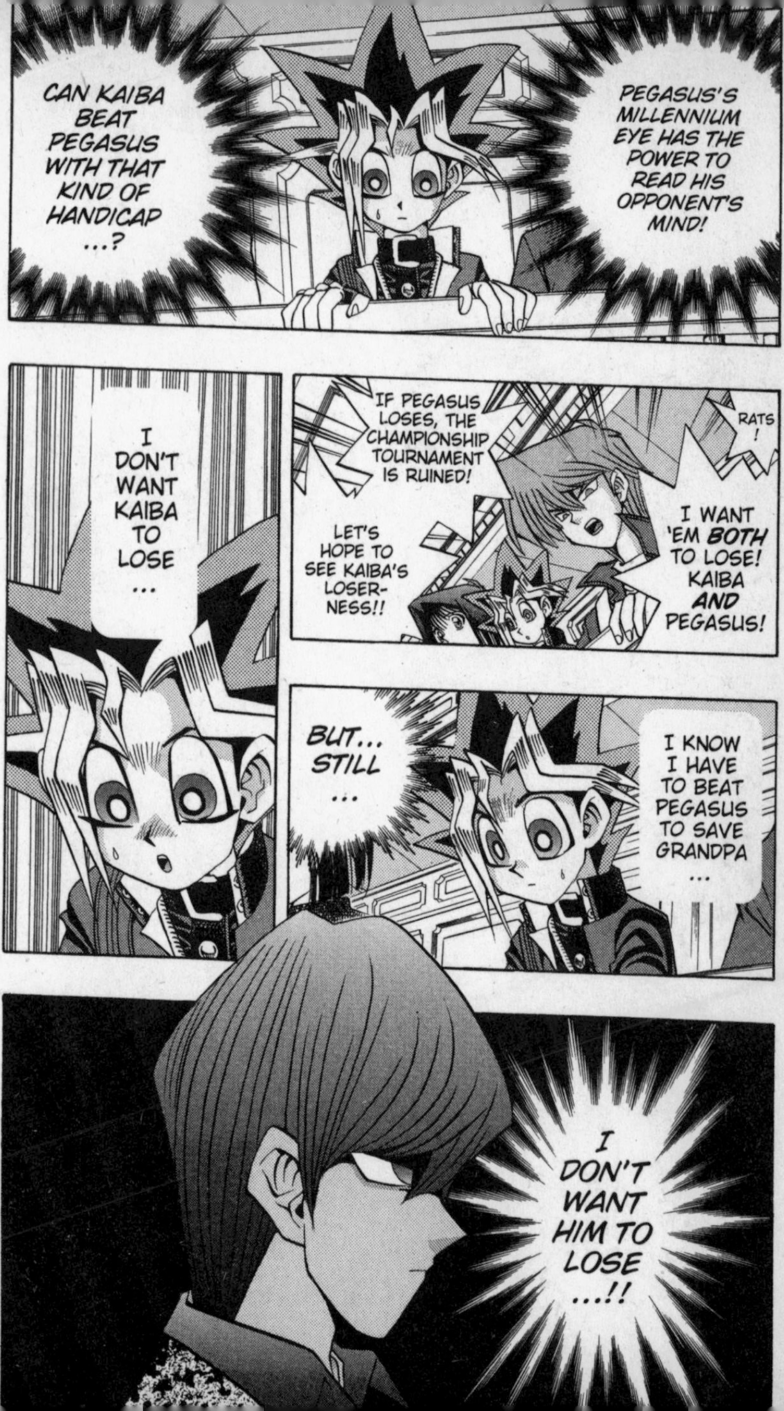
PEGASUS'S MILLENNIUM EYE HAS THE POWER TO READ HIS OPPONENT'S MIND!
CAN KAIBA BEAT PEGASUS WITH THAT KIND OF HANDICAP ...?
RATS!
IF PEGASUS LOSES, THE CHAMPIONSHIP TOURNAMENT IS RUINED!
I WANT 'EM BOTH TO LOSE! KAIBA AND PEGASUS!
LET'S HOPE TO SEE KAIBA'S LOSERNESS!!
I KNOW I HAVE TO BEAT PEGASUS TO SAVE GRANDPA ...
BUT... STILL ...
I DON'T WANT KAIBA TO LOSE ...
I DON'T WANT HIM TO LOSE ...!!

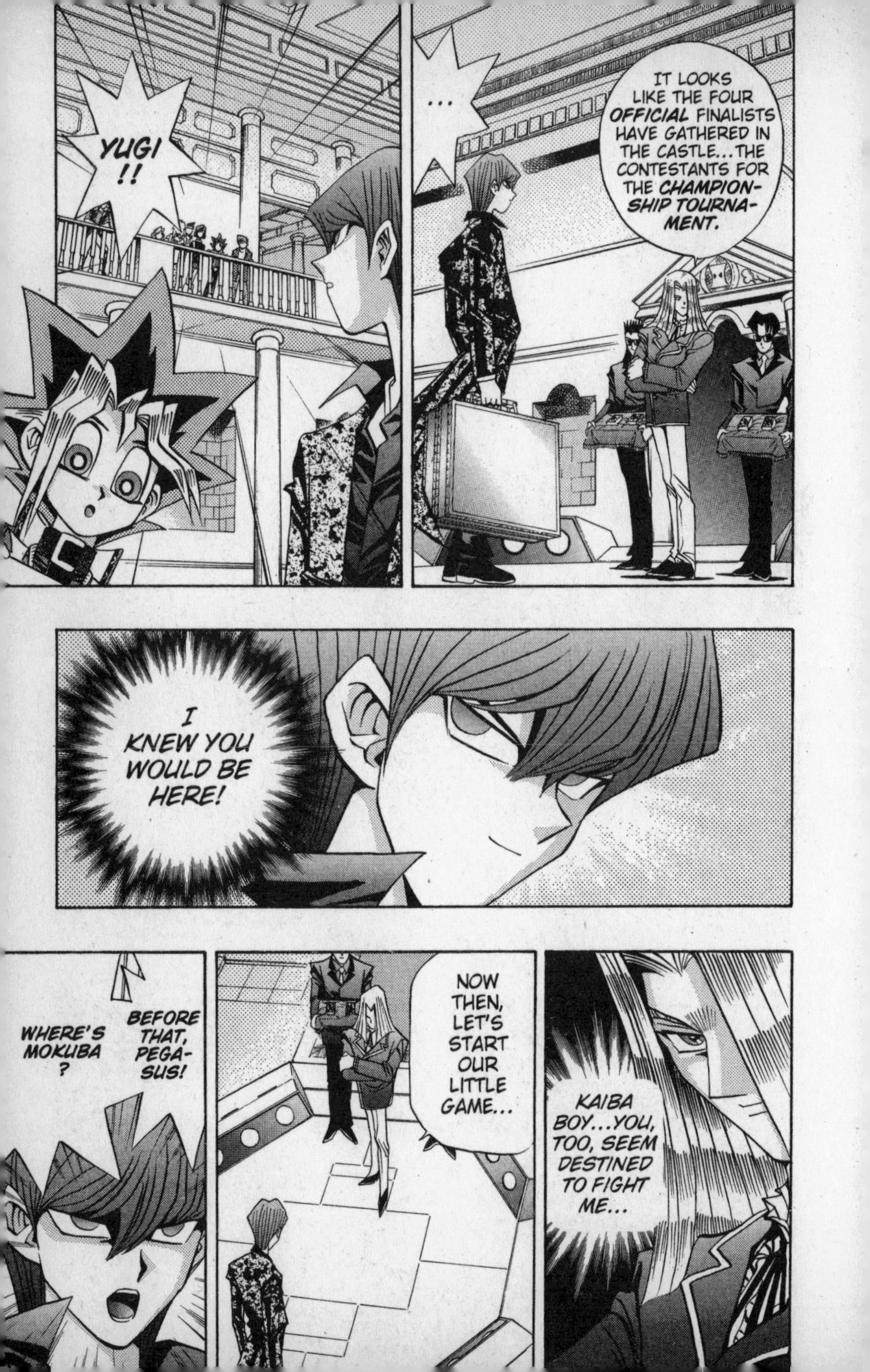
IT LOOKS LIKE THE FOUR OFFICIAL FINALISTS HAVE GATHERED IN THE CASTLE...THE CONTESTANTS FOR THE CHAMPIONSHIP TOURNAMENT.
...
YUGI !!
I KNEW YOU WOULD BE HERE!
KAIBA BOY...YOU, TOO, SEEM DESTINED TO FIGHT ME...
NOW THEN, LET'S START OUR LITTLE GAME...
BEFORE THAT, PEGASUS!
WHERE'S MOKUBA?

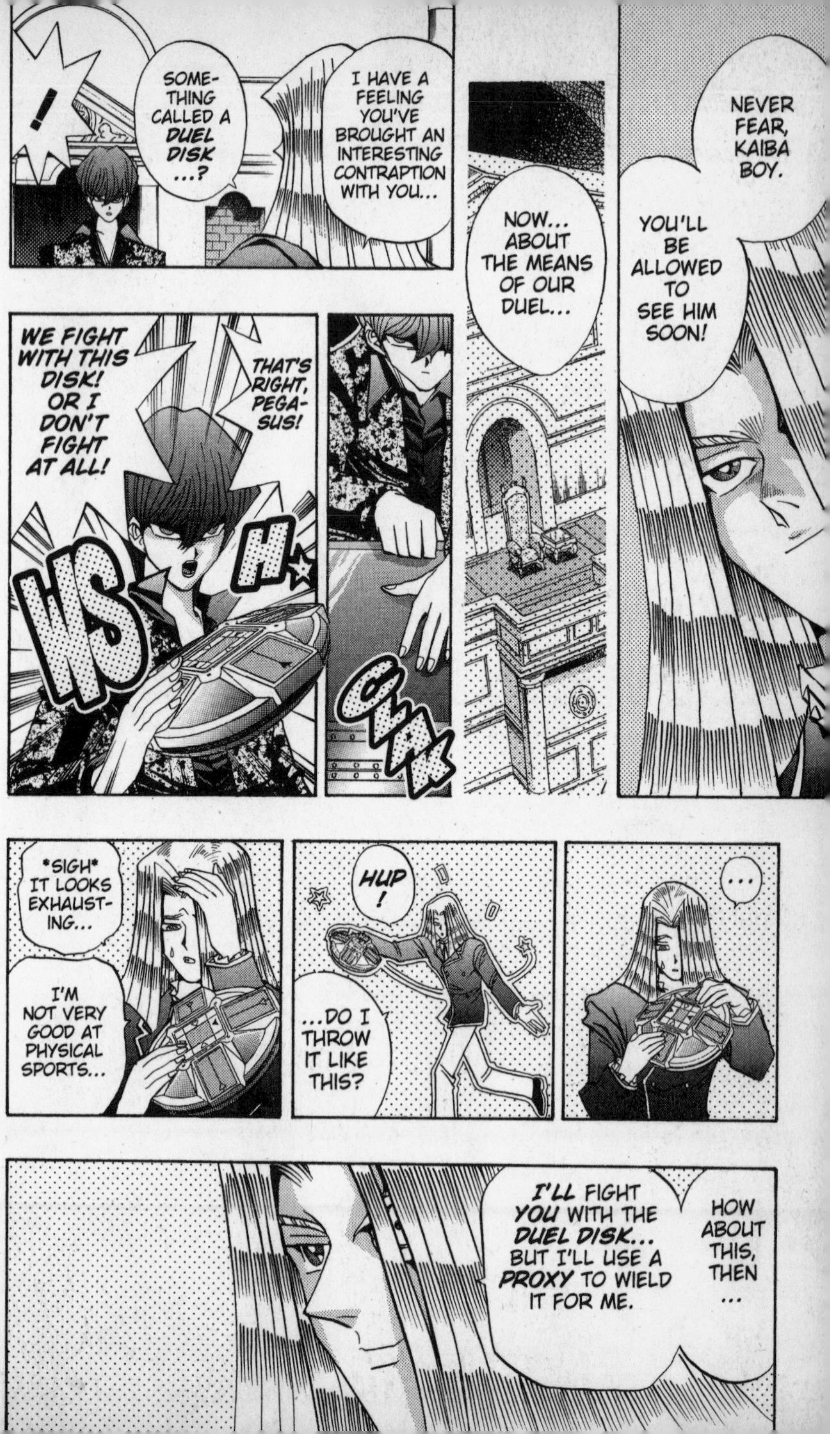
NEVER FEAR, KAIBA BOY.
YOU'LL BE ALLOWED TO SEE HIM SOON!
NOW... ABOUT THE MEANS OF OUR DUEL...
I HAVE A FEELING YOU'VE BROUGHT AN INTERESTING CONTRAPTION WITH YOU...
SOME-THING CALLED A DUEL DISK ...?
!
THAT'S RIGHT, PEGA-SUS!
WE FIGHT WITH THIS DISK! OR I DON'T FIGHT AT ALL!
...
HUP!
...DO I THROW IT LIKE THIS?
SIGH IT LOOKS EXHAUST-ING...
I'M NOT VERY GOOD AT PHYSICAL SPORTS...
HOW ABOUT THIS, THEN ...
I'LL FIGHT YOU WITH THE DUEL DISK... BUT I'LL USE A PROXY TO WIELD IT FOR ME.

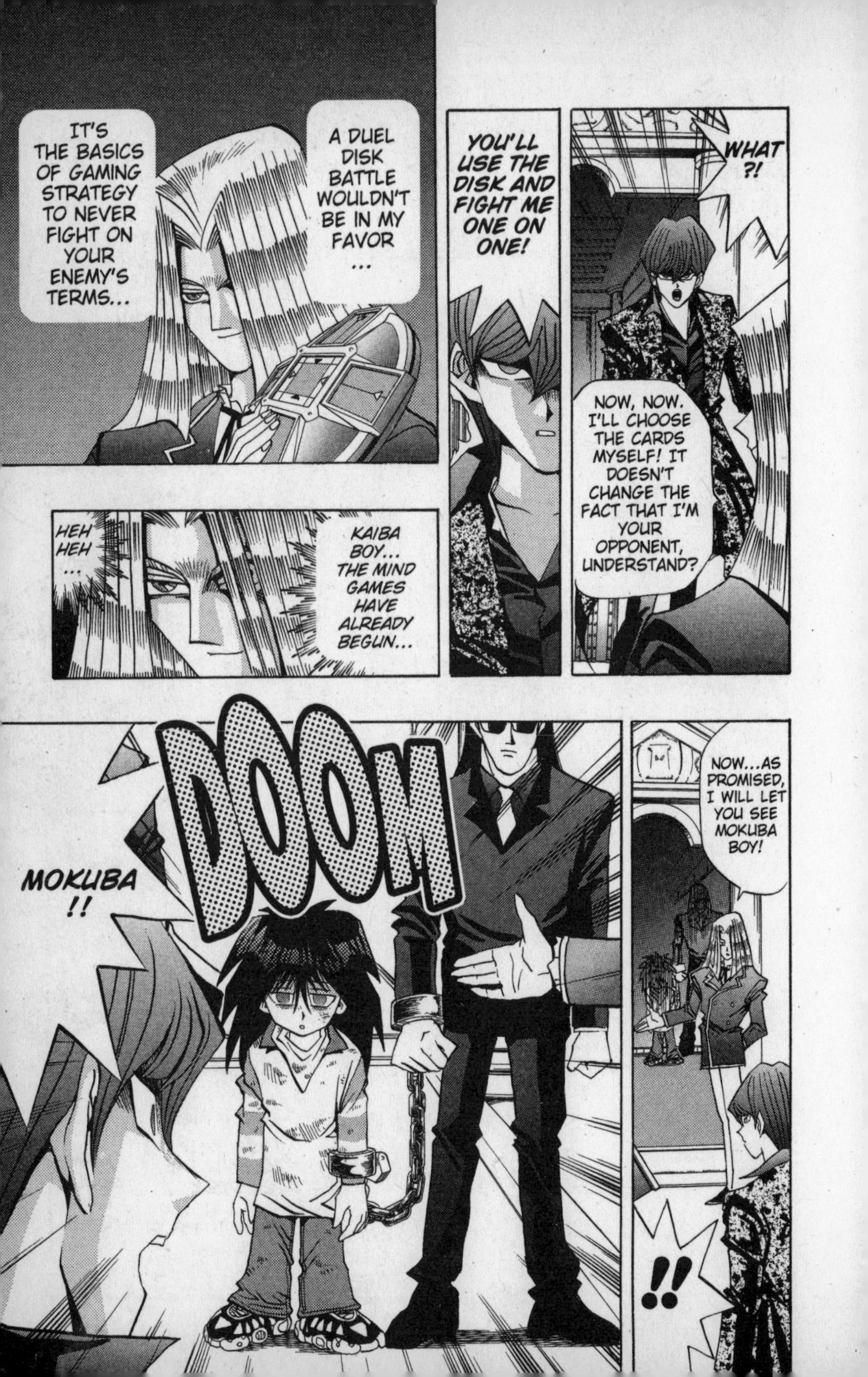
WHAT?!
NOW, NOW. I'LL CHOOSE THE CARDS MYSELF! IT DOESN'T CHANGE THE FACT THAT I'M YOUR OPPONENT, UNDERSTAND?
YOU'LL USE THE DISK AND FIGHT ME ONE ON ONE!
A DUEL DISK BATTLE WOULDN'T BE IN MY FAVOR...
IT'S THE BASICS OF GAMING STRATEGY TO NEVER FIGHT ON YOUR ENEMY'S TERMS...
KAIBA BOY... THE MIND GAMES HAVE ALREADY BEGUN...
HEH HEH...
NOW...AS PROMISED, I WILL LET YOU SEE MOKUBA BOY!
!!
DOOM
MOKUBA!!

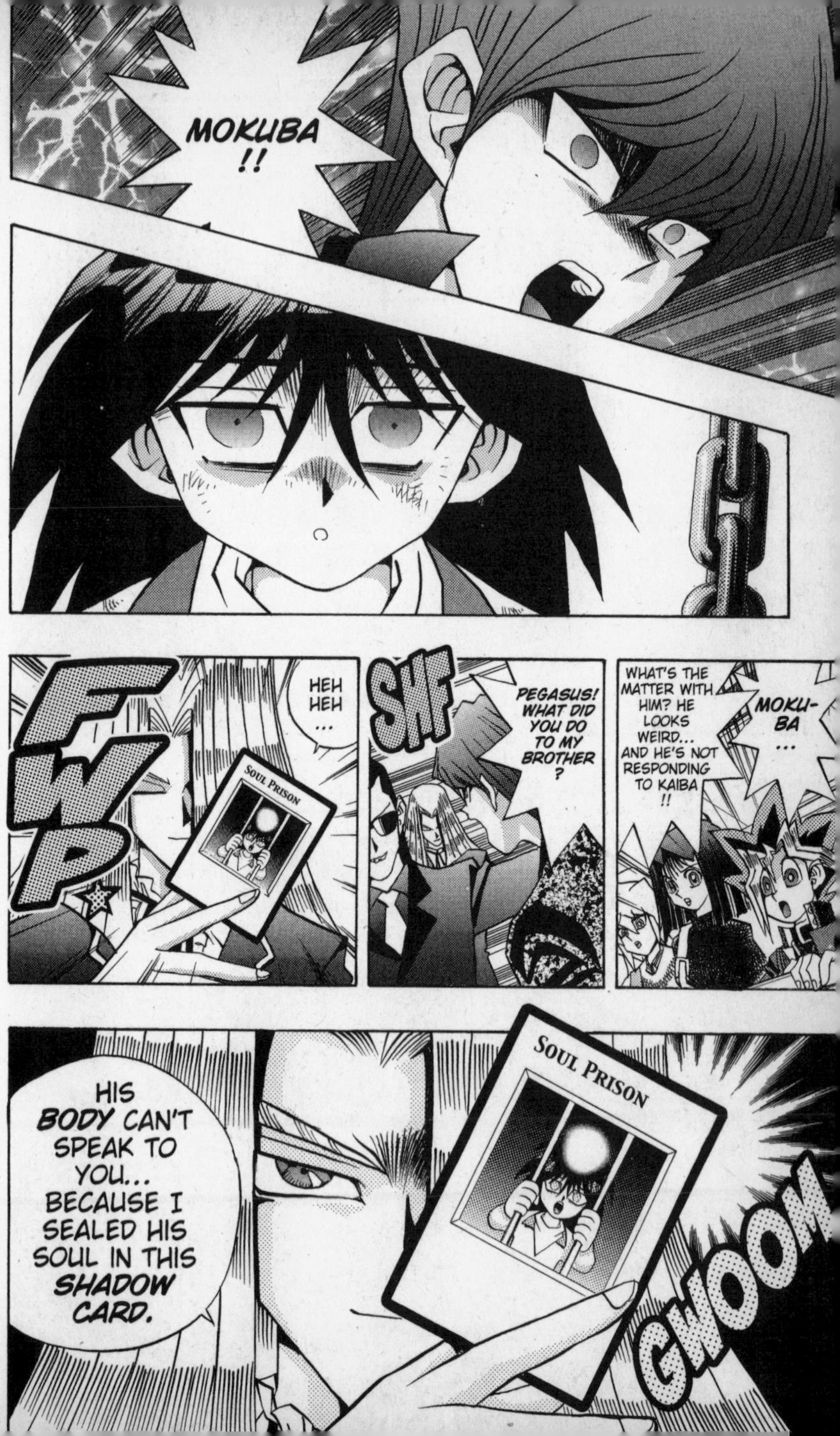
MOKUBA !!
MOKU-BA ...
WHAT'S THE MATTER WITH HIM? HE LOOKS WEIRD... AND HE'S NOT RESPONDING TO KAIBA !!
SHF
PEGASUS! WHAT DID YOU DO TO MY BROTHER ?
HEH HEH ...
FWP
SOUL PRISON
SOUL PRISON
HIS BODY CAN'T SPEAK TO YOU... BECAUSE I SEALED HIS SOUL IN THIS SHADOW CARD.
CHOOM

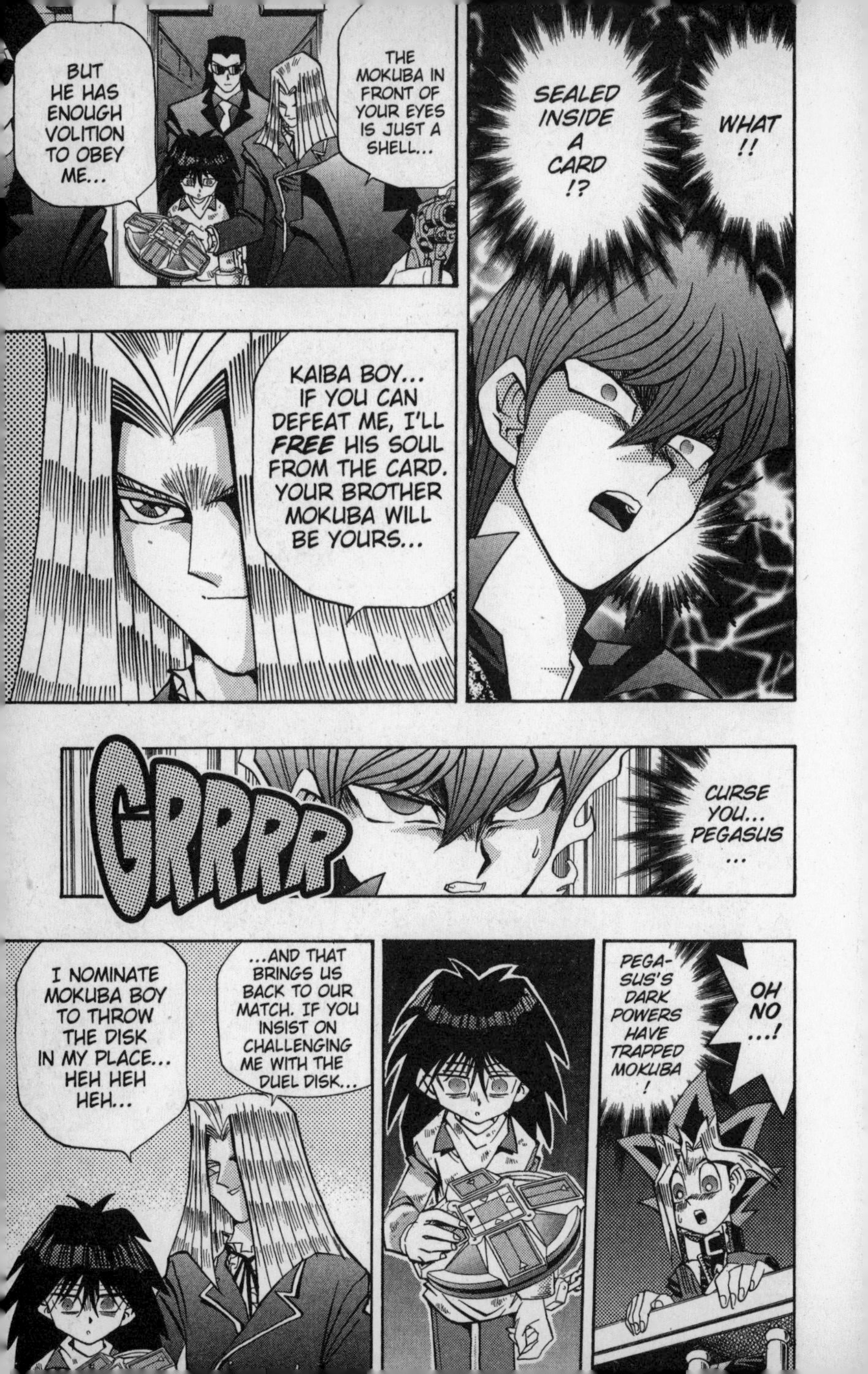
WHAT!!
SEALED INSIDE A CARD!?
THE MOKUBA IN FRONT OF YOUR EYES IS JUST A SHELL...
BUT HE HAS ENOUGH VOLITION TO OBEY ME...
KAIBA BOY... IF YOU CAN DEFEAT ME, I'LL *FREE* HIS SOUL FROM THE CARD. YOUR BROTHER MOKUBA WILL BE YOURS...
CURSE YOU... PEGASUS...
GRRRRR
OH NO...!
PEGA-SUS'S DARK POWERS HAVE TRAPPED MOKUBA!
...AND THAT BRINGS US BACK TO OUR MATCH. IF YOU INSIST ON CHALLENGING ME WITH THE DUEL DISK...
I NOMINATE MOKUBA BOY TO THROW THE DISK IN MY PLACE... HEH HEH HEH...

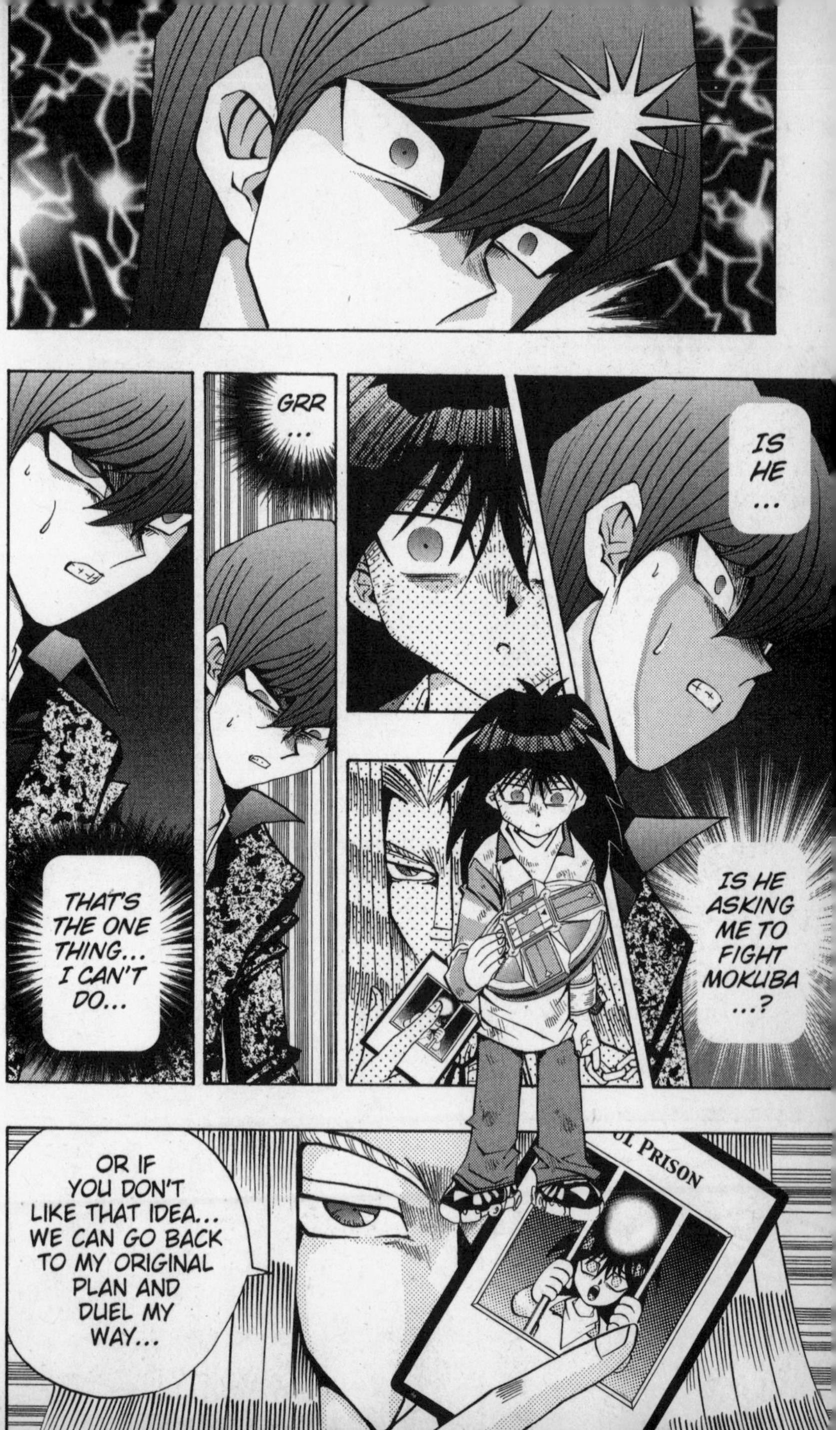
IS HE ...
IS HE ASKING ME TO FIGHT MOKUBA ...?
GRR ...
THAT'S THE ONE THING... I CAN'T DO...
OR IF YOU DON'T LIKE THAT IDEA... WE CAN GO BACK TO MY ORIGINAL PLAN AND DUEL MY WAY...

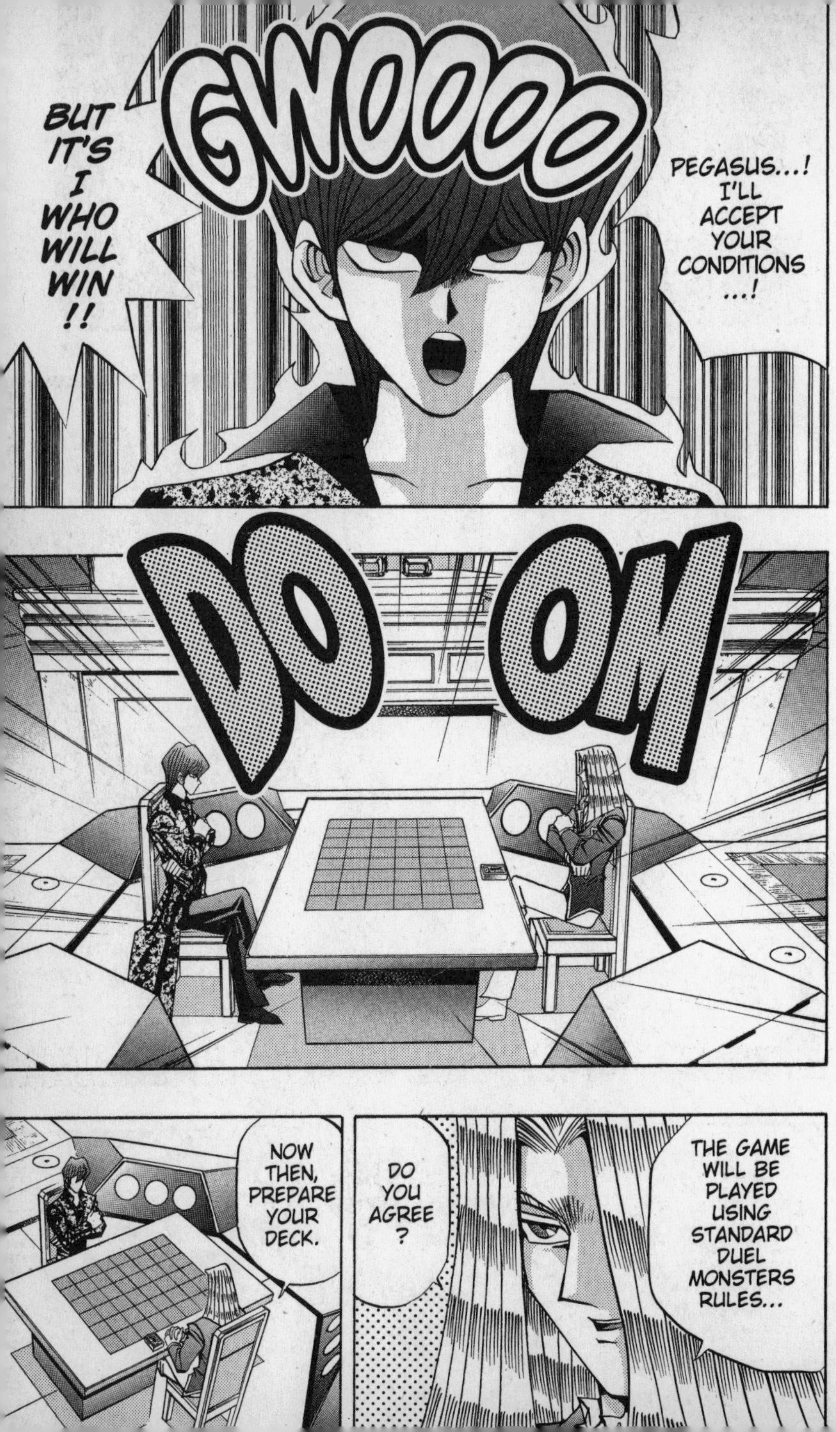
PEGASUS...! I'LL ACCEPT YOUR CONDITIONS ...!
GWOOOO
BUT IT'S I WHO WILL WIN !!
DO OM
THE GAME WILL BE PLAYED USING STANDARD DUEL MONSTERS RULES...
DO YOU AGREE ?
NOW THEN, PREPARE YOUR DECK.

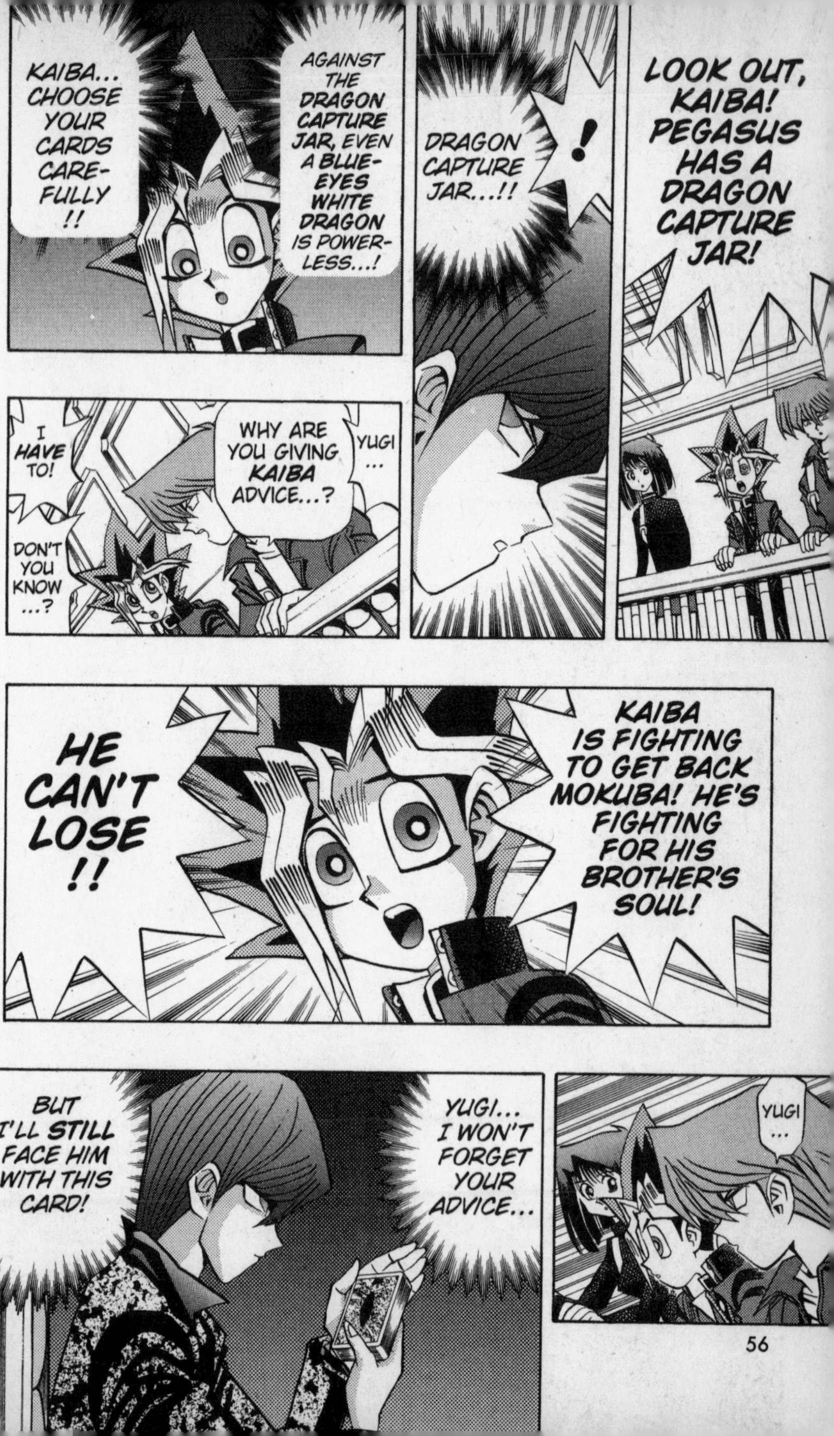
LOOK OUT, KAIBA! PEGASUS HAS A DRAGON CAPTURE JAR!
!
DRAGON CAPTURE JAR...!!
AGAINST THE DRAGON CAPTURE JAR, EVEN A BLUE-EYES WHITE DRAGON IS POWERLESS...!
KAIBA... CHOOSE YOUR CARDS CAREFULLY!!
YUGI ...
WHY ARE YOU GIVING KAIBA ADVICE...?
I HAVE TO!
DON'T YOU KNOW ...?
KAIBA IS FIGHTING TO GET BACK MOKUBA! HE'S FIGHTING FOR HIS BROTHER'S SOUL!
HE CAN'T LOSE!!
YUGI ...
YUGI... I WON'T FORGET YOUR ADVICE...
BUT I'LL STILL FACE HIM WITH THIS CARD!

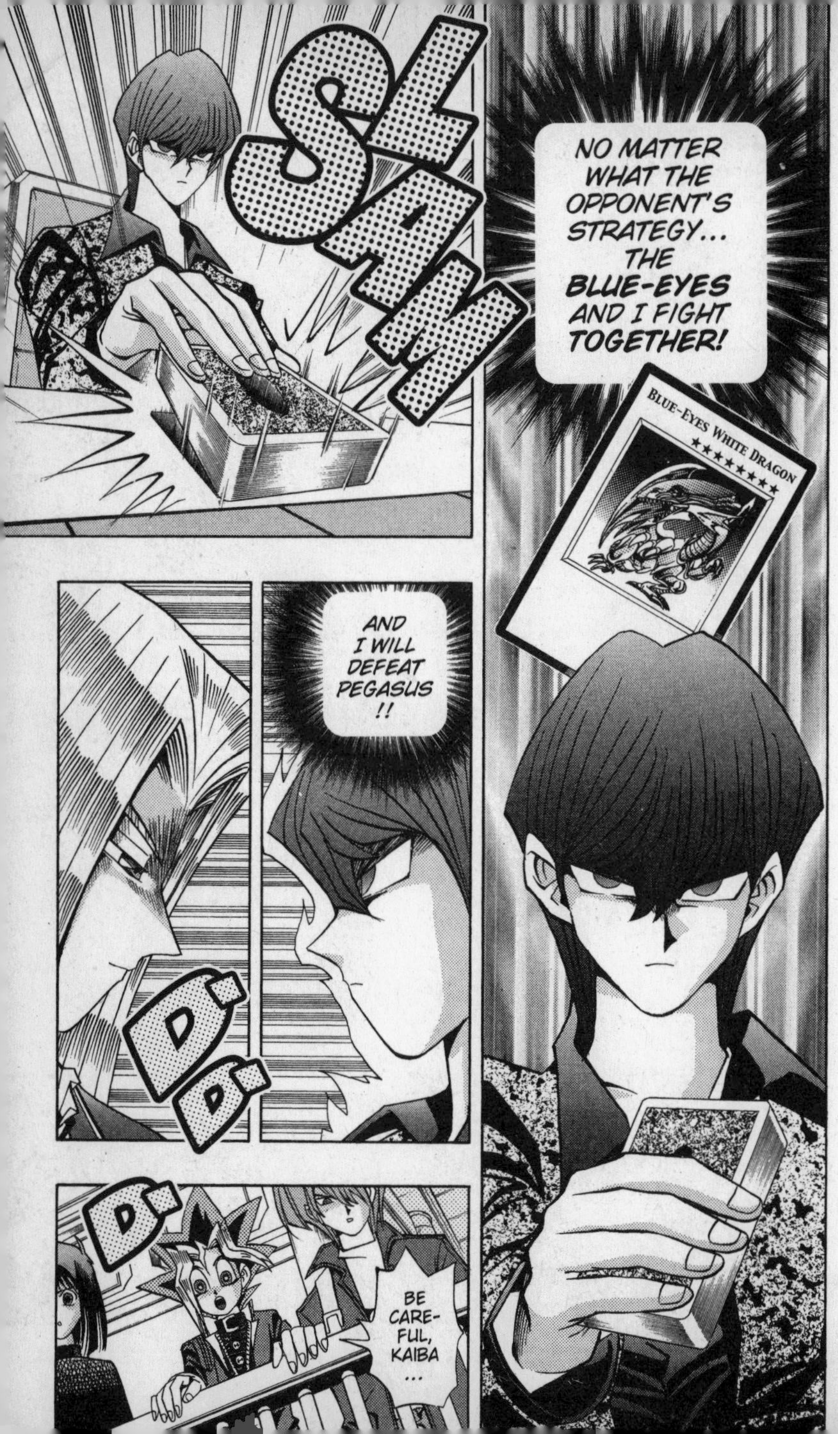
NO MATTER WHAT THE OPPONENT'S STRATEGY... THE BLUE-EYES AND I FIGHT TOGETHER!
BLUE-EYES WHITE DRAGON
SLAM!!
AND I WILL DEFEAT PEGASUS !!
D D D
D
BE CARE-FUL, KAIBA ...

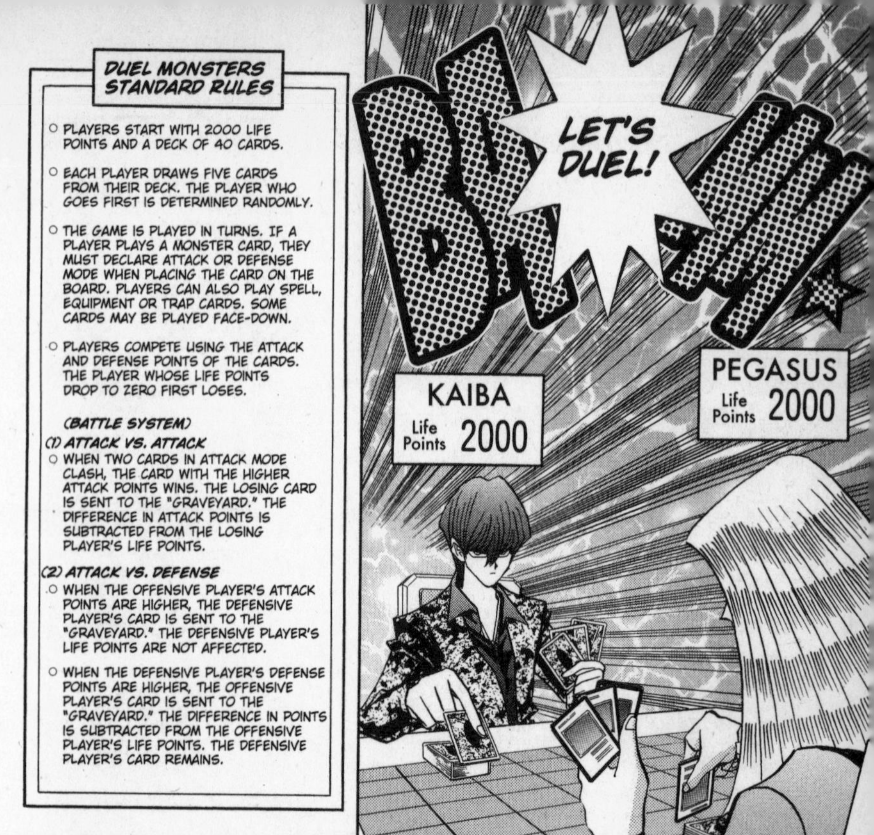
LET'S DUEL!
PEGASUS Life Points 2000
KAIBA Life Points 2000

DUEL MONSTERS STANDARD RULES

- PLAYERS START WITH 2000 LIFE POINTS AND A DECK OF 40 CARDS.
- EACH PLAYER DRAWS FIVE CARDS FROM THEIR DECK. THE PLAYER WHO GOES FIRST IS DETERMINED RANDOMLY.
- THE GAME IS PLAYED IN TURNS. IF A PLAYER PLAYS A MONSTER CARD, THEY MUST DECLARE ATTACK OR DEFENSE MODE WHEN PLACING THE CARD ON THE BOARD. PLAYERS CAN ALSO PLAY SPELL, EQUIPMENT OR TRAP CARDS. SOME CARDS MAY BE PLAYED FACE-DOWN.
- PLAYERS COMPETE USING THE ATTACK AND DEFENSE POINTS OF THE CARDS. THE PLAYER WHOSE LIFE POINTS DROP TO ZERO FIRST LOSES.

(BATTLE SYSTEM)

(1) ATTACK VS. ATTACK

- WHEN TWO CARDS IN ATTACK MODE CLASH, THE CARD WITH THE HIGHER ATTACK POINTS WINS. THE LOSING CARD IS SENT TO THE "GRAVEYARD." THE DIFFERENCE IN ATTACK POINTS IS SUBTRACTED FROM THE LOSING PLAYER'S LIFE POINTS.

(2) ATTACK VS. DEFENSE

- WHEN THE OFFENSIVE PLAYER'S ATTACK POINTS ARE HIGHER, THE DEFENSIVE PLAYER'S CARD IS SENT TO THE "GRAVEYARD." THE DEFENSIVE PLAYER'S LIFE POINTS ARE NOT AFFECTED.
- WHEN THE DEFENSIVE PLAYER'S DEFENSE POINTS ARE HIGHER, THE OFFENSIVE PLAYER'S CARD IS SENT TO THE "GRAVEYARD." THE DIFFERENCE IN POINTS IS SUBTRACTED FROM THE OFFENSIVE PLAYER'S LIFE POINTS. THE DEFENSIVE PLAYER'S CARD REMAINS.

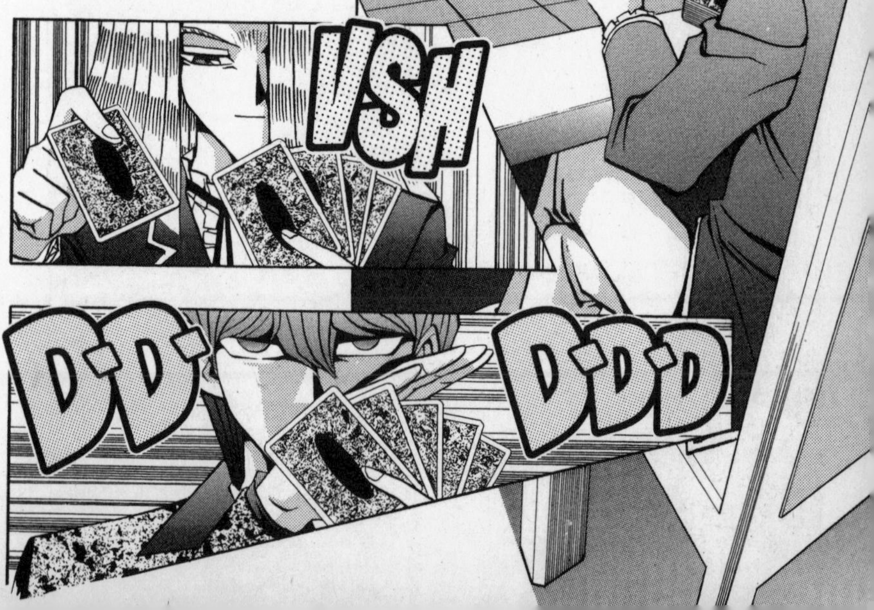
VSH
D-D-D
D-D-

READ THIS WAY

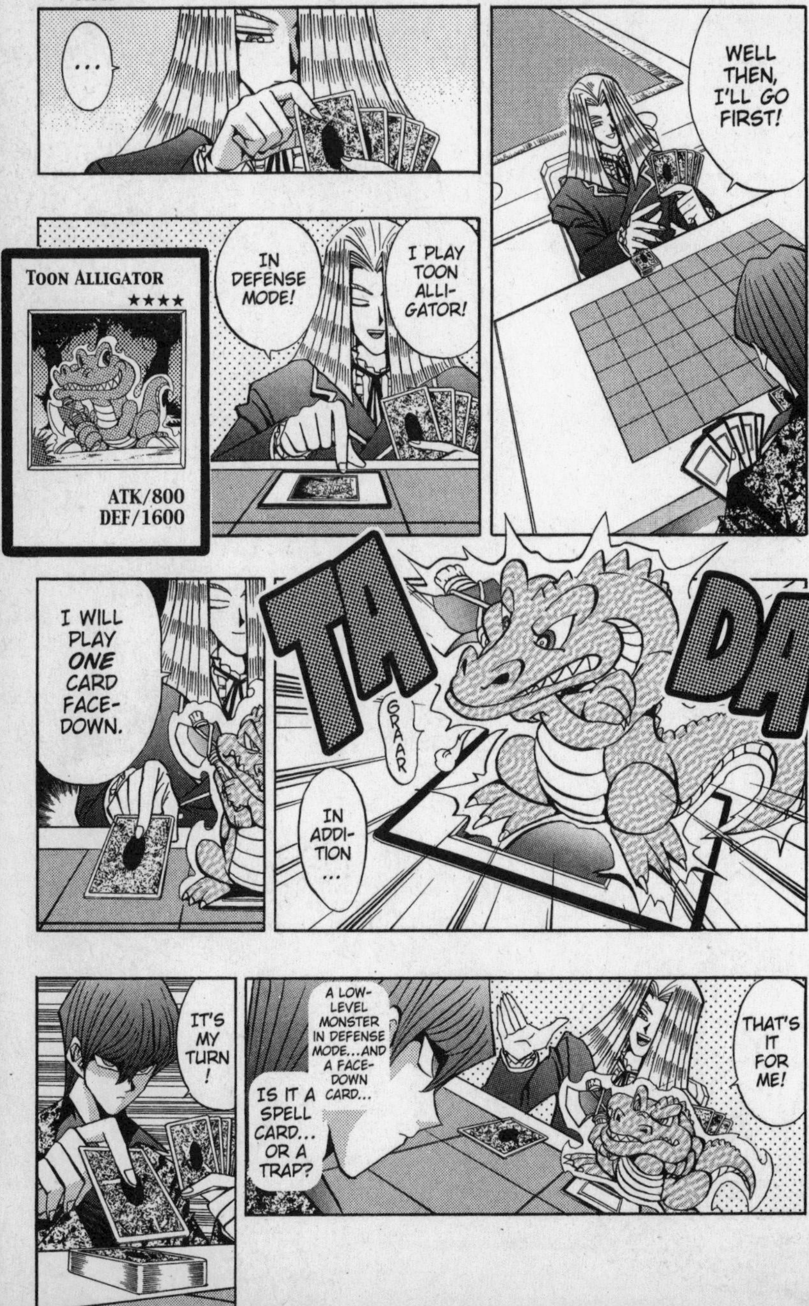
WELL THEN, I'LL GO FIRST!
...
I PLAY TOON ALLIGATOR!
IN DEFENSE MODE!
TOON ALLIGATOR
★★★★
ATK/800
DEF/1600
TA
DA
GRAAAR
IN ADDITION...
I WILL PLAY ONE CARD FACE-DOWN.
THAT'S IT FOR ME!
A LOW-LEVEL MONSTER IN DEFENSE MODE...AND A FACE-DOWN CARD...
IS IT A SPELL CARD... OR A TRAP?
IT'S MY TURN!

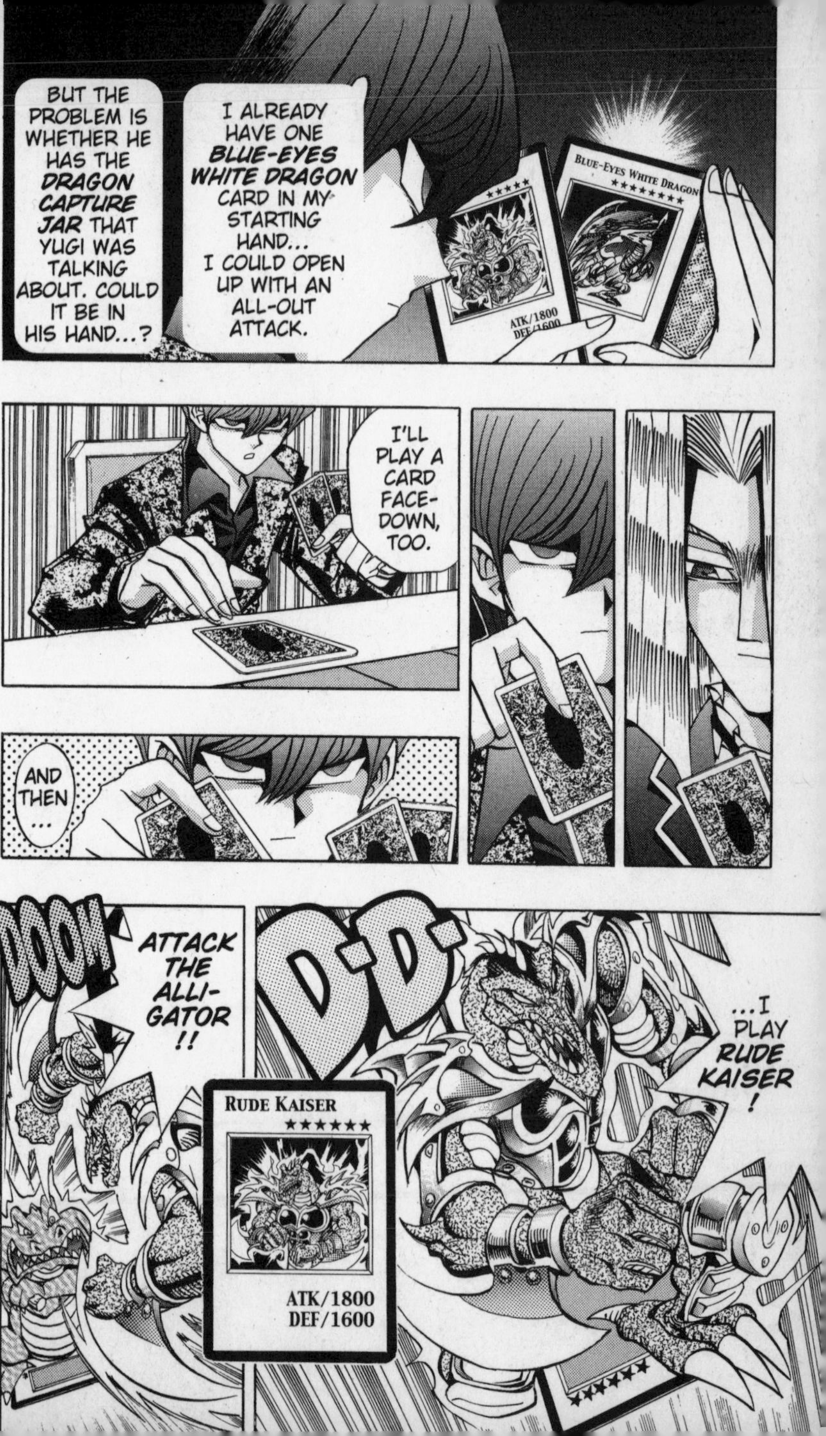
I ALREADY HAVE ONE BLUE-EYES WHITE DRAGON CARD IN MY STARTING HAND... I COULD OPEN UP WITH AN ALL-OUT ATTACK.
BUT THE PROBLEM IS WHETHER HE HAS THE DRAGON CAPTURE JAR THAT YUGI WAS TALKING ABOUT. COULD IT BE IN HIS HAND...?
BLUE-EYES WHITE DRAGON
ATK/1800
DEF/1600
I'LL PLAY A CARD FACE-DOWN, TOO.
AND THEN ...
D-D-
...I PLAY RUDE KAISER!
RUDE KAISER
ATK/1800
DEF/1600
DOOM
ATTACK THE ALLI-GATOR!!

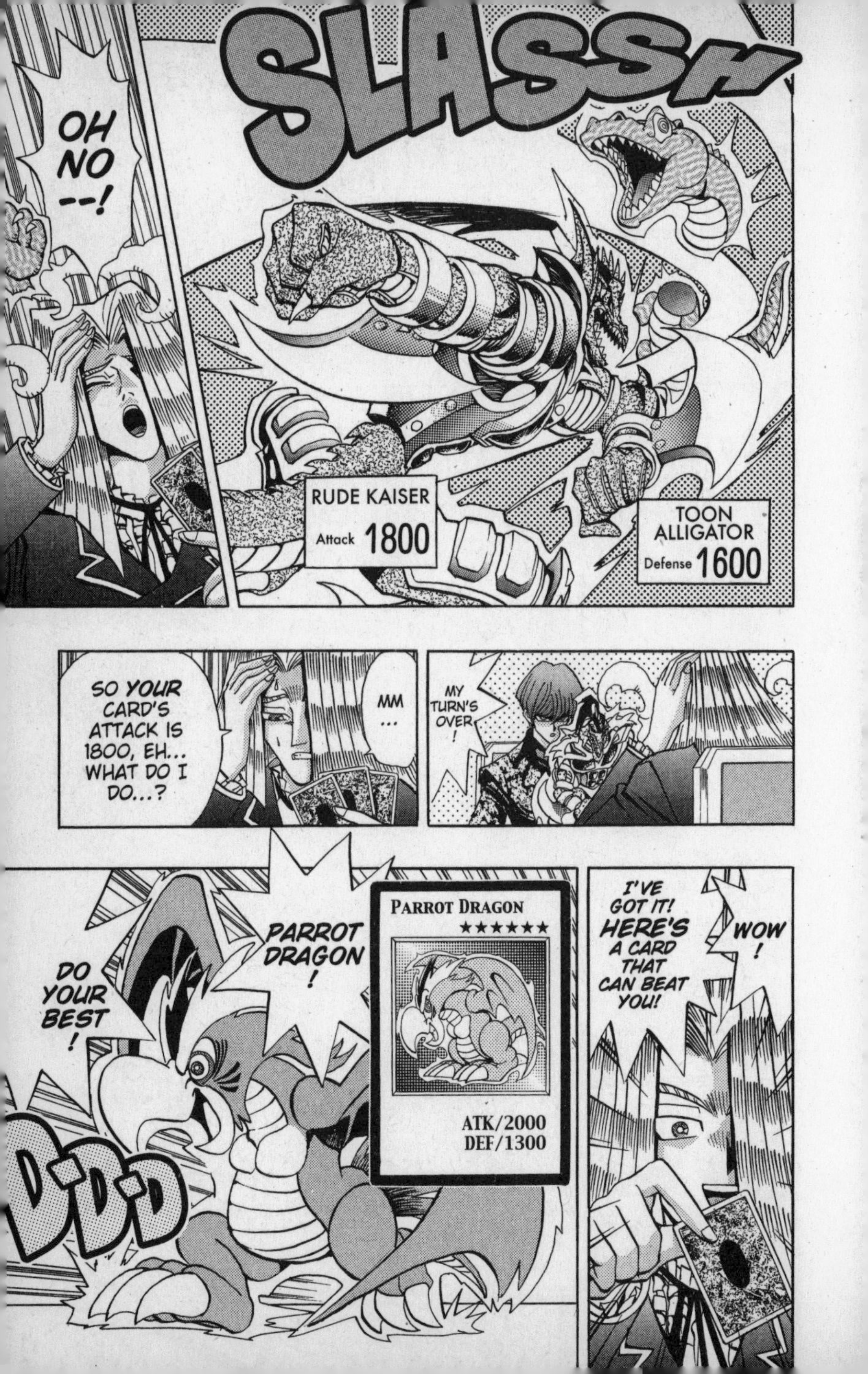
SLASSH
TOON ALLIGATOR Defense 1600
RUDE KAISER Attack 1800
OH NO --!
MY TURN'S OVER!
MM ...
SO YOUR CARD'S ATTACK IS 1800, EH... WHAT DO I DO...?
WOW!
I'VE GOT IT! HERE'S A CARD THAT CAN BEAT YOU!
PARROT DRAGON ★★★★★★
ATK/2000 DEF/1300
PARROT DRAGON!
DO YOUR BEST!
D-D-D

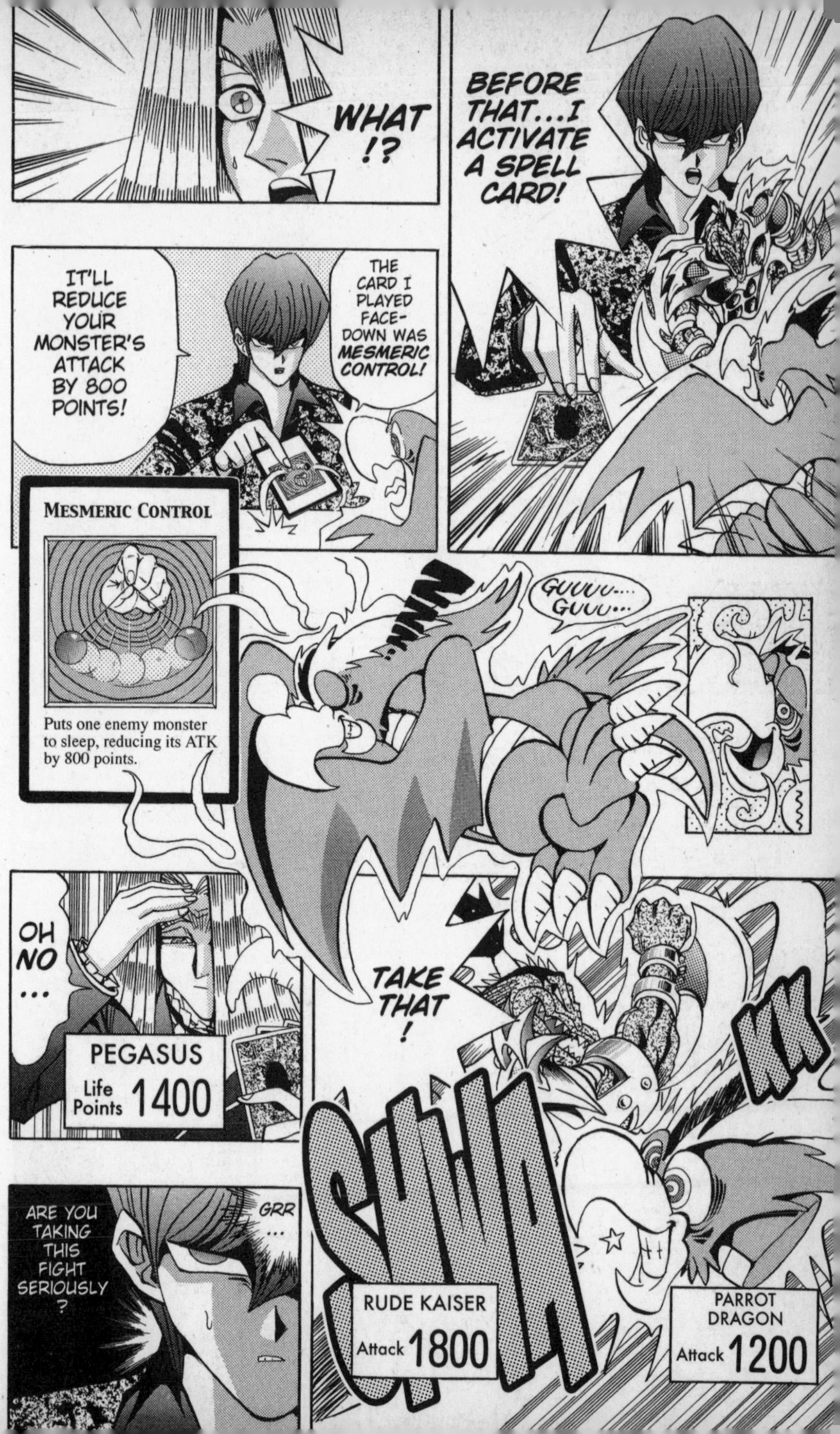
BEFORE THAT...I ACTIVATE A SPELL CARD!
WHAT !?
THE CARD I PLAYED FACE-DOWN WAS MESMERIC CONTROL!
IT'LL REDUCE YOUR MONSTER'S ATTACK BY 800 POINTS!
MESMERIC CONTROL
Puts one enemy monster to sleep, reducing its ATK by 800 points.
GUUUU.... GUUU...
TAKE THAT!
KK
SHWA
RUDE KAISER Attack 1800
PARROT DRAGON Attack 1200
OH NO ...
PEGASUS Life Points 1400
GRR ...
ARE YOU TAKING THIS FIGHT SERIOUSLY?

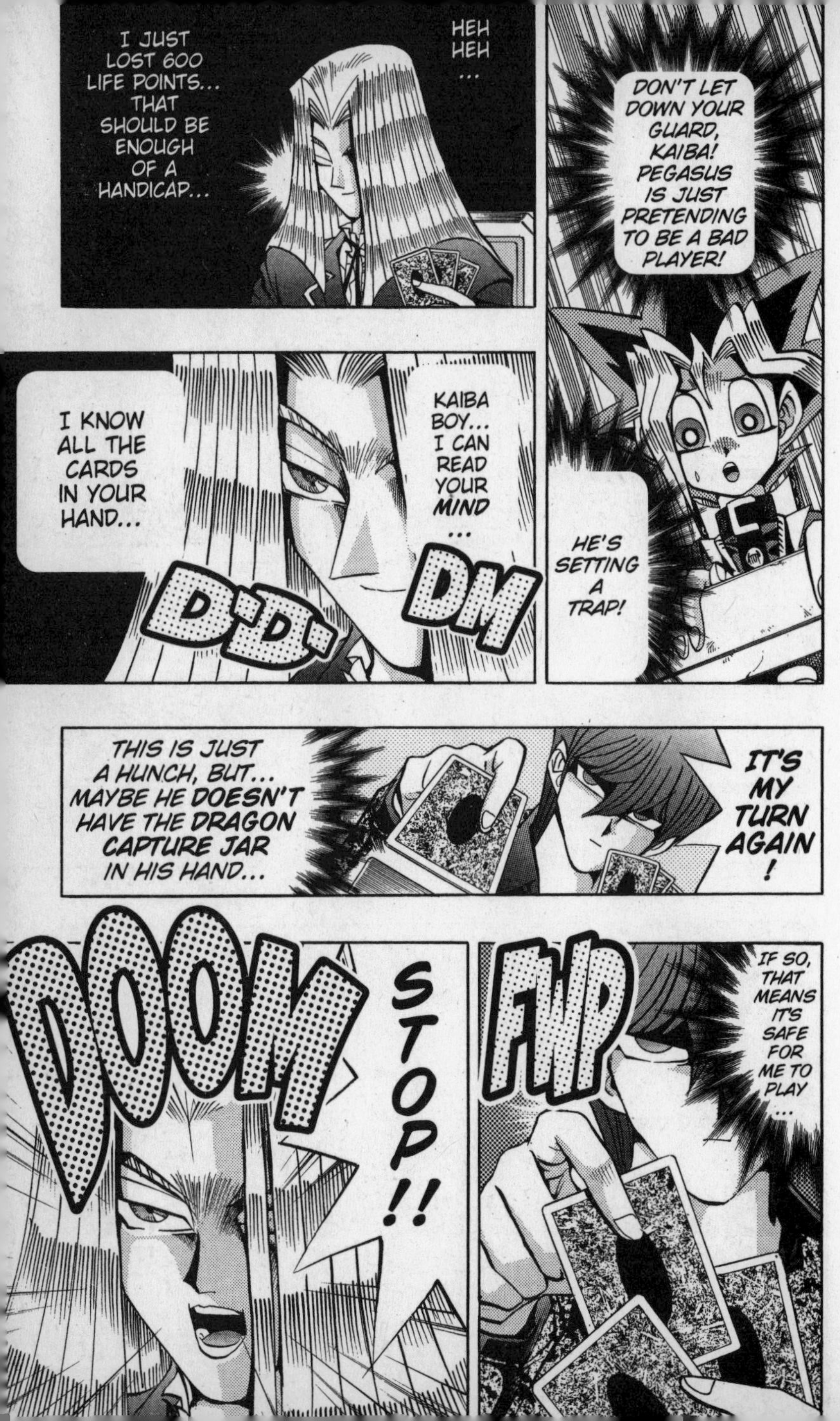
DON'T LET DOWN YOUR GUARD, KAIBA! PEGASUS IS JUST PRETENDING TO BE A BAD PLAYER!
HE'S SETTING A TRAP!
HEH HEH ...
I JUST LOST 600 LIFE POINTS... THAT SHOULD BE ENOUGH OF A HANDICAP...
KAIBA BOY... I CAN READ YOUR MIND ...
DM
I KNOW ALL THE CARDS IN YOUR HAND...
D'D'
IT'S MY TURN AGAIN!
THIS IS JUST A HUNCH, BUT... MAYBE HE DOESN'T HAVE THE DRAGON CAPTURE JAR IN HIS HAND...
IF SO, THAT MEANS IT'S SAFE FOR ME TO PLAY ...
FWP
STOP!!
DOOM

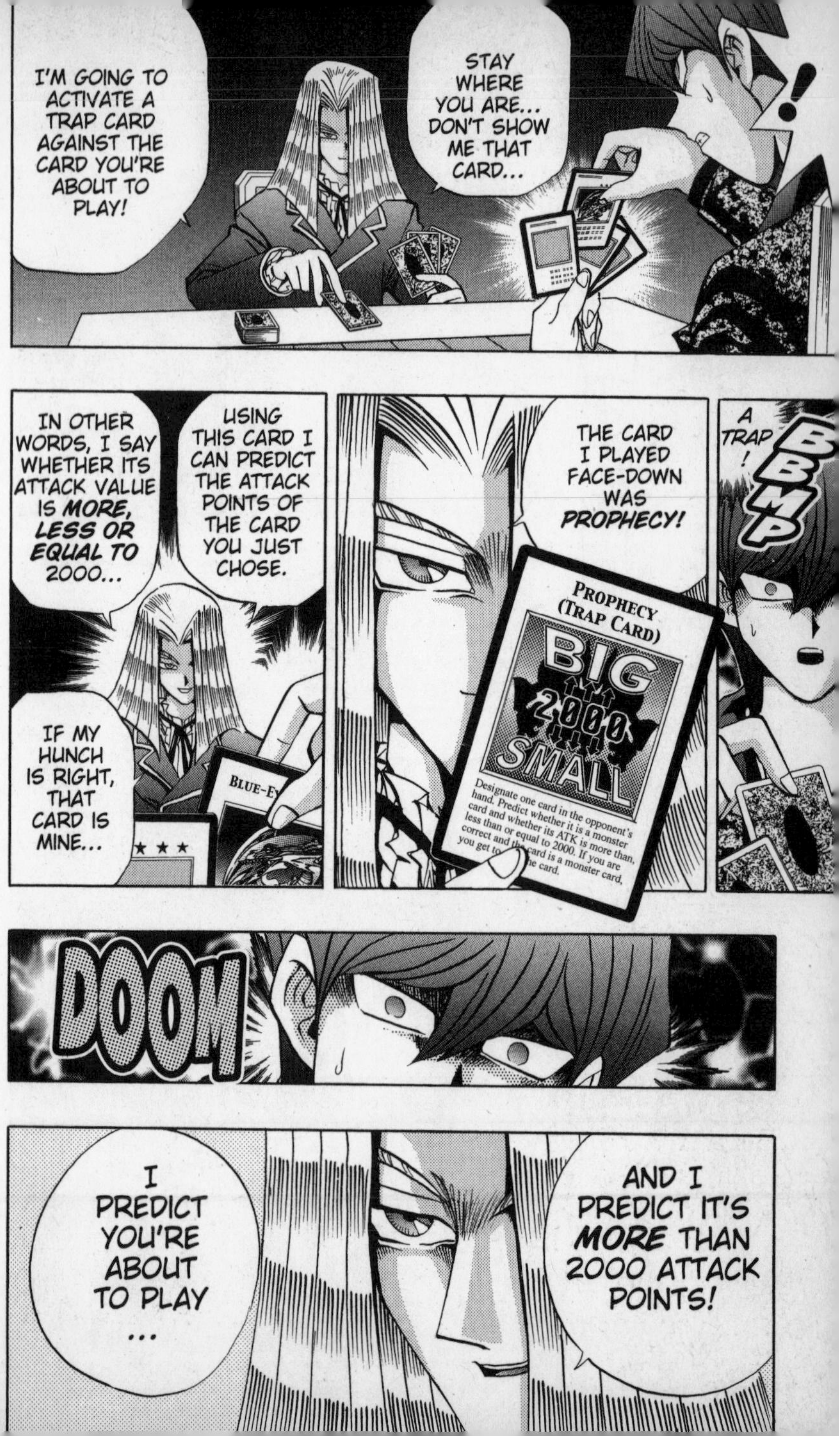
!
STAY WHERE YOU ARE... DON'T SHOW ME THAT CARD...
I'M GOING TO ACTIVATE A TRAP CARD AGAINST THE CARD YOU'RE ABOUT TO PLAY!
A TRAP!
BBMP
THE CARD I PLAYED FACE-DOWN WAS ***PROPHECY!***
PROPHECY (TRAP CARD)
BIG
2000
SMALL
Designate one card in the opponent's hand. Predict whether it is a monster card and whether its ATK is more than, less than or equal to 2000. If you are correct and the card is a monster card, you get to
USING THIS CARD I CAN PREDICT THE ATTACK POINTS OF THE CARD YOU JUST CHOSE.
IN OTHER WORDS, I SAY WHETHER ITS ATTACK VALUE IS ***MORE, LESS OR EQUAL TO*** 2000...
IF MY HUNCH IS RIGHT, THAT CARD IS MINE...
DOOM
I PREDICT YOU'RE ABOUT TO PLAY ...
AND I PREDICT IT'S ***MORE*** THAN 2000 ATTACK POINTS!

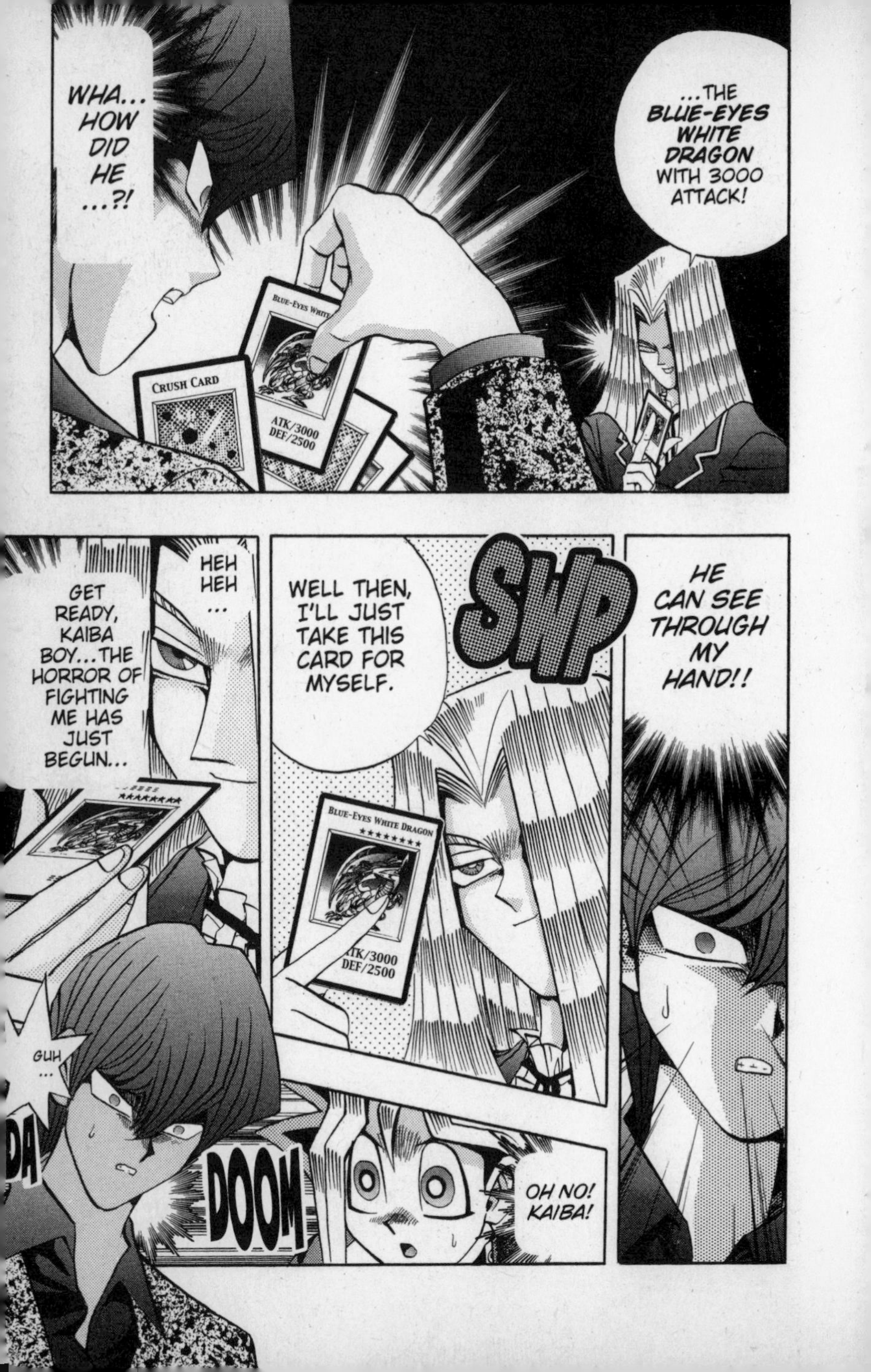
...THE BLUE-EYES WHITE DRAGON WITH 3000 ATTACK!
WHA... HOW DID HE ...?!
BLUE-EYES WHITE
ATK/3000 DEF/2500
CRUSH CARD
HE CAN SEE THROUGH MY HAND!!
SWP
WELL THEN, I'LL JUST TAKE THIS CARD FOR MYSELF.
BLUE-EYES WHITE DRAGON
ATK/3000 DEF/2500
HEH HEH ...
GET READY, KAIBA BOY...THE HORROR OF FIGHTING ME HAS JUST BEGUN...
OH NO! KAIBA!
DOOM
DA
GUH ...

Duel 50: The Deadly Duelist King

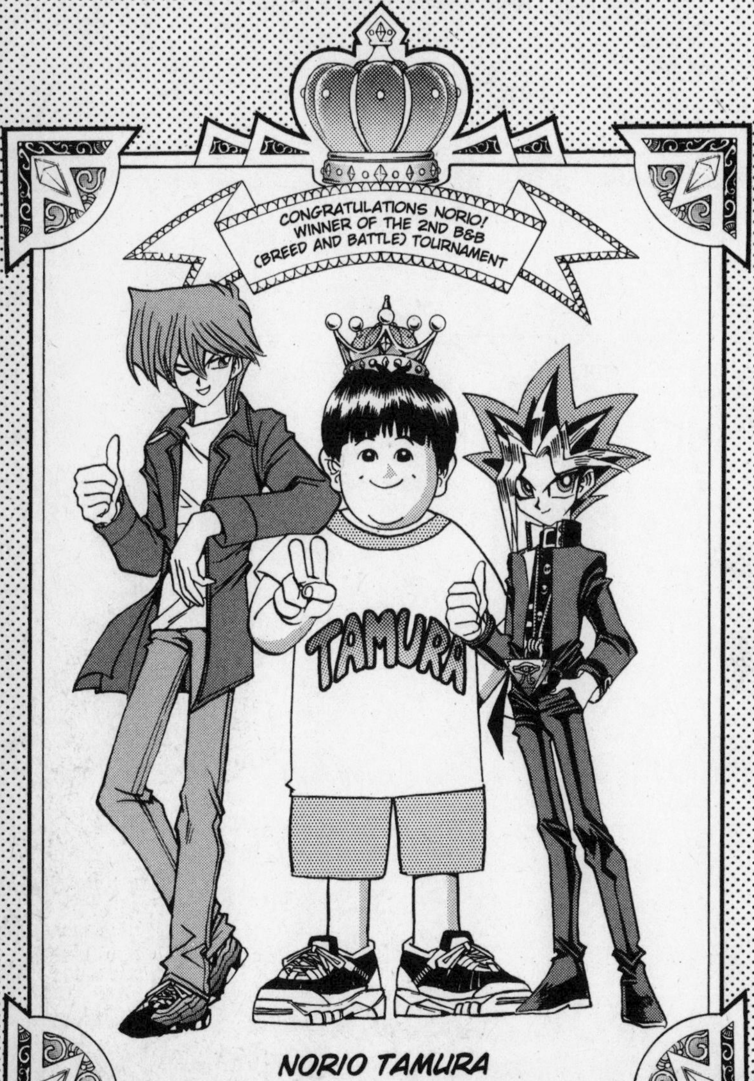
CONGRATULATIONS NORIO!
WINNER OF THE 2ND B&B
(BREED AND BATTLE) TOURNAMENT
TAMURA
NORIO TAMURA

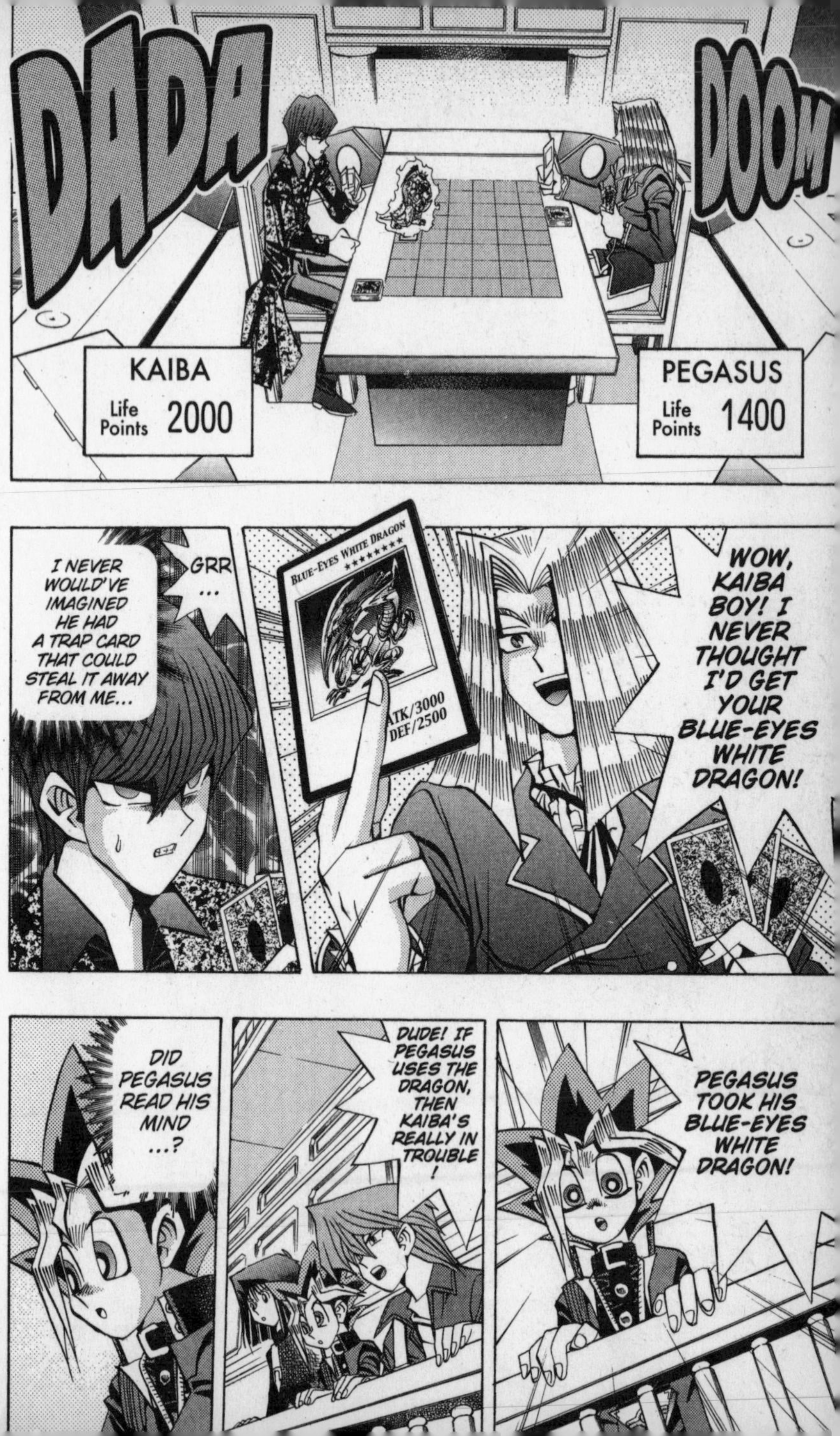
DADA DOOM
PEGASUS
Life Points 1400
KAIBA
Life Points 2000
WOW, KAIBA BOY! I NEVER THOUGHT I'D GET YOUR BLUE-EYES WHITE DRAGON!
BLUE-EYES WHITE DRAGON
ATK/3000 DEF/2500
GRR ...
I NEVER WOULD'VE IMAGINED HE HAD A TRAP CARD THAT COULD STEAL IT AWAY FROM ME...
PEGASUS TOOK HIS BLUE-EYES WHITE DRAGON!
DUDE! IF PEGASUS USES THE DRAGON, THEN KAIBA'S REALLY IN TROUBLE!
DID PEGASUS READ HIS MIND ...?

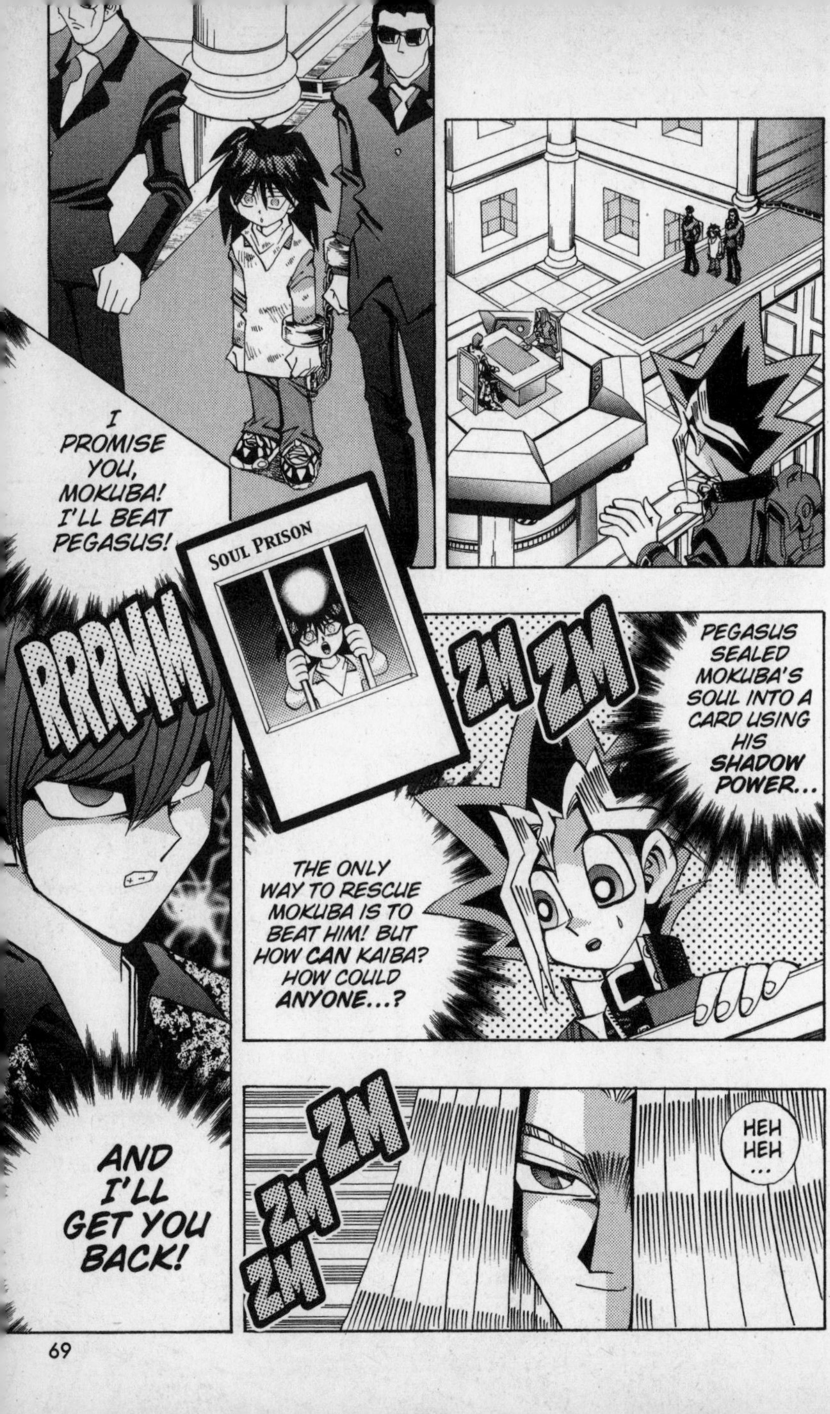
PEGASUS SEALED MOKUBA'S SOUL INTO A CARD USING HIS SHADOW POWER...
ZM ZM
SOUL PRISON
THE ONLY WAY TO RESCUE MOKUBA IS TO BEAT HIM! BUT HOW CAN KAIBA? HOW COULD ANYONE...?
HEH HEH ...
ZM ZM ZM
I PROMISE YOU, MOKUBA! I'LL BEAT PEGASUS!
RRRMM
AND I'LL GET YOU BACK!

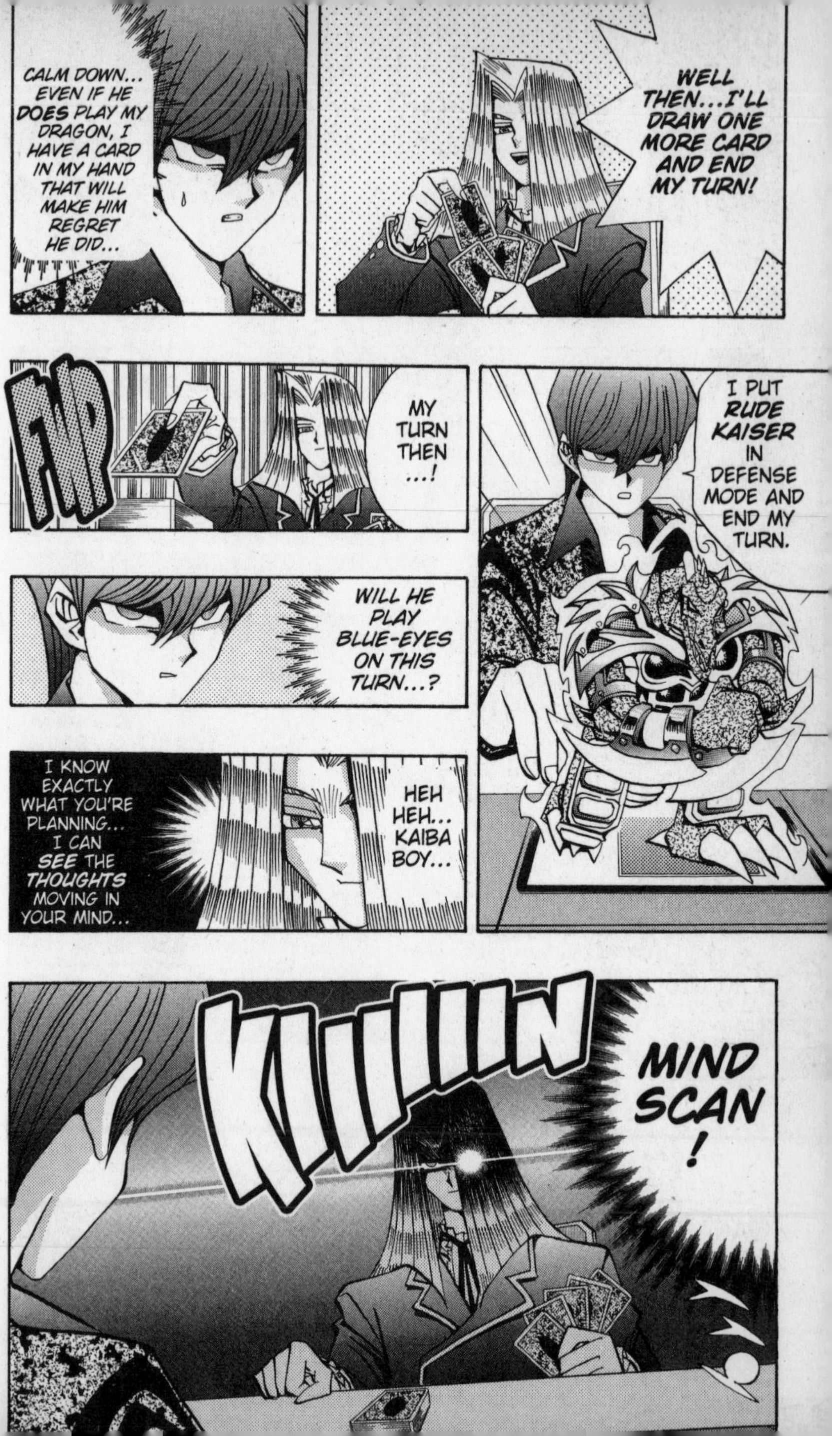
WELL THEN...I'LL DRAW ONE MORE CARD AND END MY TURN!
CALM DOWN... EVEN IF HE DOES PLAY MY DRAGON, I HAVE A CARD IN MY HAND THAT WILL MAKE HIM REGRET HE DID...
I PUT RUDE KAISER IN DEFENSE MODE AND END MY TURN.
FWIP
MY TURN THEN ...!
WILL HE PLAY BLUE-EYES ON THIS TURN...?
HEH HEH... KAIBA BOY...
I KNOW EXACTLY WHAT YOU'RE PLANNING... I CAN SEE THE THOUGHTS MOVING IN YOUR MIND...
KIIIIIIN
MIND SCAN !

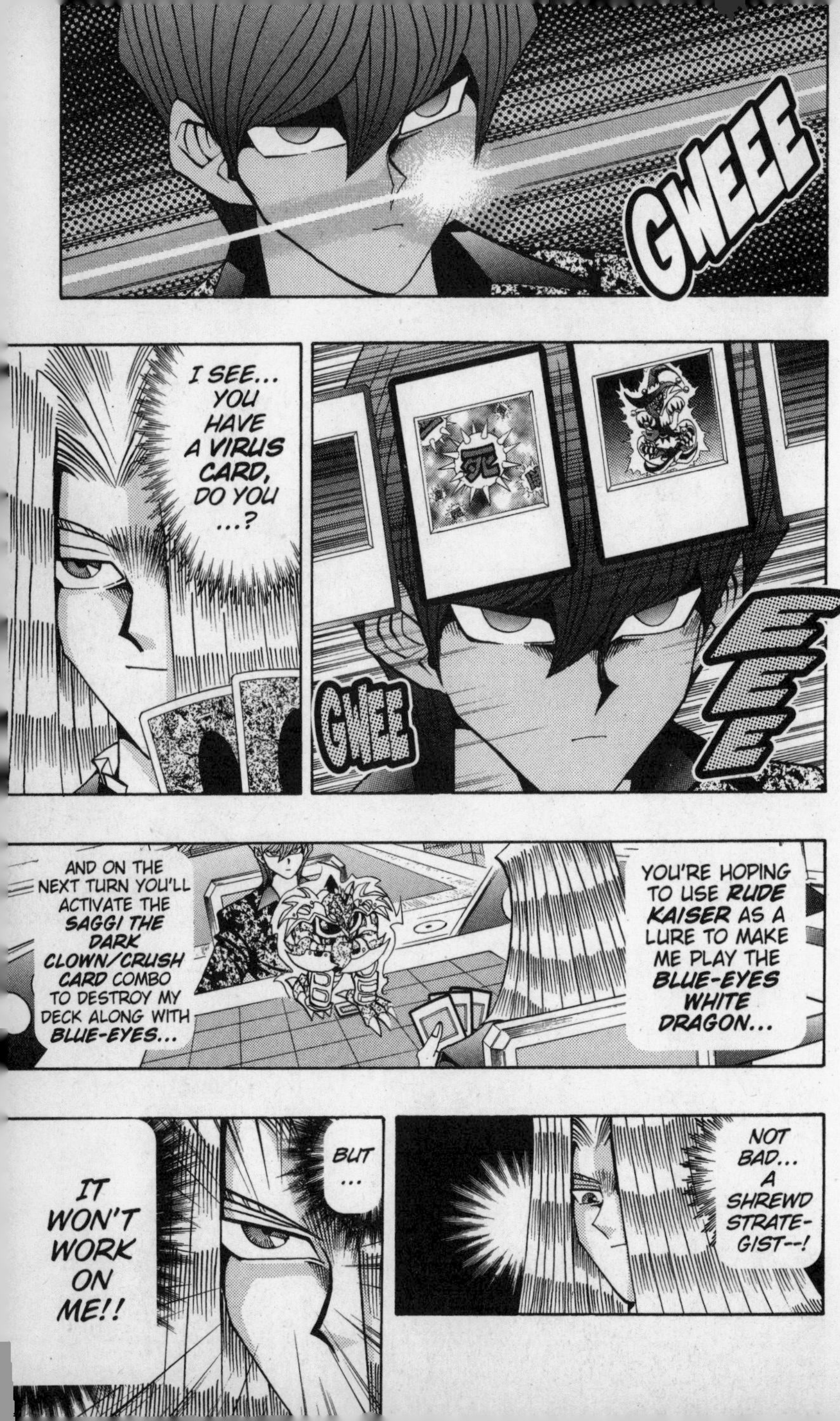
GWEEE
EEEE
GWEE
I SEE... YOU HAVE A VIRUS CARD, DO YOU ...?
YOU'RE HOPING TO USE RUDE KAISER AS A LURE TO MAKE ME PLAY THE BLUE-EYES WHITE DRAGON...
AND ON THE NEXT TURN YOU'LL ACTIVATE THE SAGGI THE DARK CLOWN/CRUSH CARD COMBO TO DESTROY MY DECK ALONG WITH BLUE-EYES...
NOT BAD... A SHREWD STRATE-GIST--!
BUT ...
IT WON'T WORK ON ME!!

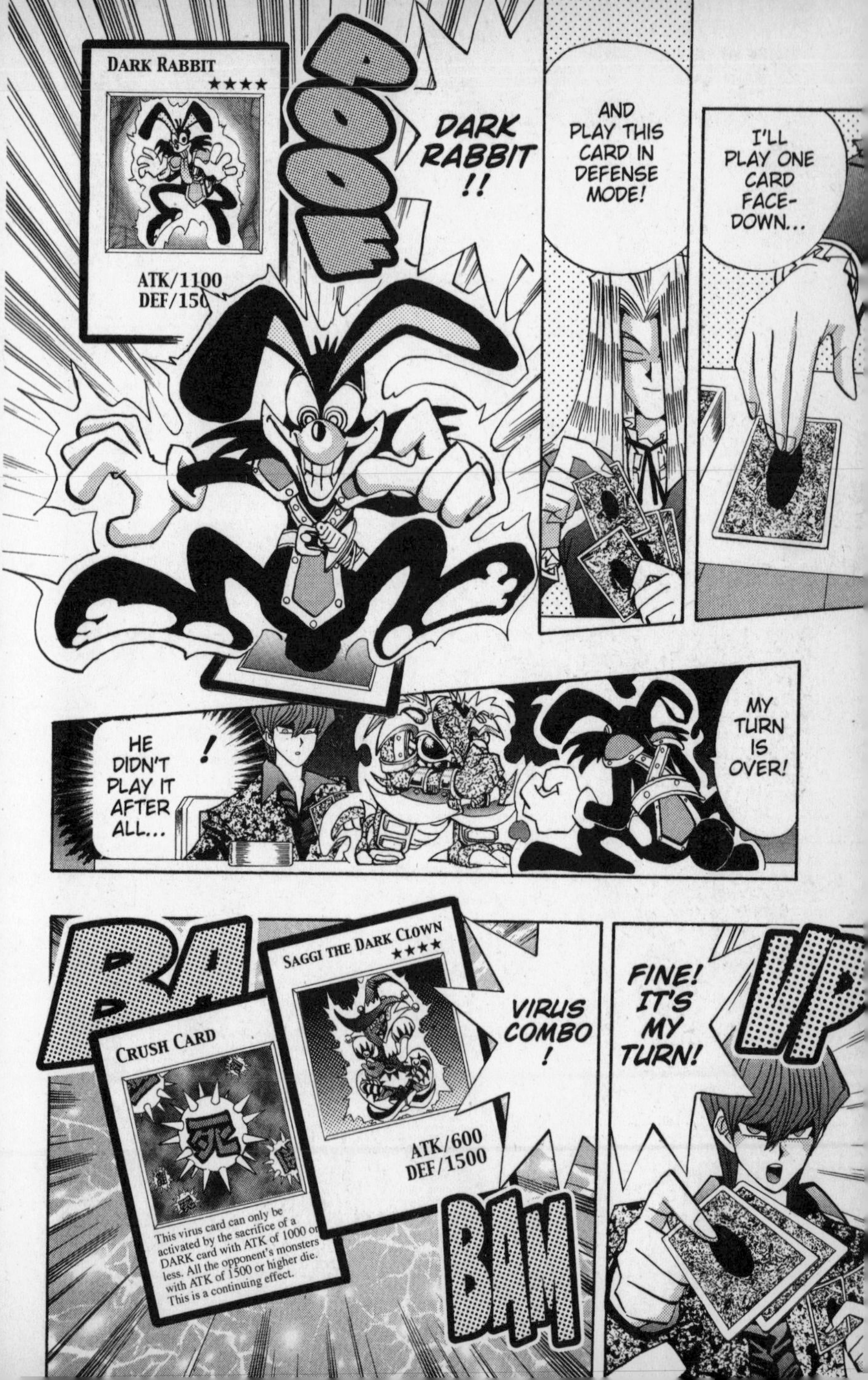
I'LL PLAY ONE CARD FACE-DOWN...
AND PLAY THIS CARD IN DEFENSE MODE!
POOF
DARK RABBIT!!
DARK RABBIT ★★★★
ATK/1100
DEF/150
MY TURN IS OVER!
!
HE DIDN'T PLAY IT AFTER ALL...
FINE! IT'S MY TURN!
VIRUS COMBO!
SAGGI THE DARK CLOWN ★★★★
ATK/600
DEF/1500
CRUSH CARD
This virus card can only be activated by the sacrifice of a DARK card with ATK of 1000 or less. All the opponent's monsters with ATK of 1500 or higher die. This is a continuing effect.
BAM

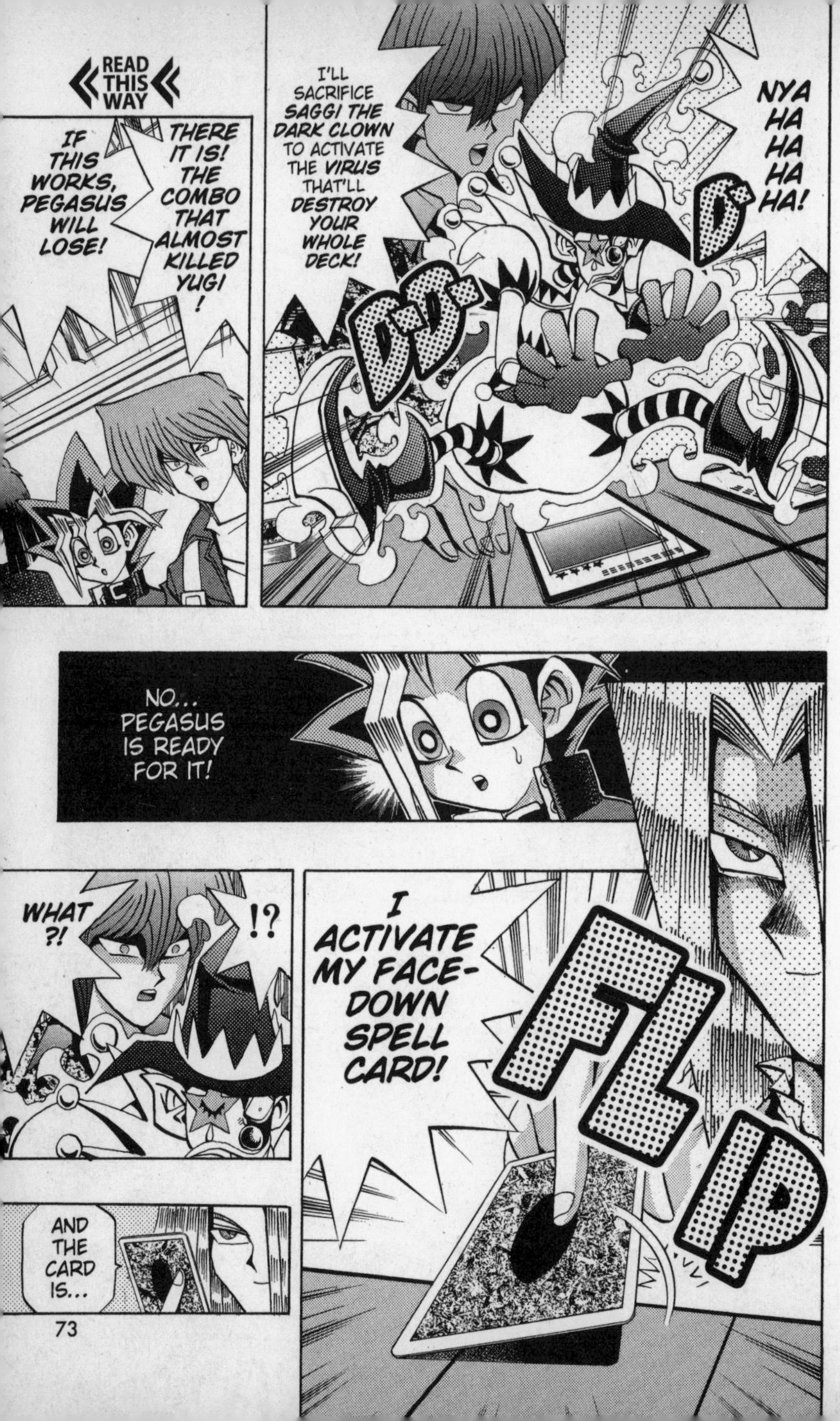
READ THIS WAY
NYA HA HA HA HA!
I'LL SACRIFICE SAGGI THE DARK CLOWN TO ACTIVATE THE VIRUS THAT'LL DESTROY YOUR WHOLE DECK!
THERE IT IS! THE COMBO THAT ALMOST KILLED YUGI!
IF THIS WORKS, PEGASUS WILL LOSE!
NO... PEGASUS IS READY FOR IT!
I ACTIVATE MY FACE-DOWN SPELL CARD!
FLIP
!?
WHAT?!
AND THE CARD IS...

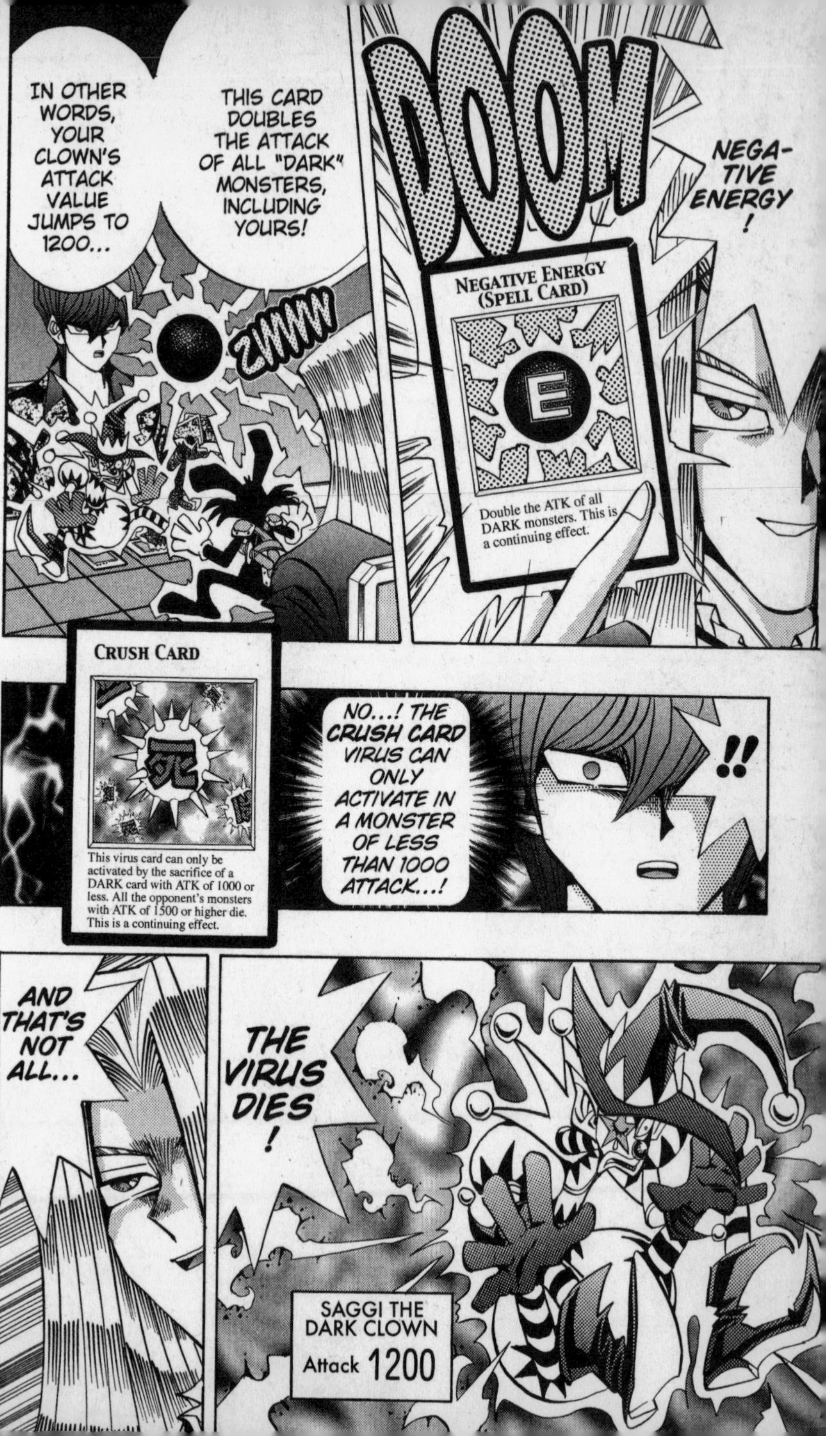
DOOM
NEGATIVE ENERGY!
NEGATIVE ENERGY (SPELL CARD)
E
Double the ATK of all DARK monsters. This is a continuing effect.
THIS CARD DOUBLES THE ATTACK OF ALL "DARK" MONSTERS, INCLUDING YOURS!
IN OTHER WORDS, YOUR CLOWN'S ATTACK VALUE JUMPS TO 1200...
ZWWW
!!
NO...! THE CRUSH CARD VIRUS CAN ONLY ACTIVATE IN A MONSTER OF LESS THAN 1000 ATTACK...!
CRUSH CARD
This virus card can only be activated by the sacrifice of a DARK card with ATK of 1000 or less. All the opponent's monsters with ATK of 1500 or higher die. This is a continuing effect.
THE VIRUS DIES!
SAGGI THE DARK CLOWN
Attack 1200
AND THAT'S NOT ALL...

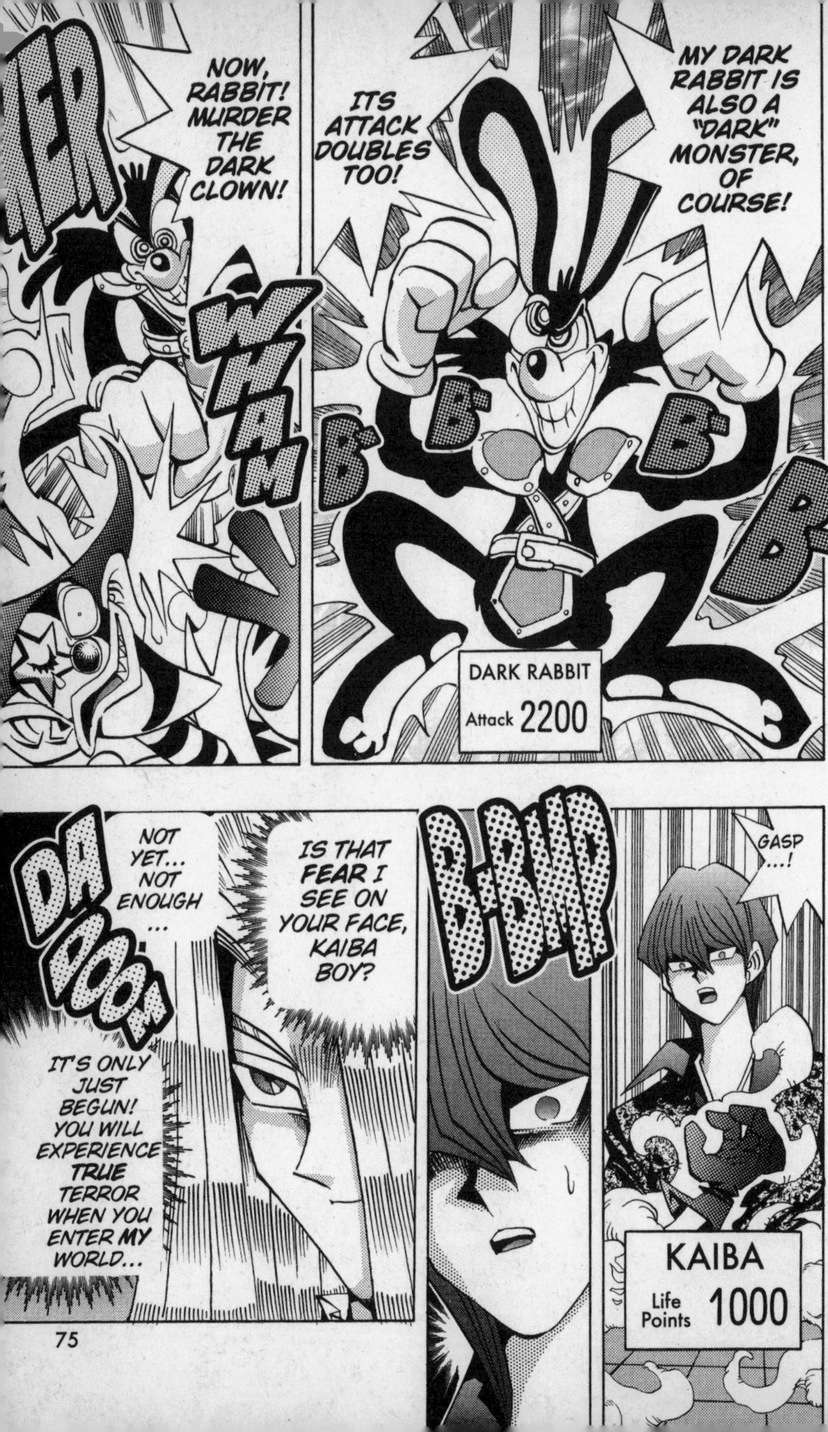
MY DARK RABBIT IS ALSO A "DARK" MONSTER, OF COURSE!
ITS ATTACK DOUBLES TOO!
B B B B
DARK RABBIT Attack 2200
NOW, RABBIT! MURDER THE DARK CLOWN!
ER
WHAM
GASP ...!
KAIBA Life Points 1000
B-BMP
IS THAT FEAR I SEE ON YOUR FACE, KAIBA BOY?
NOT YET... NOT ENOUGH ...
DA DOOM
IT'S ONLY JUST BEGUN! YOU WILL EXPERIENCE TRUE TERROR WHEN YOU ENTER MY WORLD...

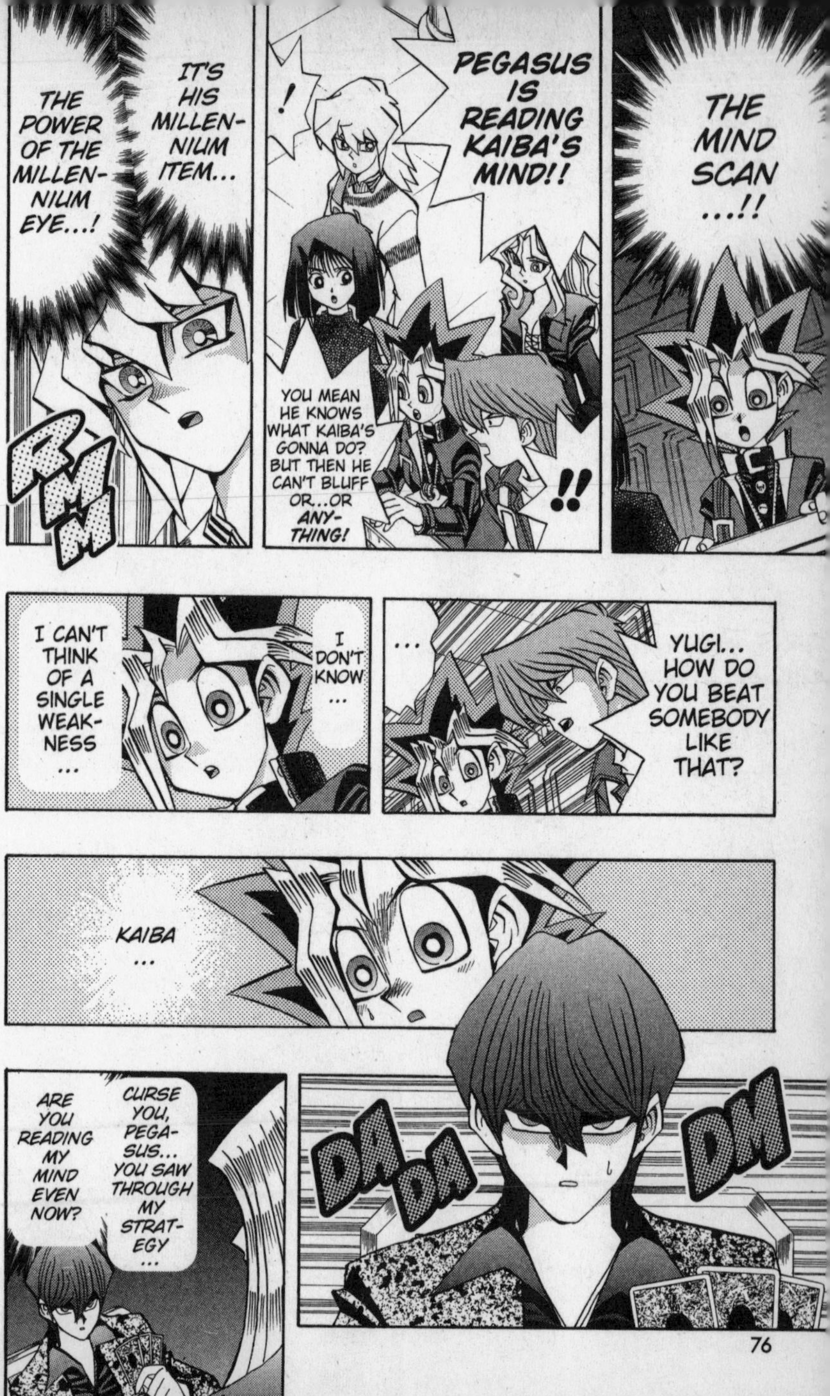
THE MIND SCAN ...!!
PEGASUS IS READING KAIBA'S MIND!!
!
YOU MEAN HE KNOWS WHAT KAIBA'S GONNA DO? BUT THEN HE CAN'T BLUFF OR...OR ANYTHING!
!!
IT'S HIS MILLENNIUM ITEM...
THE POWER OF THE MILLENNIUM EYE...!
RMM
YUGI... HOW DO YOU BEAT SOMEBODY LIKE THAT?
...
I DON'T KNOW ...
I CAN'T THINK OF A SINGLE WEAKNESS ...
KAIBA ...
DA DA DM
CURSE YOU, PEGASUS... YOU SAW THROUGH MY STRATEGY ...
ARE YOU READING MY MIND EVEN NOW?

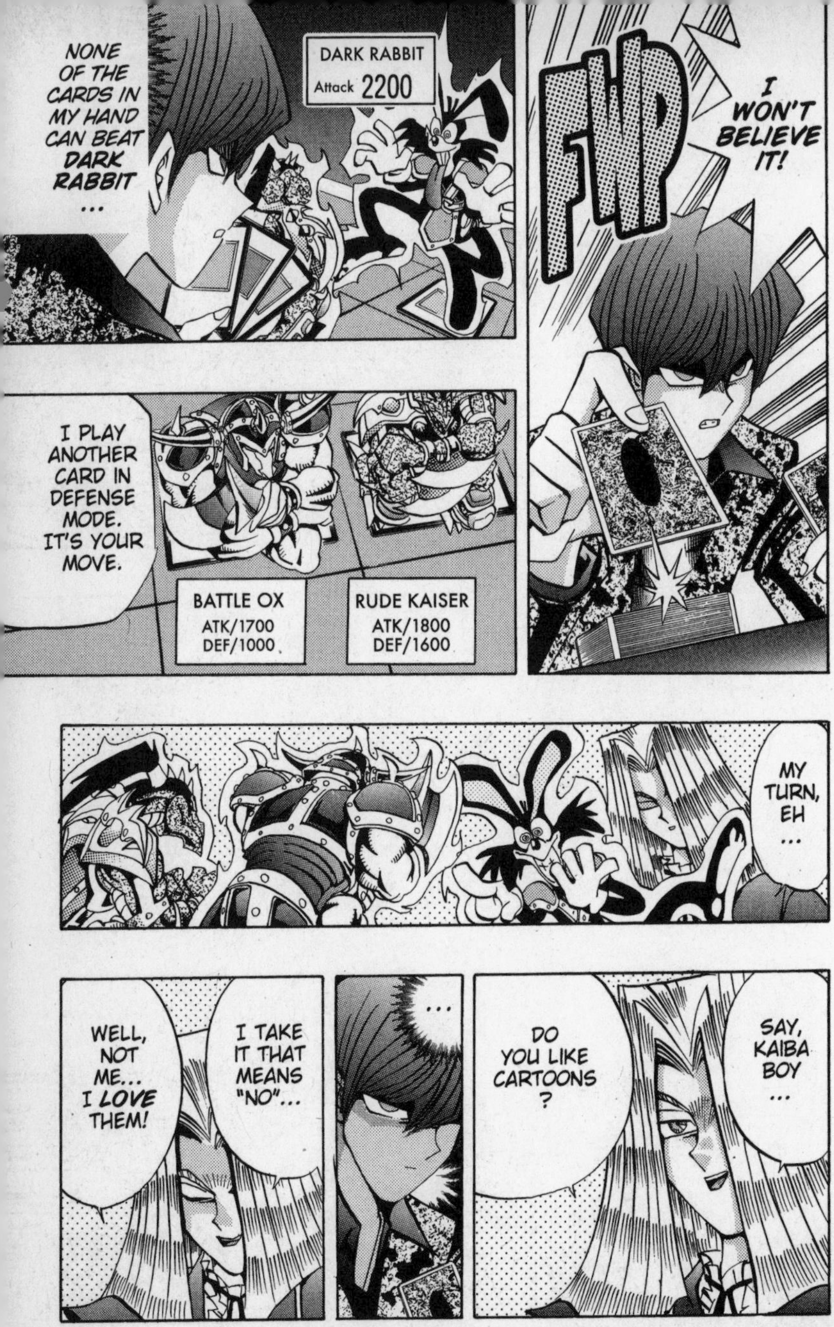
FWP
I WON'T BELIEVE IT!
NONE OF THE CARDS IN MY HAND CAN BEAT DARK RABBIT ...
DARK RABBIT Attack 2200
I PLAY ANOTHER CARD IN DEFENSE MODE. IT'S YOUR MOVE.
RUDE KAISER ATK/1800 DEF/1600
BATTLE OX ATK/1700 DEF/1000
MY TURN, EH ...
SAY, KAIBA BOY ...
DO YOU LIKE CARTOONS ?
...
I TAKE IT THAT MEANS "NO"...
WELL, NOT ME... I LOVE THEM!

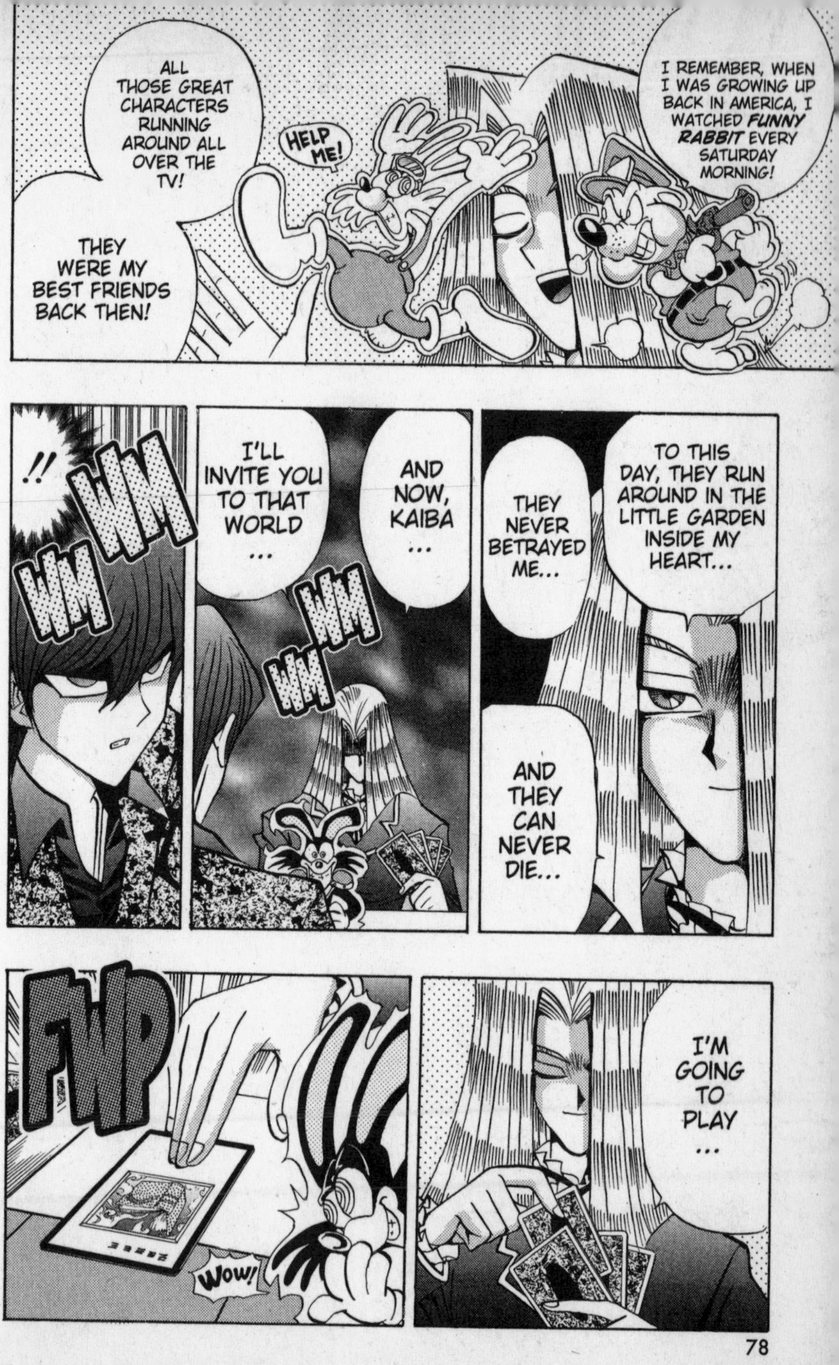
I REMEMBER, WHEN I WAS GROWING UP BACK IN AMERICA, I WATCHED ***FUNNY RABBIT*** EVERY SATURDAY MORNING!
ALL THOSE GREAT CHARACTERS RUNNING AROUND ALL OVER THE TV!
HELP ME!
THEY WERE MY BEST FRIENDS BACK THEN!
TO THIS DAY, THEY RUN AROUND IN THE LITTLE GARDEN INSIDE MY HEART...
THEY NEVER BETRAYED ME...
AND THEY CAN NEVER DIE...
AND NOW, KAIBA ...
I'LL INVITE YOU TO THAT WORLD ...
WM WM
!!
WM WM
I'M GOING TO PLAY ...
FWIP
WOW!

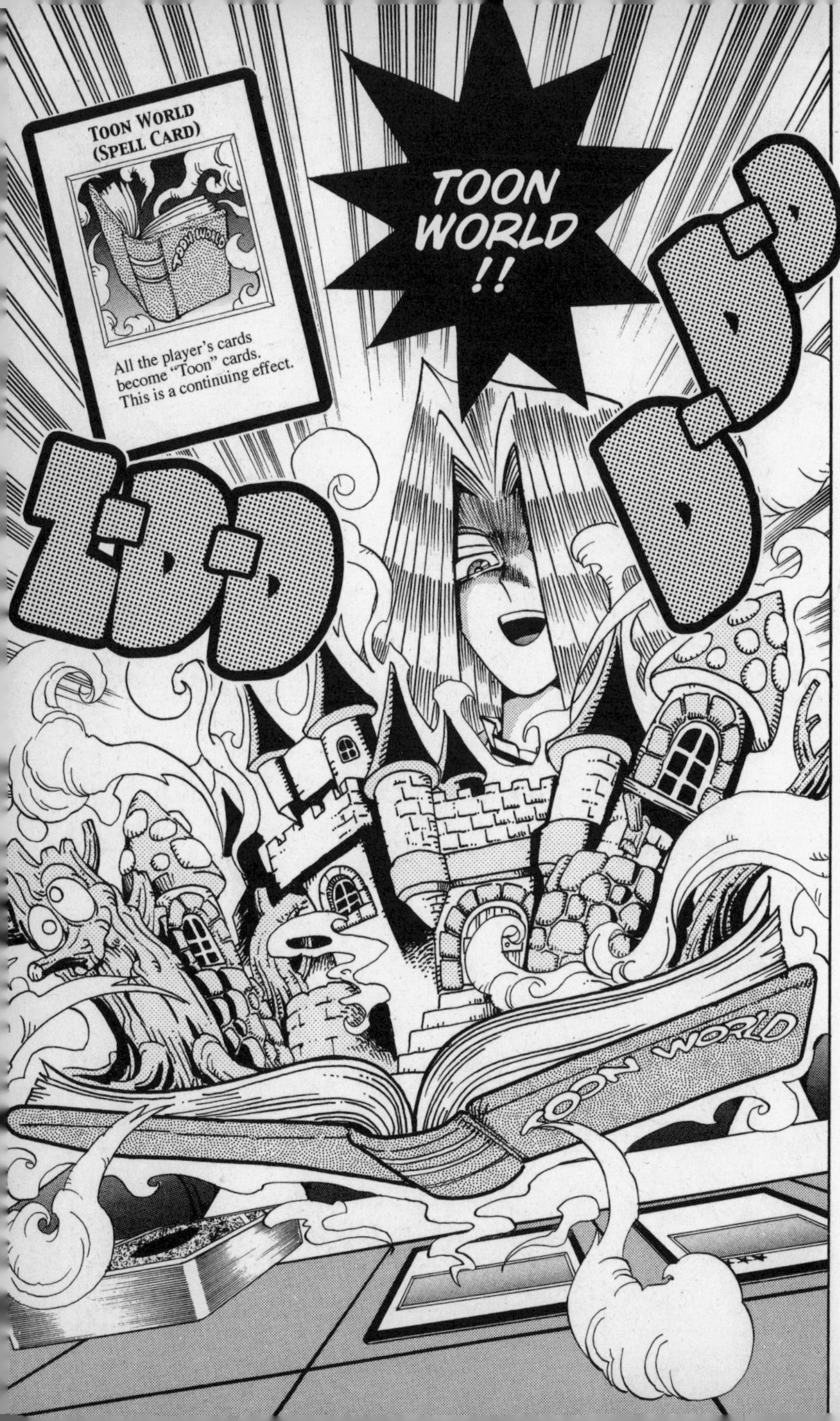
TOON WORLD !!
TOON WORLD (SPELL CARD)
All the player's cards become "Toon" cards. This is a continuing effect.
TOON WORLD

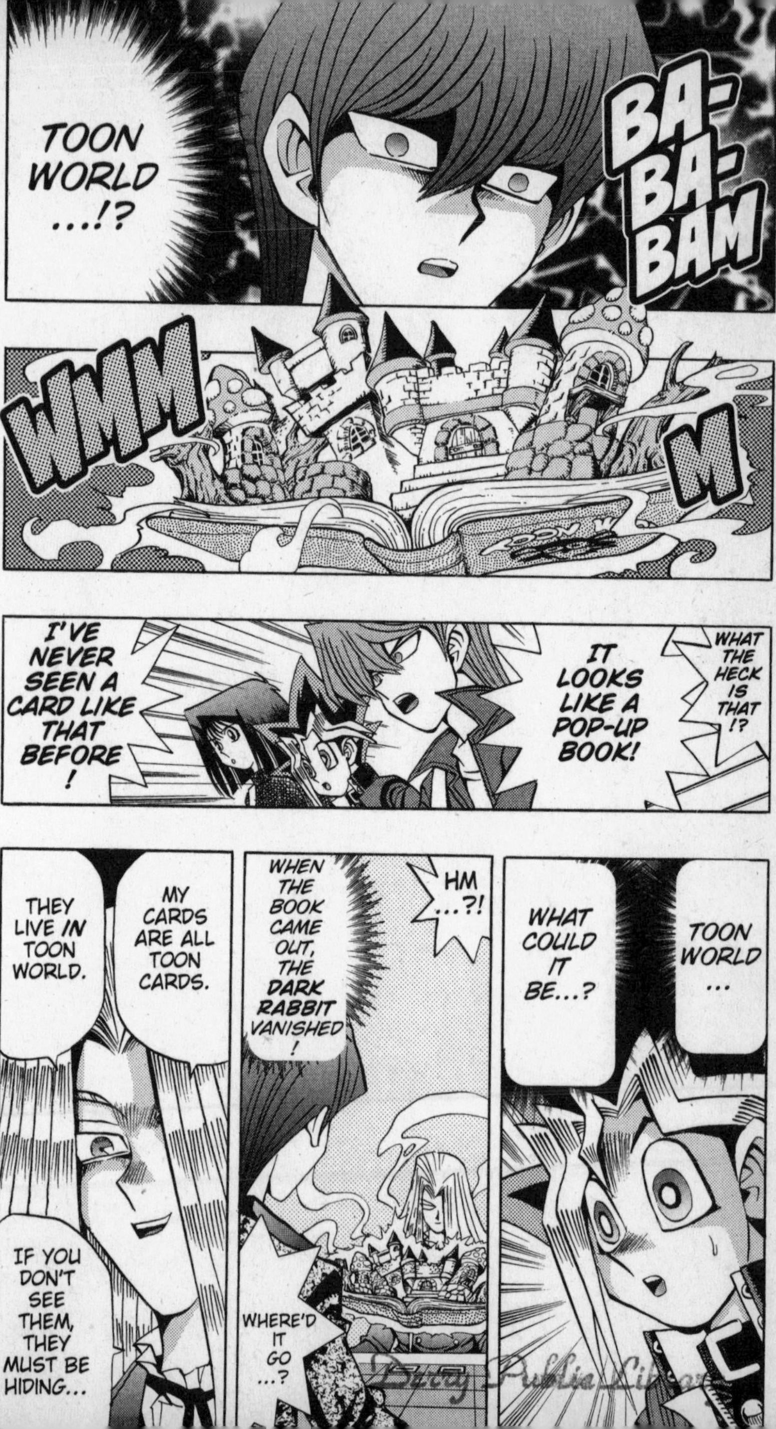
BA-BA-BAM
TOON WORLD ...!?
WMMM
WHAT THE HECK IS THAT!?
IT LOOKS LIKE A POP-UP BOOK!
I'VE NEVER SEEN A CARD LIKE THAT BEFORE!
TOON WORLD ...
WHAT COULD IT BE...?
HM ...?!
WHEN THE BOOK CAME OUT, THE DARK RABBIT VANISHED!
WHERE'D IT GO ...?
MY CARDS ARE ALL TOON CARDS.
THEY LIVE IN TOON WORLD.
IF YOU DON'T SEE THEM, THEY MUST BE HIDING...

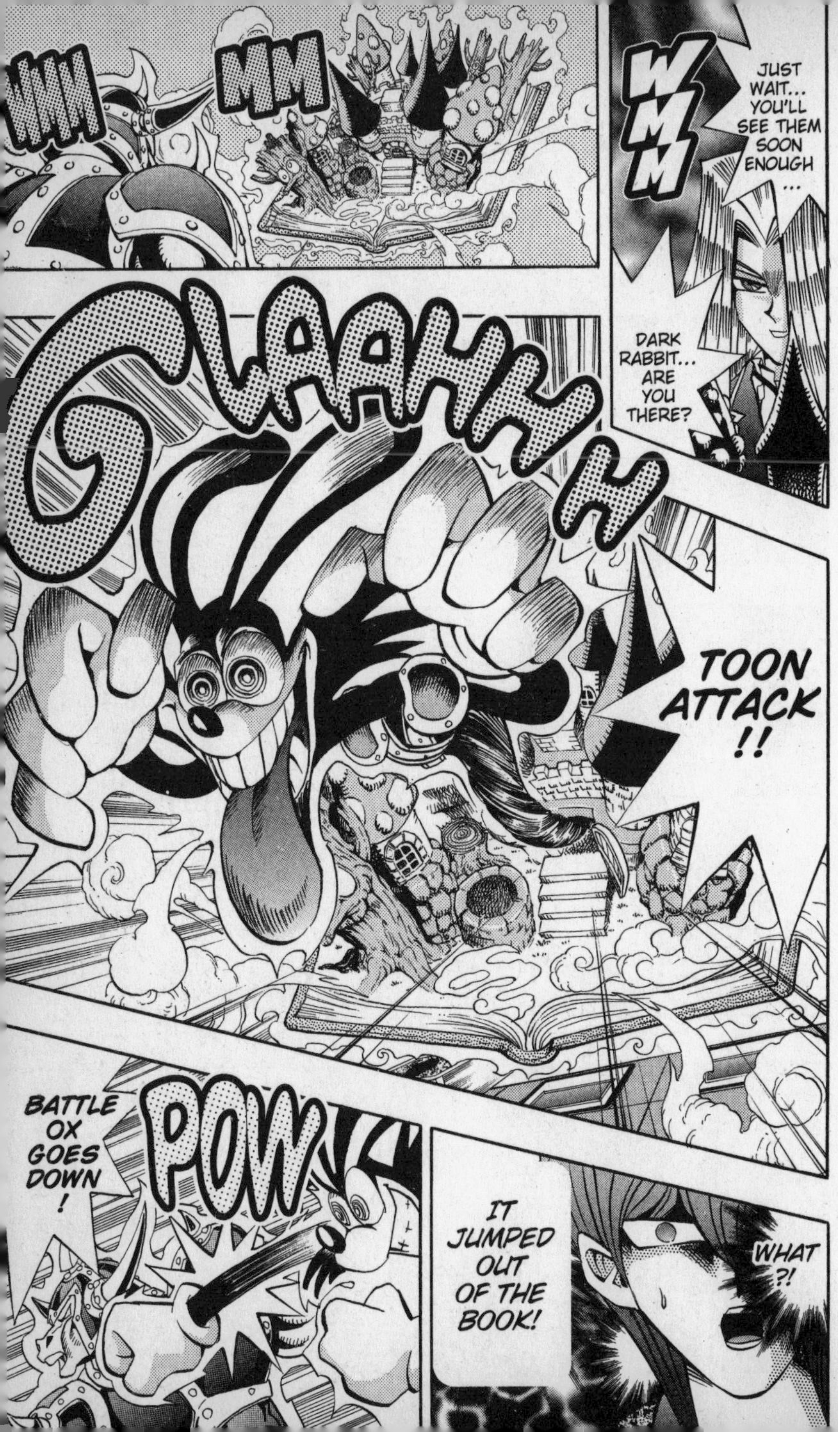
WMM
JUST WAIT... YOU'LL SEE THEM SOON ENOUGH ...
DARK RABBIT... ARE YOU THERE?
MM
GWAHHHH
TOON ATTACK !!
WHAT ?!
IT JUMPED OUT OF THE BOOK!
POW
BATTLE OX GOES DOWN !

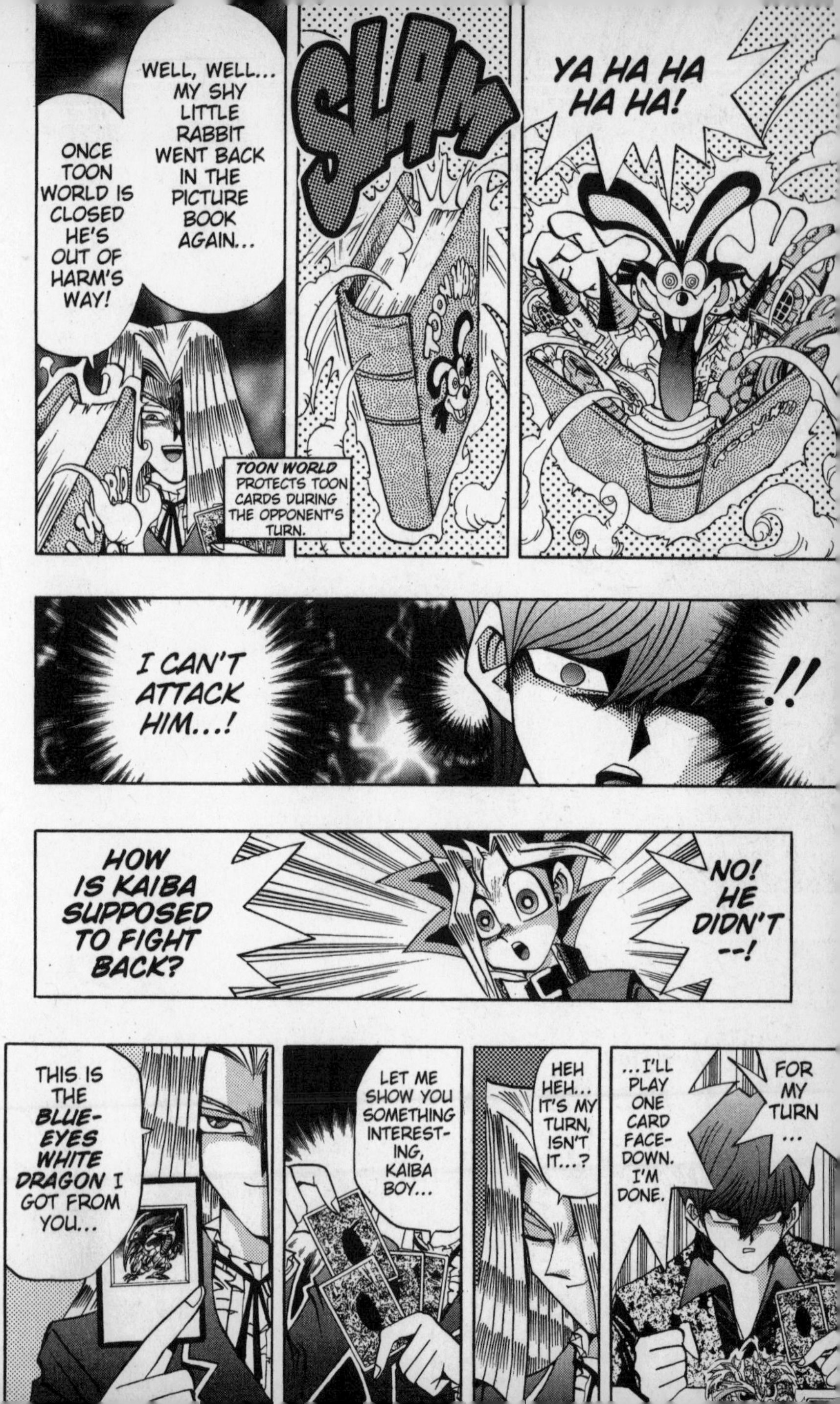
YA HA HA HA HA!
SLAM
TOON WORLD PROTECTS TOON CARDS DURING THE OPPONENT'S TURN.
WELL, WELL... MY SHY LITTLE RABBIT WENT BACK IN THE PICTURE BOOK AGAIN...
ONCE TOON WORLD IS CLOSED HE'S OUT OF HARM'S WAY!
!!
I CAN'T ATTACK HIM...!
NO! HE DIDN'T --!
HOW IS KAIBA SUPPOSED TO FIGHT BACK?
FOR MY TURN ...
...I'LL PLAY ONE CARD FACE-DOWN. I'M DONE.
HEH HEH... IT'S MY TURN, ISN'T IT...?
LET ME SHOW YOU SOMETHING INTEREST-ING, KAIBA BOY...
THIS IS THE BLUE-EYES WHITE DRAGON I GOT FROM YOU...

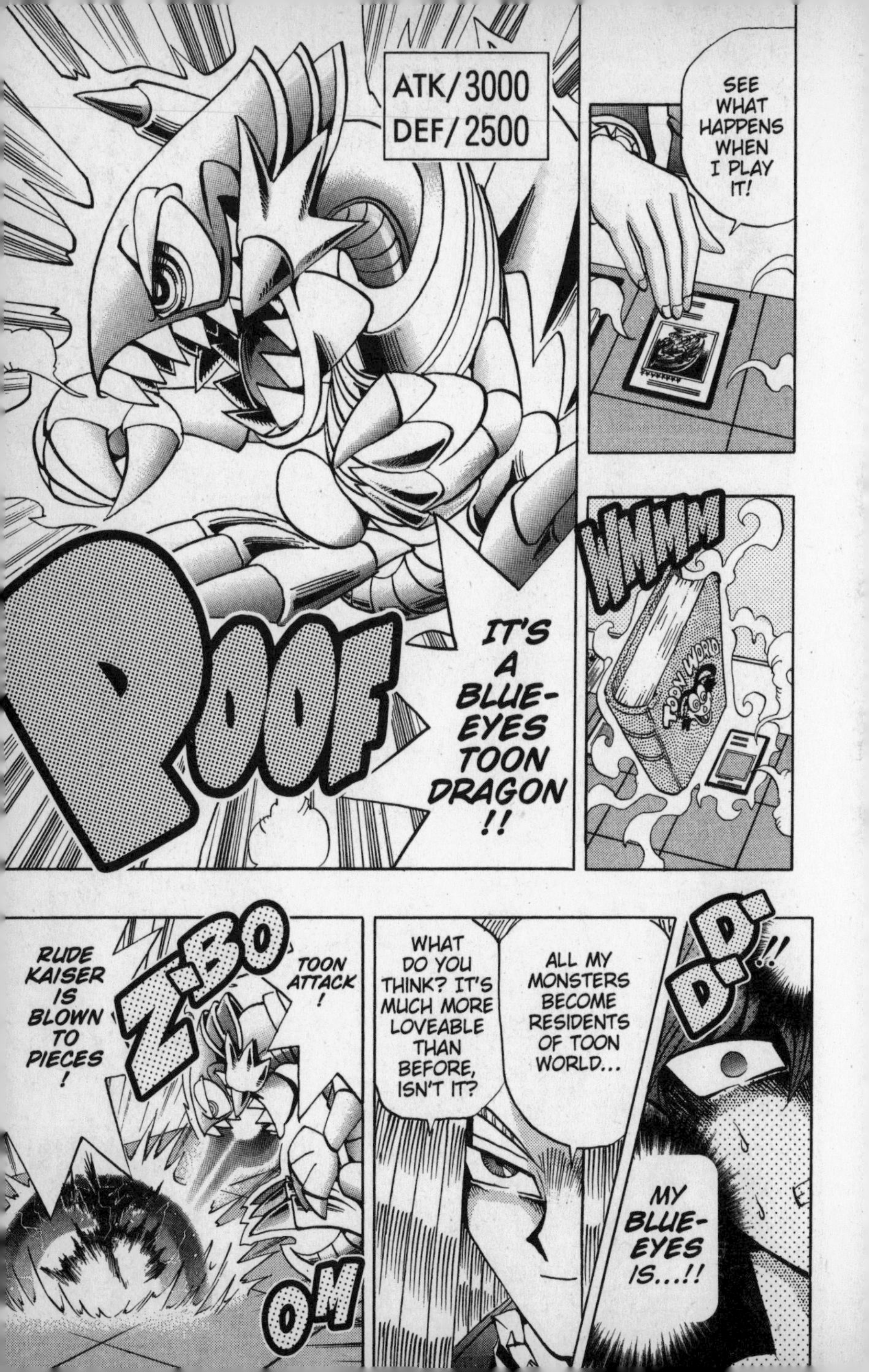
SEE WHAT HAPPENS WHEN I PLAY IT!
WMMM
TOON WORLD
ATK/3000
DEF/2500
POOF
IT'S A BLUE-EYES TOON DRAGON!!
D-D-!!
MY BLUE-EYES IS...!!
ALL MY MONSTERS BECOME RESIDENTS OF TOON WORLD...
WHAT DO YOU THINK? IT'S MUCH MORE LOVEABLE THAN BEFORE, ISN'T IT?
TOON ATTACK!
Z-BO
RUDE KAISER IS BLOWN TO PIECES!

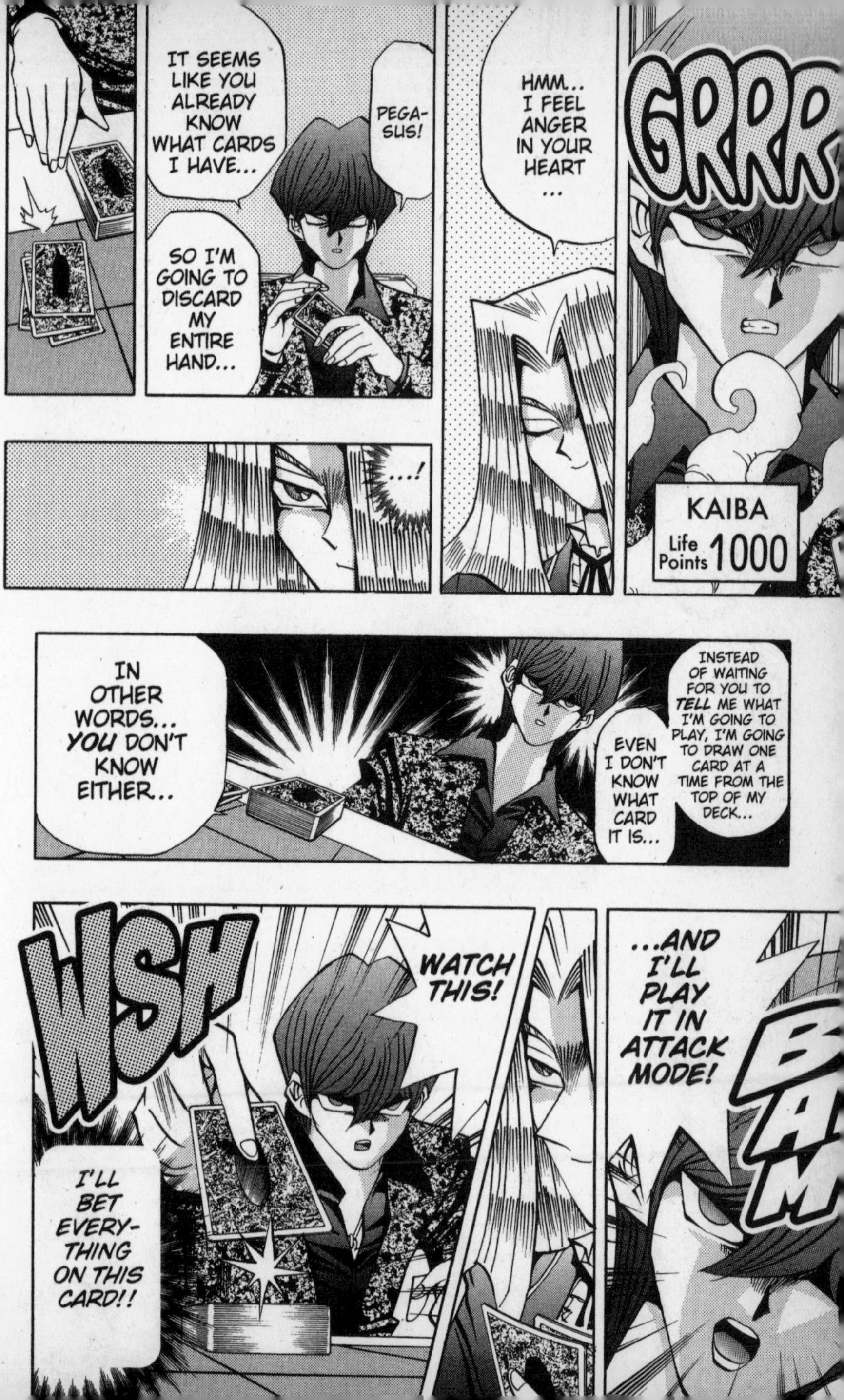
GRRR
KAIBA
Life Points 1000
HMM... I FEEL ANGER IN YOUR HEART ...
PEGA-SUS!
IT SEEMS LIKE YOU ALREADY KNOW WHAT CARDS I HAVE...
SO I'M GOING TO DISCARD MY ENTIRE HAND...
...!
INSTEAD OF WAITING FOR YOU TO *TELL* ME WHAT I'M GOING TO PLAY, I'M GOING TO DRAW ONE CARD AT A TIME FROM THE TOP OF MY DECK...
EVEN I DON'T KNOW WHAT CARD IT IS...
IN OTHER WORDS... *YOU* DON'T KNOW EITHER...
BAM
...AND I'LL PLAY IT IN ATTACK MODE!
WATCH THIS!
WSH
I'LL BET EVERY-THING ON THIS CARD!!

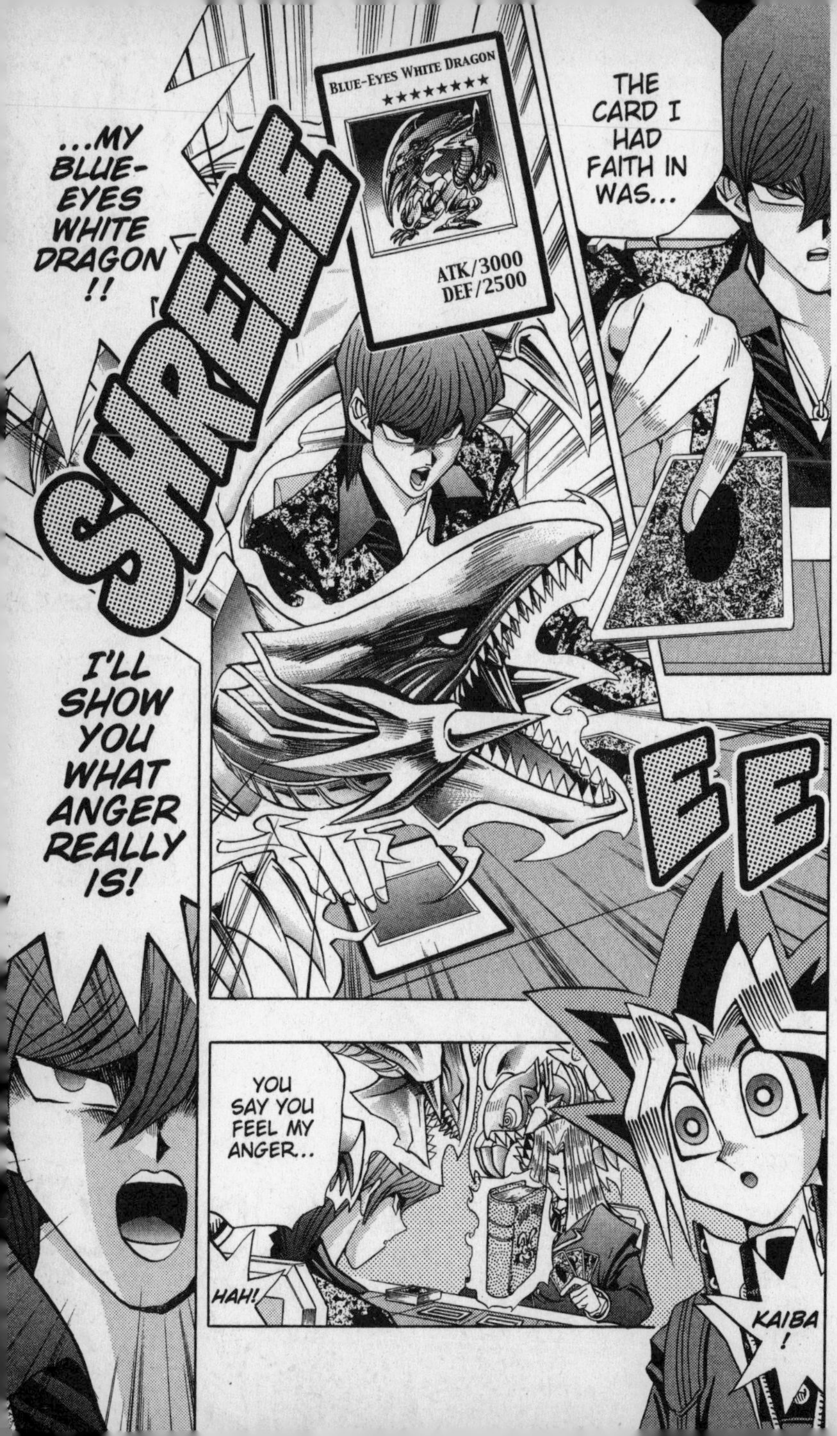

THE CARD I HAD FAITH IN WAS...
BLUE-EYES WHITE DRAGON
ATK/3000 DEF/2500
...MY BLUE-EYES WHITE DRAGON!!
SHREEE
EE
I'LL SHOW YOU WHAT ANGER REALLY IS!
KAIBA!
YOU SAY YOU FEEL MY ANGER...
HAH!

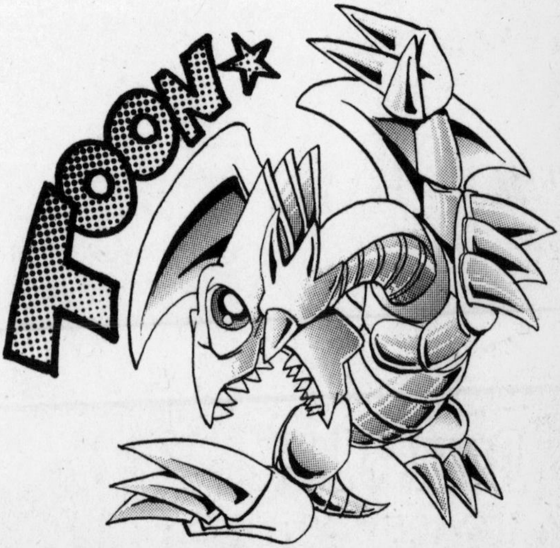
TOON☆

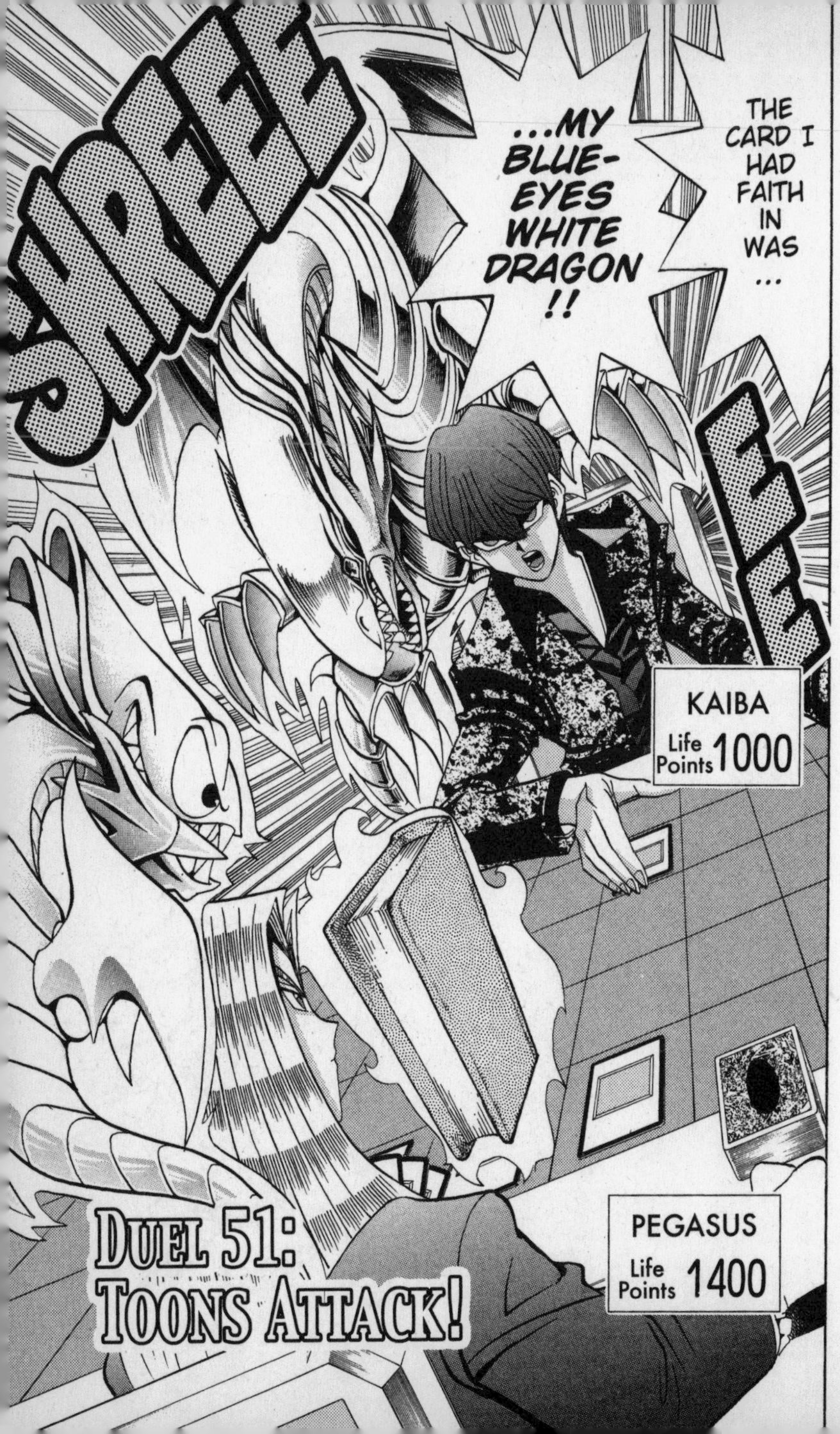
THE CARD I HAD FAITH IN WAS...
...MY BLUE-EYES WHITE DRAGON!!
KAIBA
Life Points 1000
PEGASUS
Life Points 1400
DUEL 51: TOONS ATTACK!

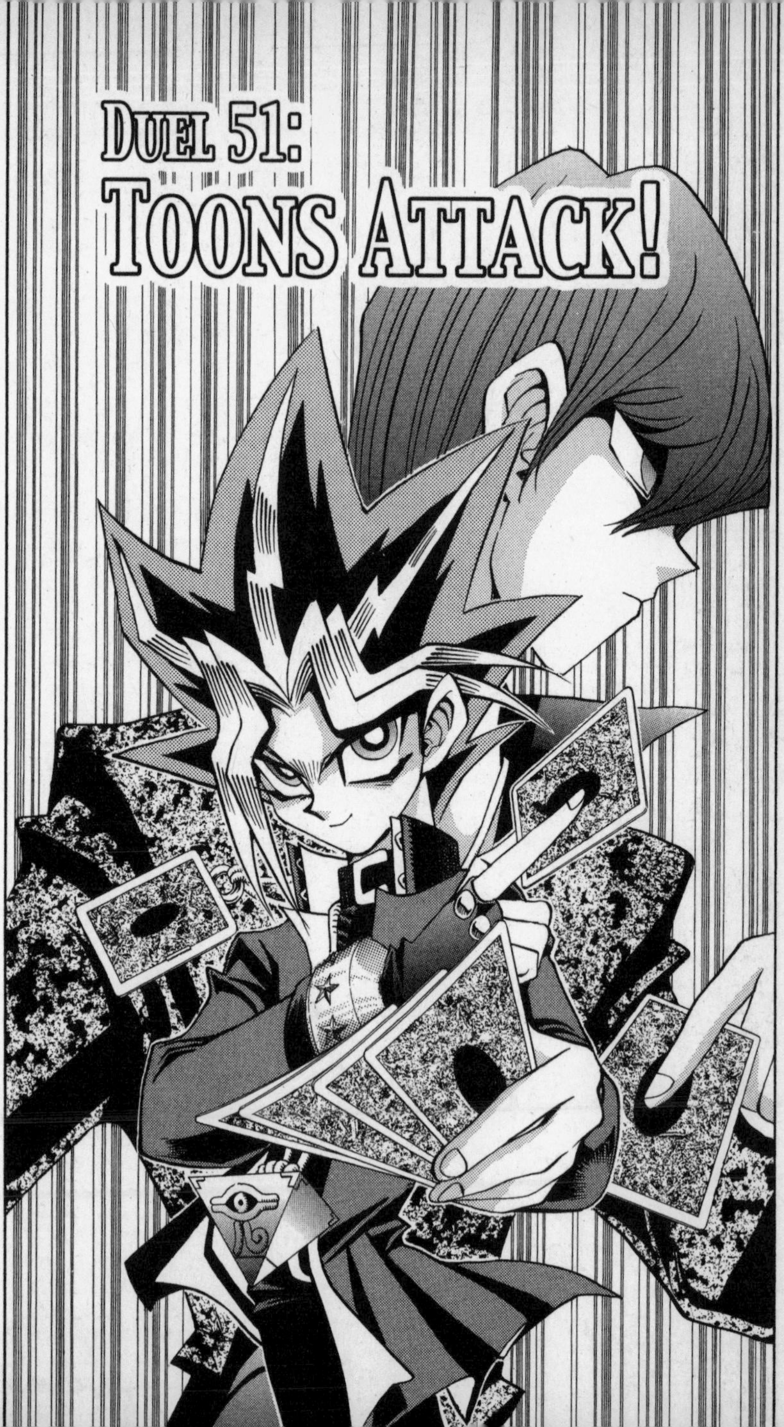
DUEL 51:
TOONS ATTACK!

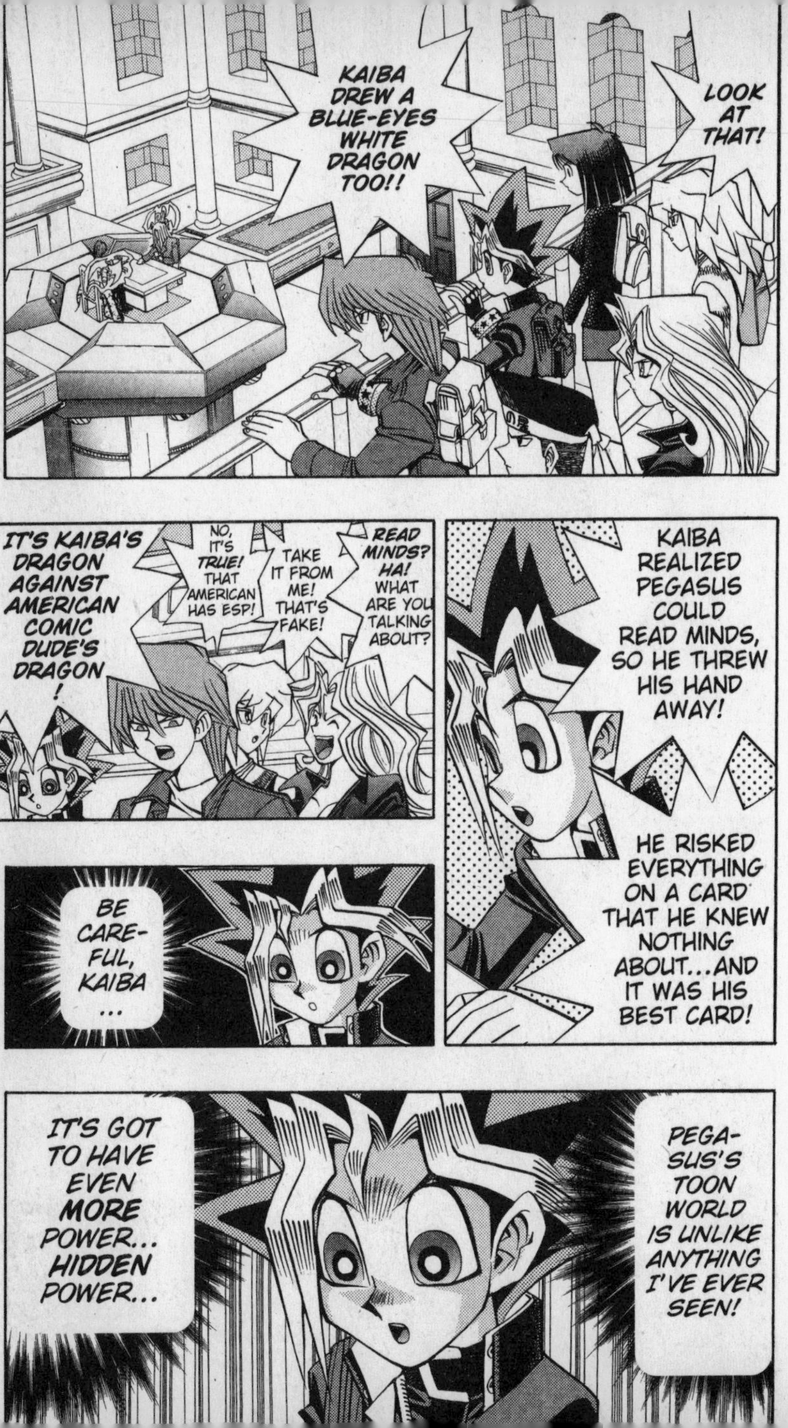
LOOK AT THAT!
KAIBA DREW A BLUE-EYES WHITE DRAGON TOO!!
KAIBA REALIZED PEGASUS COULD READ MINDS, SO HE THREW HIS HAND AWAY!
HE RISKED EVERYTHING ON A CARD THAT HE KNEW NOTHING ABOUT...AND IT WAS HIS BEST CARD!
READ MINDS? HA! WHAT ARE YOU TALKING ABOUT?
TAKE IT FROM ME! THAT'S FAKE!
NO, IT'S TRUE! THAT AMERICAN HAS ESP!
IT'S KAIBA'S DRAGON AGAINST AMERICAN COMIC DUDE'S DRAGON!
BE CAREFUL, KAIBA...
PEGASUS'S TOON WORLD IS UNLIKE ANYTHING I'VE EVER SEEN!
IT'S GOT TO HAVE EVEN MORE POWER... HIDDEN POWER...

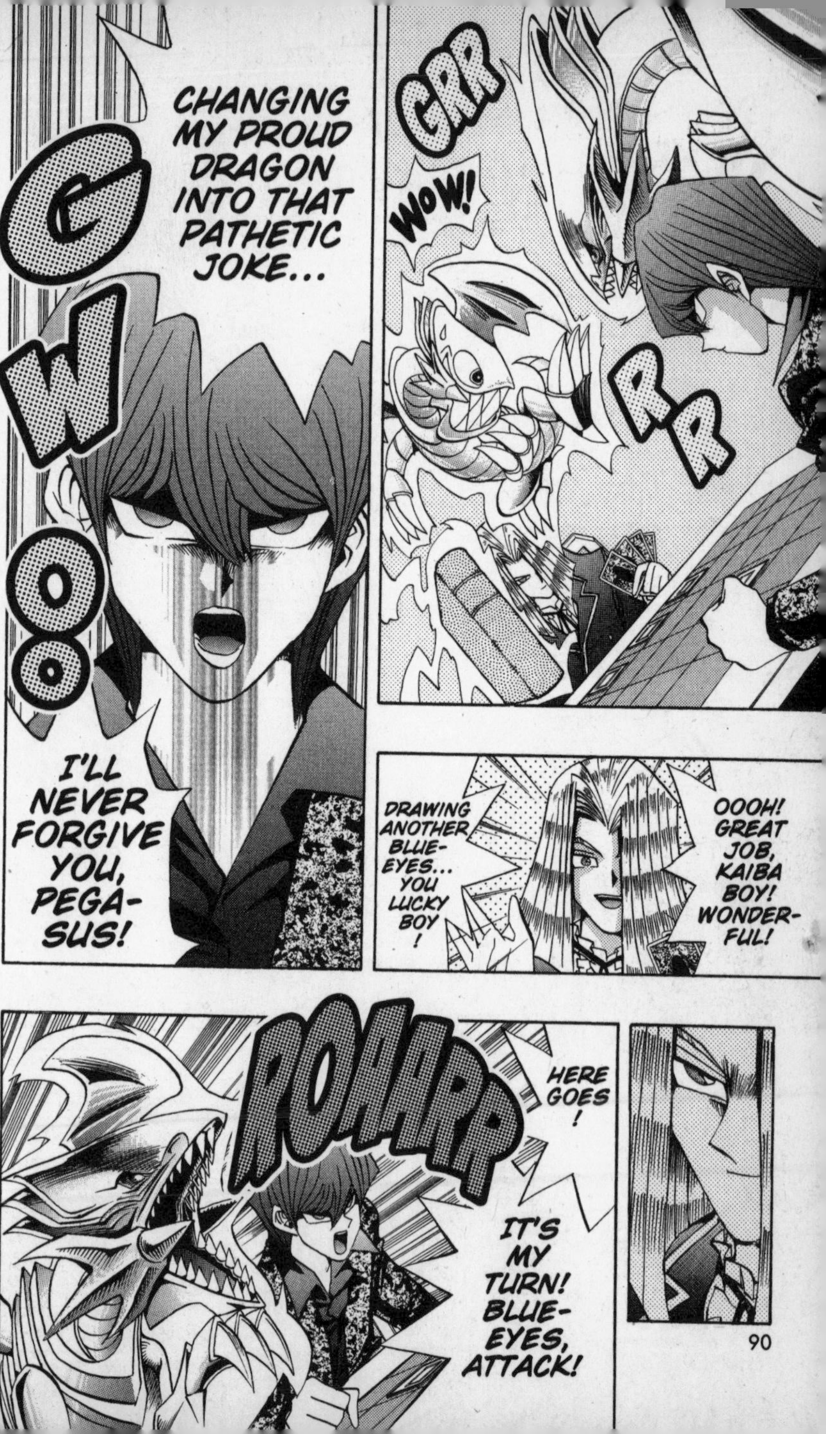
GRR
WOW!
RR
OOOH! GREAT JOB, KAIBA BOY! WONDERFUL!
DRAWING ANOTHER BLUE-EYES... YOU LUCKY BOY!
CHANGING MY PROUD DRAGON INTO THAT PATHETIC JOKE...
I'LL NEVER FORGIVE YOU, PEGASUS!
ROARR
HERE GOES!
IT'S MY TURN! BLUE-EYES, ATTACK!

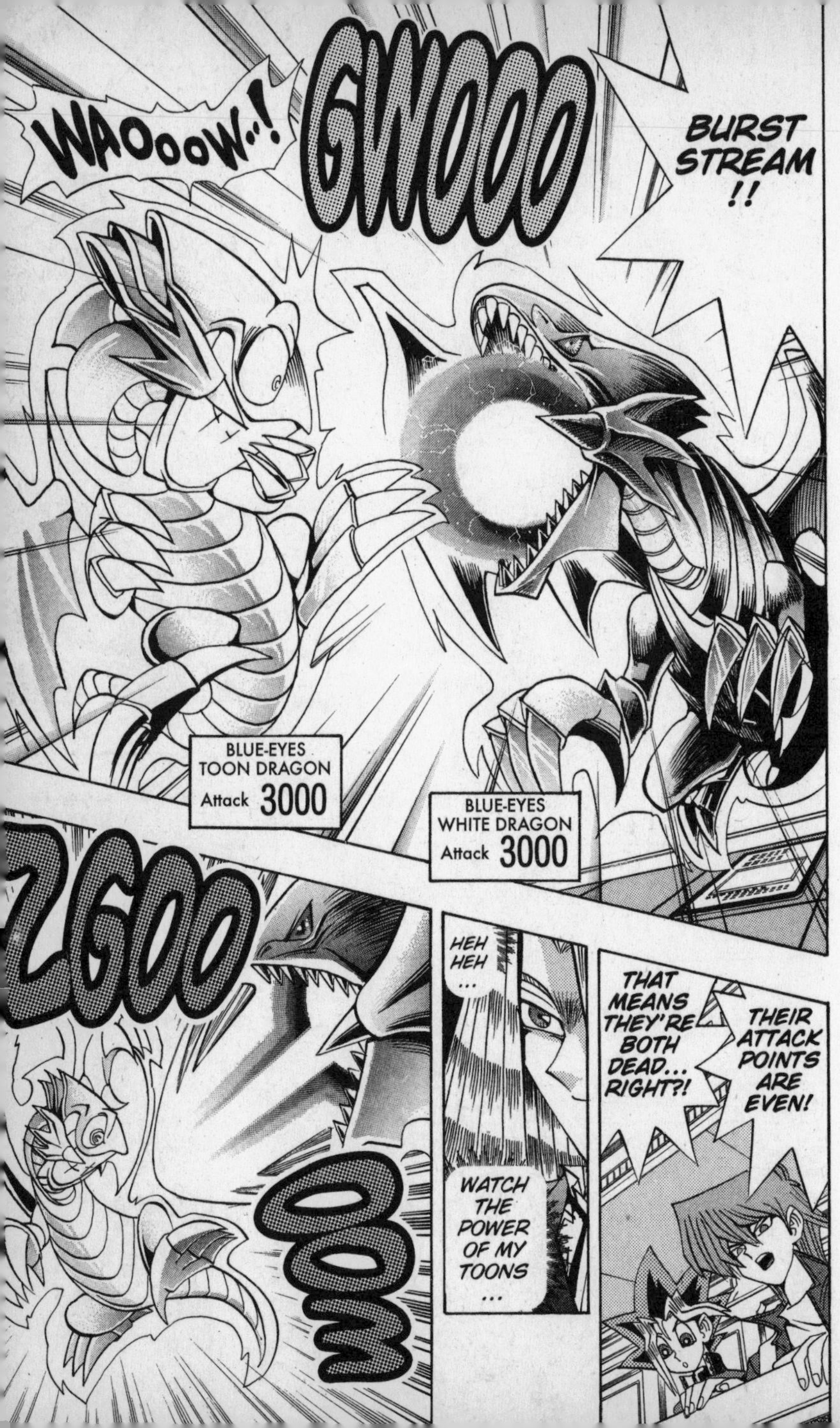
BURST STREAM!!
GWOOO
WAOOOW..!
BLUE-EYES WHITE DRAGON Attack 3000
BLUE-EYES TOON DRAGON Attack 3000
THEIR ATTACK POINTS ARE EVEN!
THAT MEANS THEY'RE BOTH DEAD... RIGHT?!
HEH HEH ...
WATCH THE POWER OF MY TOONS ...
ZGOO
OOOM

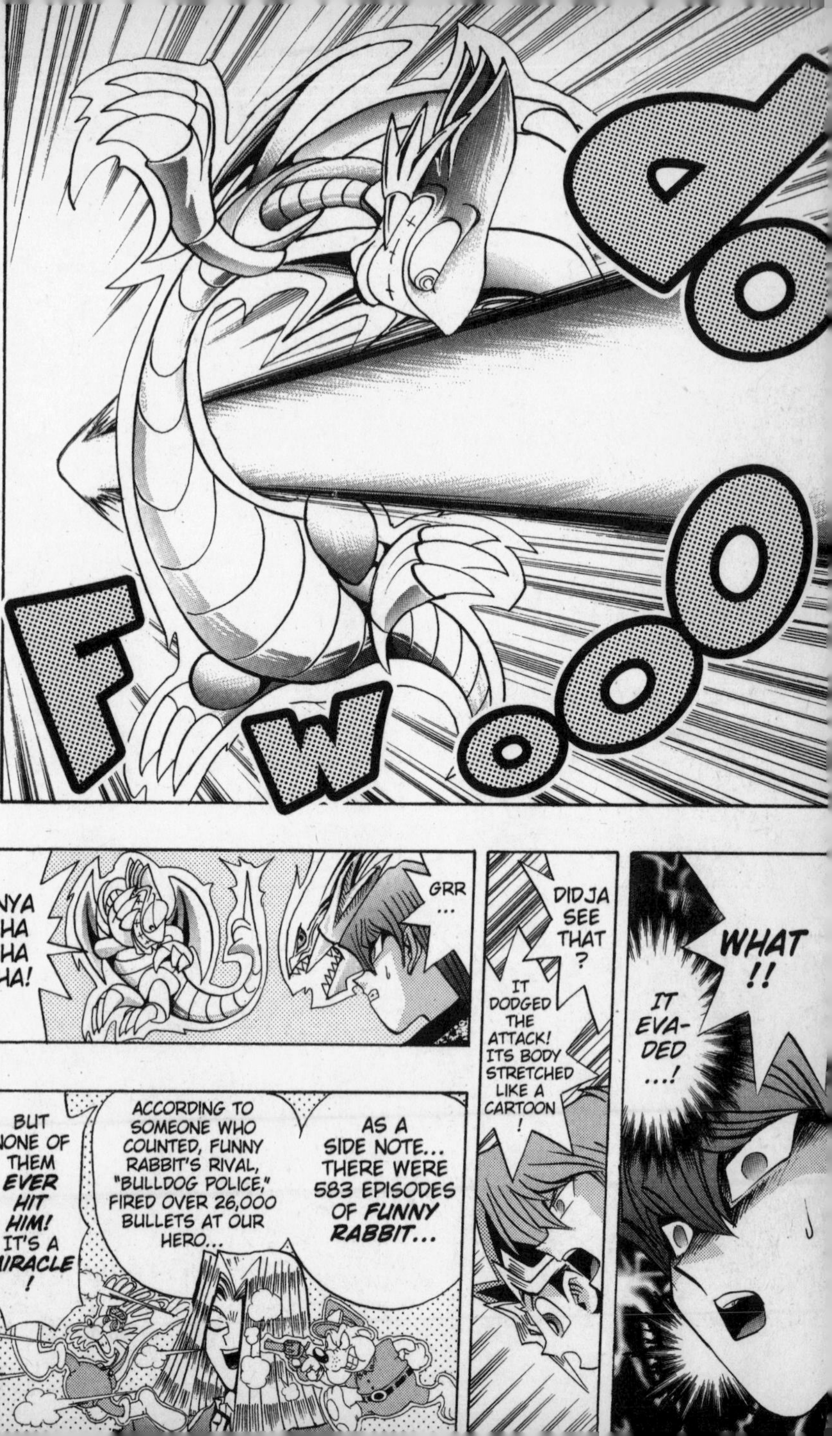
FWOOOOO
WHAT!!
IT EVADED...!
DIDJA SEE THAT?
IT DODGED THE ATTACK! ITS BODY STRETCHED LIKE A CARTOON!
GRR...
NYA HA HA HA!
AS A SIDE NOTE... THERE WERE 583 EPISODES OF *FUNNY RABBIT*...
ACCORDING TO SOMEONE WHO COUNTED, FUNNY RABBIT'S RIVAL, "BULLDOG POLICE," FIRED OVER 26,000 BULLETS AT OUR HERO...
BUT NONE OF THEM *EVER HIT HIM!* IT'S A *MIRACLE*!

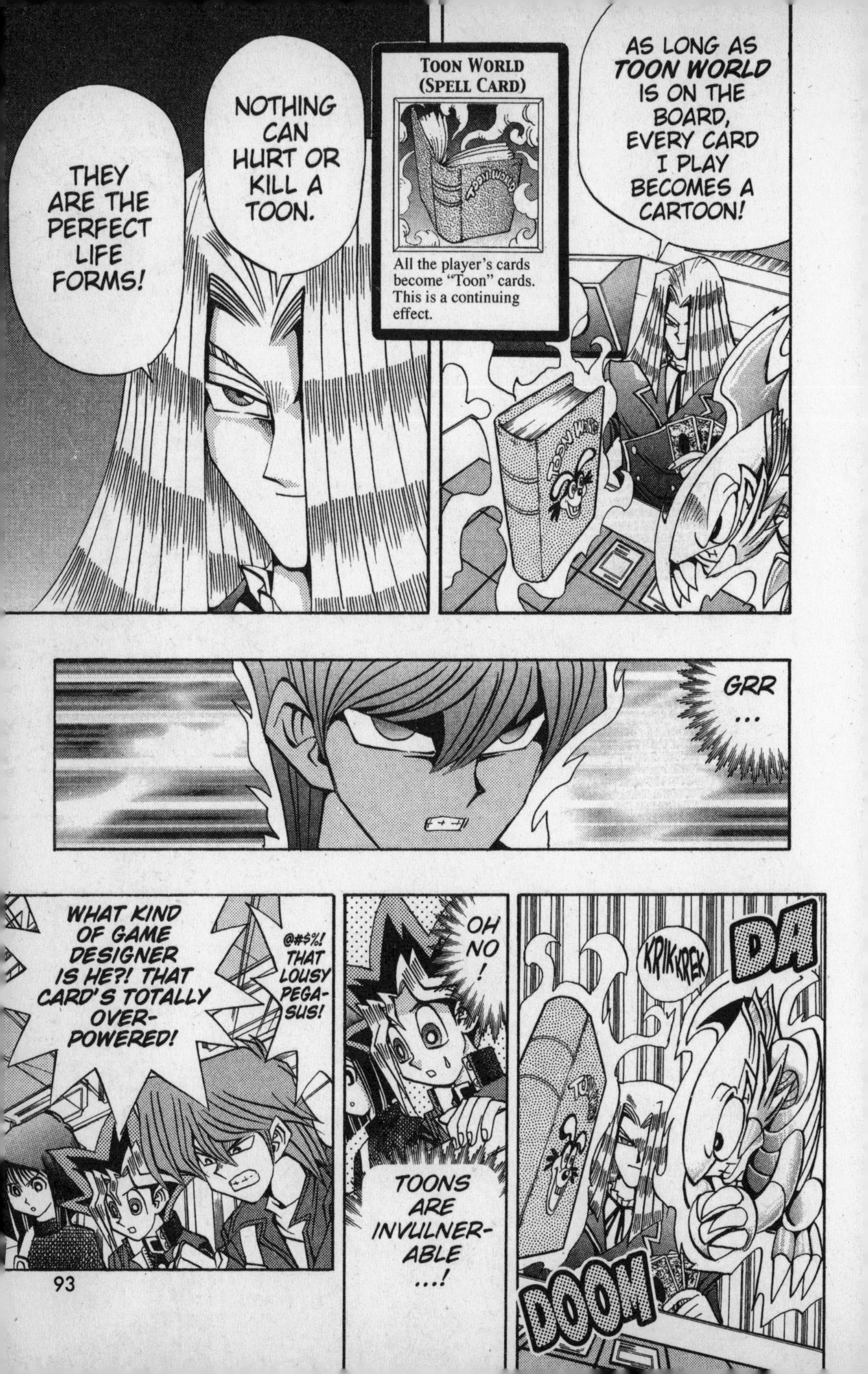
AS LONG AS TOON WORLD IS ON THE BOARD, EVERY CARD I PLAY BECOMES A CARTOON!
TOON WORLD (SPELL CARD)
All the player's cards become "Toon" cards. This is a continuing effect.
NOTHING CAN HURT OR KILL A TOON.
THEY ARE THE PERFECT LIFE FORMS!
GRR ...
DA
KRIKKREK
DOOM
OH NO!
TOONS ARE INVULNERABLE ...!
@#$%! THAT LOUSY PEGASUS!
WHAT KIND OF GAME DESIGNER IS HE?! THAT CARD'S TOTALLY OVERPOWERED!

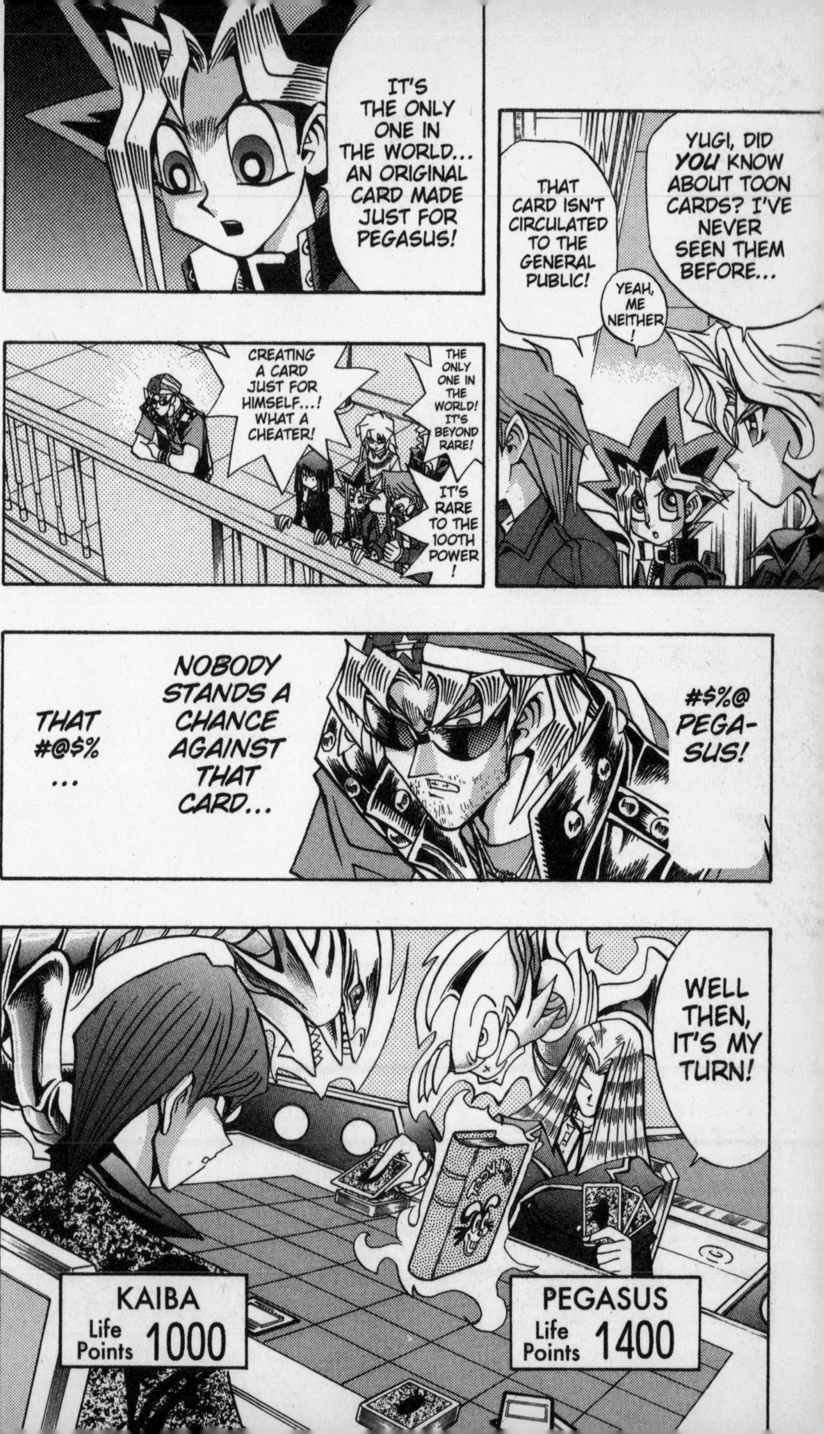

YUGI, DID YOU KNOW ABOUT TOON CARDS? I'VE NEVER SEEN THEM BEFORE...
THAT CARD ISN'T CIRCULATED TO THE GENERAL PUBLIC!
YEAH, ME NEITHER!
IT'S THE ONLY ONE IN THE WORLD... AN ORIGINAL CARD MADE JUST FOR PEGASUS!
THE ONLY ONE IN THE WORLD! IT'S BEYOND RARE!
IT'S RARE TO THE 100TH POWER!
CREATING A CARD JUST FOR HIMSELF...! WHAT A CHEATER!
#$%@ PEGA-SUS!
NOBODY STANDS A CHANCE AGAINST THAT CARD...
THAT #@$% ...
WELL THEN, IT'S MY TURN!
PEGASUS Life Points 1400
KAIBA Life Points 1000

READ THIS WAY

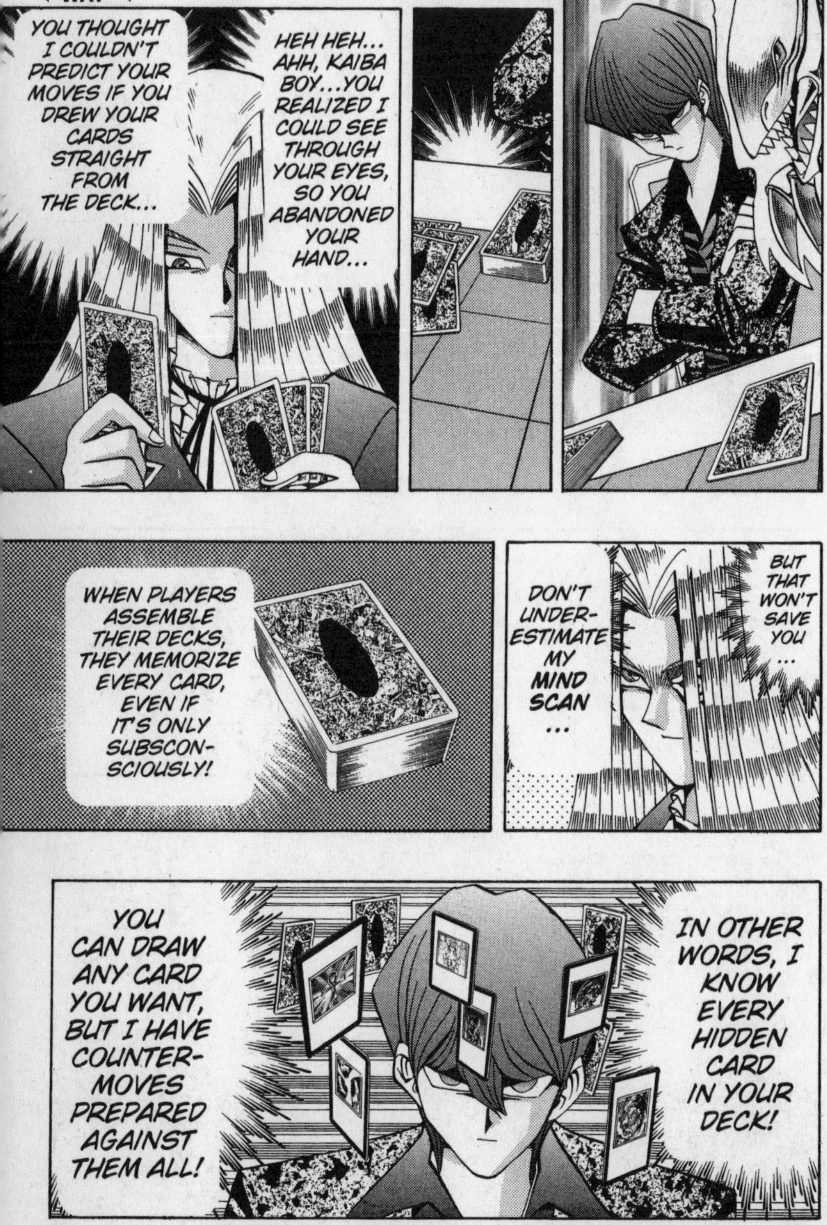
HEH HEH... AHH, KAIBA BOY...YOU REALIZED I COULD SEE THROUGH YOUR EYES, SO YOU ABANDONED YOUR HAND...
YOU THOUGHT I COULDN'T PREDICT YOUR MOVES IF YOU DREW YOUR CARDS STRAIGHT FROM THE DECK...
BUT THAT WON'T SAVE YOU ...
DON'T UNDER-ESTIMATE MY MIND SCAN ...
WHEN PLAYERS ASSEMBLE THEIR DECKS, THEY MEMORIZE EVERY CARD, EVEN IF IT'S ONLY SUBSCON-SCIOUSLY!
IN OTHER WORDS, I KNOW EVERY HIDDEN CARD IN YOUR DECK!
YOU CAN DRAW ANY CARD YOU WANT, BUT I HAVE COUNTER-MOVES PREPARED AGAINST THEM ALL!

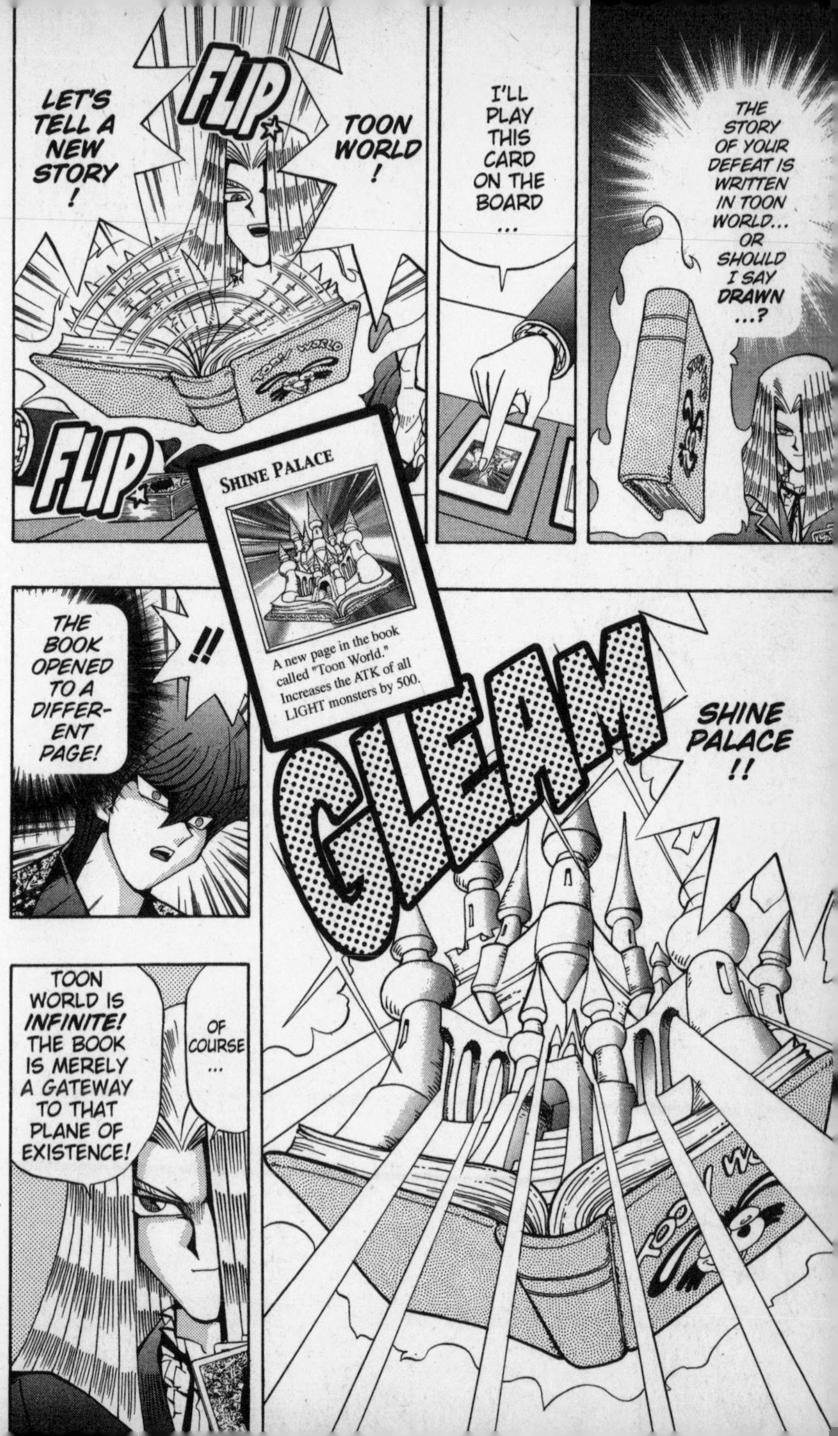
THE STORY OF YOUR DEFEAT IS WRITTEN IN TOON WORLD... OR SHOULD I SAY *DRAWN*...?
I'LL PLAY THIS CARD ON THE BOARD...
TOON WORLD!
FLIP
LET'S TELL A NEW STORY!
FLIP
SHINE PALACE!!
GLEAM
SHINE PALACE
A new page in the book called "Toon World." Increases the ATK of all LIGHT monsters by 500.
!!
THE BOOK OPENED TO A DIFFERENT PAGE!
OF COURSE...
TOON WORLD IS *INFINITE!* THE BOOK IS MERELY A GATEWAY TO THAT PLANE OF EXISTENCE!

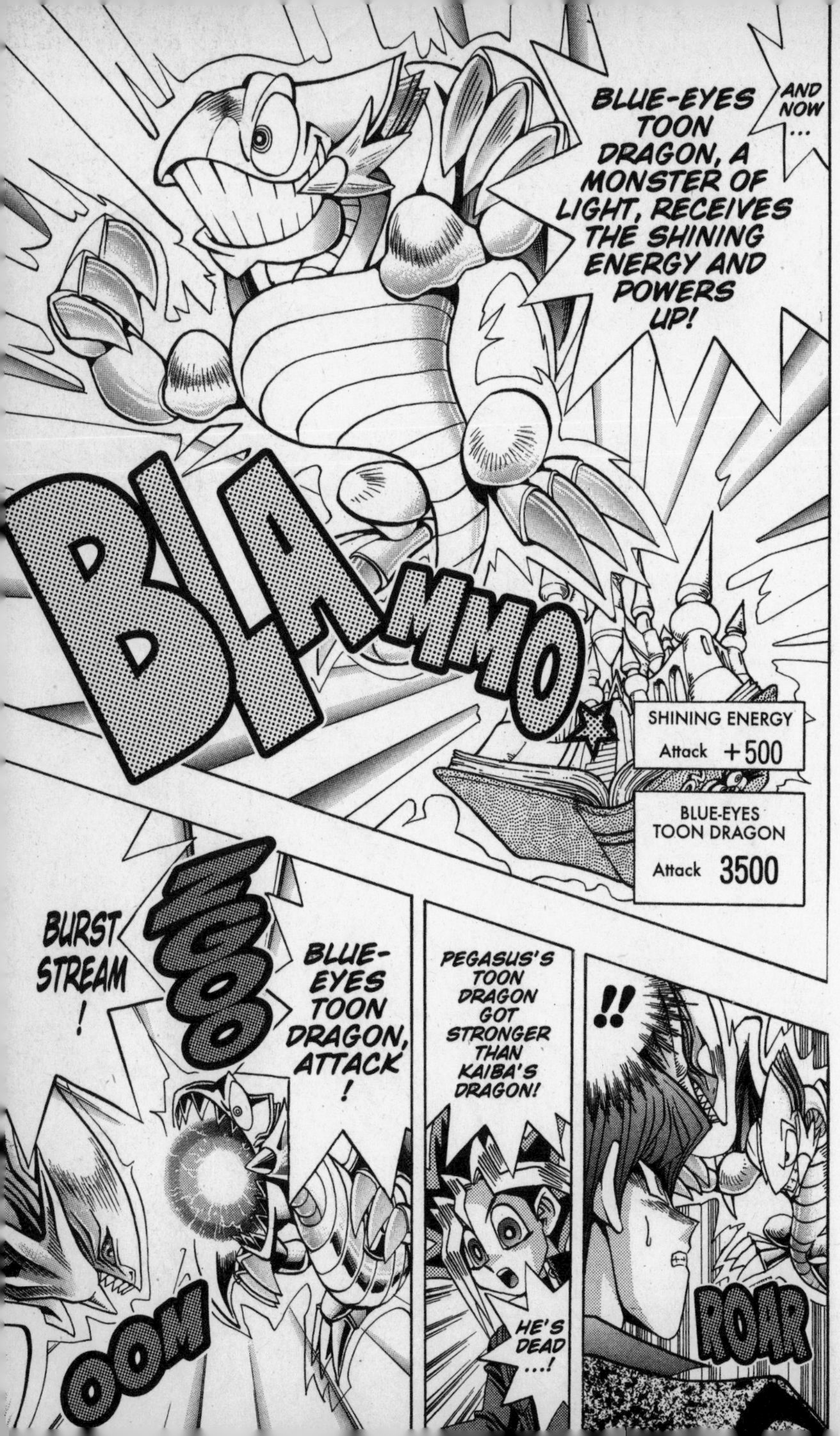

AND NOW...
BLUE-EYES TOON DRAGON, A MONSTER OF LIGHT, RECEIVES THE SHINING ENERGY AND POWERS UP!
BLAMMO
SHINING ENERGY
Attack +500
BLUE-EYES TOON DRAGON
Attack 3500
!!
ROAR
PEGASUS'S TOON DRAGON GOT STRONGER THAN KAIBA'S DRAGON!
HE'S DEAD...!
BLUE-EYES TOON DRAGON, ATTACK!
BURST STREAM!
OOM

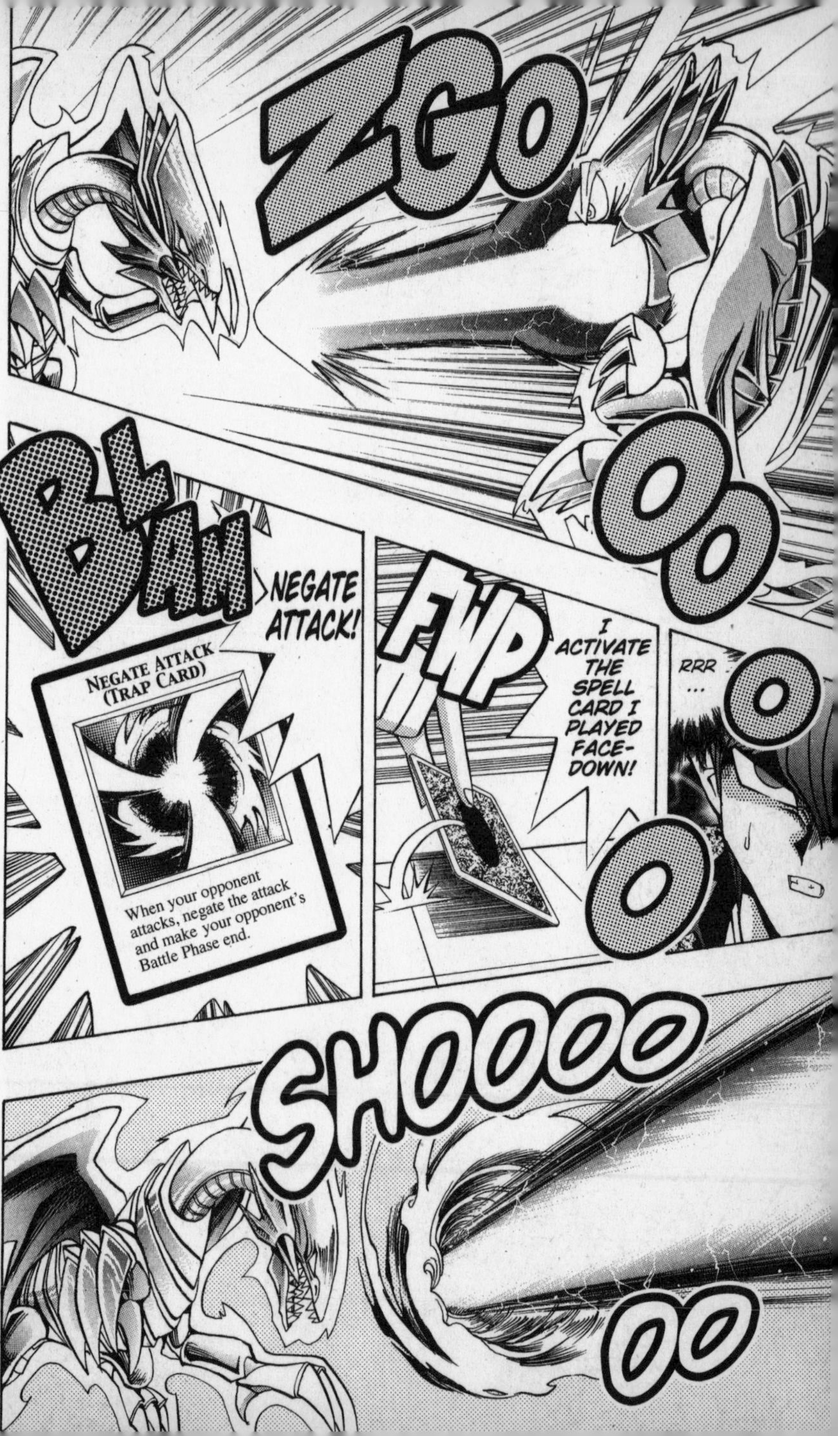
ZGO
OOOO
RRR …
FWP
I ACTIVATE THE SPELL CARD I PLAYED FACE-DOWN!
BLAM
NEGATE ATTACK!
NEGATE ATTACK (TRAP CARD)
When your opponent attacks, negate the attack and make your opponent's Battle Phase end.
SHOOOOO
OO

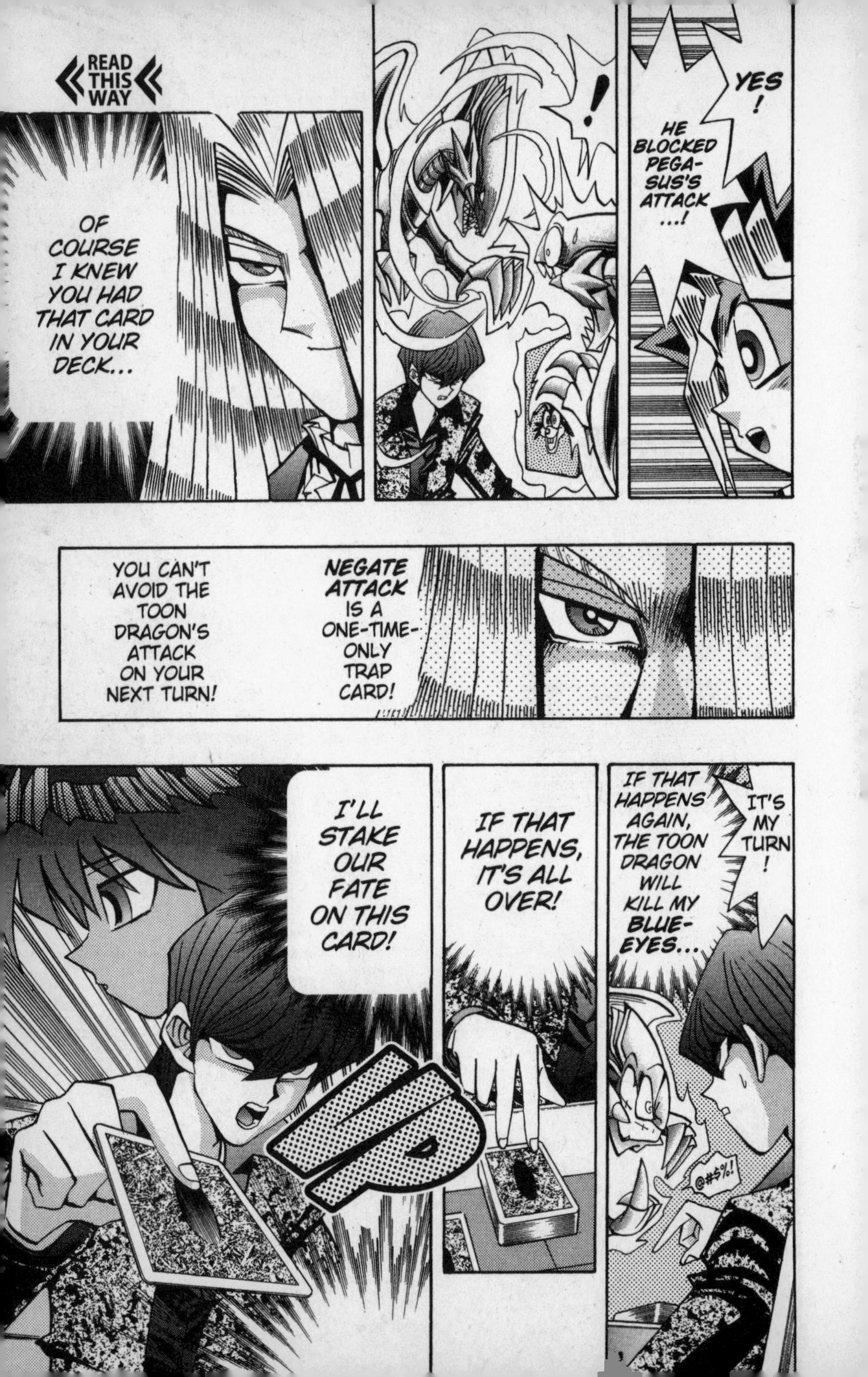
READ THIS WAY
YES!
HE BLOCKED PEGASUS'S ATTACK...!
!
OF COURSE I KNEW YOU HAD THAT CARD IN YOUR DECK...
NEGATE ATTACK IS A ONE-TIME-ONLY TRAP CARD!
YOU CAN'T AVOID THE TOON DRAGON'S ATTACK ON YOUR NEXT TURN!
IT'S MY TURN!
IF THAT HAPPENS AGAIN, THE TOON DRAGON WILL KILL MY BLUE-EYES...
@#$%!
IF THAT HAPPENS, IT'S ALL OVER!
I'LL STAKE OUR FATE ON THIS CARD!

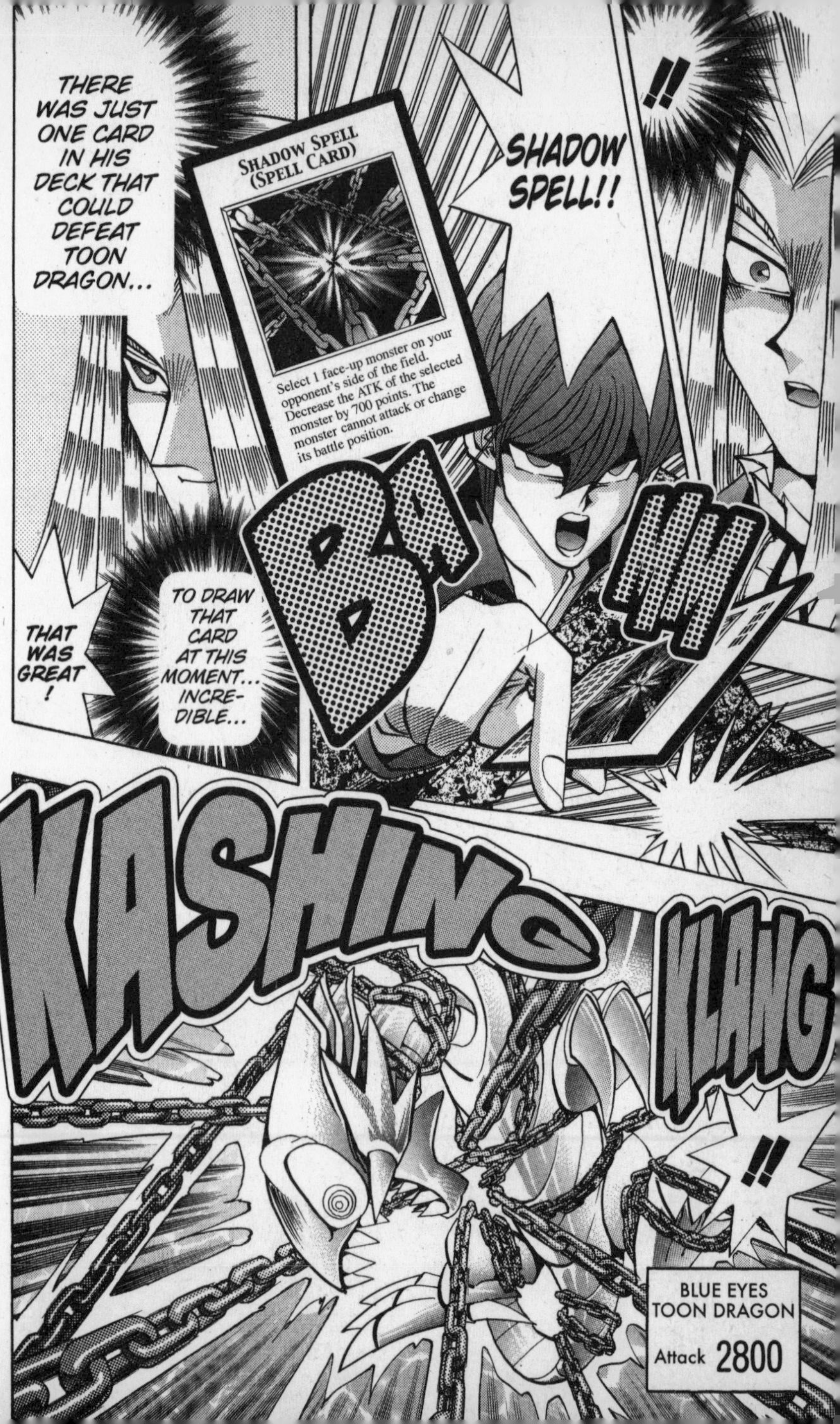
!!
SHADOW SPELL!!
SHADOW SPELL (SPELL CARD)
Select 1 face-up monster on your opponent's side of the field. Decrease the ATK of the selected monster by 700 points. The monster cannot attack or change its battle position.
BAMM
THERE WAS JUST ONE CARD IN HIS DECK THAT COULD DEFEAT TOON DRAGON...
TO DRAW THAT CARD AT THIS MOMENT... INCREDIBLE...
THAT WAS GREAT!
KASHING
KLANG
!!
BLUE EYES TOON DRAGON
Attack 2800

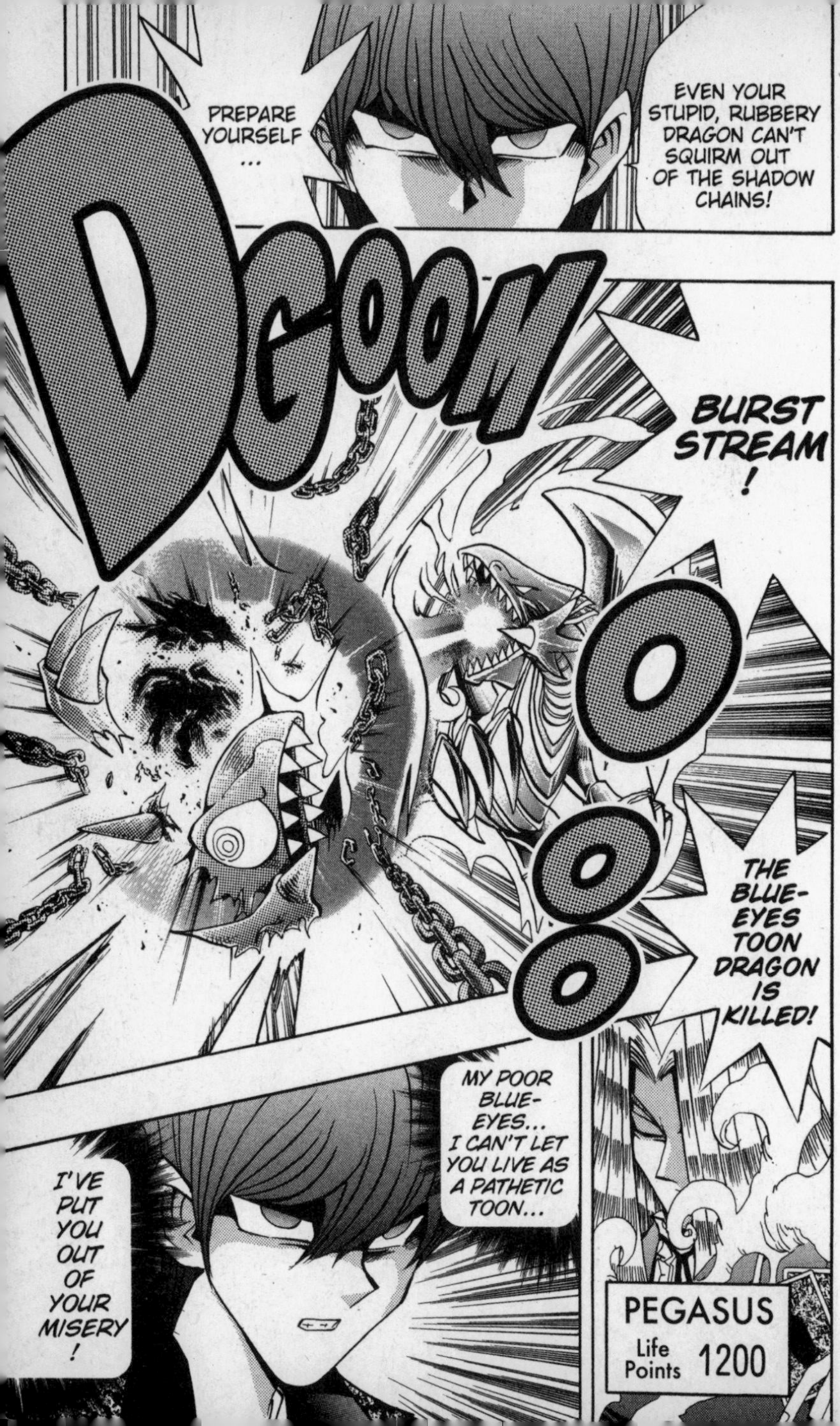

EVEN YOUR STUPID, RUBBERY DRAGON CAN'T SQUIRM OUT OF THE SHADOW CHAINS!
PREPARE YOURSELF ...
BURST STREAM!
DGOOM
OOOO
THE BLUE-EYES TOON DRAGON IS KILLED!
PEGASUS
Life Points 1200
MY POOR BLUE-EYES... I CAN'T LET YOU LIVE AS A PATHETIC TOON...
I'VE PUT YOU OUT OF YOUR MISERY!

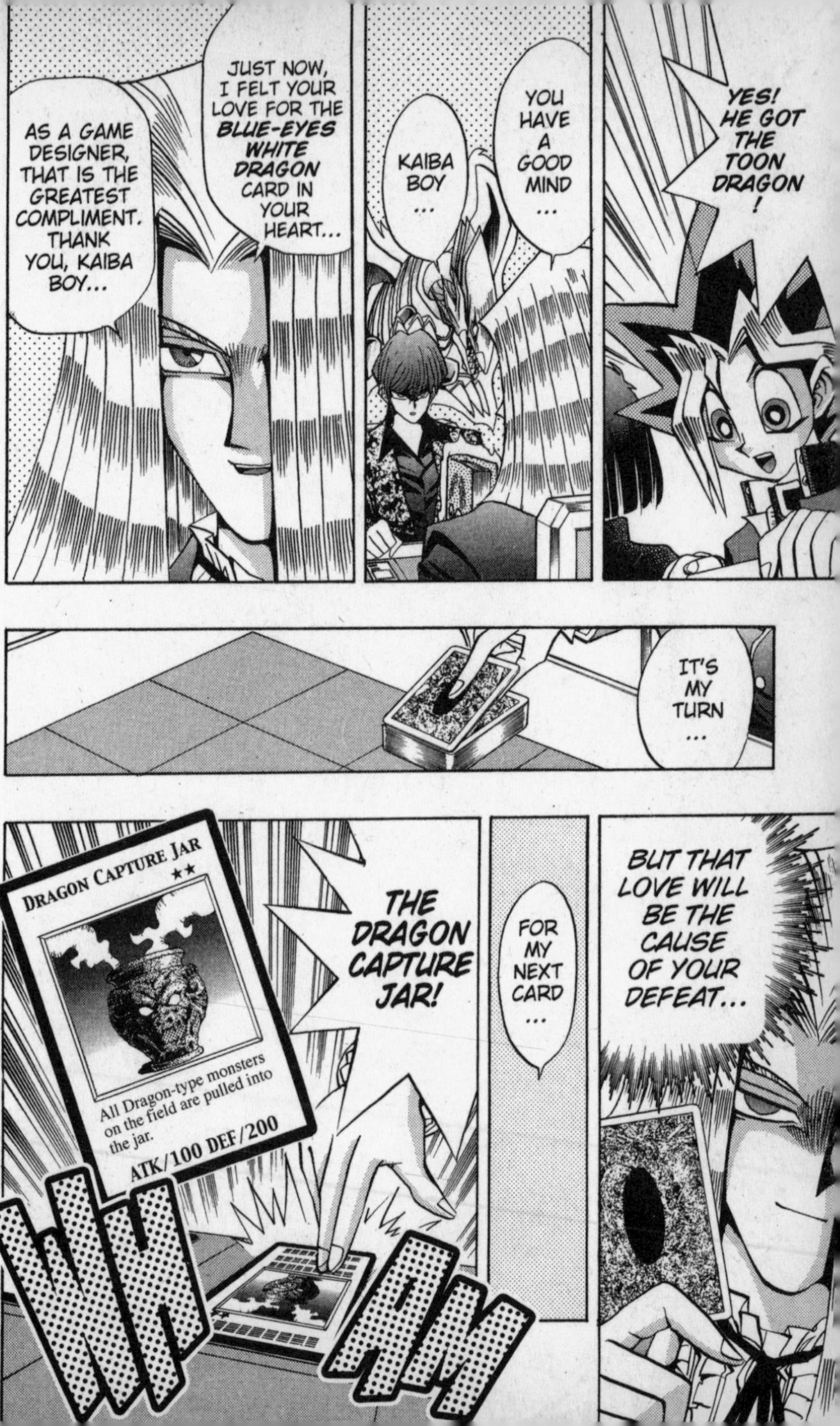
YES! HE GOT THE TOON DRAGON!
YOU HAVE A GOOD MIND...
KAIBA BOY...
JUST NOW, I FELT YOUR LOVE FOR THE BLUE-EYES WHITE DRAGON CARD IN YOUR HEART...
AS A GAME DESIGNER, THAT IS THE GREATEST COMPLIMENT. THANK YOU, KAIBA BOY...
IT'S MY TURN...
BUT THAT LOVE WILL BE THE CAUSE OF YOUR DEFEAT...
FOR MY NEXT CARD...
THE DRAGON CAPTURE JAR!
DRAGON CAPTURE JAR ★★
All Dragon-type monsters on the field are pulled into the jar.
ATK/100 DEF/200
WHAM

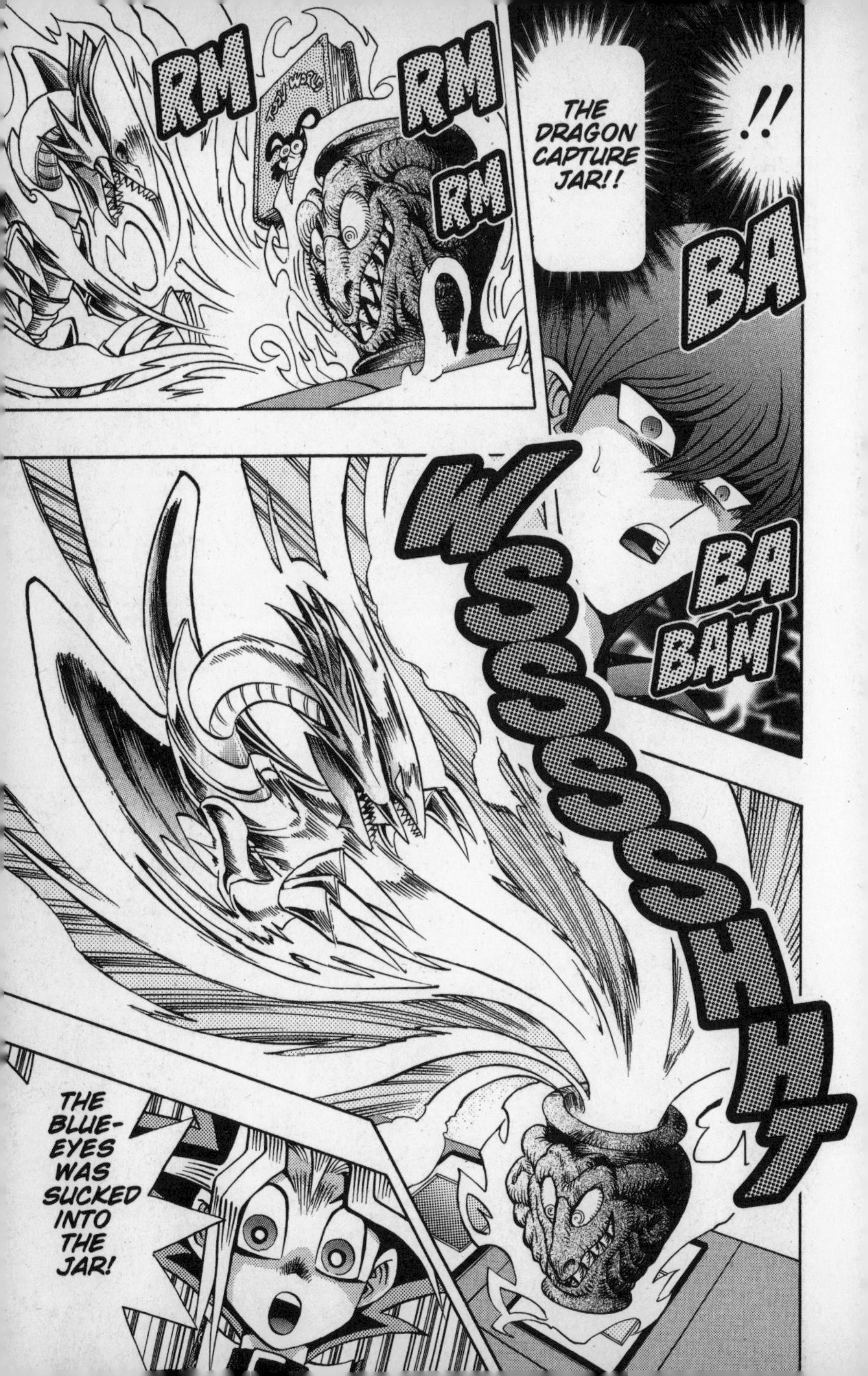
THE DRAGON CAPTURE JAR!!
!!
BA
BA BAM
RM
RM
RM
WSSSSHHHT
THE BLUE-EYES WAS SUCKED INTO THE JAR!

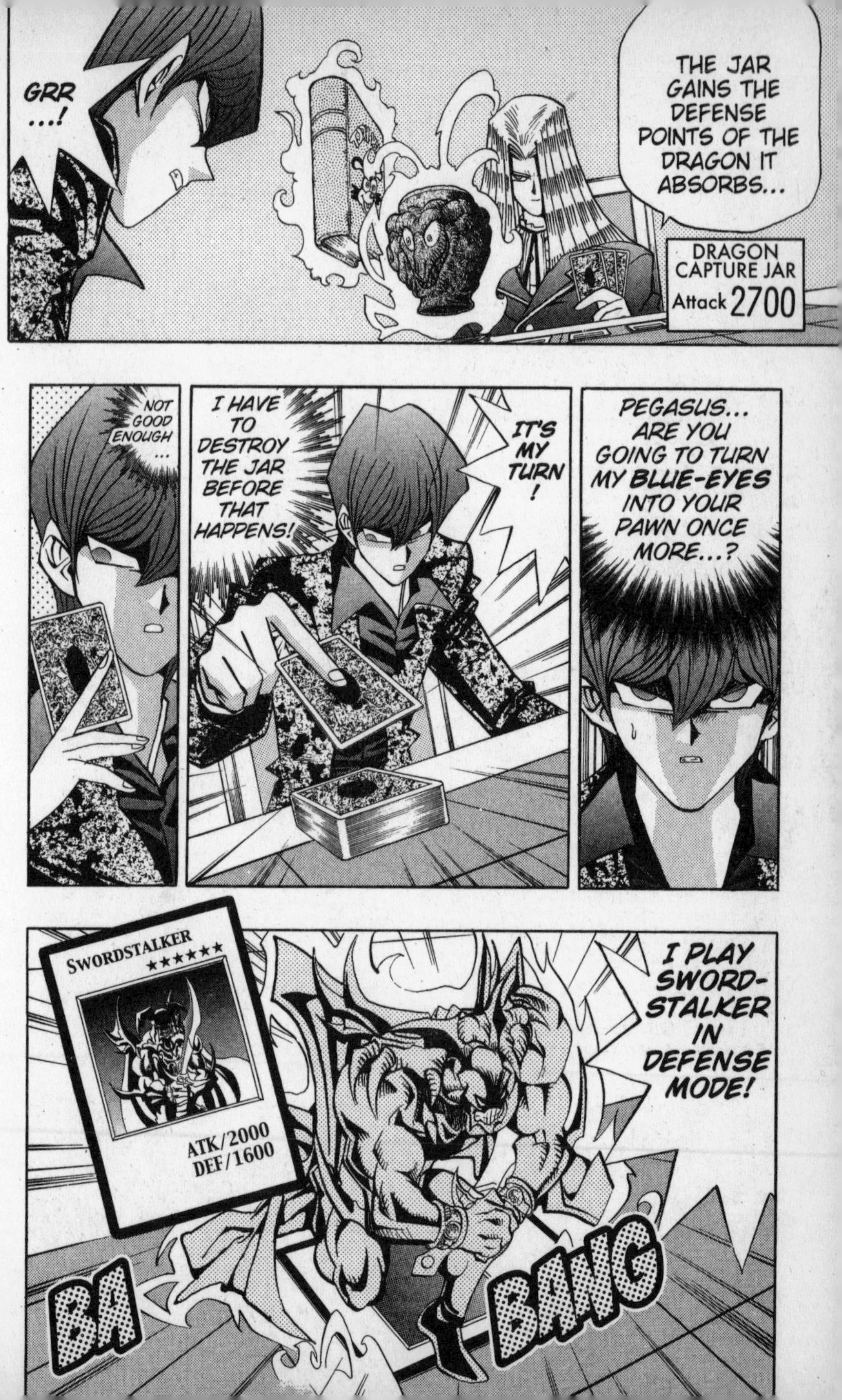
THE JAR GAINS THE DEFENSE POINTS OF THE DRAGON IT ABSORBS...
DRAGON CAPTURE JAR
Attack 2700
GRR ...!
PEGASUS... ARE YOU GOING TO TURN MY BLUE-EYES INTO YOUR PAWN ONCE MORE...?
IT'S MY TURN!
I HAVE TO DESTROY THE JAR BEFORE THAT HAPPENS!
NOT GOOD ENOUGH...
I PLAY SWORD-STALKER IN DEFENSE MODE!
SWORDSTALKER ★★★★★★
ATK/2000
DEF/1600
BA
BANG

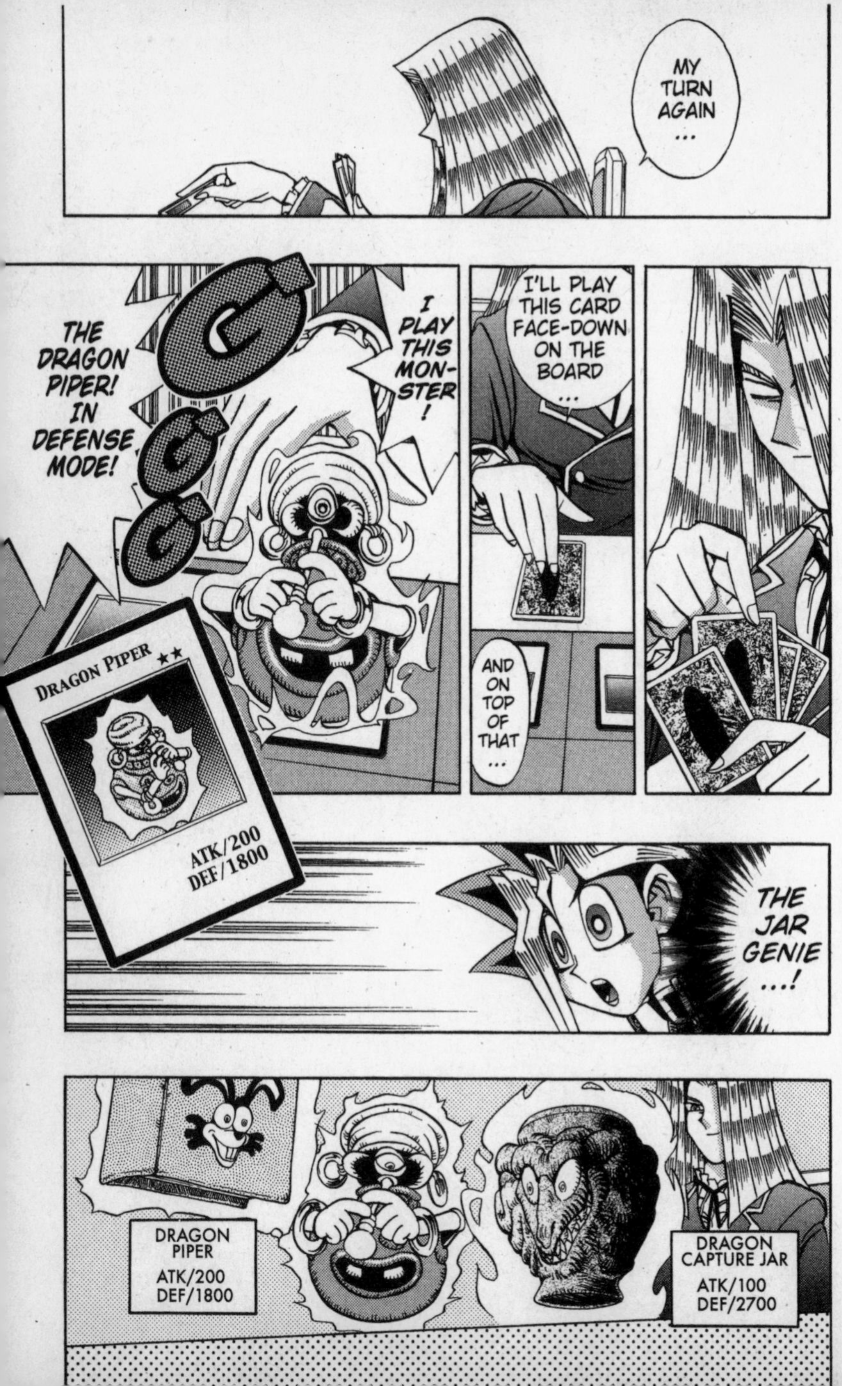
MY TURN AGAIN ...
I'LL PLAY THIS CARD FACE-DOWN ON THE BOARD ...
AND ON TOP OF THAT ...
I PLAY THIS MONSTER!
THE DRAGON PIPER! IN DEFENSE MODE!
DRAGON PIPER ★★
ATK/200 DEF/1800
THE JAR GENIE ...!
DRAGON CAPTURE JAR
ATK/100 DEF/2700
DRAGON PIPER
ATK/200 DEF/1800

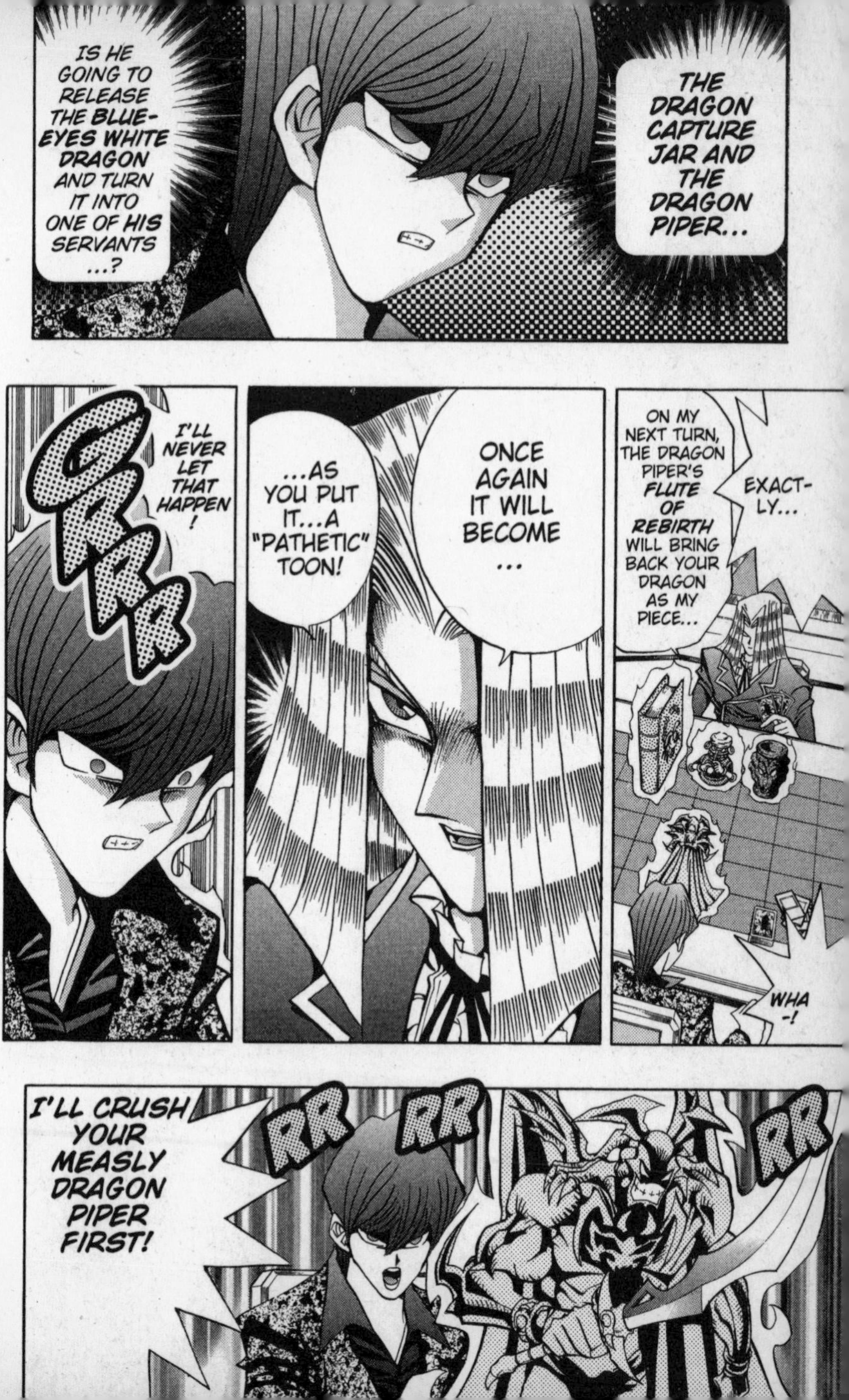
THE DRAGON CAPTURE JAR AND THE DRAGON PIPER...
IS HE GOING TO RELEASE THE BLUE-EYES WHITE DRAGON AND TURN IT INTO ONE OF HIS SERVANTS ...?
EXACT-LY...
ON MY NEXT TURN, THE DRAGON PIPER'S FLUTE OF REBIRTH WILL BRING BACK YOUR DRAGON AS MY PIECE...
WHA-!
ONCE AGAIN IT WILL BECOME ...
...AS YOU PUT IT...A "PATHETIC" TOON!
I'LL NEVER LET THAT HAPPEN!
CRRR
RR
RR
RR
I'LL CRUSH YOUR MEASLY DRAGON PIPER FIRST!

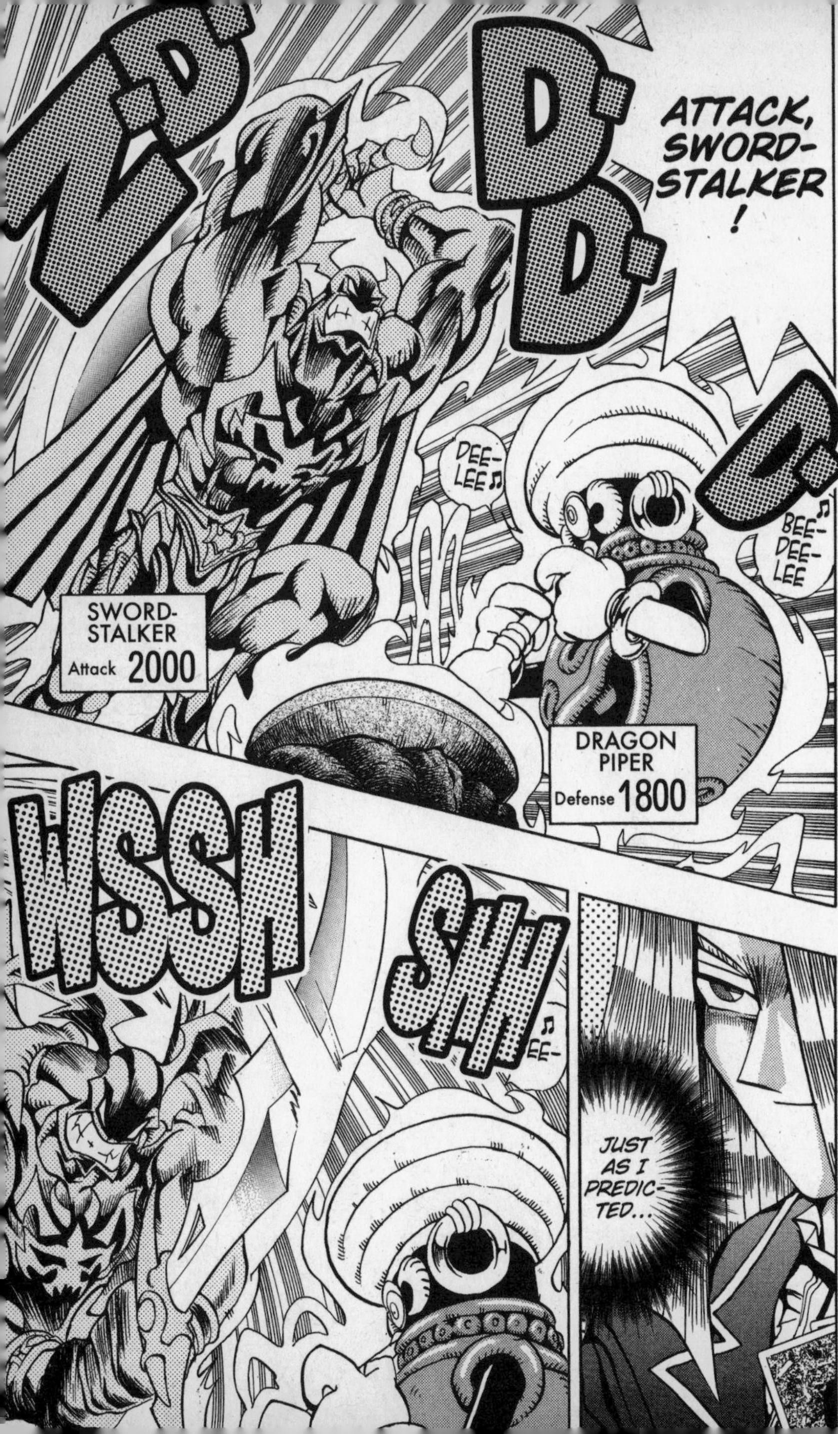
ATTACK, SWORD-STALKER!
BEE-DEE-LEE
DEE-LEE
SWORD-STALKER Attack 2000
DRAGON PIPER Defense 1800
JUST AS I PREDICTED...
EE-
SHH
WSSH

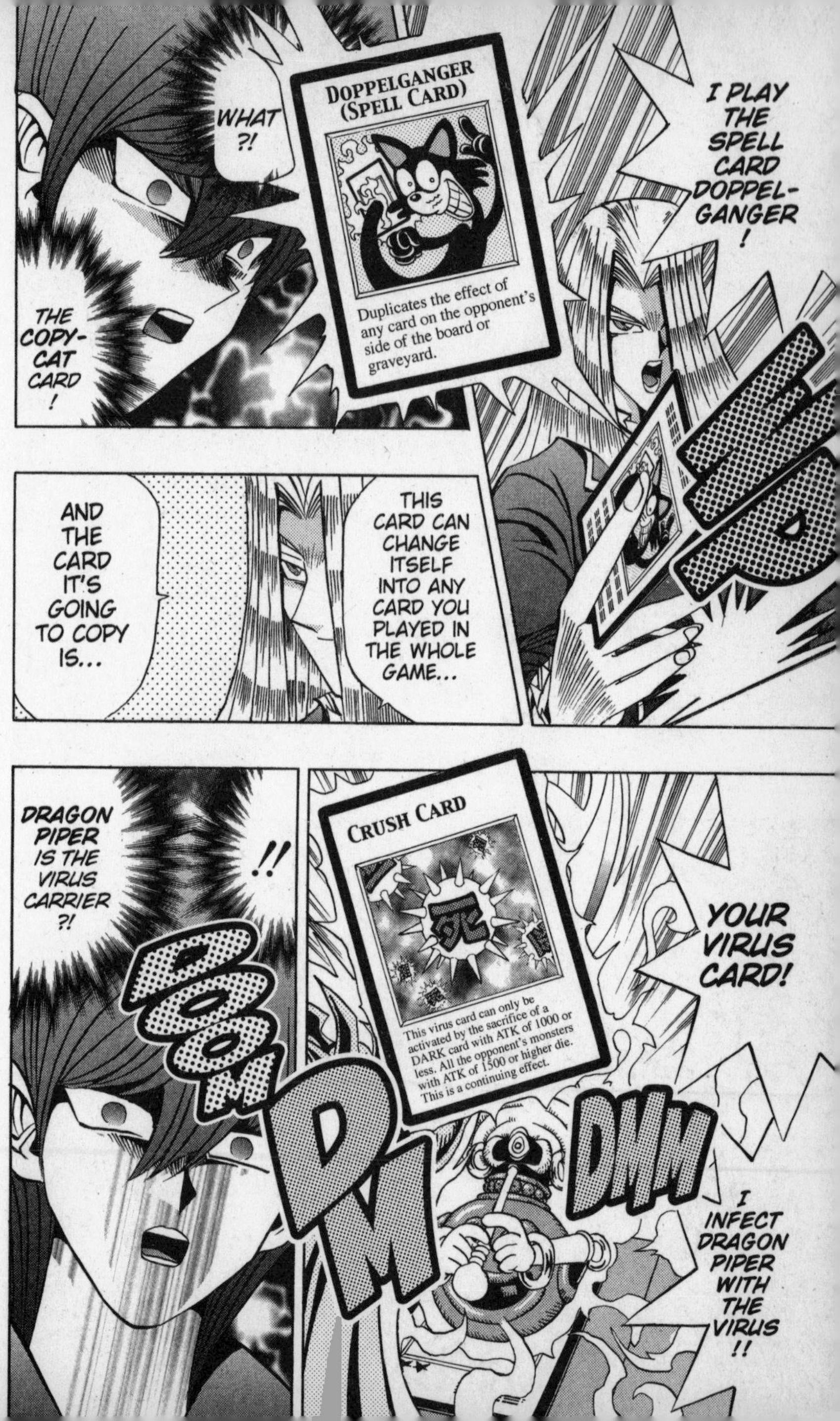
I PLAY THE SPELL CARD DOPPELGANGER!
WHAT?!
DOPPELGANGER (SPELL CARD)
Duplicates the effect of any card on the opponent's side of the board or graveyard.
THE COPY-CAT CARD!
THIS CARD CAN CHANGE ITSELF INTO ANY CARD YOU PLAYED IN THE WHOLE GAME...
AND THE CARD IT'S GOING TO COPY IS...
YOUR VIRUS CARD!
CRUSH CARD
This virus card can only be activated by the sacrifice of a DARK card with ATK of 1000 or less. All the opponent's monsters with ATK of 1500 or higher die. This is a continuing effect.
DMM
I INFECT DRAGON PIPER WITH THE VIRUS!!
!!
DRAGON PIPER IS THE VIRUS CARRIER?!

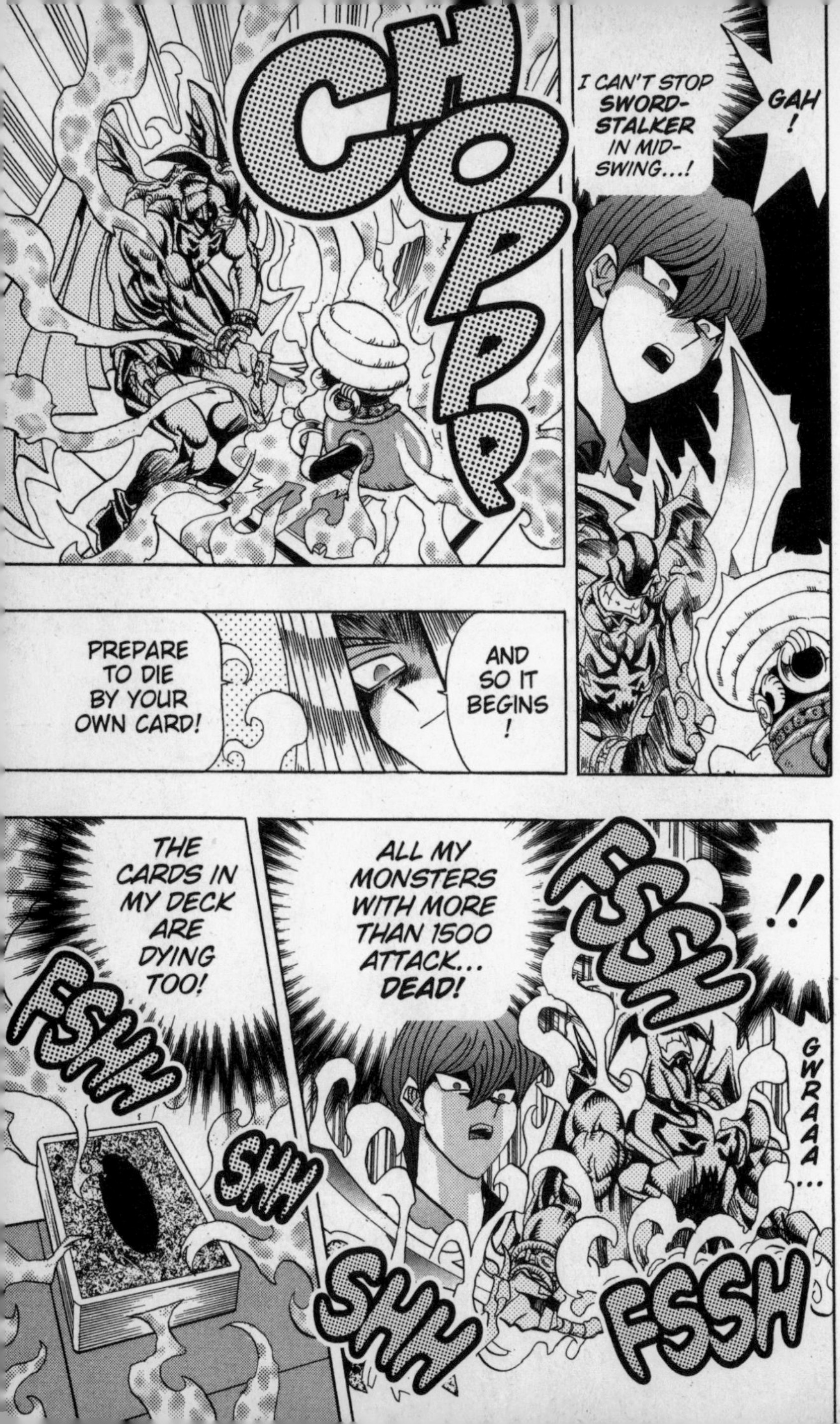
GAH!
I CAN'T STOP SWORD-STALKER IN MID-SWING...!
CHOPPP
AND SO IT BEGINS!
PREPARE TO DIE BY YOUR OWN CARD!
!!
FSSH
GWRAAA...
ALL MY MONSTERS WITH MORE THAN 1500 ATTACK... DEAD!
FSSH
SHH
THE CARDS IN MY DECK ARE DYING TOO!
FSSH
SHH

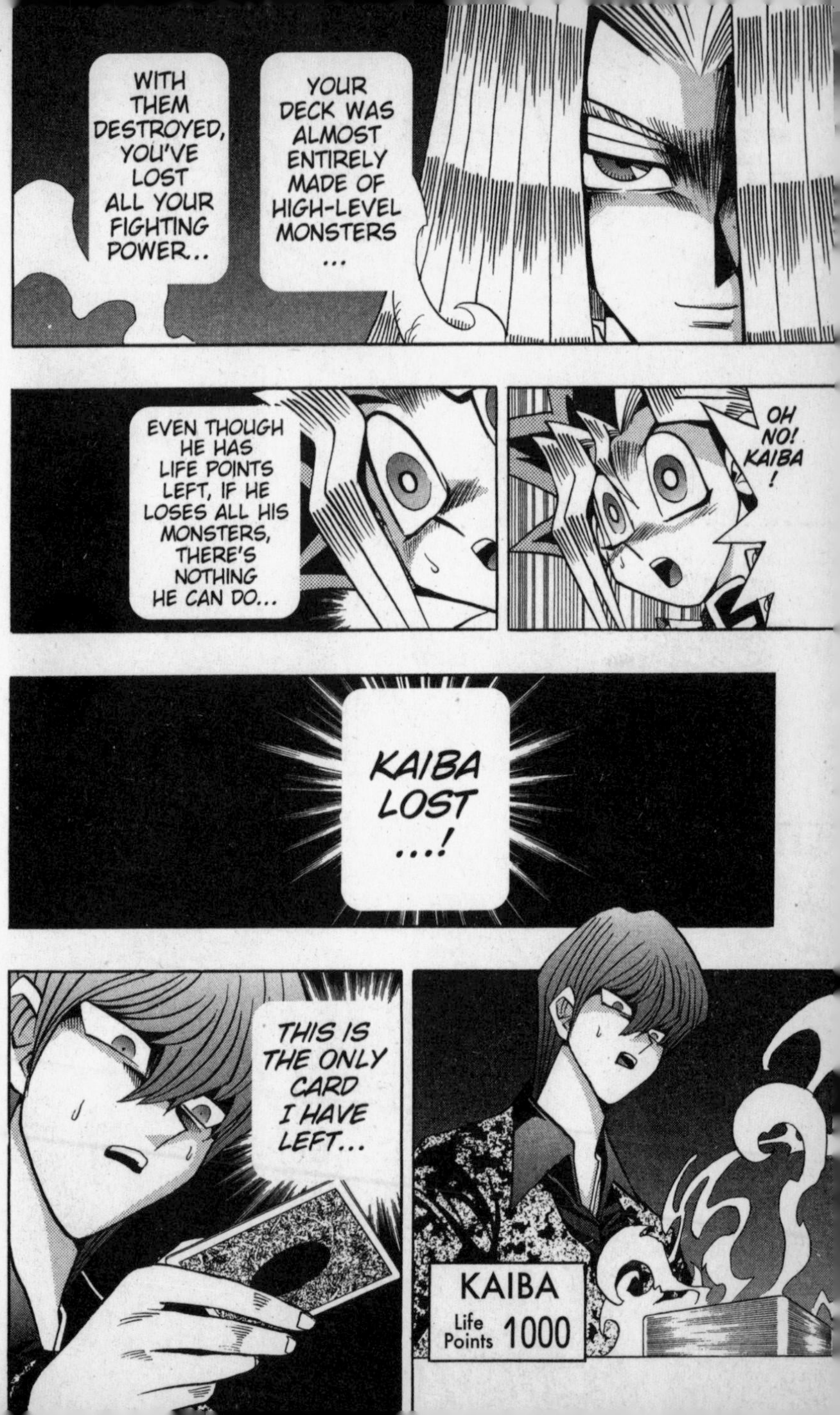
YOUR DECK WAS ALMOST ENTIRELY MADE OF HIGH-LEVEL MONSTERS ...
WITH THEM DESTROYED, YOU'VE LOST ALL YOUR FIGHTING POWER...
OH NO! KAIBA!
EVEN THOUGH HE HAS LIFE POINTS LEFT, IF HE LOSES ALL HIS MONSTERS, THERE'S NOTHING HE CAN DO...
KAIBA LOST ...!
KAIBA
Life Points 1000
THIS IS THE ONLY CARD I HAVE LEFT...

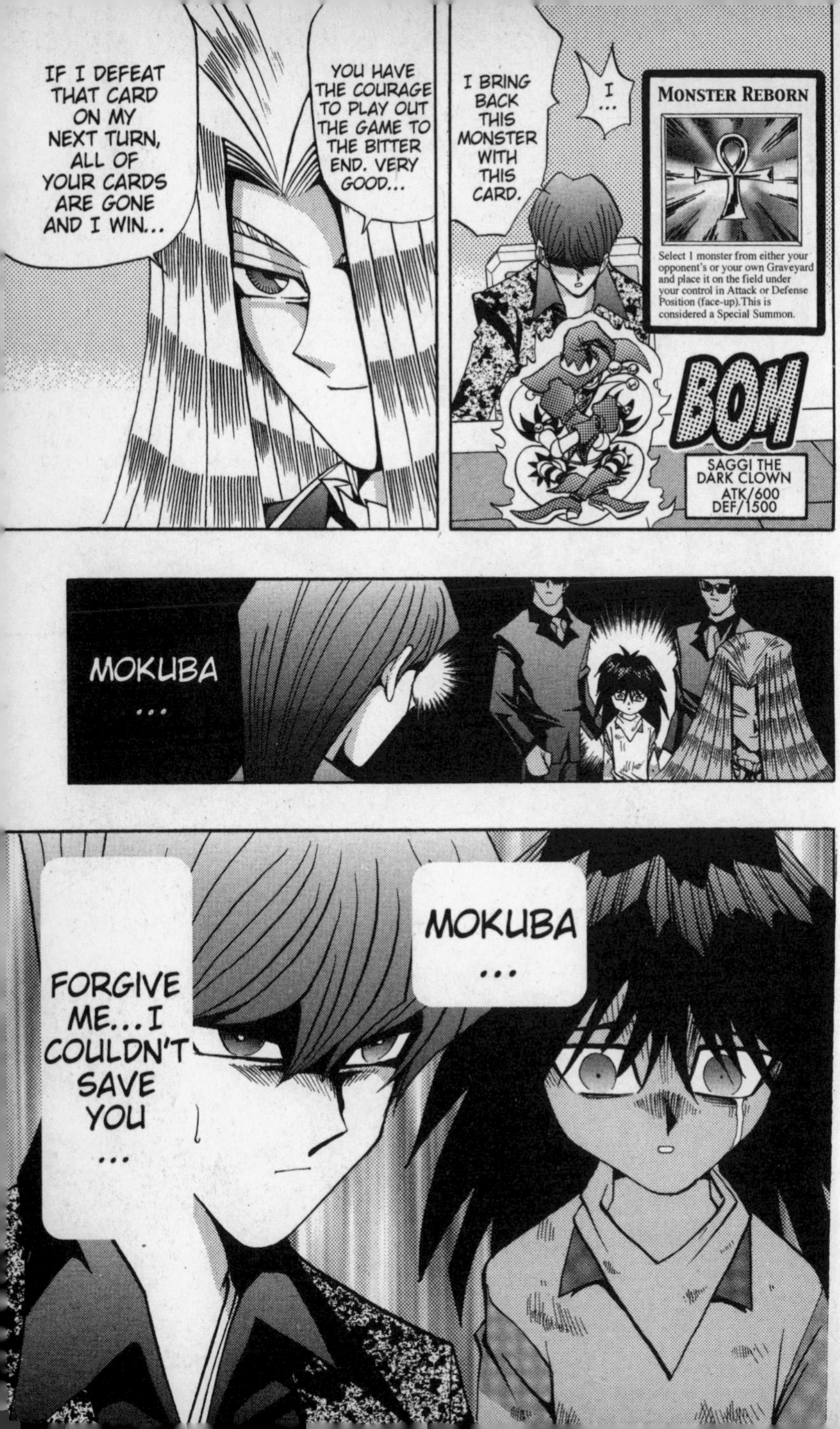
I ...
I BRING BACK THIS MONSTER WITH THIS CARD.
MONSTER REBORN
Select 1 monster from either your opponent's or your own Graveyard and place it on the field under your control in Attack or Defense Position (face-up).This is considered a Special Summon.
BOM
SAGGI THE DARK CLOWN ATK/600 DEF/1500
YOU HAVE THE COURAGE TO PLAY OUT THE GAME TO THE BITTER END. VERY GOOD...
IF I DEFEAT THAT CARD ON MY NEXT TURN, ALL OF YOUR CARDS ARE GONE AND I WIN...
MOKUBA ...
MOKUBA ...
FORGIVE ME...I COULDN'T SAVE YOU ...

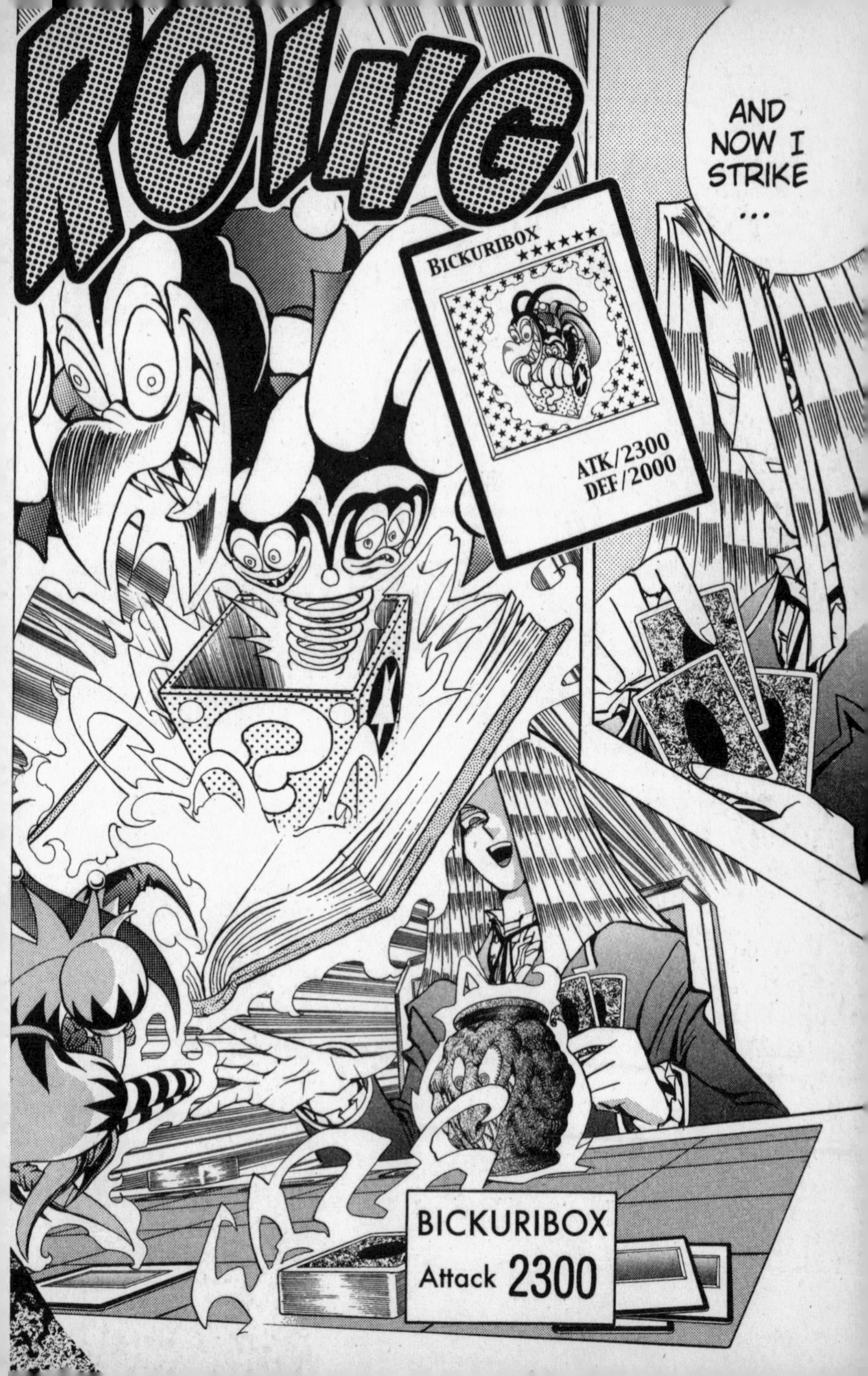
AND NOW I STRIKE ...
BICKURIBOX
ATK/2300
DEF/2000
BICKURIBOX
Attack 2300

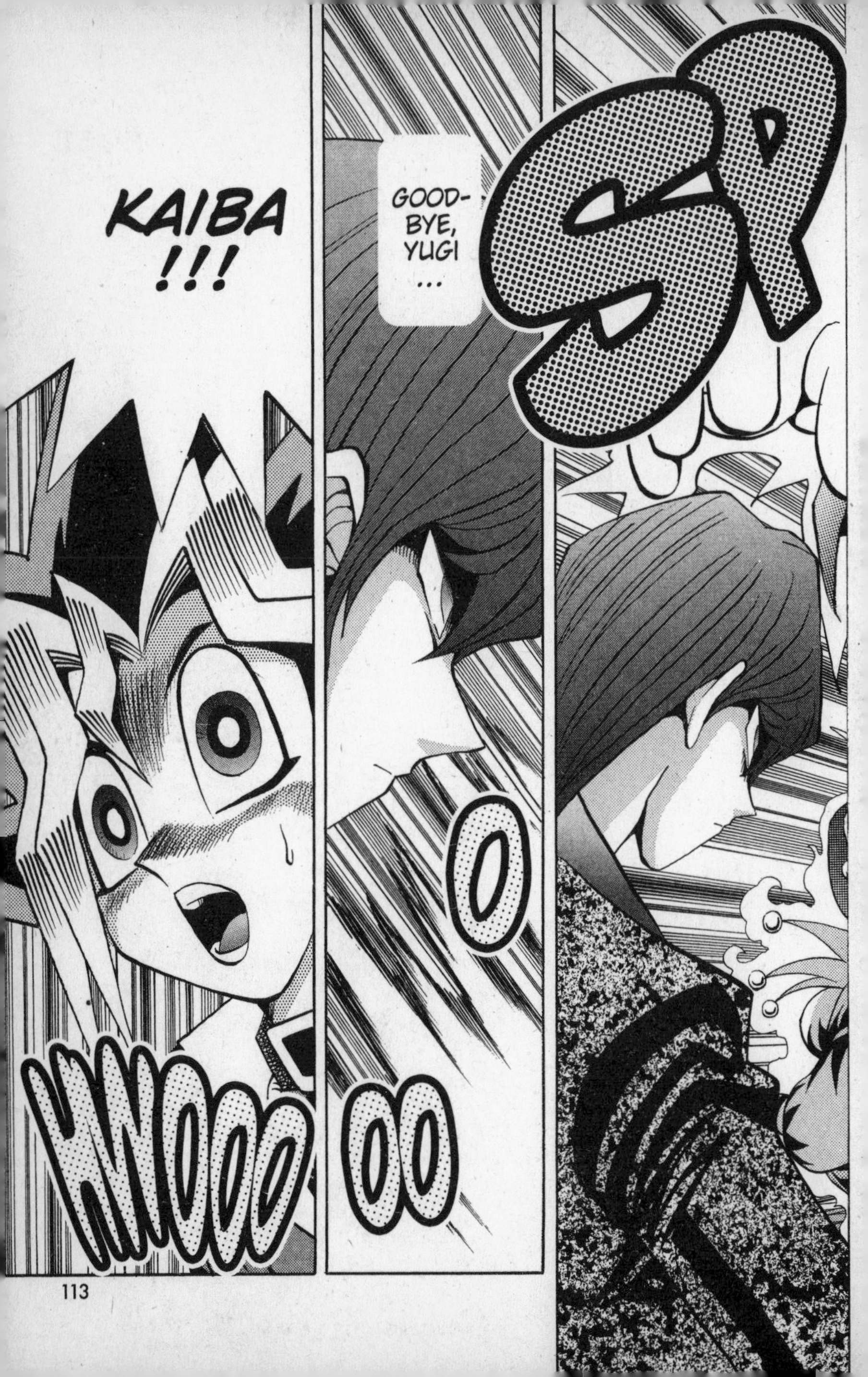
SP
GOOD-BYE, YUGI ...
O
KAIBA !!!
WHOOO
OO

SOUL PRISON

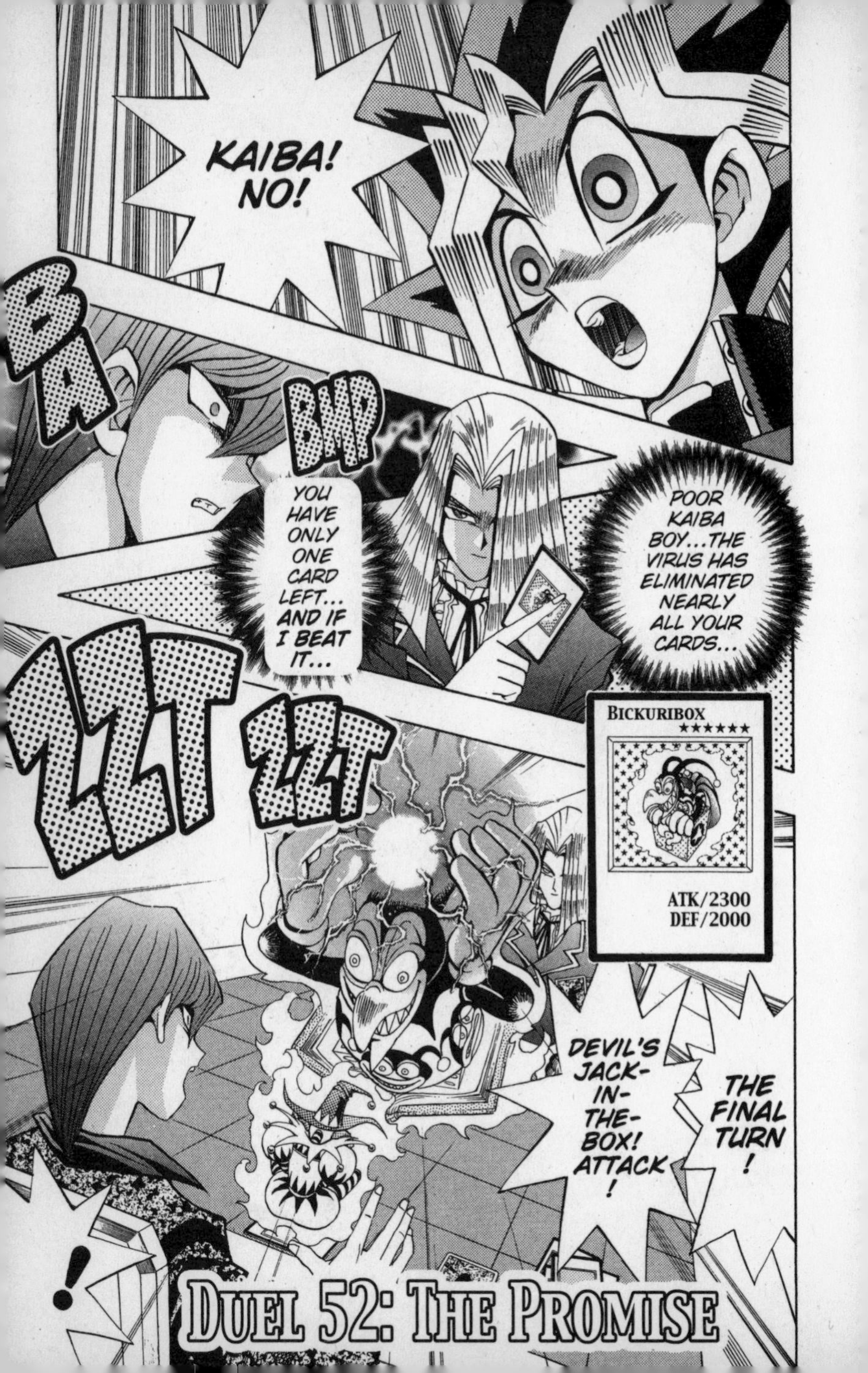
KAIBA! NO!
POOR KAIBA BOY...THE VIRUS HAS ELIMINATED NEARLY ALL YOUR CARDS...
YOU HAVE ONLY ONE CARD LEFT... AND IF I BEAT IT...
BMP
BA
ZZT
ZZT
BICKURIBOX
ATK/2300
DEF/2000
THE FINAL TURN!
DEVIL'S JACK-IN-THE-BOX! ATTACK!
!
DUEL 52: THE PROMISE

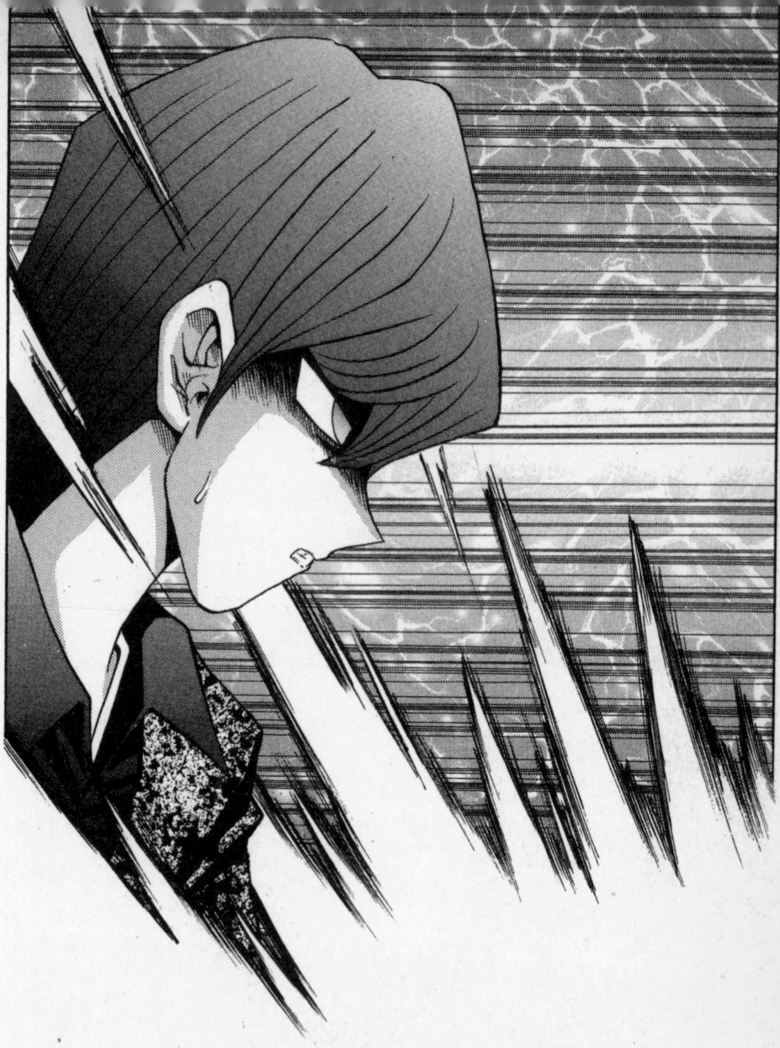

Duel 52: The Promise

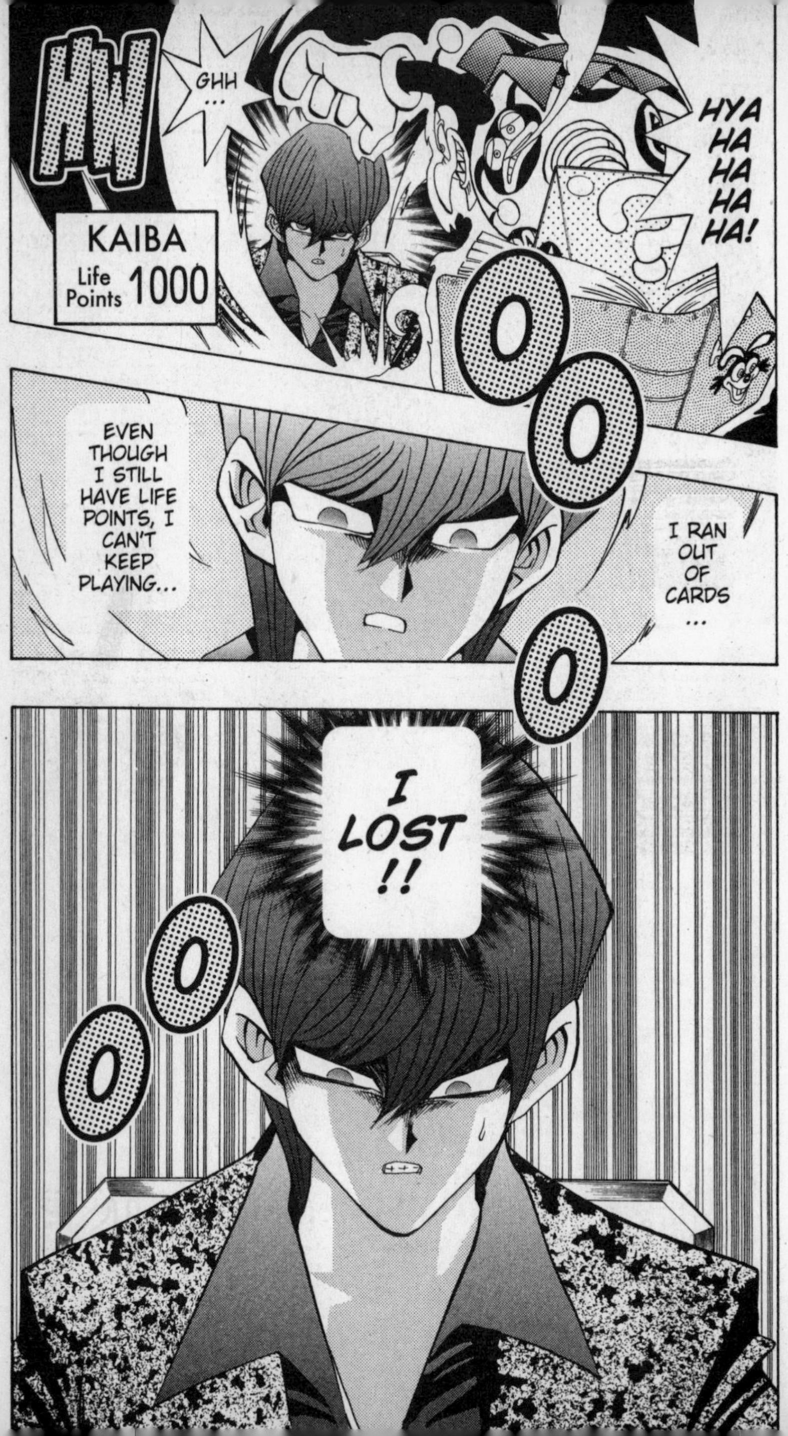
HYA HA HA HA HA!
GHH ...
HN
KAIBA Life Points 1000
OOOO
I RAN OUT OF CARDS ...
EVEN THOUGH I STILL HAVE LIFE POINTS, I CAN'T KEEP PLAYING...
I LOST!!
OOO

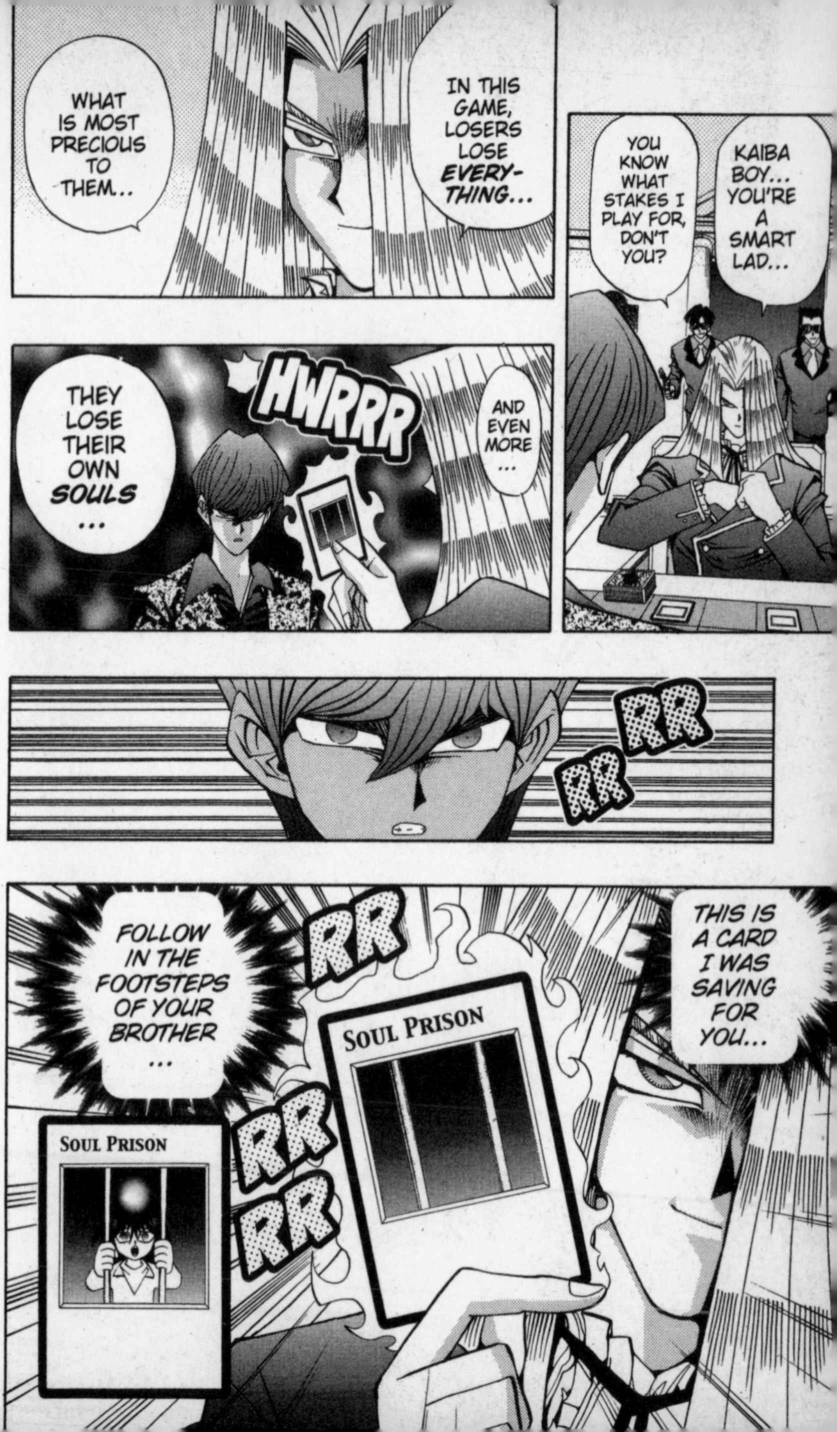

KAIBA BOY... YOU'RE A SMART LAD...
YOU KNOW WHAT STAKES I PLAY FOR, DON'T YOU?
IN THIS GAME, LOSERS LOSE EVERYTHING...
WHAT IS MOST PRECIOUS TO THEM...
AND EVEN MORE...
HWRRR
THEY LOSE THEIR OWN SOULS...
RR
RR
THIS IS A CARD I WAS SAVING FOR YOU...
RR
SOUL PRISON
FOLLOW IN THE FOOTSTEPS OF YOUR BROTHER...
RR
RR
SOUL PRISON

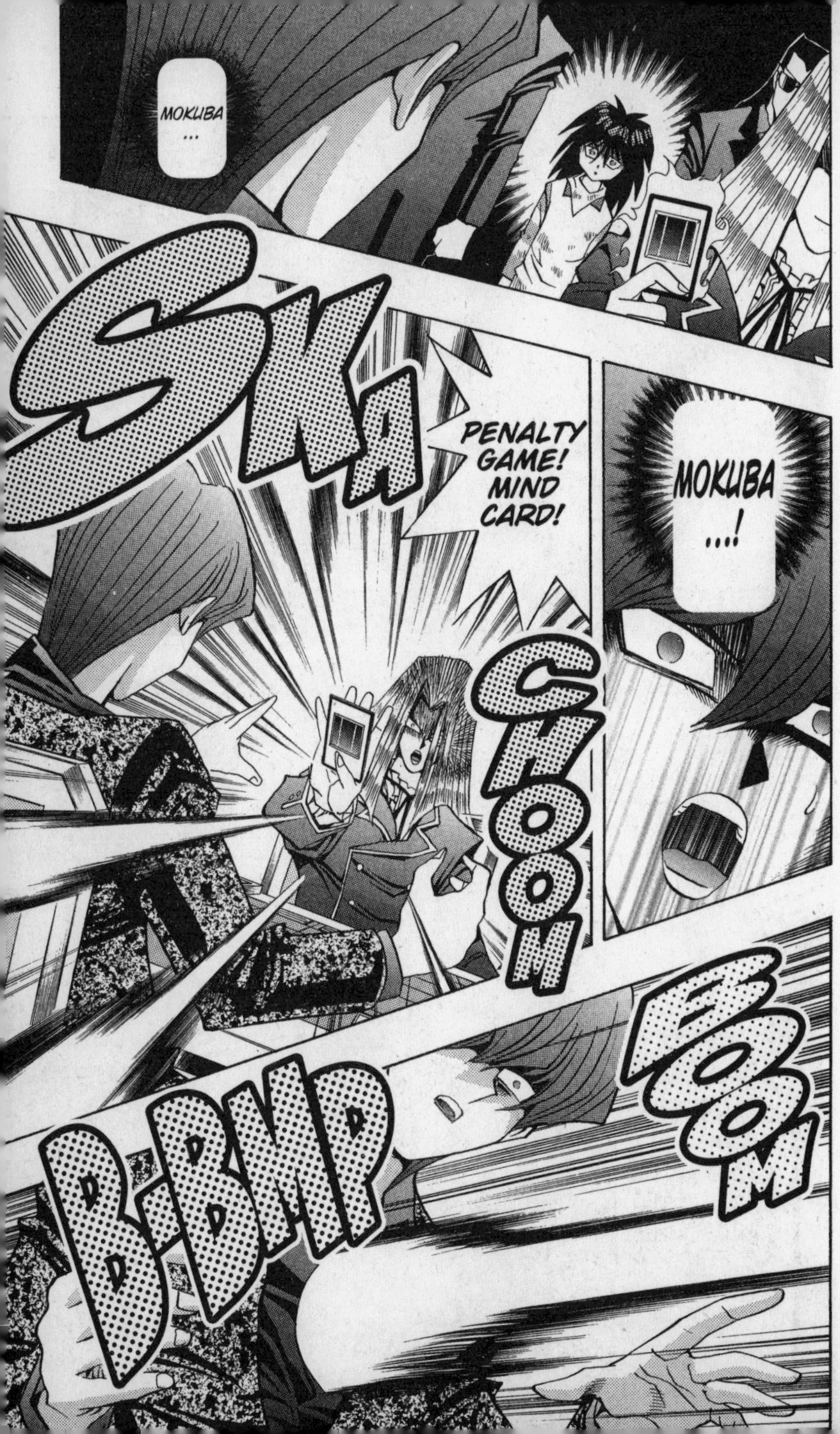
MOKUBA ...
SKA
MOKUBA ...!
PENALTY GAME! MIND CARD!
CHOOOM
ZOOOM
B-DMP
D D D D D D

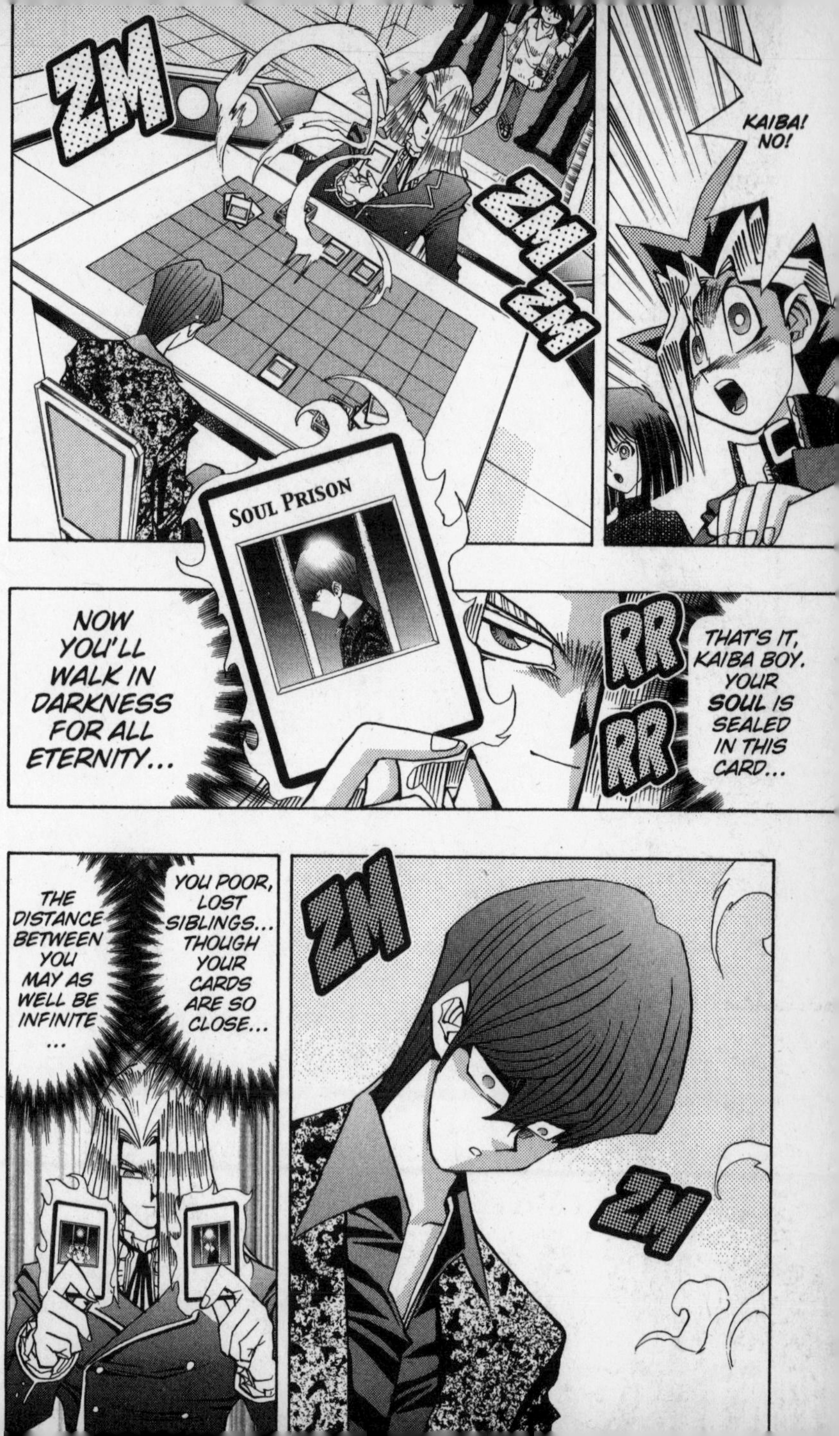
KAIBA! NO!
ZM
ZM ZM
SOUL PRISON
THAT'S IT, KAIBA BOY. YOUR SOUL IS SEALED IN THIS CARD...
RR RR
NOW YOU'LL WALK IN DARKNESS FOR ALL ETERNITY...
ZM
ZM
YOU POOR, LOST SIBLINGS... THOUGH YOUR CARDS ARE SO CLOSE...
THE DISTANCE BETWEEN YOU MAY AS WELL BE INFINITE ...

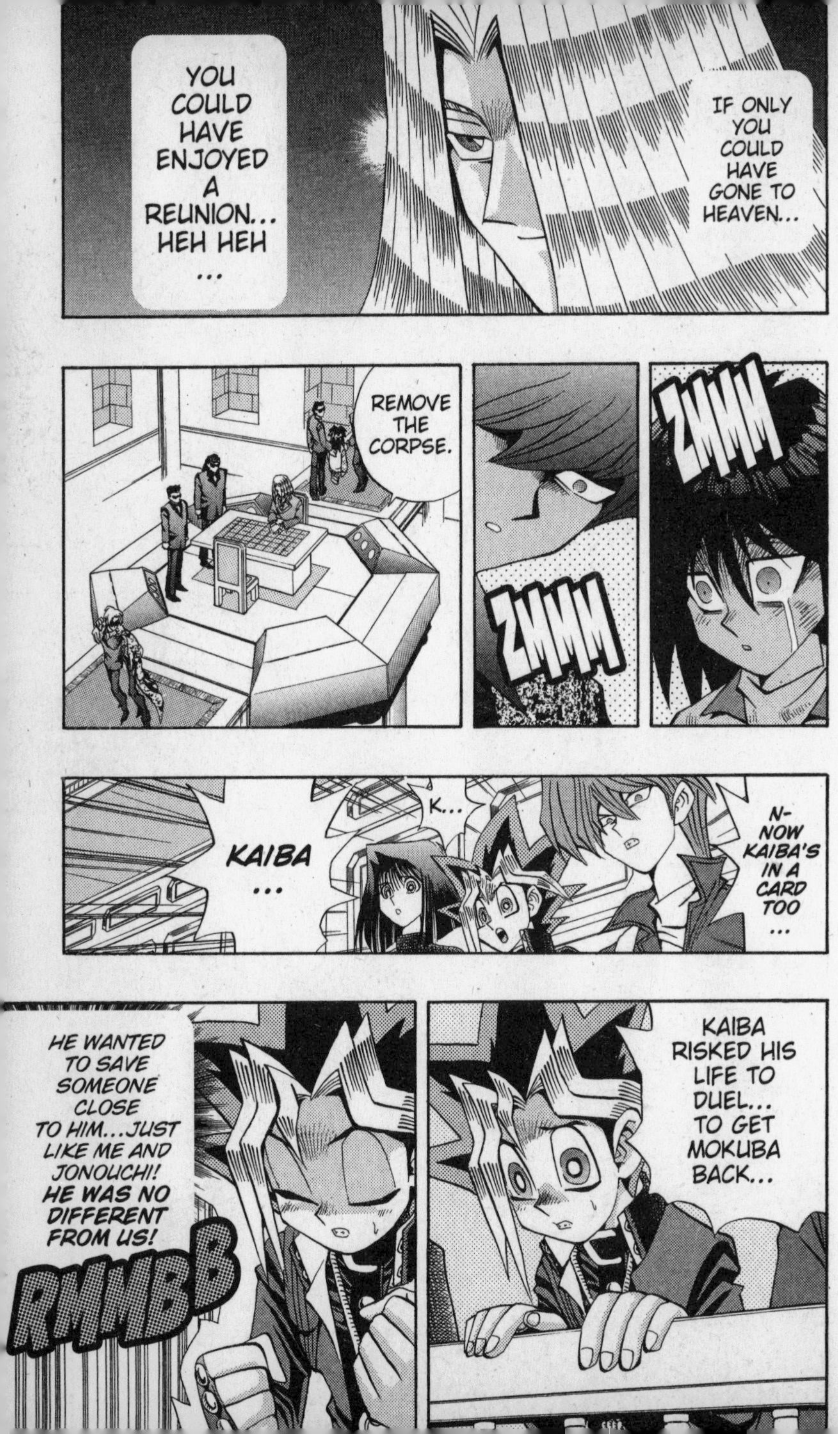
IF ONLY YOU COULD HAVE GONE TO HEAVEN...
YOU COULD HAVE ENJOYED A REUNION... HEH HEH ...
ZMMM
ZMMM
REMOVE THE CORPSE.
N-NOW KAIBA'S IN A CARD TOO ...
K...
KAIBA ...
KAIBA RISKED HIS LIFE TO DUEL... TO GET MOKUBA BACK...
HE WANTED TO SAVE SOMEONE CLOSE TO HIM...JUST LIKE ME AND JONOUCHI! HE WAS NO DIFFERENT FROM US!
RMMBB

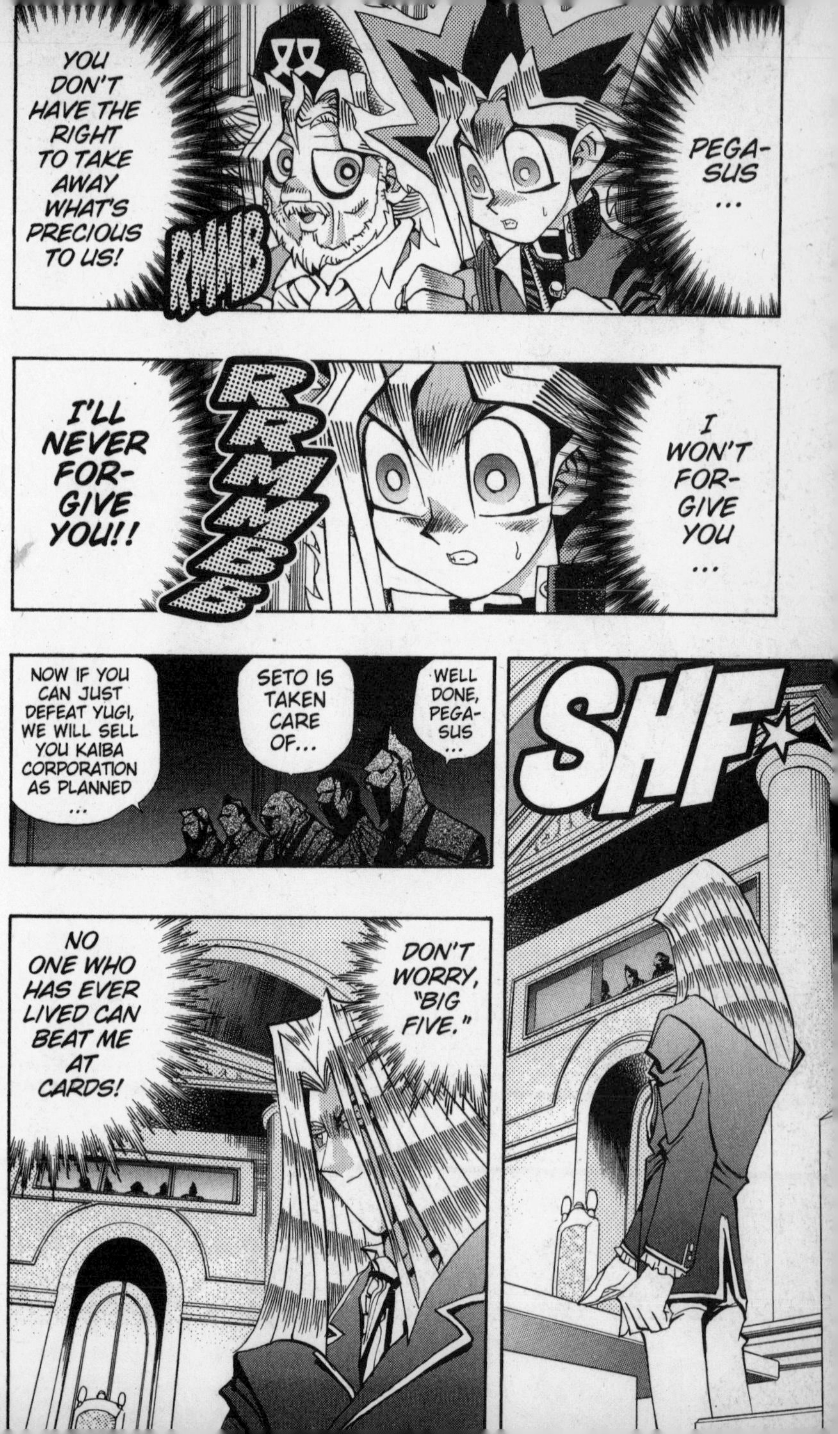
PEGA-SUS ...
YOU DON'T HAVE THE RIGHT TO TAKE AWAY WHAT'S PRECIOUS TO US!
RMMB
I WON'T FOR-GIVE YOU ...
RRMMBB
I'LL NEVER FOR-GIVE YOU!!
SHF
WELL DONE, PEGA-SUS ...
SETO IS TAKEN CARE OF...
NOW IF YOU CAN JUST DEFEAT YUGI, WE WILL SELL YOU KAIBA CORPORATION AS PLANNED ...
DON'T WORRY, "BIG FIVE."
NO ONE WHO HAS EVER LIVED CAN BEAT ME AT CARDS!

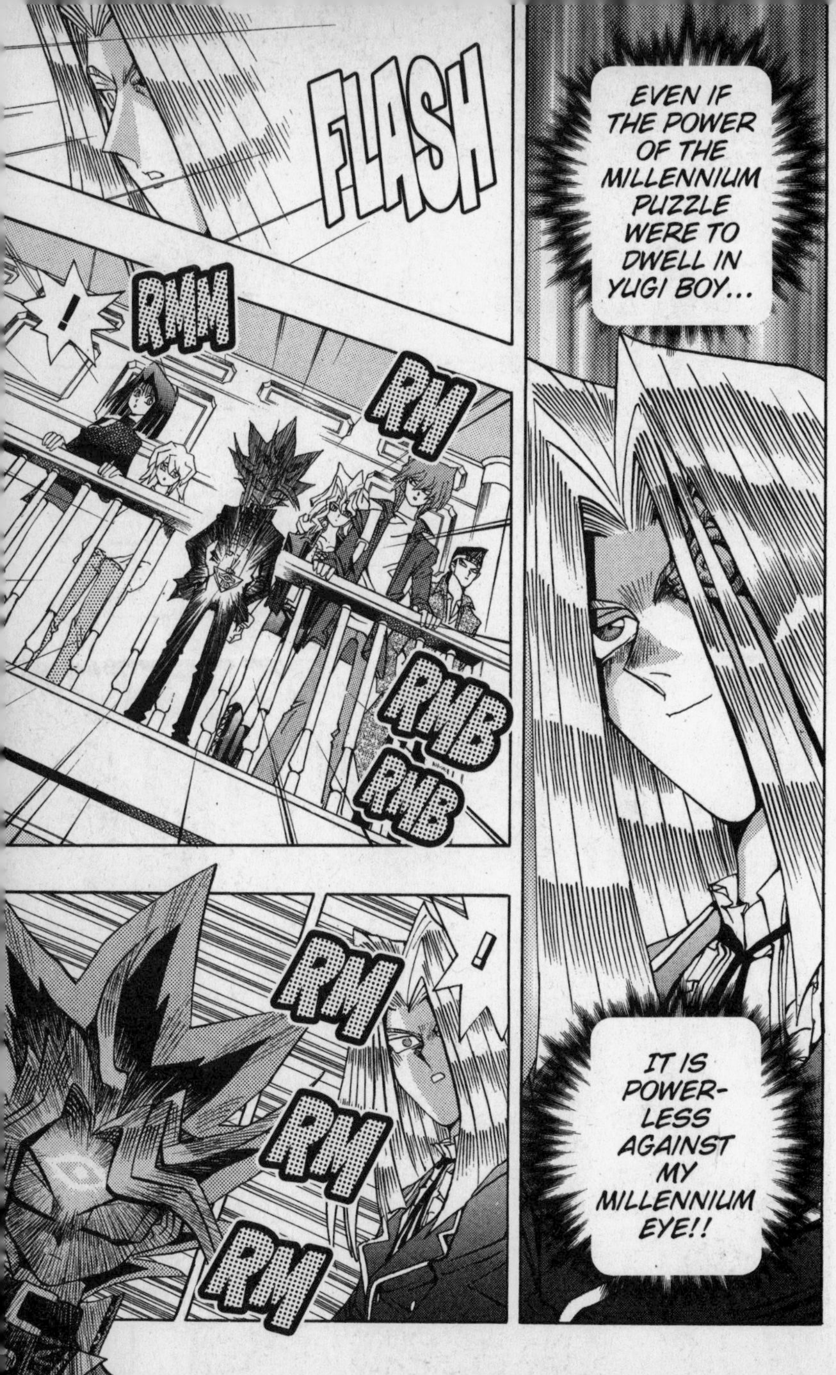
EVEN IF THE POWER OF THE MILLENNIUM PUZZLE WERE TO DWELL IN YUGI BOY...
IT IS POWER-LESS AGAINST MY MILLENNIUM EYE!!
FLASH
!
RMM
RM
RMB
RMB
!
RM
RM
RM

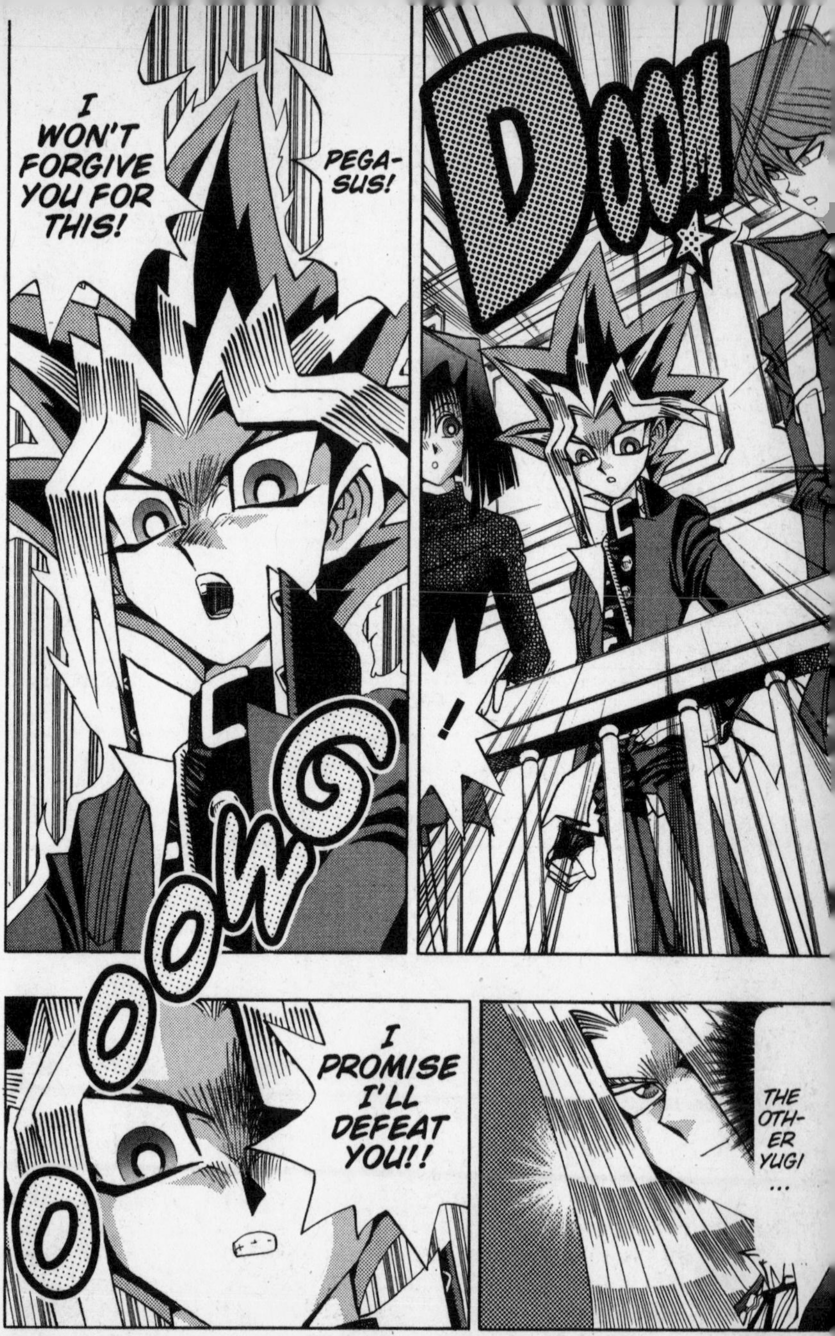
DOOOM
!
PEGASUS!
I WON'T FORGIVE YOU FOR THIS!
THE OTHER YUGI...
I PROMISE I'LL DEFEAT YOU!!

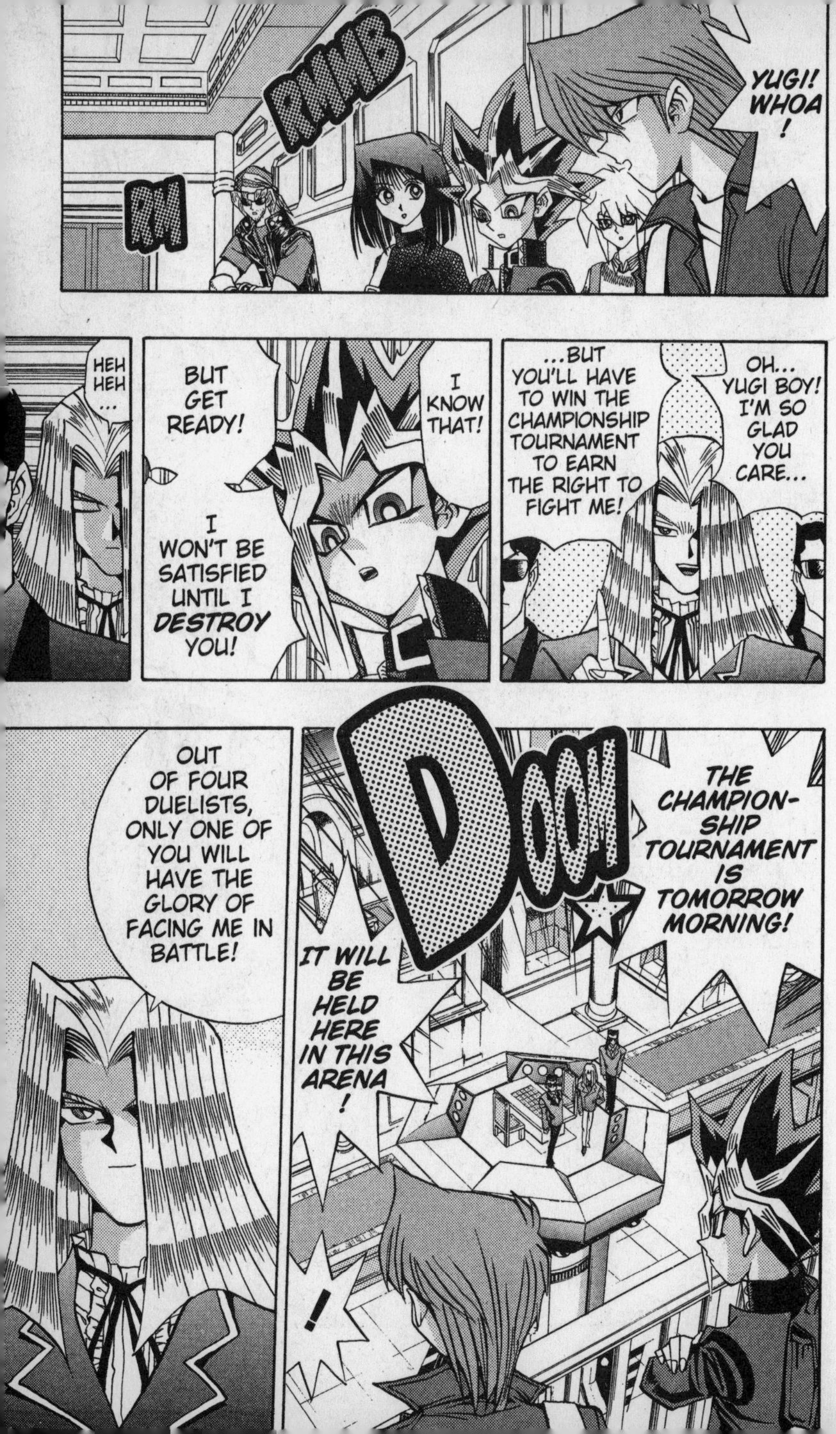
YUGI! WHOA!
RMMB
RM
OH... YUGI BOY! I'M SO GLAD YOU CARE...
...BUT YOU'LL HAVE TO WIN THE CHAMPIONSHIP TOURNAMENT TO EARN THE RIGHT TO FIGHT ME!
I KNOW THAT!
BUT GET READY!
I WON'T BE SATISFIED UNTIL I DESTROY YOU!
HEH HEH ...
THE CHAMPION-SHIP TOURNAMENT IS TOMORROW MORNING!
DOOM
IT WILL BE HELD HERE IN THIS ARENA!
!
OUT OF FOUR DUELISTS, ONLY ONE OF YOU WILL HAVE THE GLORY OF FACING ME IN BATTLE!

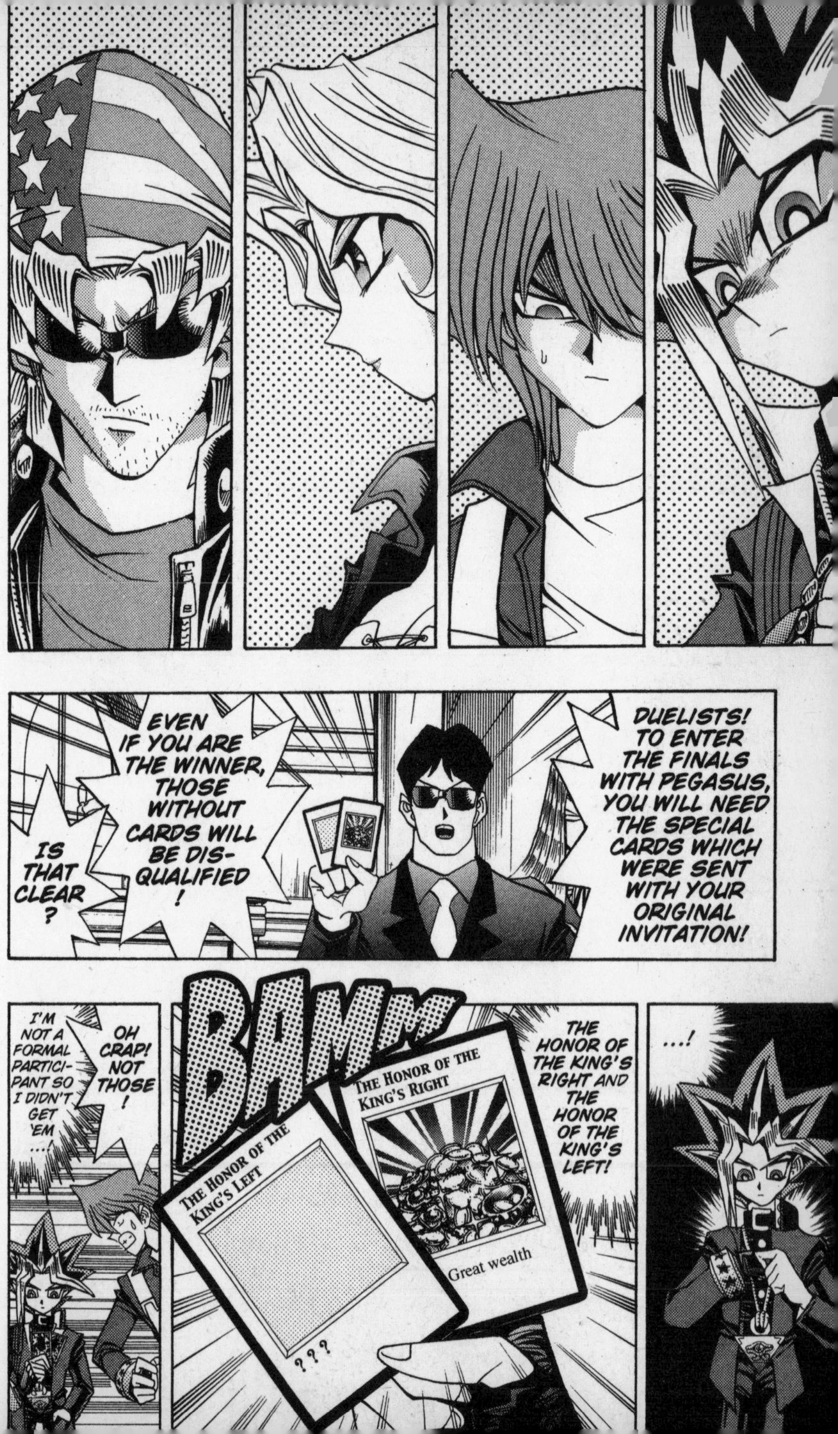
DUELISTS! TO ENTER THE FINALS WITH PEGASUS, YOU WILL NEED THE SPECIAL CARDS WHICH WERE SENT WITH YOUR ORIGINAL INVITATION!
EVEN IF YOU ARE THE WINNER, THOSE WITHOUT CARDS WILL BE DIS-QUALIFIED!
IS THAT CLEAR?
...!
THE HONOR OF THE KING'S RIGHT AND THE HONOR OF THE KING'S LEFT!
BAMM
THE HONOR OF THE KING'S RIGHT
Great wealth
THE HONOR OF THE KING'S LEFT
???
OH CRAP! NOT THOSE!
I'M NOT A FORMAL PARTICI-PANT SO I DIDN'T GET 'EM ...

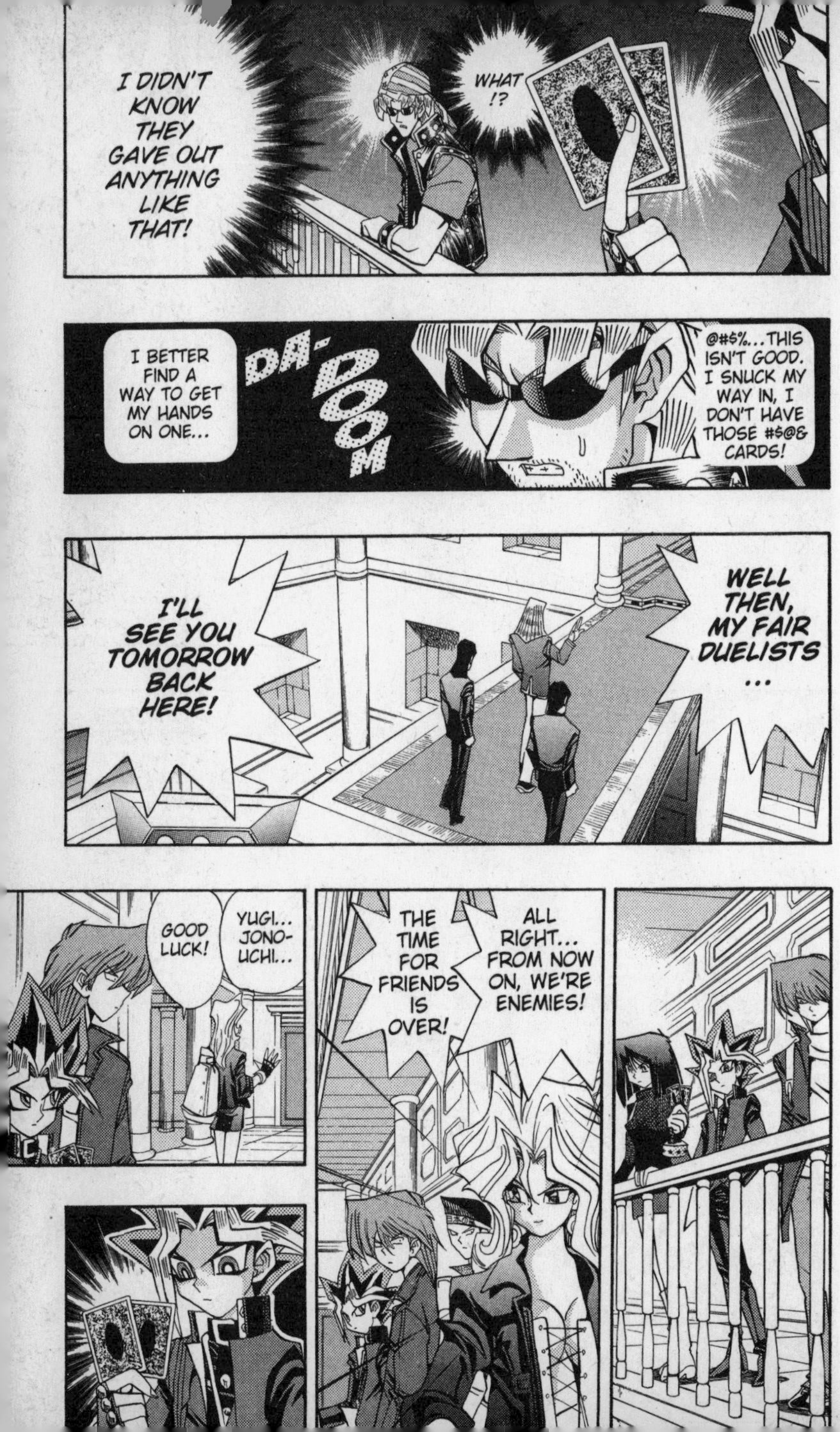
WHAT!?
I DIDN'T KNOW THEY GAVE OUT ANYTHING LIKE THAT!
@#$%... THIS ISN'T GOOD. I SNUCK MY WAY IN, I DON'T HAVE THOSE #$@& CARDS!
DA-DOOM
I BETTER FIND A WAY TO GET MY HANDS ON ONE...
WELL THEN, MY FAIR DUELISTS ...
I'LL SEE YOU TOMORROW BACK HERE!
ALL RIGHT... FROM NOW ON, WE'RE ENEMIES!
THE TIME FOR FRIENDS IS OVER!
YUGI... JONO-UCHI...
GOOD LUCK!

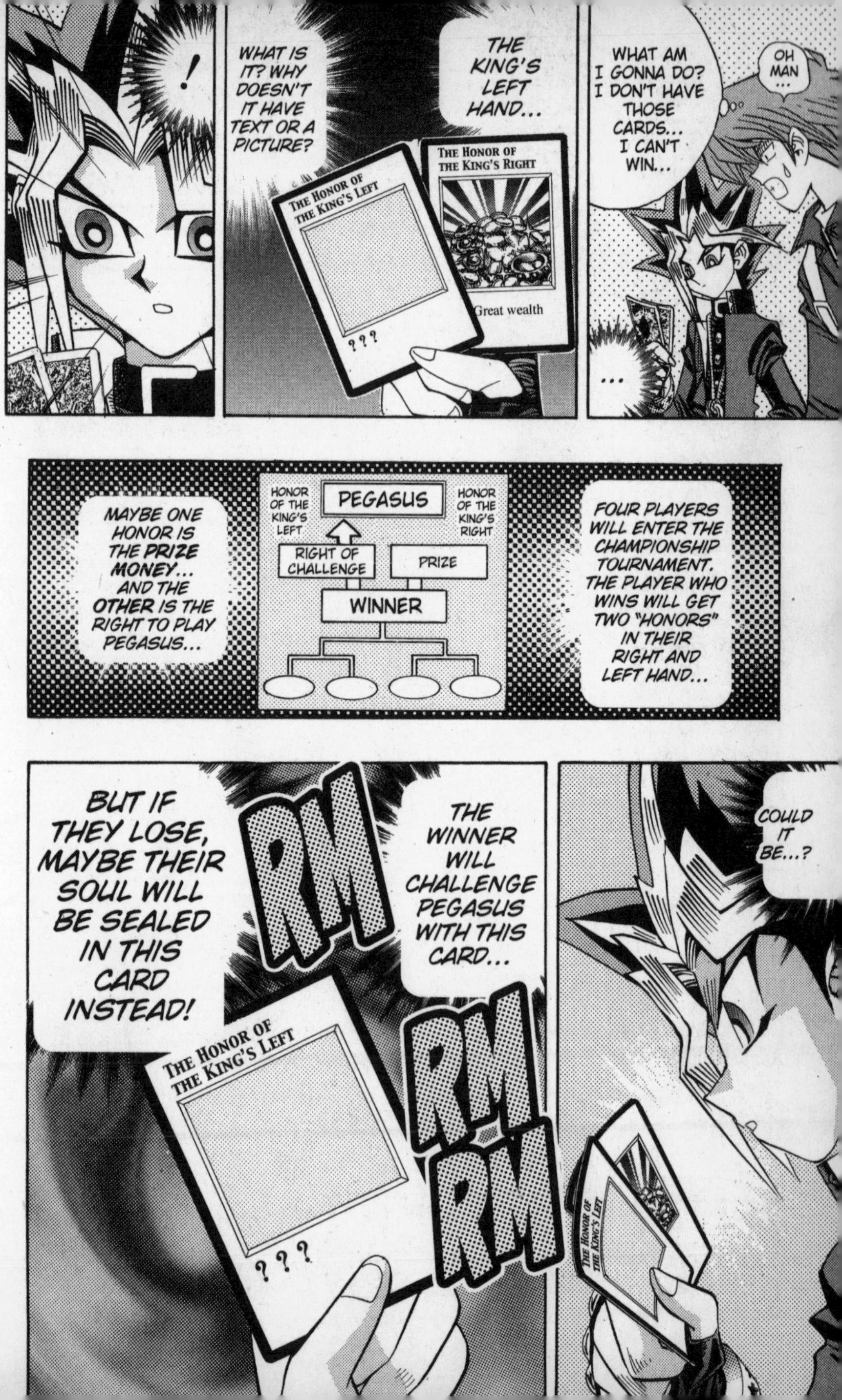
OH MAN ...
WHAT AM I GONNA DO? I DON'T HAVE THOSE CARDS... I CAN'T WIN...
...
THE KING'S LEFT HAND...
WHAT IS IT? WHY DOESN'T IT HAVE TEXT OR A PICTURE?
THE HONOR OF THE KING'S RIGHT
Great wealth
THE HONOR OF THE KING'S LEFT
???
!
FOUR PLAYERS WILL ENTER THE CHAMPIONSHIP TOURNAMENT. THE PLAYER WHO WINS WILL GET TWO "HONORS" IN THEIR RIGHT AND LEFT HAND...
HONOR OF THE KING'S RIGHT
PEGASUS
HONOR OF THE KING'S LEFT
PRIZE
RIGHT OF CHALLENGE
WINNER
MAYBE ONE HONOR IS THE PRIZE MONEY... AND THE OTHER IS THE RIGHT TO PLAY PEGASUS...
COULD IT BE...?
THE HONOR OF THE KING'S LEFT
THE WINNER WILL CHALLENGE PEGASUS WITH THIS CARD...
RM
RM RM RM
BUT IF THEY LOSE, MAYBE THEIR SOUL WILL BE SEALED IN THIS CARD INSTEAD!
THE HONOR OF THE KING'S LEFT
???

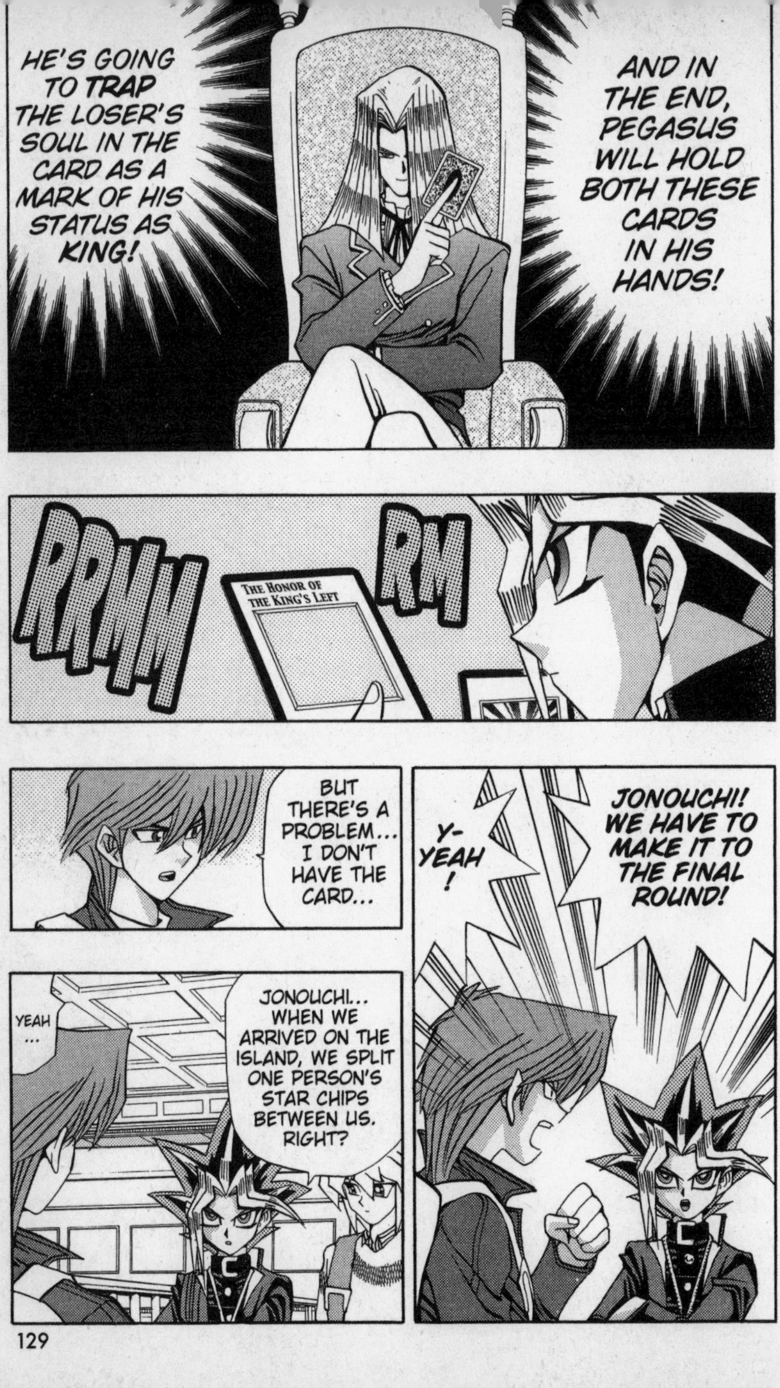
AND IN THE END, PEGASUS WILL HOLD BOTH THESE CARDS IN HIS HANDS!
HE'S GOING TO TRAP THE LOSER'S SOUL IN THE CARD AS A MARK OF HIS STATUS AS KING!
RM
THE HONOR OF THE KING'S LEFT
RRMM
JONOUCHI! WE HAVE TO MAKE IT TO THE FINAL ROUND!
Y-YEAH!
BUT THERE'S A PROBLEM... I DON'T HAVE THE CARD...
JONOUCHI... WHEN WE ARRIVED ON THE ISLAND, WE SPLIT ONE PERSON'S STAR CHIPS BETWEEN US. RIGHT?
YEAH...

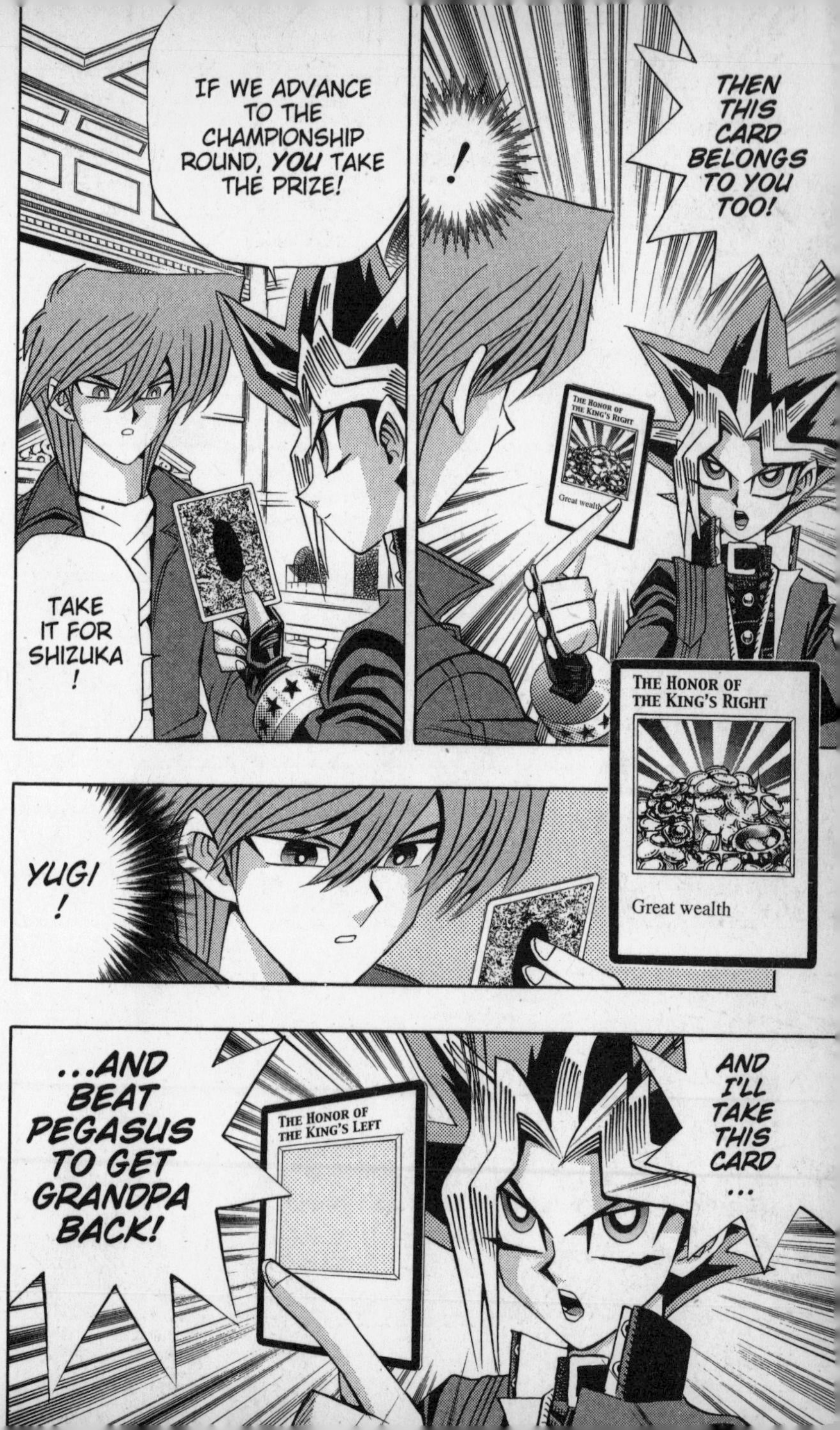
THEN THIS CARD BELONGS TO YOU TOO!
!
THE HONOR OF THE KING'S RIGHT
Great wealth
IF WE ADVANCE TO THE CHAMPIONSHIP ROUND, *YOU* TAKE THE PRIZE!
TAKE IT FOR SHIZUKA!
THE HONOR OF THE KING'S RIGHT
Great wealth
YUGI!
AND I'LL TAKE THIS CARD...
THE HONOR OF THE KING'S LEFT
...AND BEAT PEGASUS TO GET GRANDPA BACK!

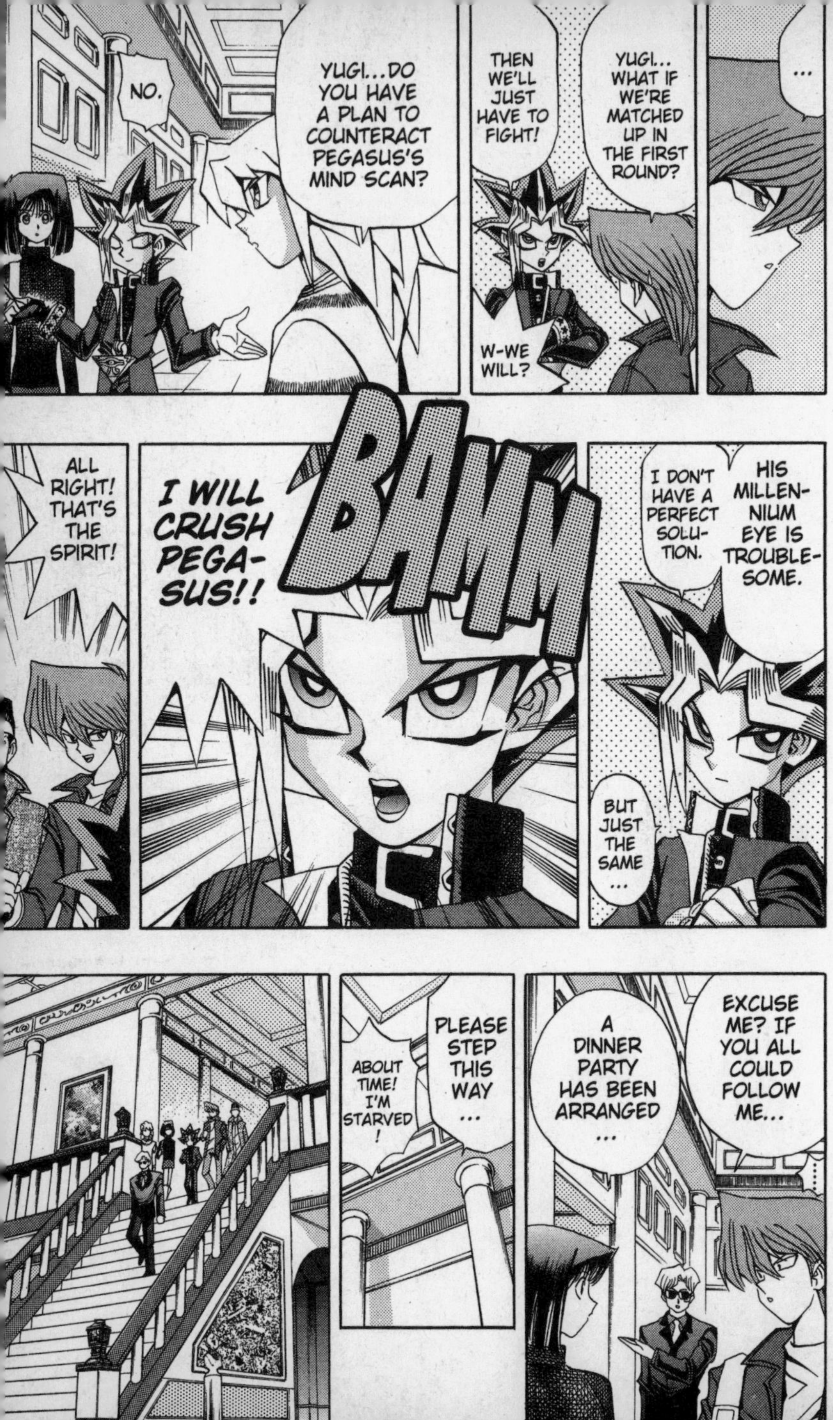
...
YUGI... WHAT IF WE'RE MATCHED UP IN THE FIRST ROUND?
THEN WE'LL JUST HAVE TO FIGHT!
W-WE WILL?
YUGI...DO YOU HAVE A PLAN TO COUNTERACT PEGASUS'S MIND SCAN?
NO.
HIS MILLEN-NIUM EYE IS TROUBLE-SOME.
I DON'T HAVE A PERFECT SOLU-TION.
BUT JUST THE SAME ...
BAMM
I WILL CRUSH PEGA-SUS!!
ALL RIGHT! THAT'S THE SPIRIT!
EXCUSE ME? IF YOU ALL COULD FOLLOW ME...
A DINNER PARTY HAS BEEN ARRANGED ...
PLEASE STEP THIS WAY ...
ABOUT TIME! I'M STARVED !

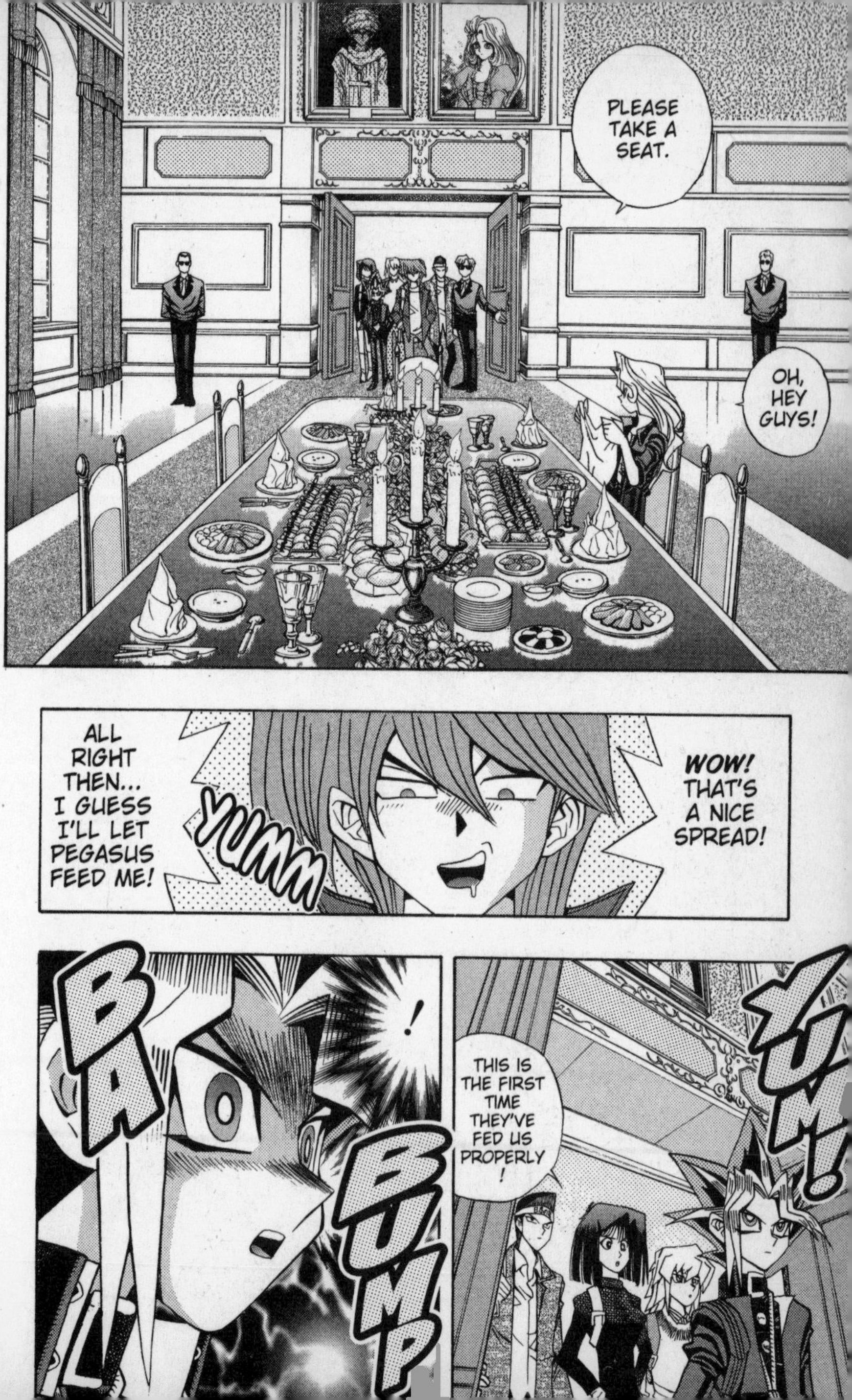

PLEASE TAKE A SEAT.
OH, HEY GUYS!
WOW! THAT'S A NICE SPREAD!
YUMM
ALL RIGHT THEN... I GUESS I'LL LET PEGASUS FEED ME!
YUMM!
THIS IS THE FIRST TIME THEY'VE FED US PROPERLY!
!
BA
BUMP

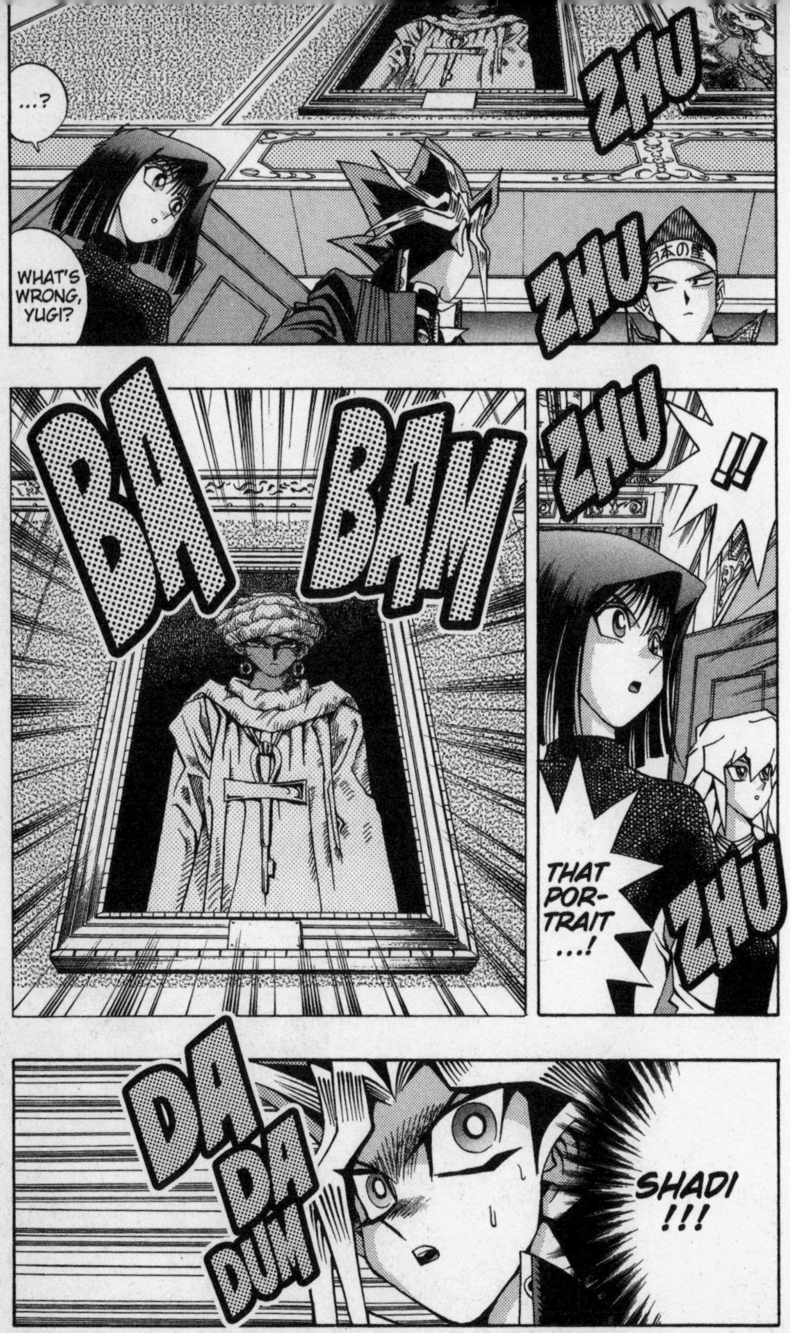
ZHU
...?
ZHU
WHAT'S WRONG, YUGI?
ZHU
!!
THAT POR-TRAIT ...!
ZHU
BA BAM
SHADI !!!
DA DA DUM

Duel 53: The Eve of Battle

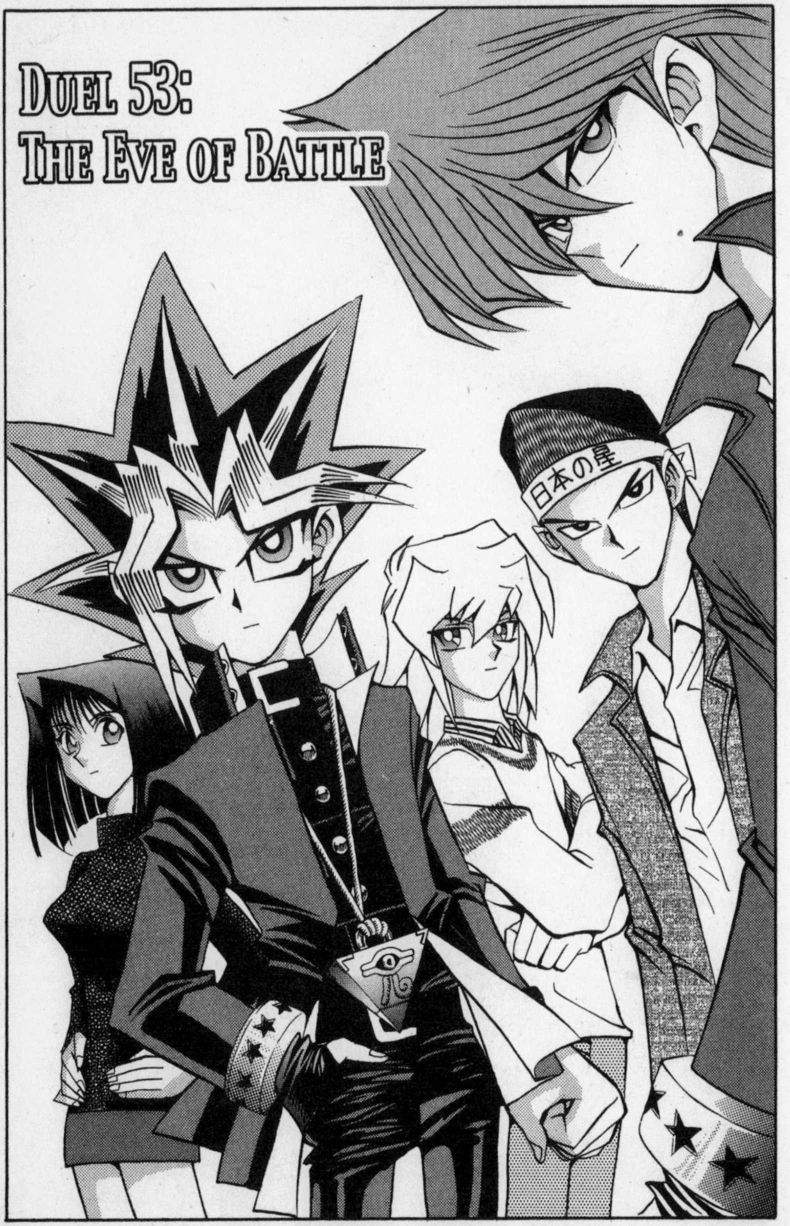
日本の星

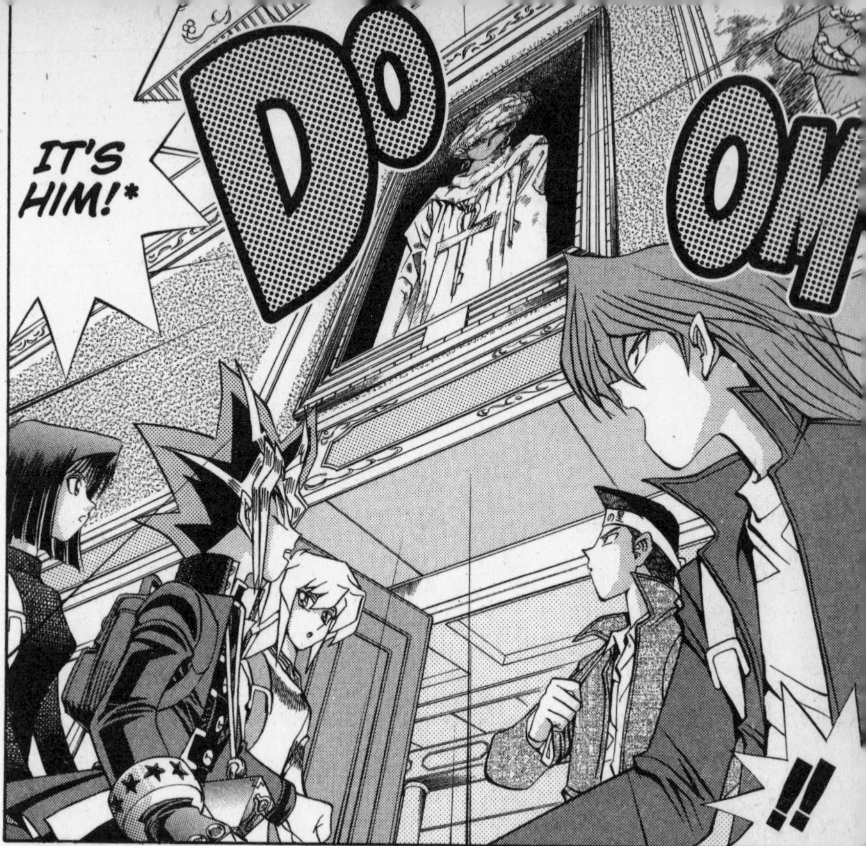
DOOM
IT'S HIM!*
!!

*SEE THE ORIGINAL *YU-GI-OH!* SERIES FOR DETAILS!

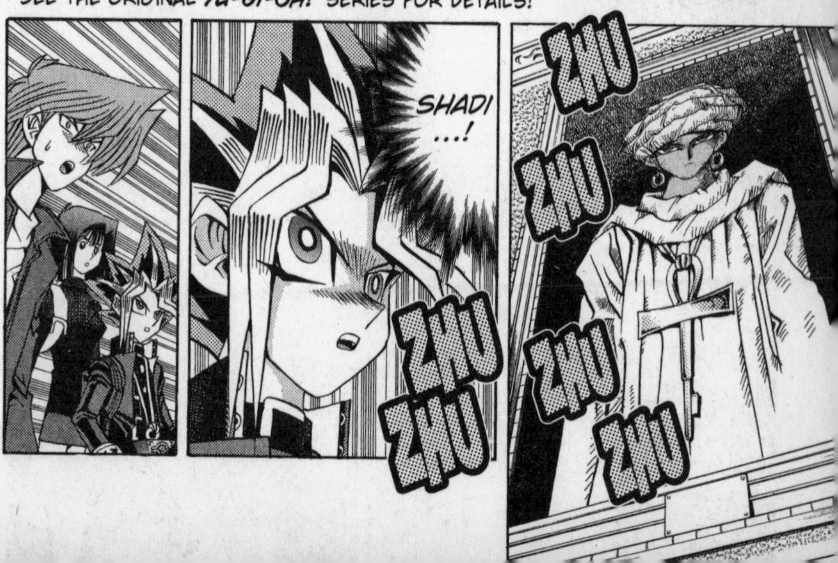
ZHU ZHU
ZHU ZHU ZHU
SHADI ...!
ZHU ZHU

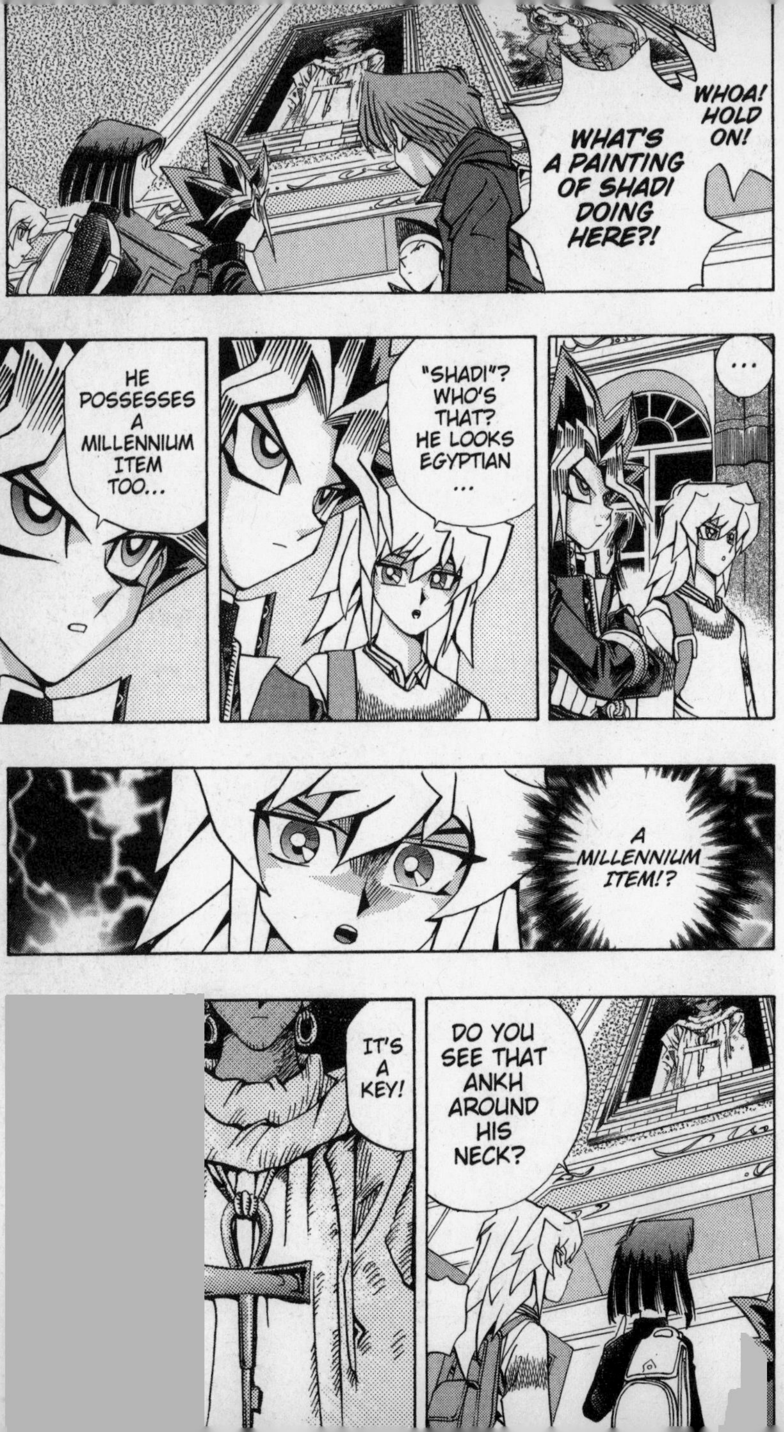
WHOA! HOLD ON!
WHAT'S A PAINTING OF SHADI DOING HERE?!
...
"SHADI"? WHO'S THAT? HE LOOKS EGYPTIAN ...
HE POSSESSES A MILLENNIUM ITEM TOO...
A MILLENNIUM ITEM!?
DO YOU SEE THAT ANKH AROUND HIS NECK?
IT'S A KEY!

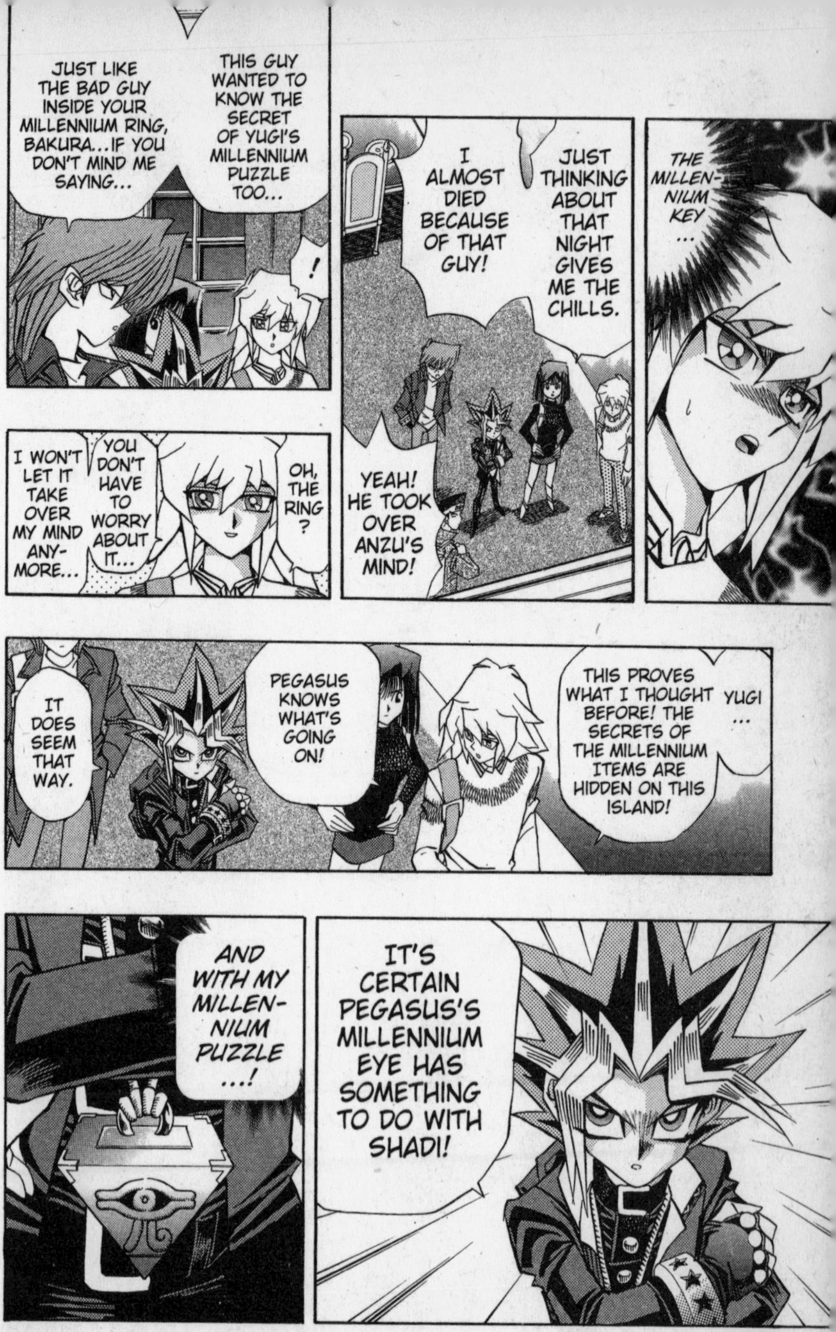
THE MILLENNIUM KEY ...
JUST THINKING ABOUT THAT NIGHT GIVES ME THE CHILLS.
I ALMOST DIED BECAUSE OF THAT GUY!
YEAH! HE TOOK OVER ANZU'S MIND!
THIS GUY WANTED TO KNOW THE SECRET OF YUGI'S MILLENNIUM PUZZLE TOO...
JUST LIKE THE BAD GUY INSIDE YOUR MILLENNIUM RING, BAKURA...IF YOU DON'T MIND ME SAYING...
!
OH, THE RING?
YOU DON'T HAVE TO WORRY ABOUT IT...
I WON'T LET IT TAKE OVER MY MIND ANYMORE...
YUGI ...
THIS PROVES WHAT I THOUGHT BEFORE! THE SECRETS OF THE MILLENNIUM ITEMS ARE HIDDEN ON THIS ISLAND!
PEGASUS KNOWS WHAT'S GOING ON!
IT DOES SEEM THAT WAY.
IT'S CERTAIN PEGASUS'S MILLENNIUM EYE HAS SOMETHING TO DO WITH SHADI!
AND WITH MY MILLENNIUM PUZZLE ...!

READ THIS WAY

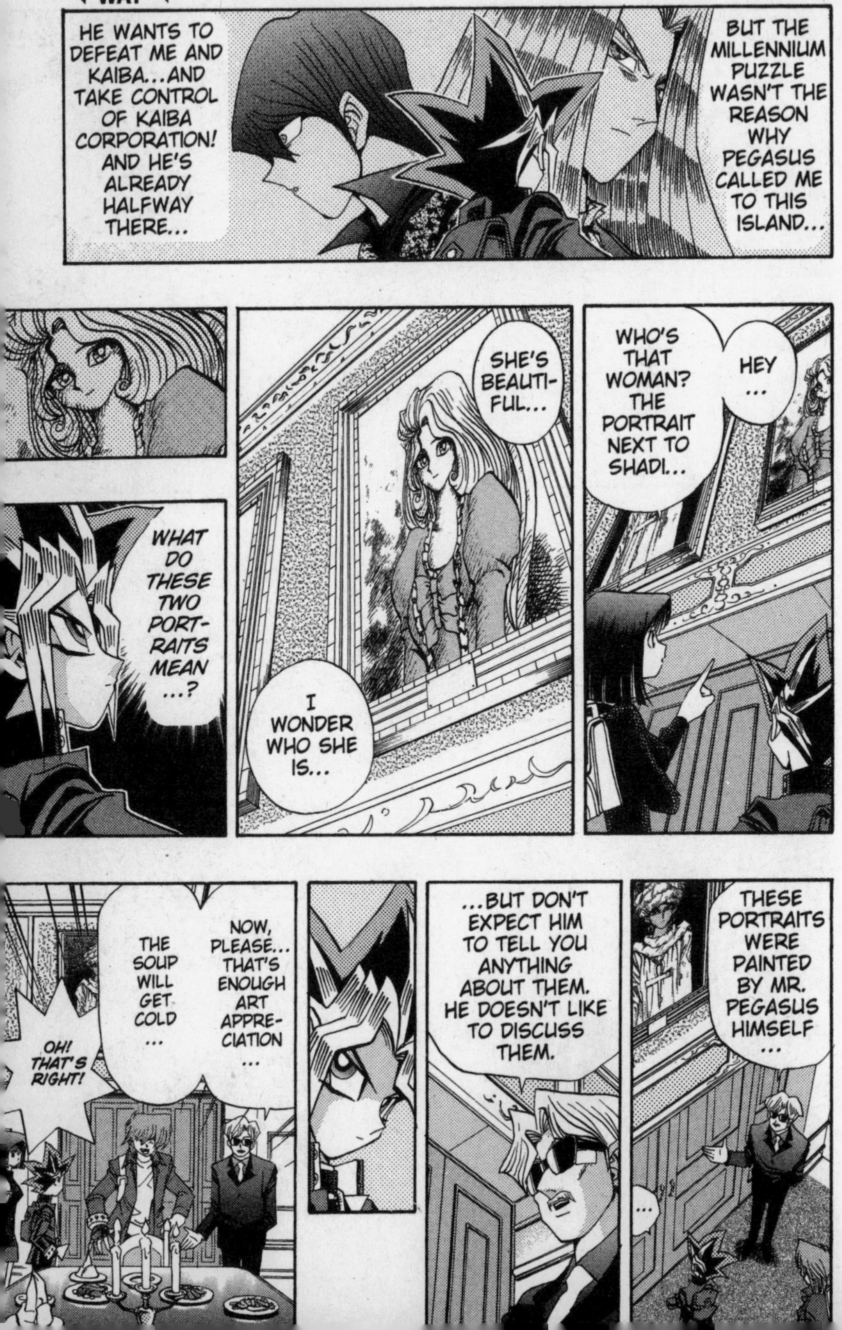
BUT THE MILLENNIUM PUZZLE WASN'T THE REASON WHY PEGASUS CALLED ME TO THIS ISLAND...
HE WANTS TO DEFEAT ME AND KAIBA...AND TAKE CONTROL OF KAIBA CORPORATION! AND HE'S ALREADY HALFWAY THERE...
HEY ...
WHO'S THAT WOMAN? THE PORTRAIT NEXT TO SHADI...
SHE'S BEAUTI-FUL...
I WONDER WHO SHE IS...
WHAT DO THESE TWO PORT-RAITS MEAN ...?
THESE PORTRAITS WERE PAINTED BY MR. PEGASUS HIMSELF ...
...
...BUT DON'T EXPECT HIM TO TELL YOU ANYTHING ABOUT THEM. HE DOESN'T LIKE TO DISCUSS THEM.
NOW, PLEASE... THAT'S ENOUGH ART APPRE-CIATION ...
THE SOUP WILL GET COLD ...
OH! THAT'S RIGHT!

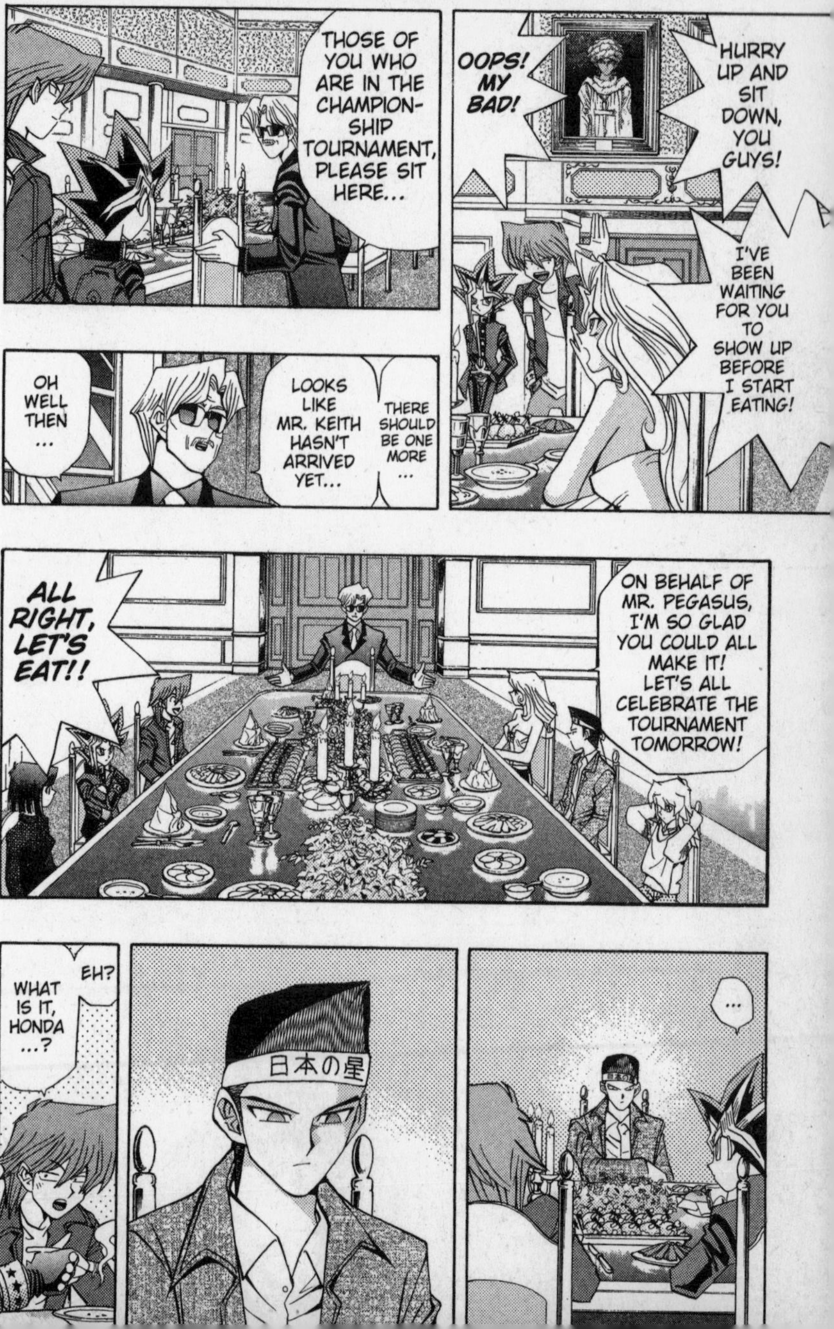
HURRY UP AND SIT DOWN, YOU GUYS!
OOPS! MY BAD!
I'VE BEEN WAITING FOR YOU TO SHOW UP BEFORE I START EATING!
THOSE OF YOU WHO ARE IN THE CHAMPIONSHIP TOURNAMENT, PLEASE SIT HERE...
THERE SHOULD BE ONE MORE ...
LOOKS LIKE MR. KEITH HASN'T ARRIVED YET...
OH WELL THEN ...
ON BEHALF OF MR. PEGASUS, I'M SO GLAD YOU COULD ALL MAKE IT! LET'S ALL CELEBRATE THE TOURNAMENT TOMORROW!
ALL RIGHT, LET'S EAT!!
...
日本の星
EH?
WHAT IS IT, HONDA ...?

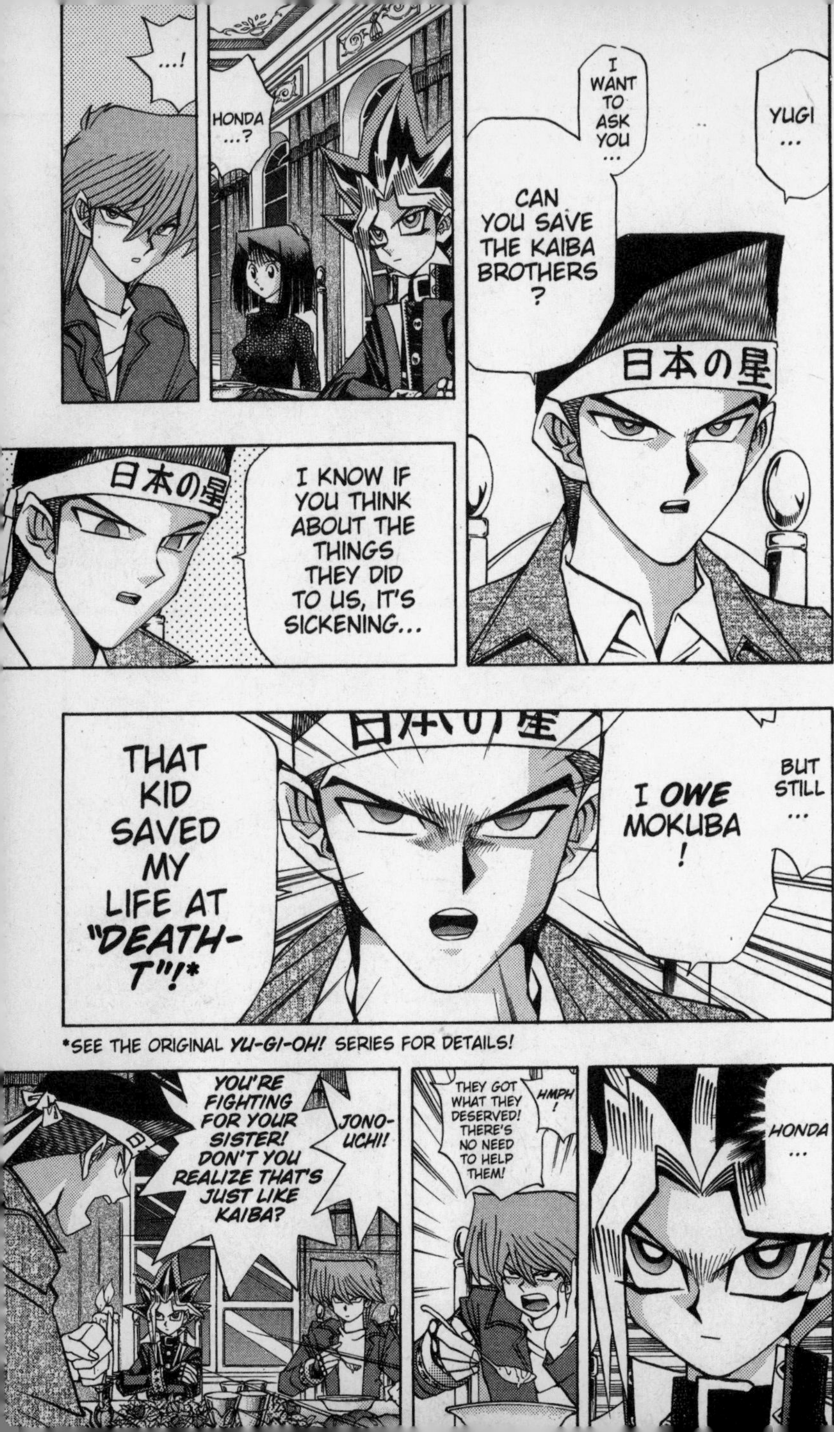
YUGI ...
I WANT TO ASK YOU ...
CAN YOU SAVE THE KAIBA BROTHERS?
日本の星
HONDA ...?
...!
日本の星
I KNOW IF YOU THINK ABOUT THE THINGS THEY DID TO US, IT'S SICKENING...
BUT STILL ...
I *OWE* MOKUBA!
THAT KID SAVED MY LIFE AT *"DEATH-T"!**
*SEE THE ORIGINAL *YU-GI-OH!* SERIES FOR DETAILS!
HONDA ...
HMPH!
THEY GOT WHAT THEY DESERVED! THERE'S NO NEED TO HELP THEM!
JONO-UCHI!
YOU'RE FIGHTING FOR YOUR SISTER! DON'T YOU REALIZE THAT'S JUST LIKE KAIBA?

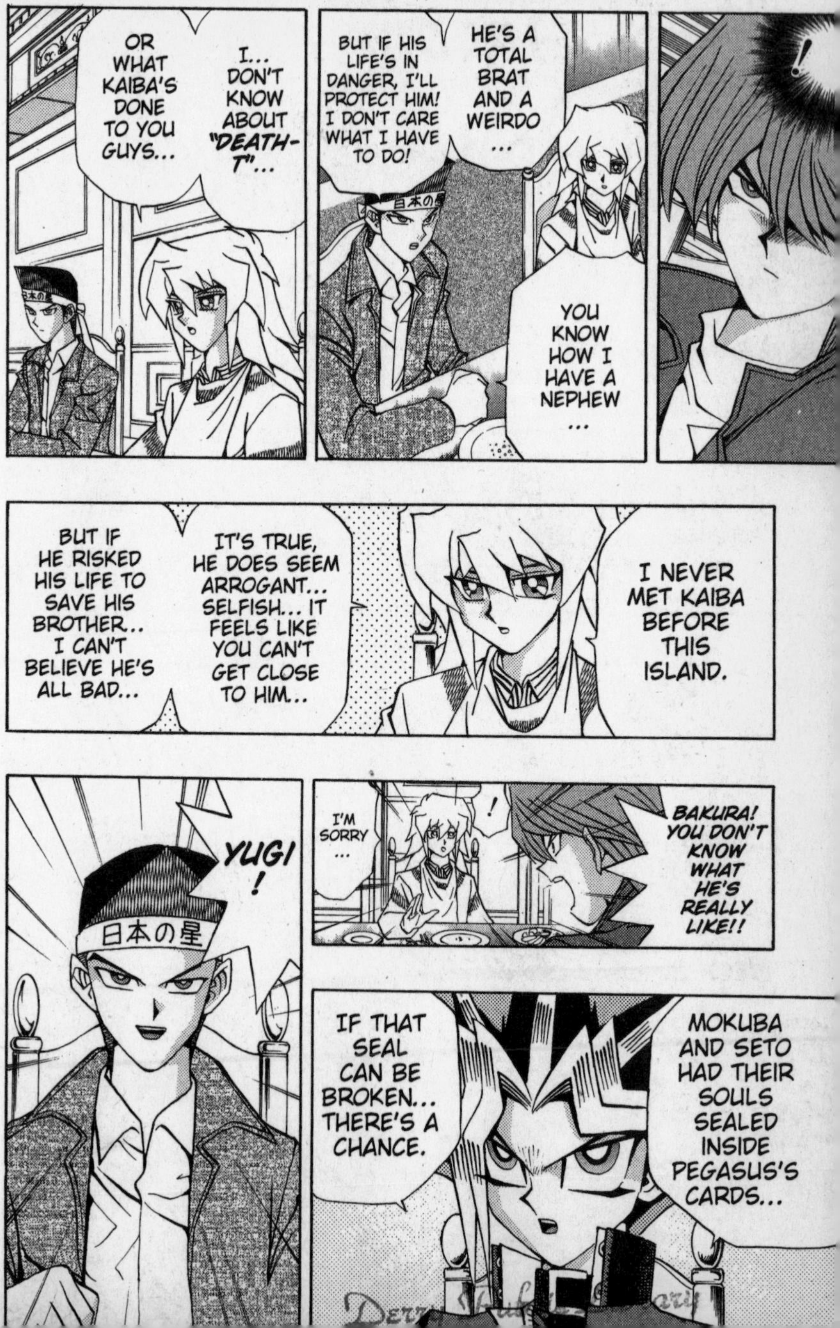
!
YOU KNOW HOW I HAVE A NEPHEW...
HE'S A TOTAL BRAT AND A WEIRDO...
BUT IF HIS LIFE'S IN DANGER, I'LL PROTECT HIM! I DON'T CARE WHAT I HAVE TO DO!
日本の星
I... DON'T KNOW ABOUT "DEATH-T"...
OR WHAT KAIBA'S DONE TO YOU GUYS...
I NEVER MET KAIBA BEFORE THIS ISLAND.
IT'S TRUE, HE DOES SEEM ARROGANT... SELFISH... IT FEELS LIKE YOU CAN'T GET CLOSE TO HIM..
BUT IF HE RISKED HIS LIFE TO SAVE HIS BROTHER.. I CAN'T BELIEVE HE'S ALL BAD...
BAKURA! YOU DON'T KNOW WHAT HE'S REALLY LIKE!!
!
I'M SORRY...
MOKUBA AND SETO HAD THEIR SOULS SEALED INSIDE PEGASUS'S CARDS...
IF THAT SEAL CAN BE BROKEN... THERE'S A CHANCE.
YUGI!
日本の星

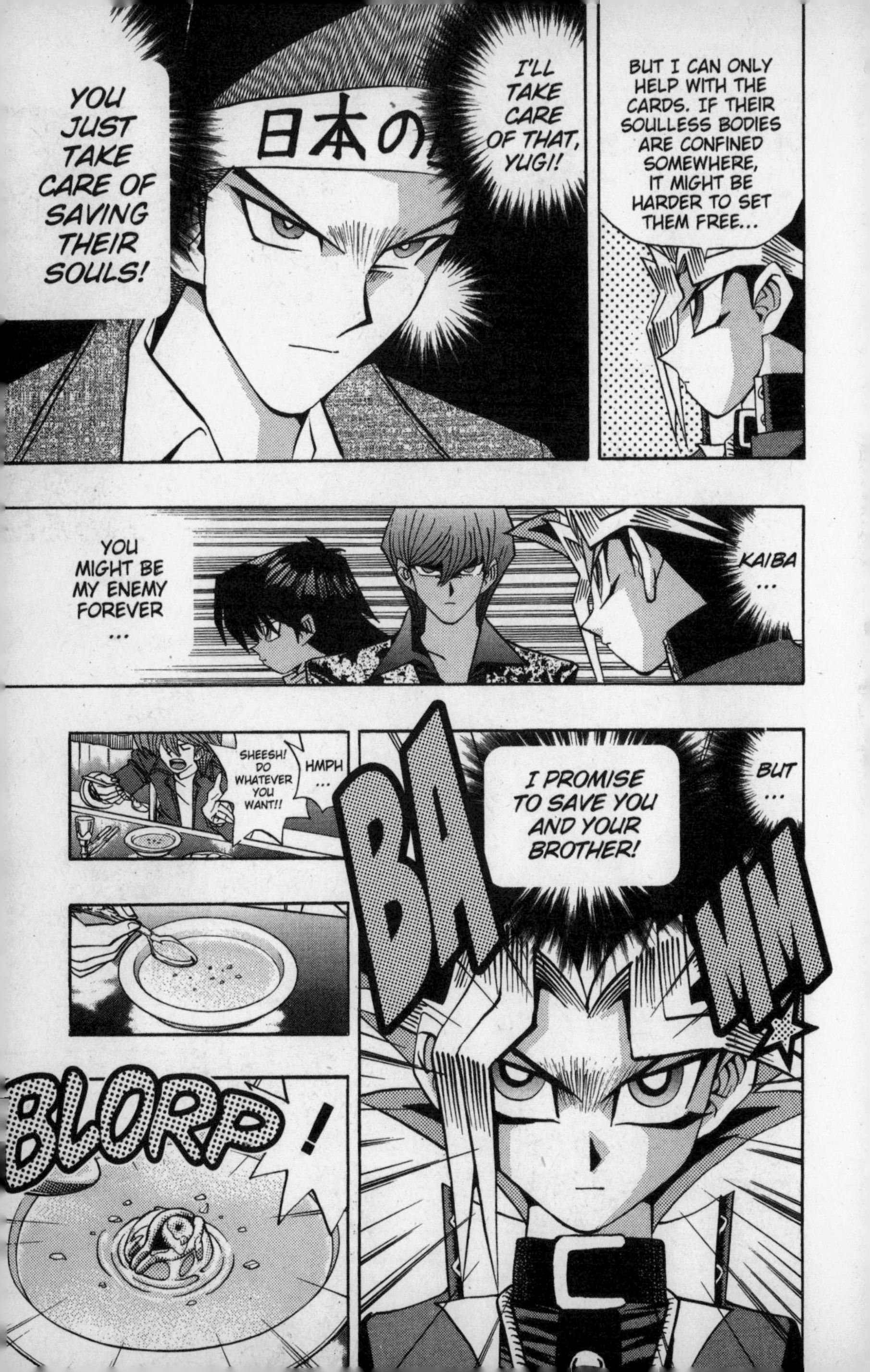
BUT I CAN ONLY HELP WITH THE CARDS. IF THEIR SOULLESS BODIES ARE CONFINED SOMEWHERE, IT MIGHT BE HARDER TO SET THEM FREE...
I'LL TAKE CARE OF THAT, YUGI!
日本の
YOU JUST TAKE CARE OF SAVING THEIR SOULS!
KAIBA ...
YOU MIGHT BE MY ENEMY FOREVER ...
BUT ...
I PROMISE TO SAVE YOU AND YOUR BROTHER!
BAMM
HMPH ...
SHEESH! DO WHATEVER YOU WANT!!
BLORP!

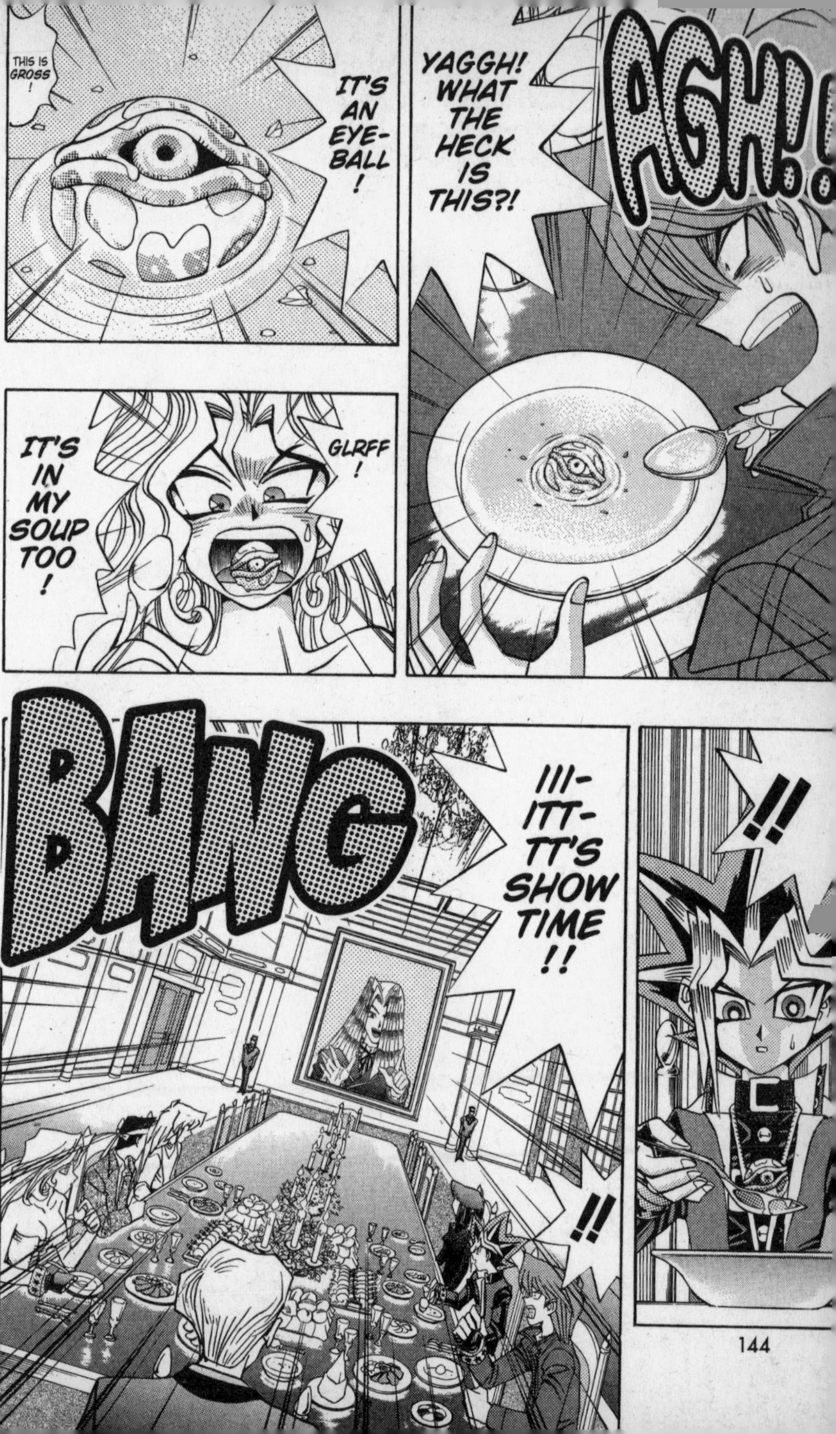
AGH!!
YAGGH! WHAT THE HECK IS THIS?!
IT'S AN EYE-BALL!
THIS IS GROSS!
GLRFF!
IT'S IN MY SOUP TOO!
!!
BANG
III-ITTT-TT'S SHOW TIME!!
!!

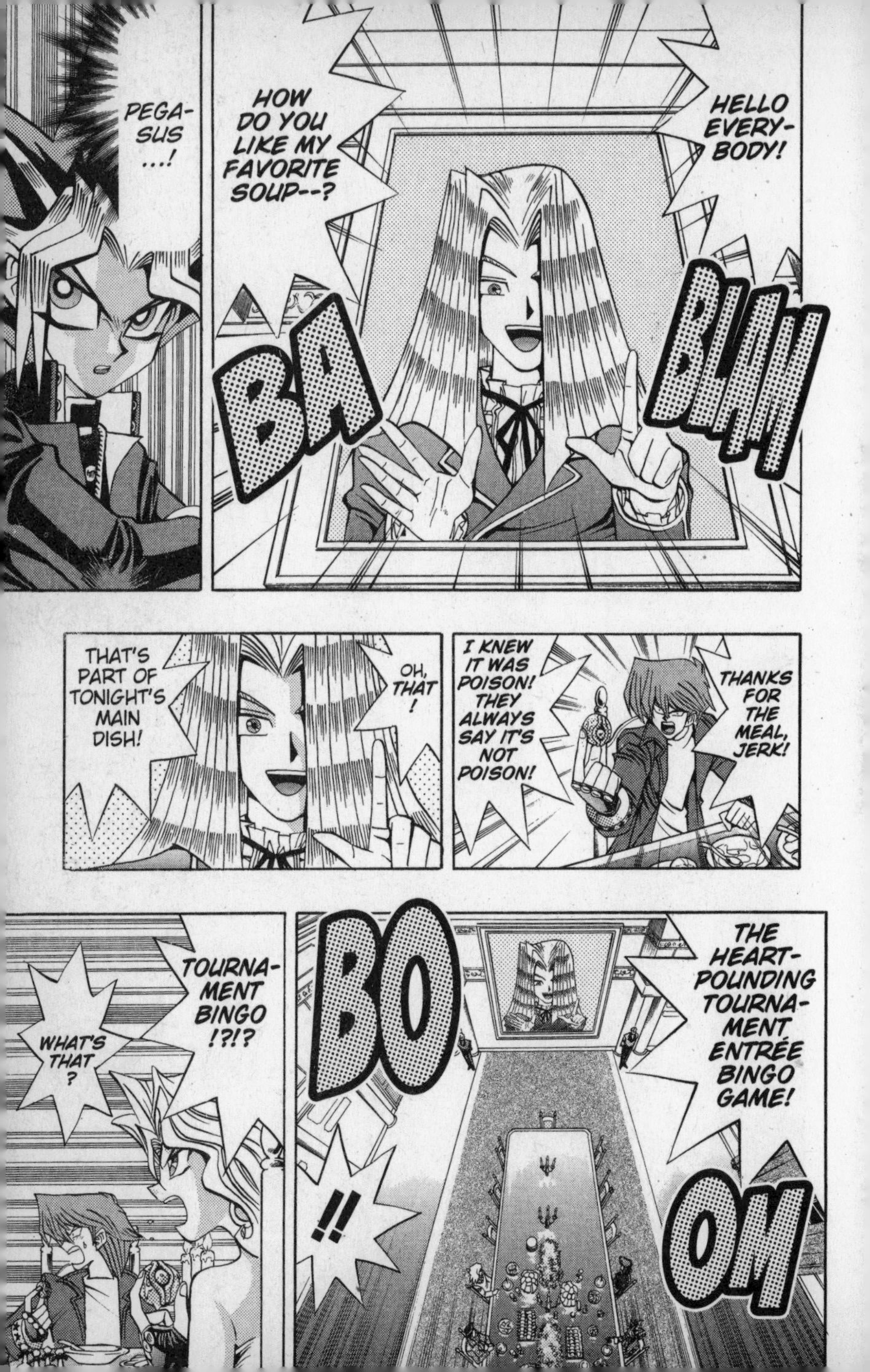
HELLO EVERYBODY!
HOW DO YOU LIKE MY FAVORITE SOUP--?
BA
BLAM
PEGASUS...!
THANKS FOR THE MEAL, JERK!
I KNEW IT WAS POISON! THEY ALWAYS SAY IT'S NOT POISON!
OH, THAT!
THAT'S PART OF TONIGHT'S MAIN DISH!
THE HEART-POUNDING TOURNAMENT ENTRÉE BINGO GAME!
BO
OM
!!
TOURNAMENT BINGO!?!?
WHAT'S THAT?

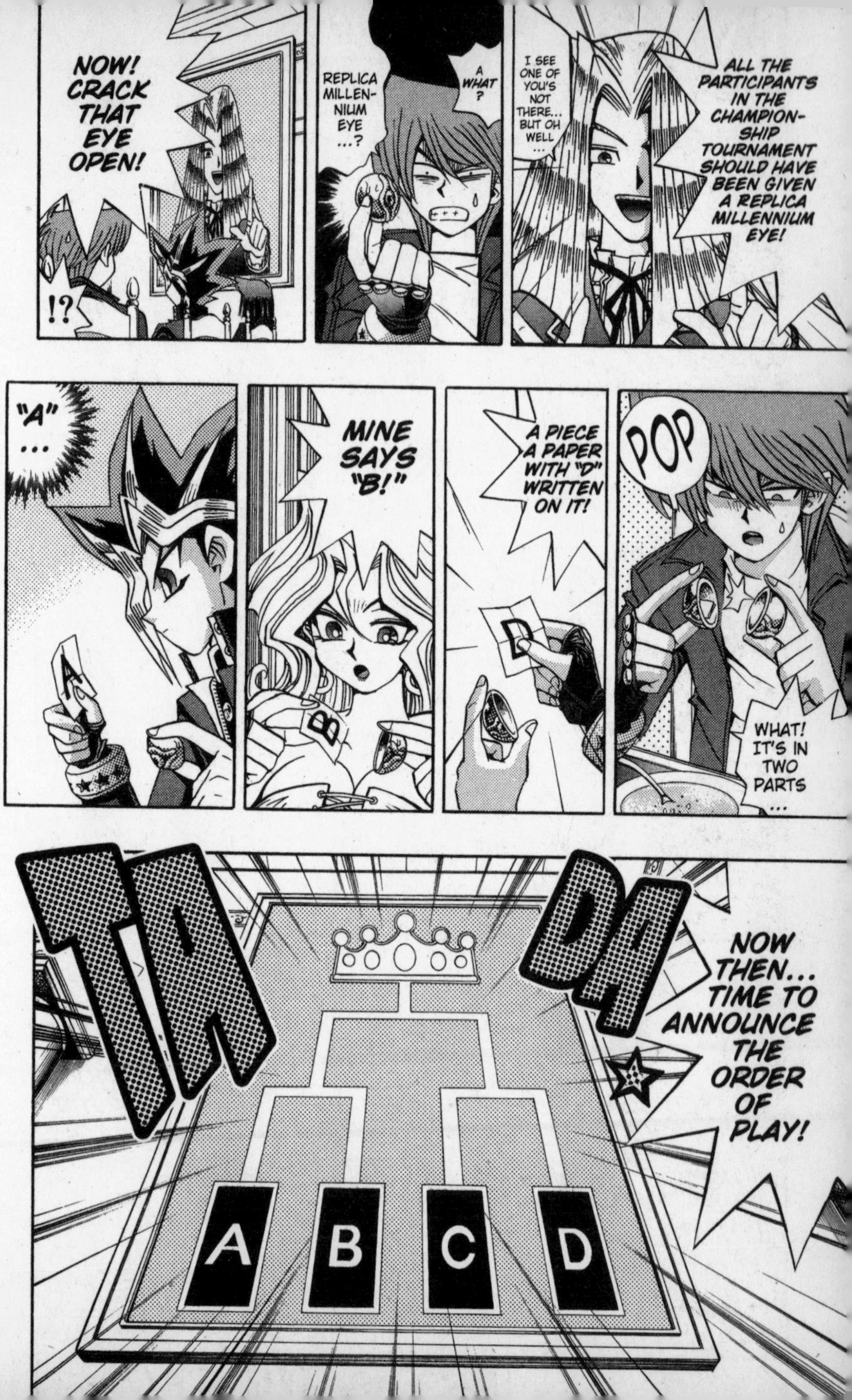
ALL THE PARTICIPANTS IN THE CHAMPIONSHIP TOURNAMENT SHOULD HAVE BEEN GIVEN A REPLICA MILLENNIUM EYE!
I SEE ONE OF YOU'S NOT THERE... BUT OH WELL...
A WHAT?
REPLICA MILLENNIUM EYE...?
NOW! CRACK THAT EYE OPEN!
!?
POP
WHAT! IT'S IN TWO PARTS...
A PIECE A PAPER WITH "D" WRITTEN ON IT!
D
MINE SAYS "B!"
B
"A"...
A
NOW THEN... TIME TO ANNOUNCE THE ORDER OF PLAY!
TA DA
A
B
C
D

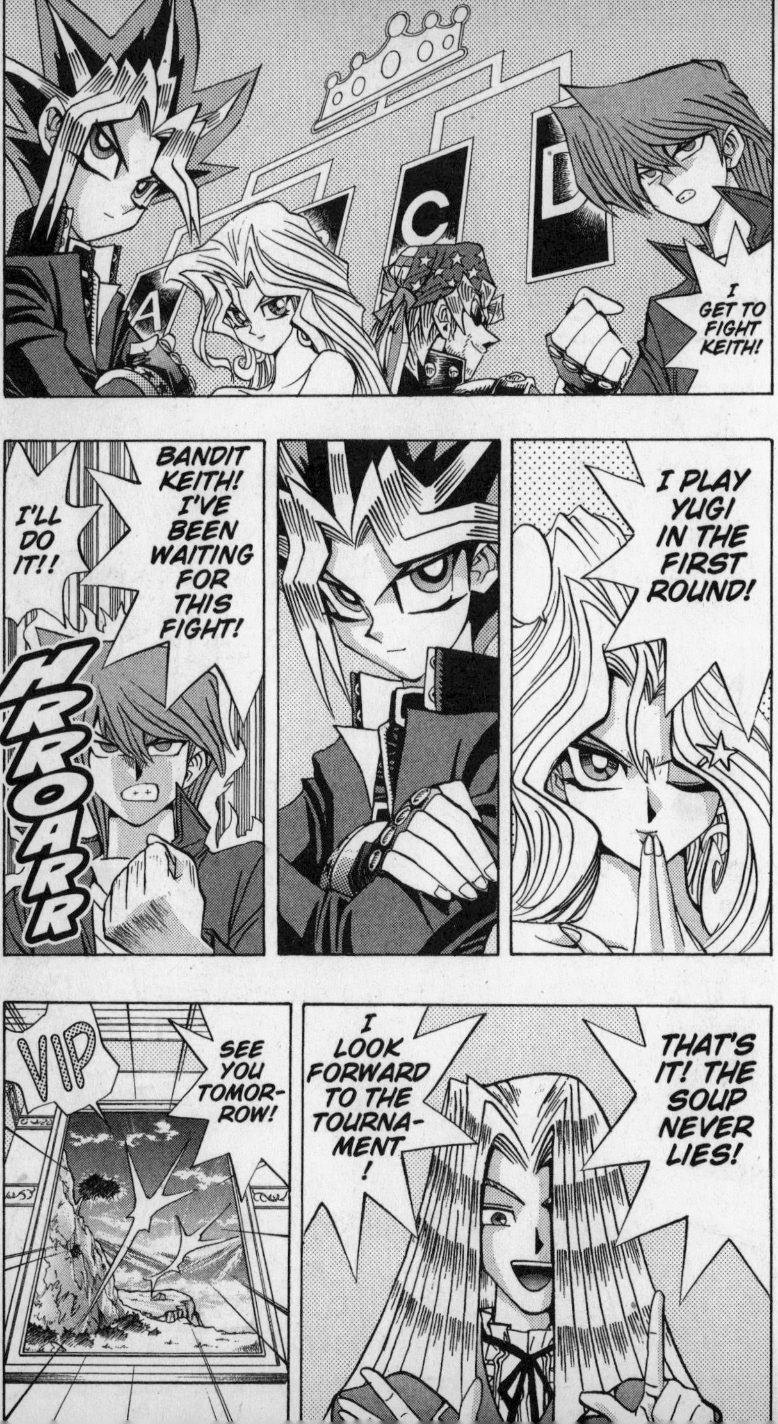
I GET TO FIGHT KEITH!
I PLAY YUGI IN THE FIRST ROUND!
BANDIT KEITH! I'VE BEEN WAITING FOR THIS FIGHT!
I'LL DO IT!!
HRROARR
THAT'S IT! THE SOUP NEVER LIES!
I LOOK FORWARD TO THE TOURNAMENT!
SEE YOU TOMORROW!
VIP

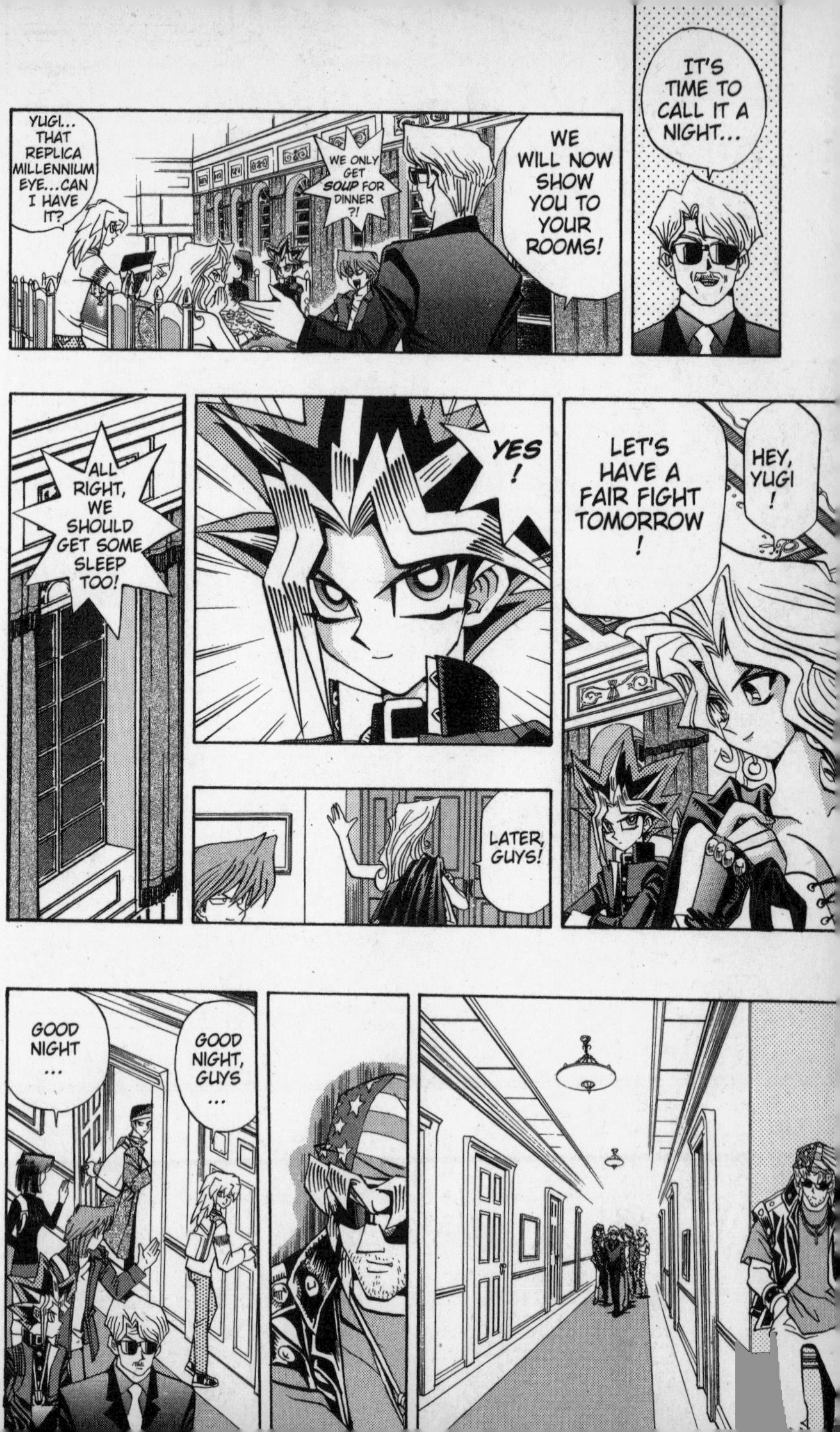
IT'S TIME TO CALL IT A NIGHT...
WE WILL NOW SHOW YOU TO YOUR ROOMS!
WE ONLY GET SOUP FOR DINNER ?!
YUGI... THAT REPLICA MILLENNIUM EYE...CAN I HAVE IT?
HEY, YUGI!
LET'S HAVE A FAIR FIGHT TOMORROW!
YES!
LATER, GUYS!
ALL RIGHT, WE SHOULD GET SOME SLEEP TOO!
GOOD NIGHT, GUYS...
GOOD NIGHT...

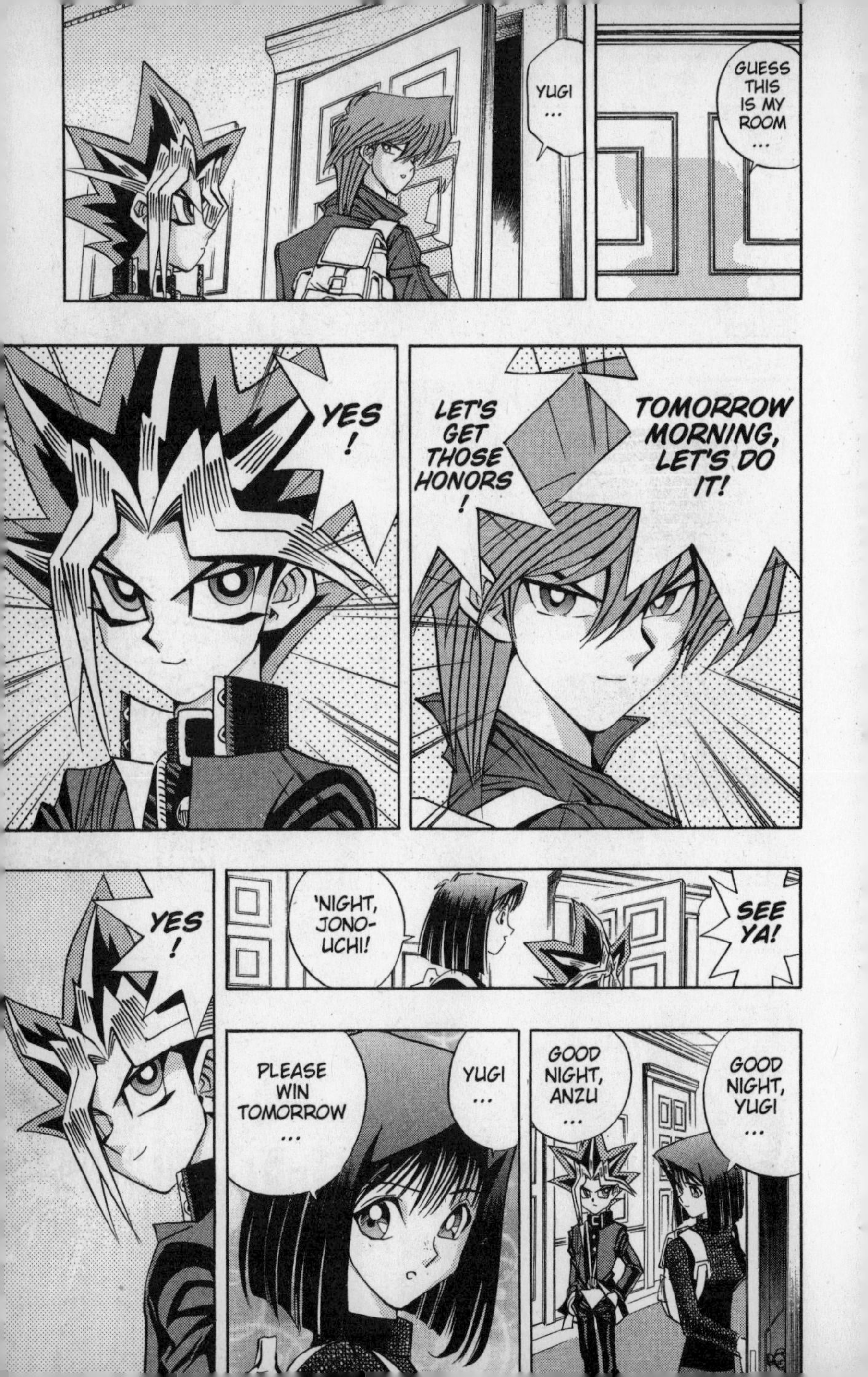
GUESS THIS IS MY ROOM ...
YUGI ...
TOMORROW MORNING, LET'S DO IT!
LET'S GET THOSE HONORS !
YES !
SEE YA!
'NIGHT, JONO-UCHI!
GOOD NIGHT, YUGI ...
GOOD NIGHT, ANZU ...
YUGI ...
PLEASE WIN TOMORROW ...
YES !

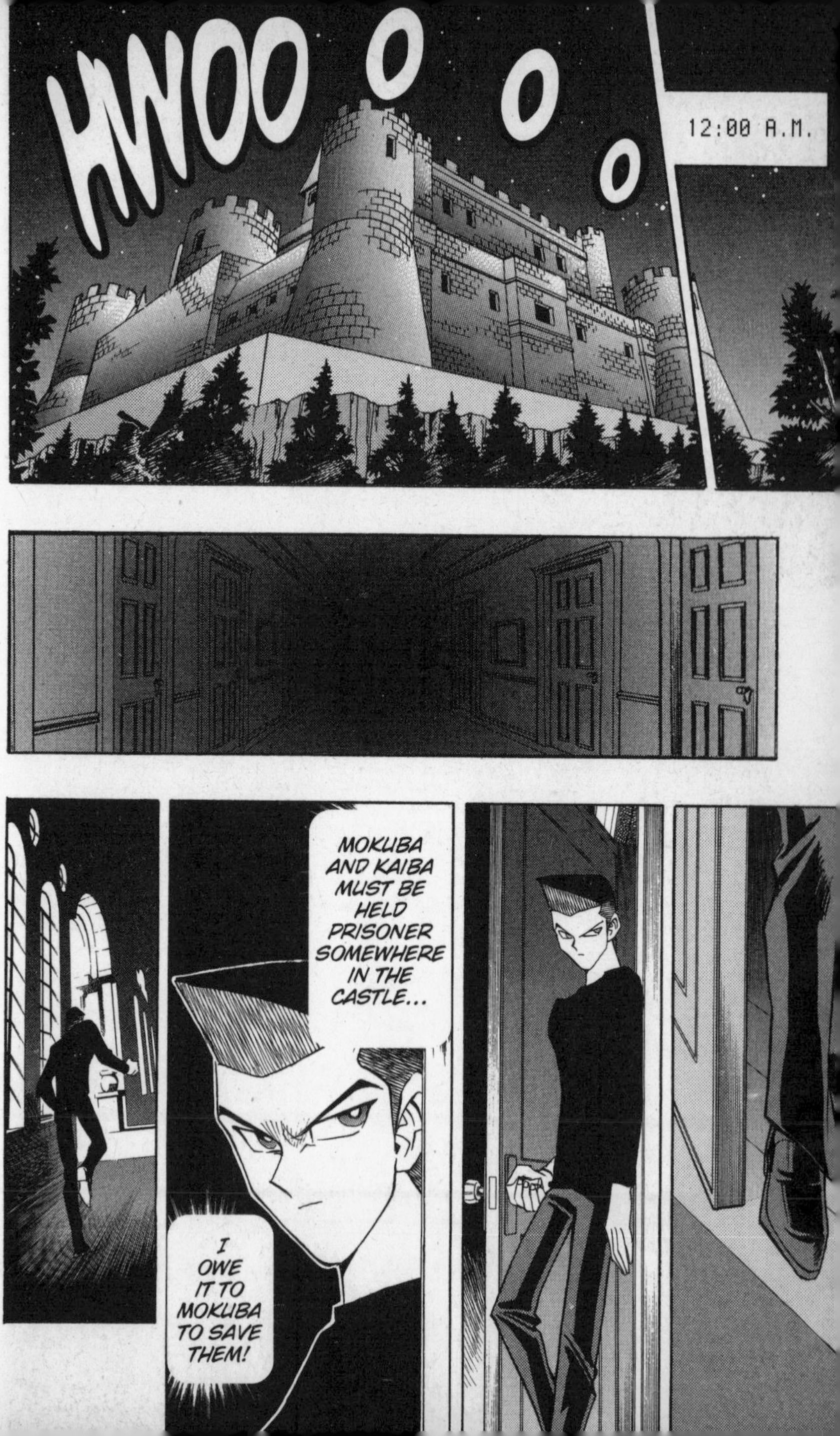
12:00 A.M.
HWOO O O O
MOKUBA AND KAIBA MUST BE HELD PRISONER SOMEWHERE IN THE CASTLE...
I OWE IT TO MOKUBA TO SAVE THEM!

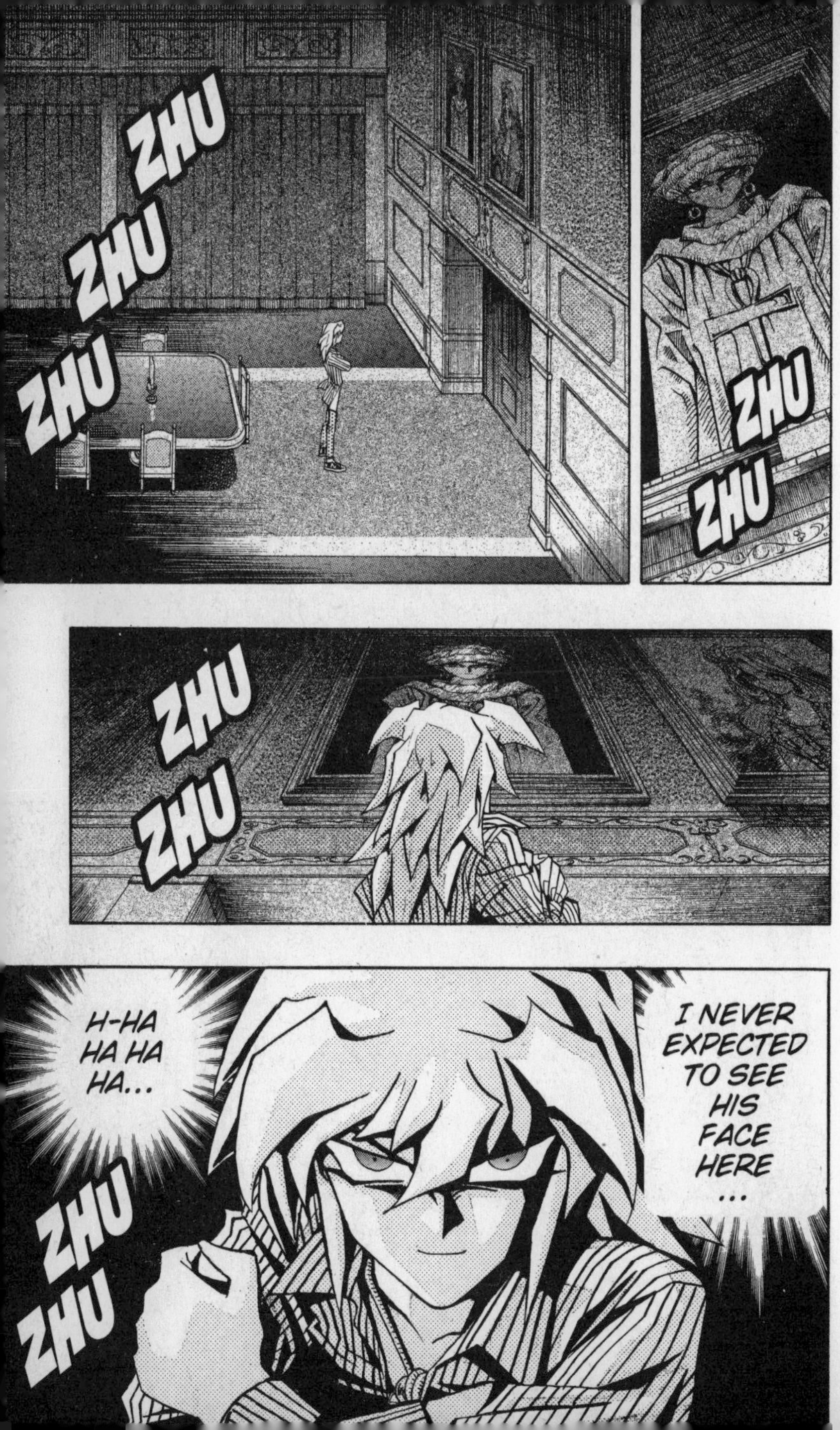
ZHU
ZHU
ZHU
ZHU
ZHU
ZHU
ZHU
ZHU
I NEVER EXPECTED TO SEE HIS FACE HERE ...
H-HA HA HA HA...
ZHU
ZHU

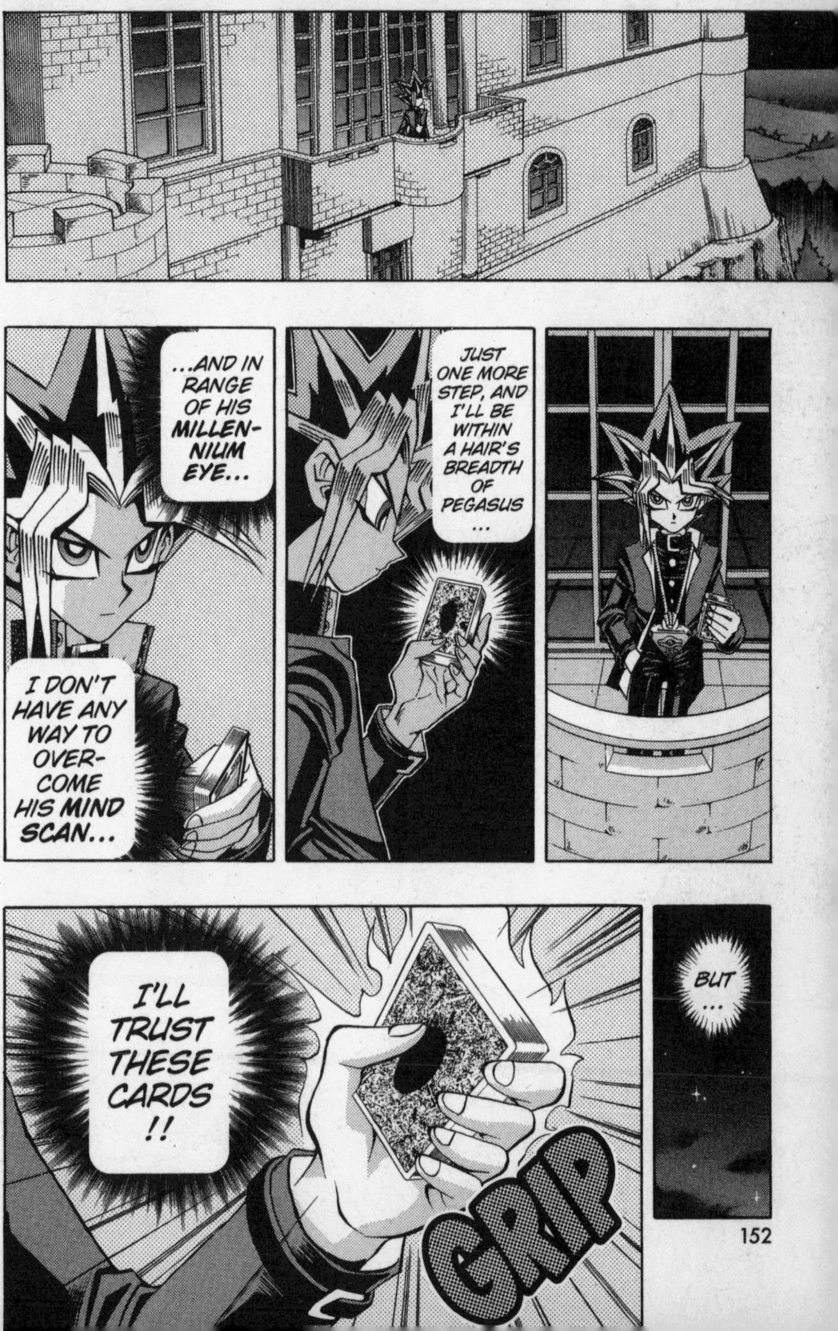
JUST ONE MORE STEP, AND I'LL BE WITHIN A HAIR'S BREADTH OF PEGASUS ...
...AND IN RANGE OF HIS MILLENNIUM EYE...
I DON'T HAVE ANY WAY TO OVERCOME HIS MIND SCAN...
BUT ...
I'LL TRUST THESE CARDS !!
GRIP

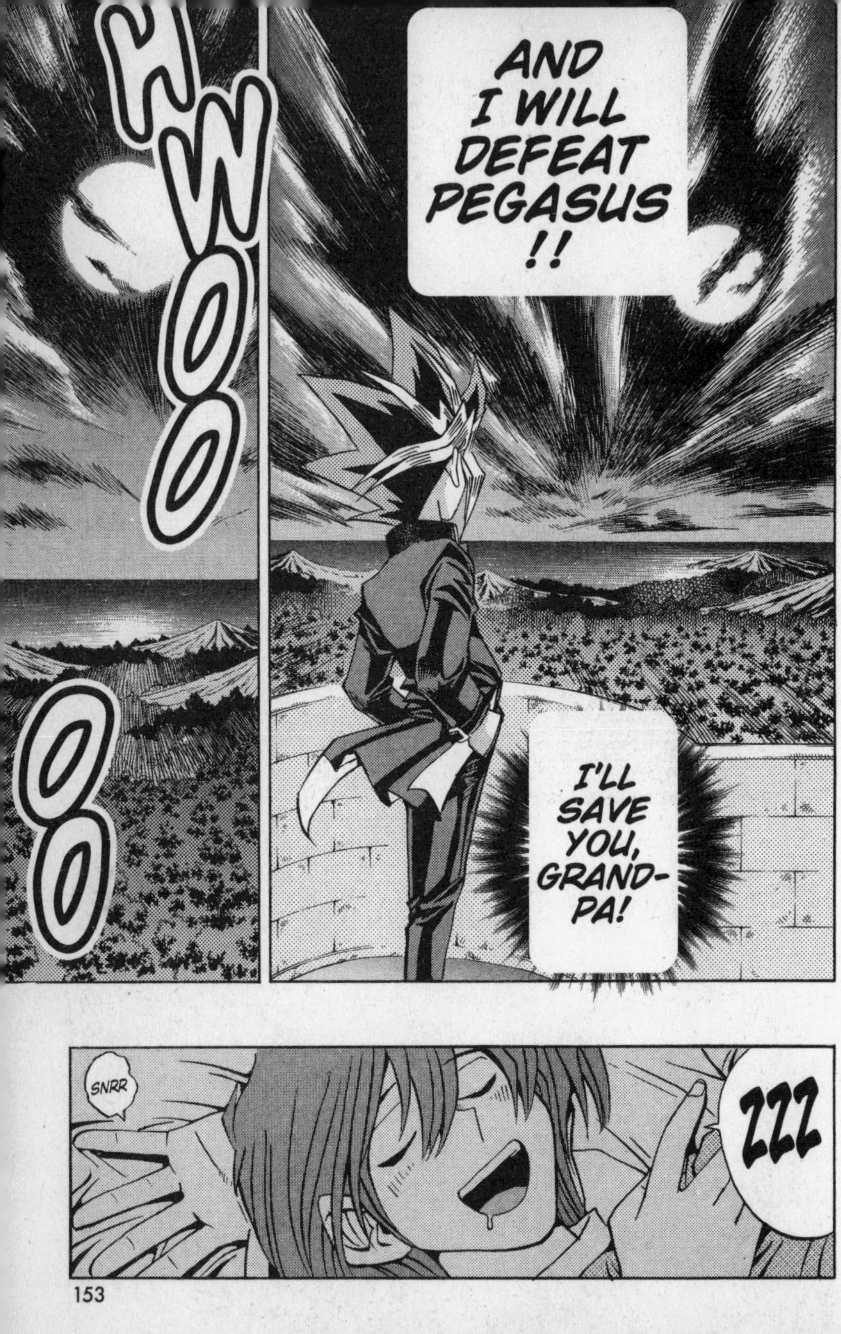
AND I WILL DEFEAT PEGASUS!!
I'LL SAVE YOU, GRAND-PA!
HWOOOOO
ZZZ
SNRR

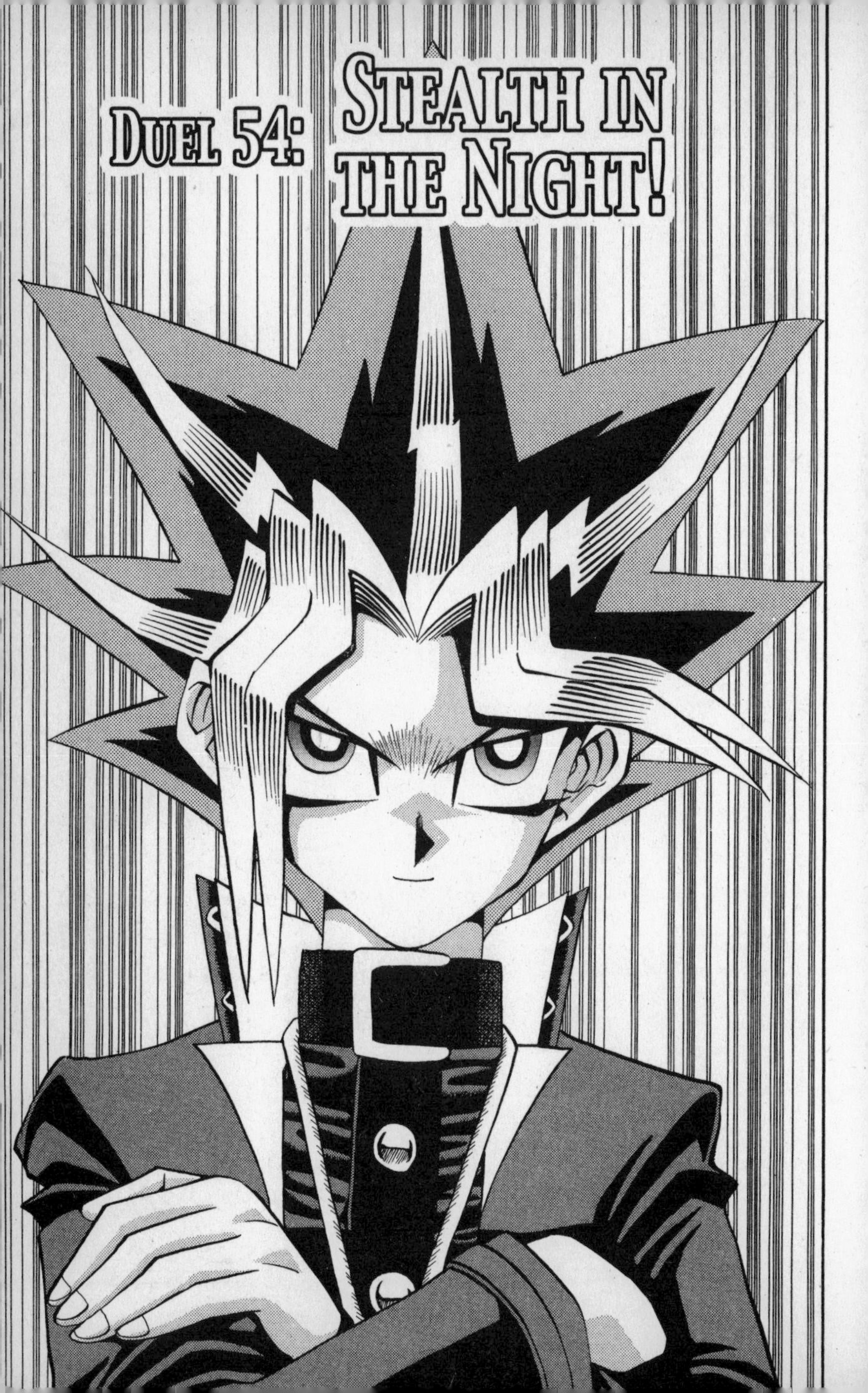
DUEL 54:
STEALTH IN THE NIGHT!

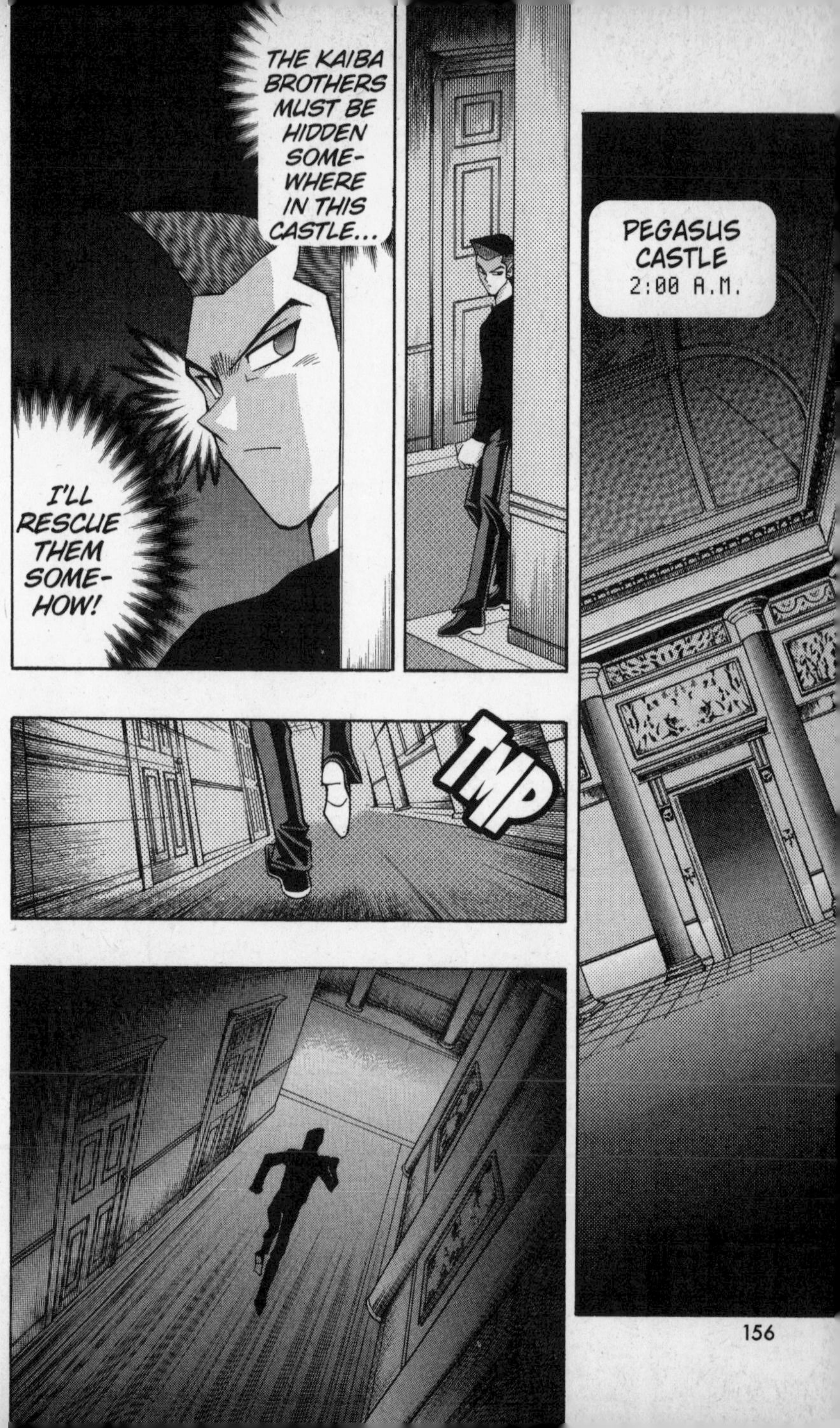
PEGASUS CASTLE
2:00 A.M.
THE KAIBA BROTHERS MUST BE HIDDEN SOME-WHERE IN THIS CASTLE...
I'LL RESCUE THEM SOME-HOW!
TMP

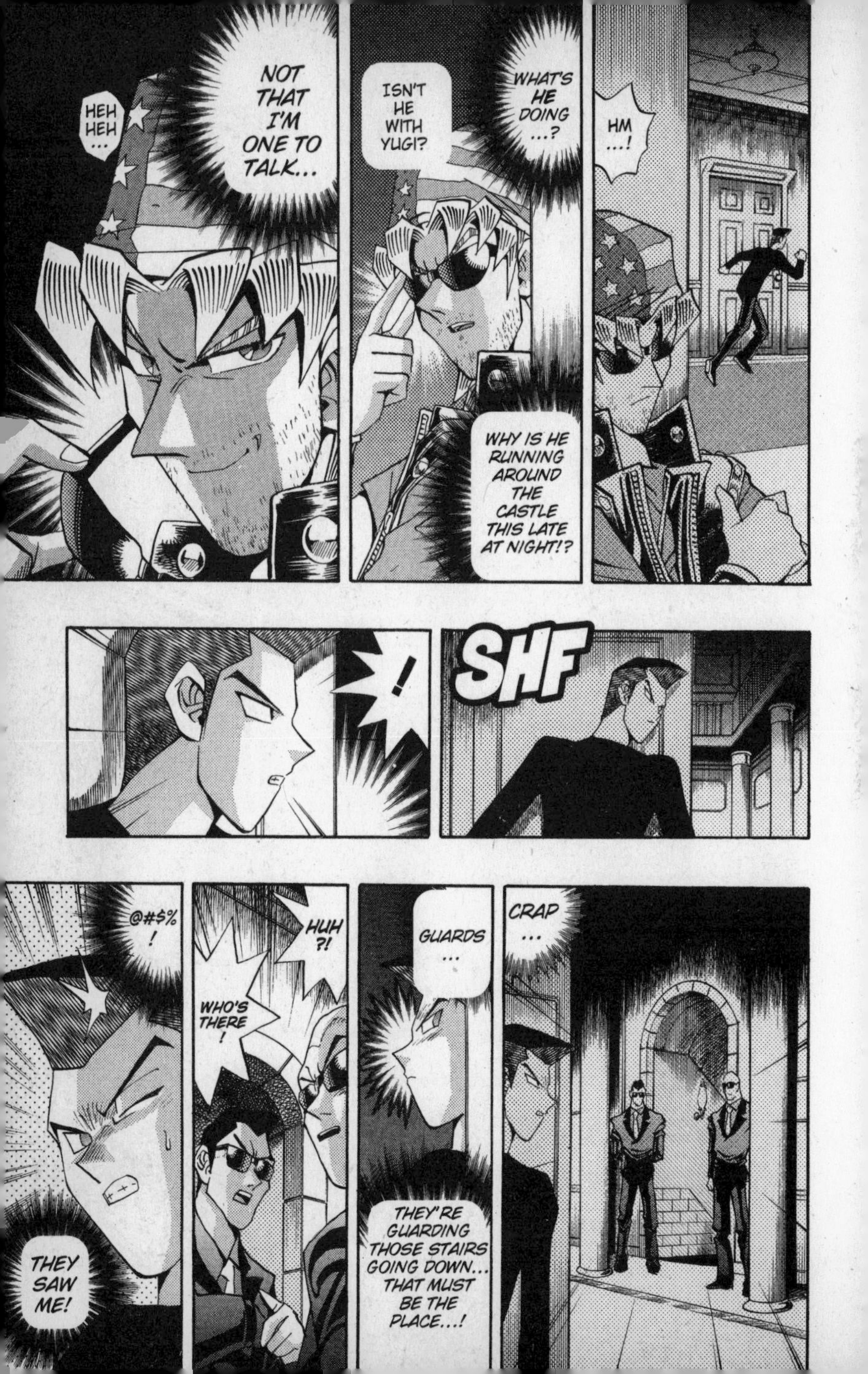
HM ...!
WHAT'S HE DOING ...?
ISN'T HE WITH YUGI?
WHY IS HE RUNNING AROUND THE CASTLE THIS LATE AT NIGHT!?
NOT THAT I'M ONE TO TALK...
HEH HEH ...
SHF
!
CRAP ...
GUARDS ...
THEY'RE GUARDING THOSE STAIRS GOING DOWN... THAT MUST BE THE PLACE...!
HUH ?!
WHO'S THERE !
@#$% !
THEY SAW ME!

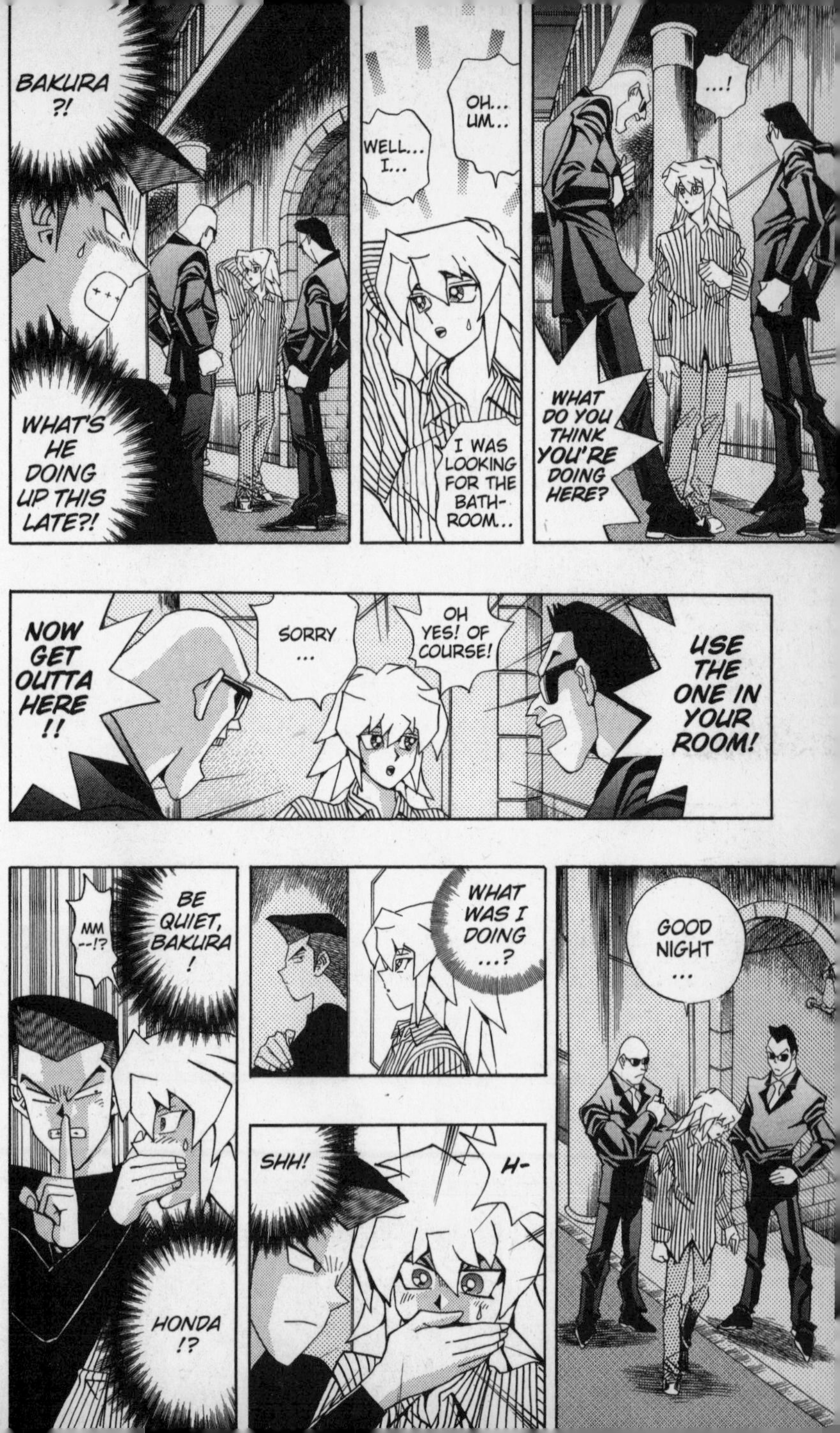
...!
WHAT DO YOU THINK YOU'RE DOING HERE?
OH... UM...
WELL... I...
I WAS LOOKING FOR THE BATH-ROOM...
BAKURA ?!
WHAT'S HE DOING UP THIS LATE?!
USE THE ONE IN YOUR ROOM!
OH YES! OF COURSE!
SORRY ...
NOW GET OUTTA HERE !!
GOOD NIGHT ...
WHAT WAS I DOING ...?
H-
SHH!
BE QUIET, BAKURA !
MM --!?
HONDA !?

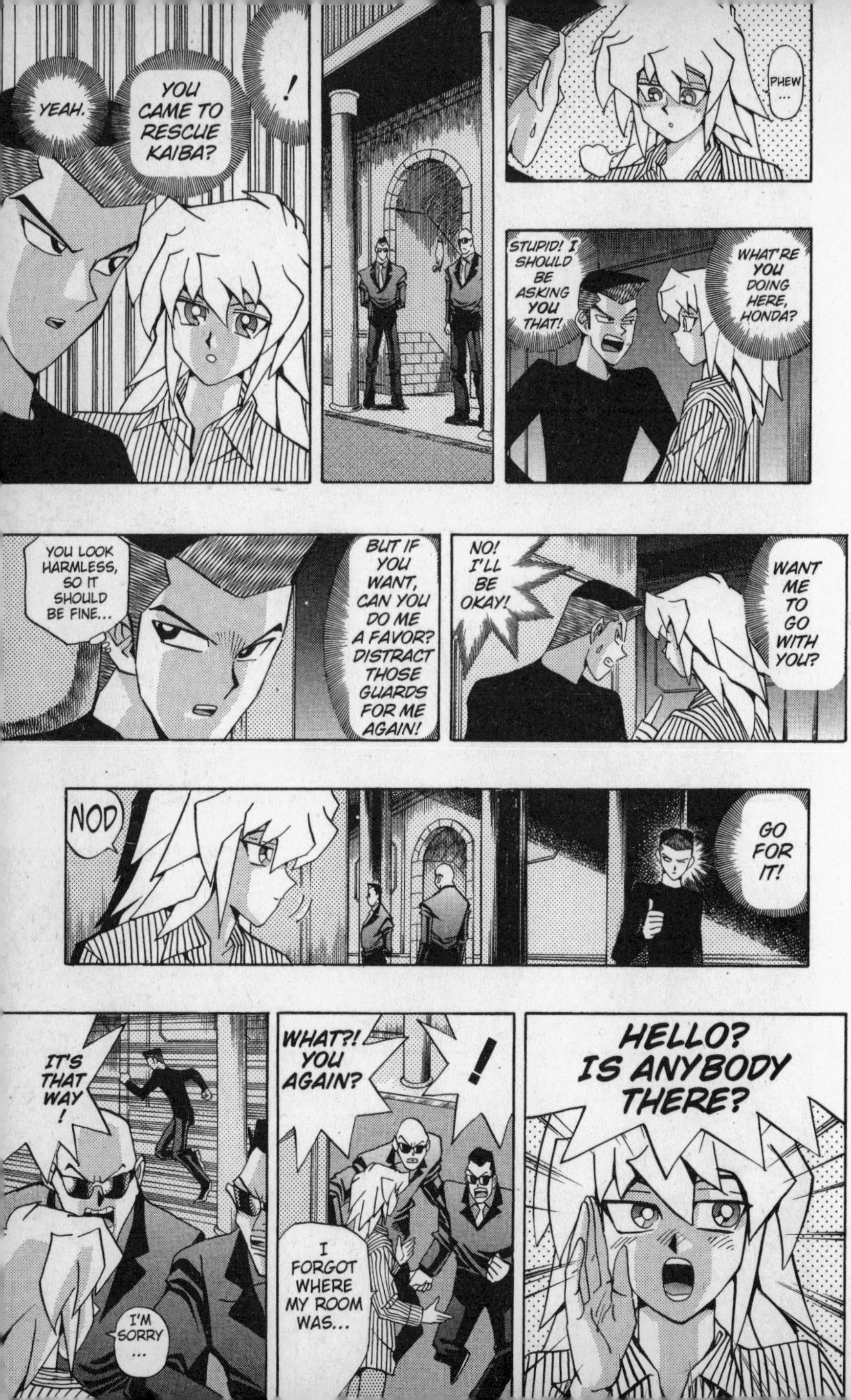
PHEW...
WHAT'RE YOU DOING HERE, HONDA?
STUPID! I SHOULD BE ASKING YOU THAT!
!
YOU CAME TO RESCUE KAIBA?
YEAH.
WANT ME TO GO WITH YOU?
NO! I'LL BE OKAY!
BUT IF YOU WANT, CAN YOU DO ME A FAVOR? DISTRACT THOSE GUARDS FOR ME AGAIN!
YOU LOOK HARMLESS, SO IT SHOULD BE FINE...
GO FOR IT!
NOD
HELLO? IS ANYBODY THERE?
!
WHAT?! YOU AGAIN?
I FORGOT WHERE MY ROOM WAS...
IT'S THAT WAY!
I'M SORRY...

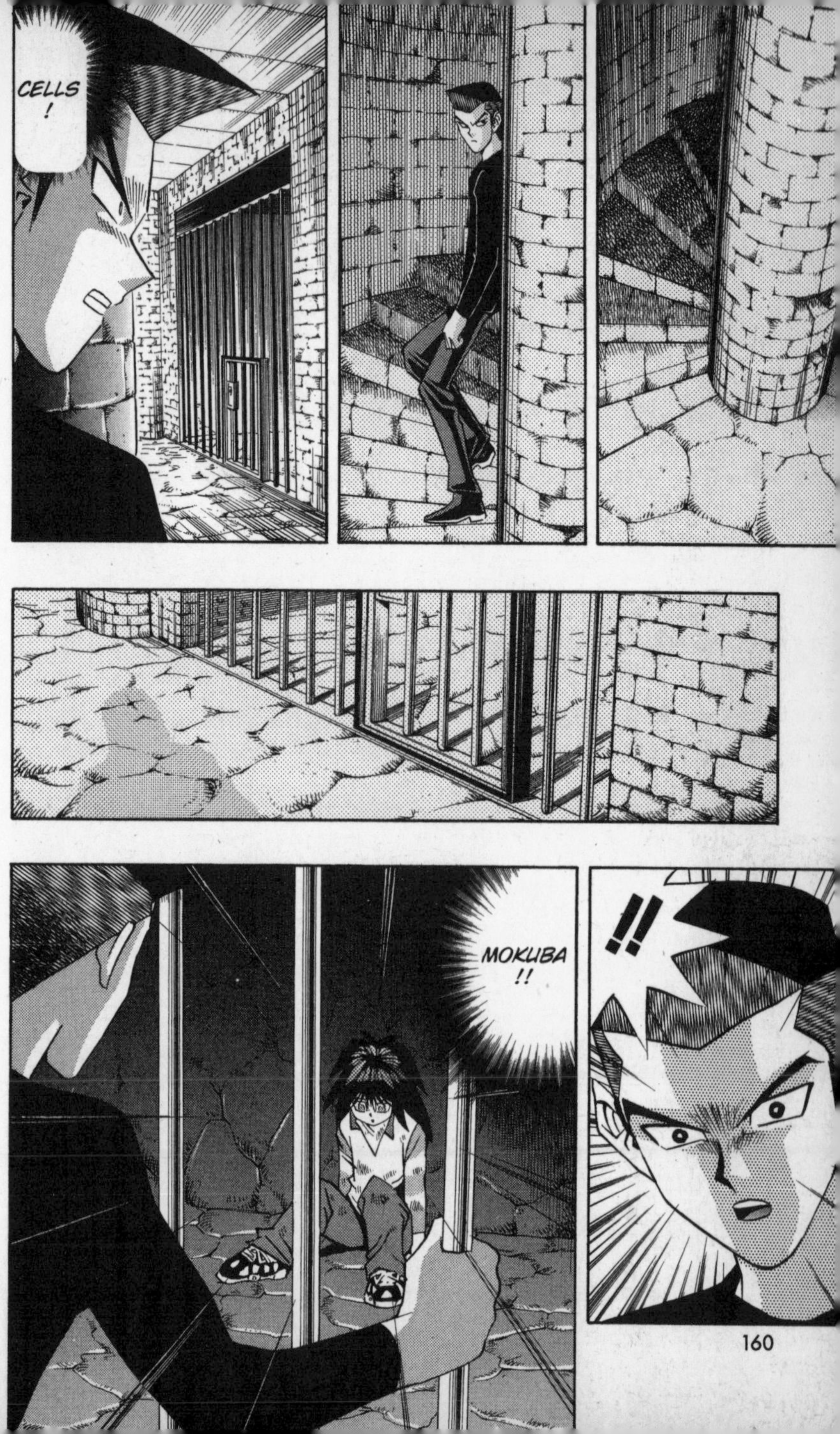
CELLS !
!!
MOKUBA !!

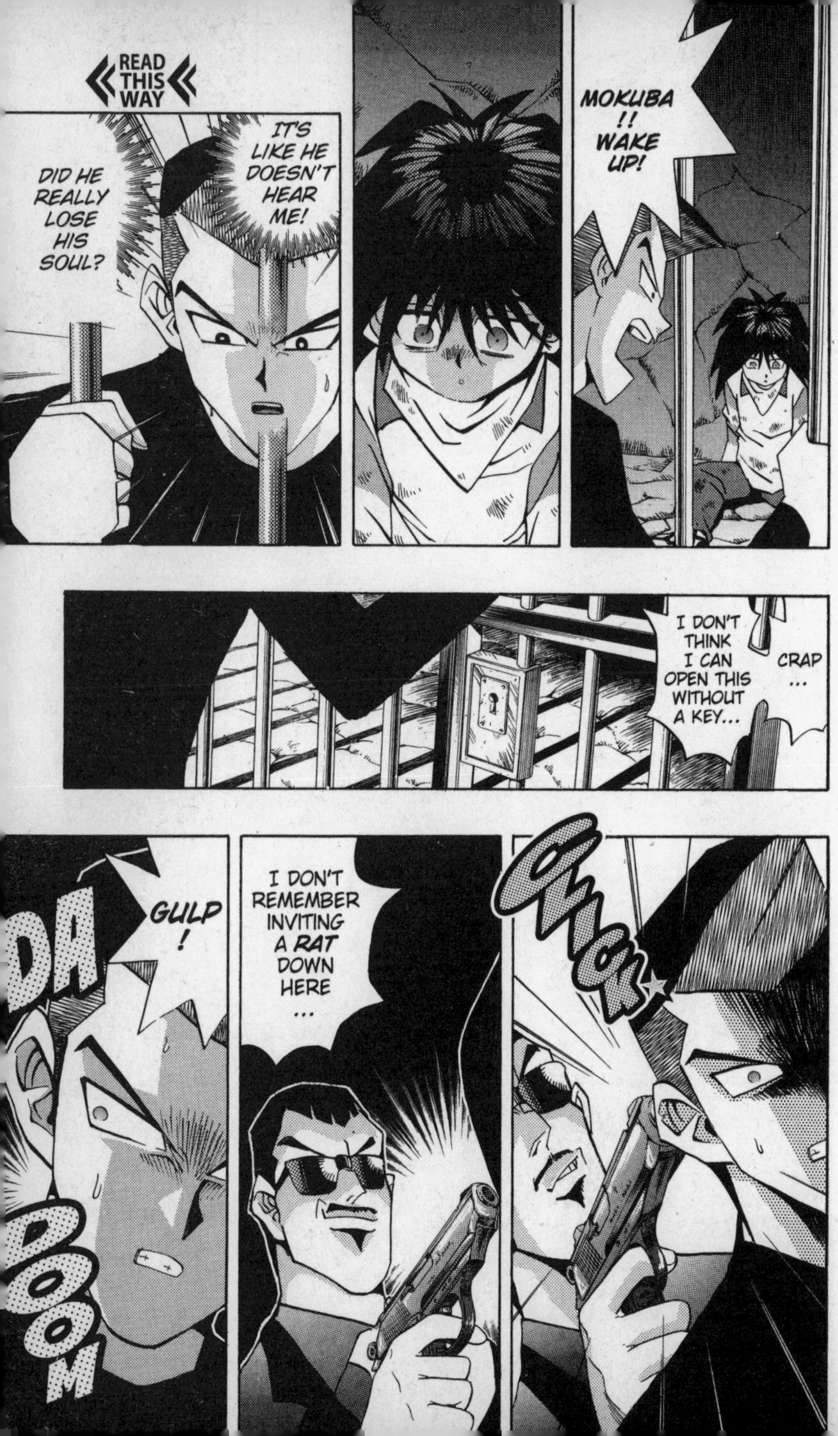
READ THIS WAY
MOKUBA!! WAKE UP!
IT'S LIKE HE DOESN'T HEAR ME!
DID HE REALLY LOSE HIS SOUL?
CRAP...
I DON'T THINK I CAN OPEN THIS WITHOUT A KEY...
CHACK★
I DON'T REMEMBER INVITING A RAT DOWN HERE...
GULP!
DA
DOOM

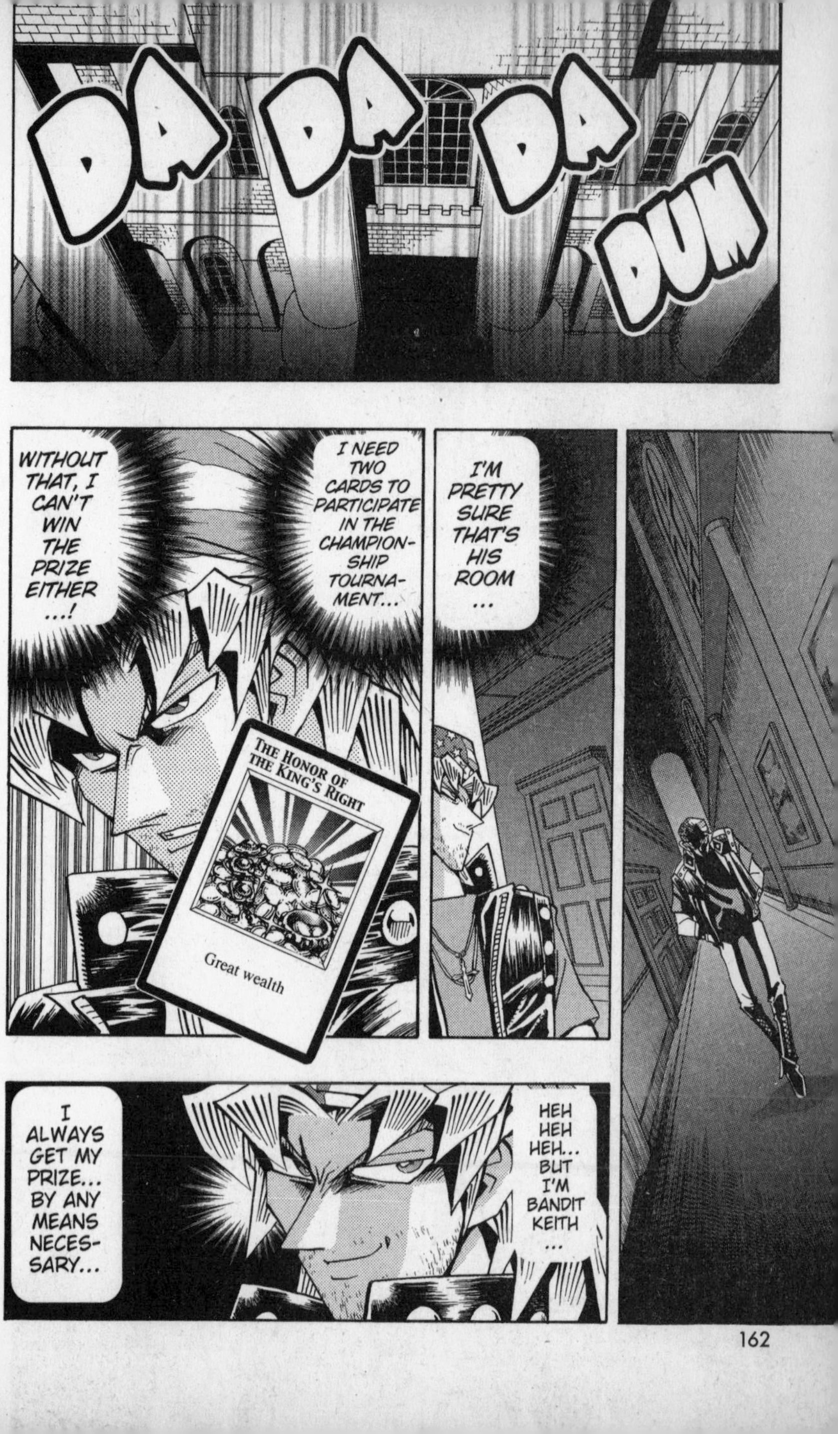
DA DA DA DUM
I'M PRETTY SURE THAT'S HIS ROOM ...
I NEED TWO CARDS TO PARTICIPATE IN THE CHAMPIONSHIP TOURNAMENT...
WITHOUT THAT, I CAN'T WIN THE PRIZE EITHER ...!
THE HONOR OF THE KING'S RIGHT
Great wealth
HEH HEH HEH... BUT I'M BANDIT KEITH ...
I ALWAYS GET MY PRIZE... BY ANY MEANS NECESSARY...

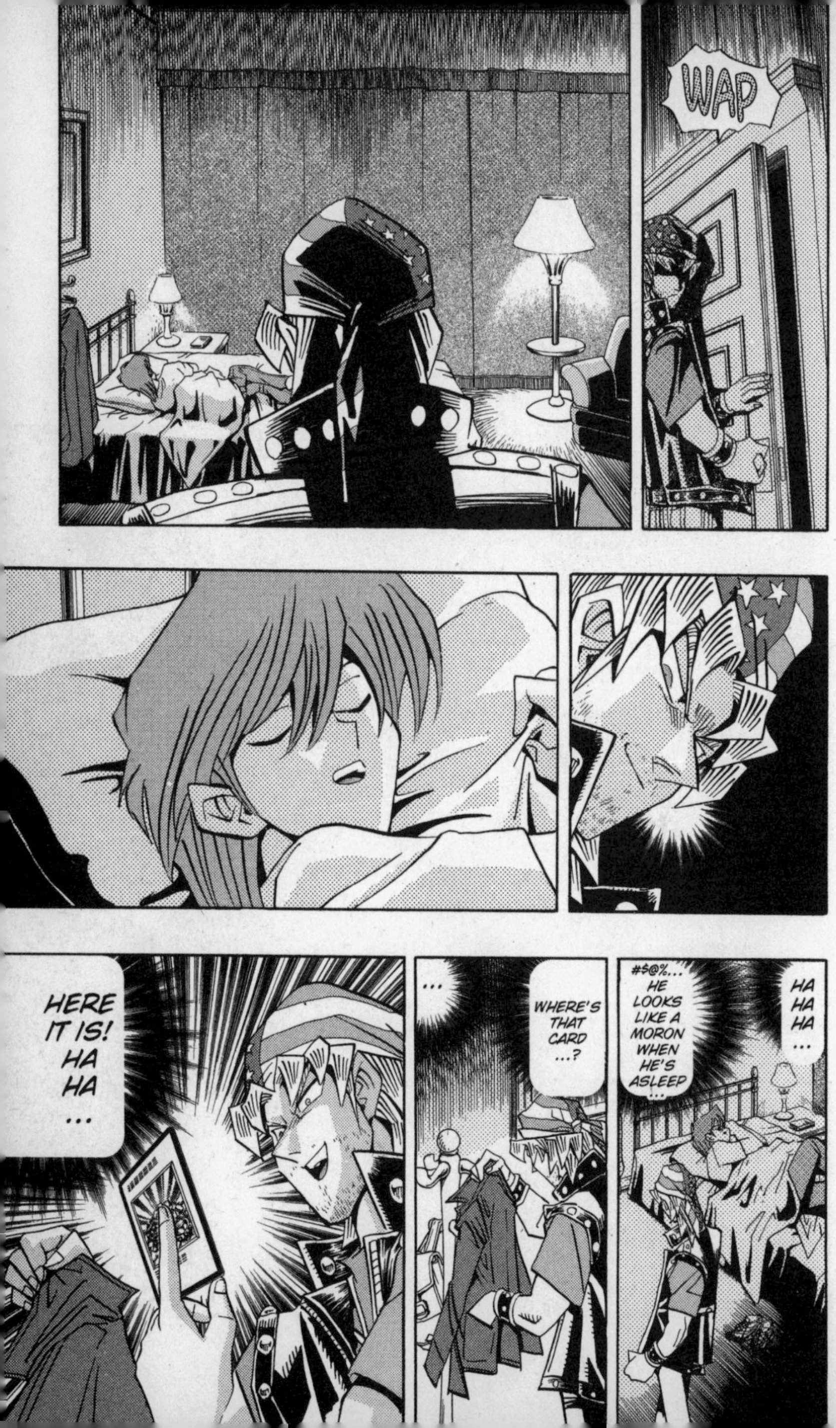
WAP
HA HA HA ...
#$@%... HE LOOKS LIKE A MORON WHEN HE'S ASLEEP ...
WHERE'S THAT CARD ...?
...
HERE IT IS! HA HA ...

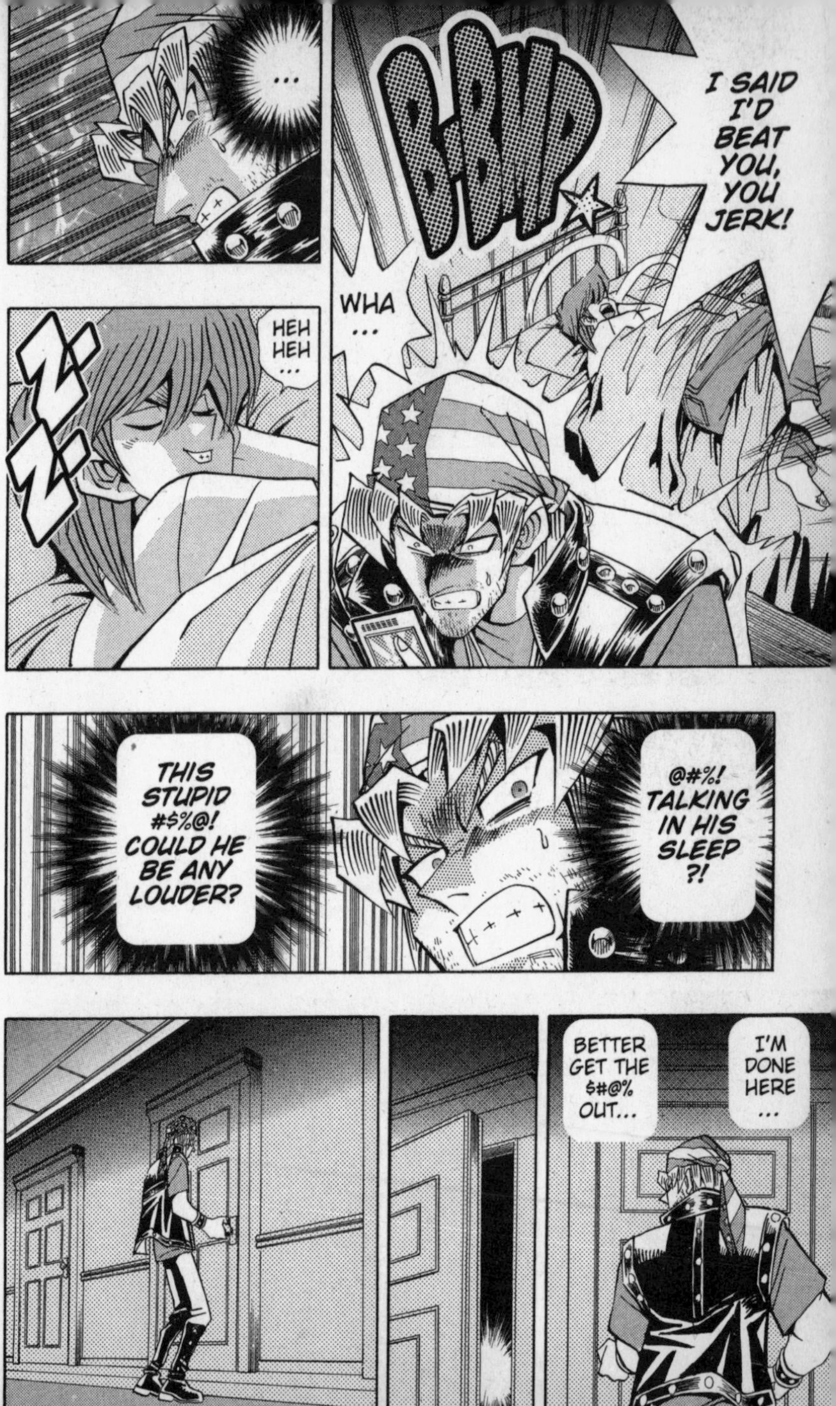
B-BMP
I SAID I'D BEAT YOU, YOU JERK!
WHA ...
...
Z-Z-
HEH HEH ...
@#%! TALKING IN HIS SLEEP ?!
THIS STUPID #$%@! COULD HE BE ANY LOUDER?
I'M DONE HERE ...
BETTER GET THE $#@% OUT...

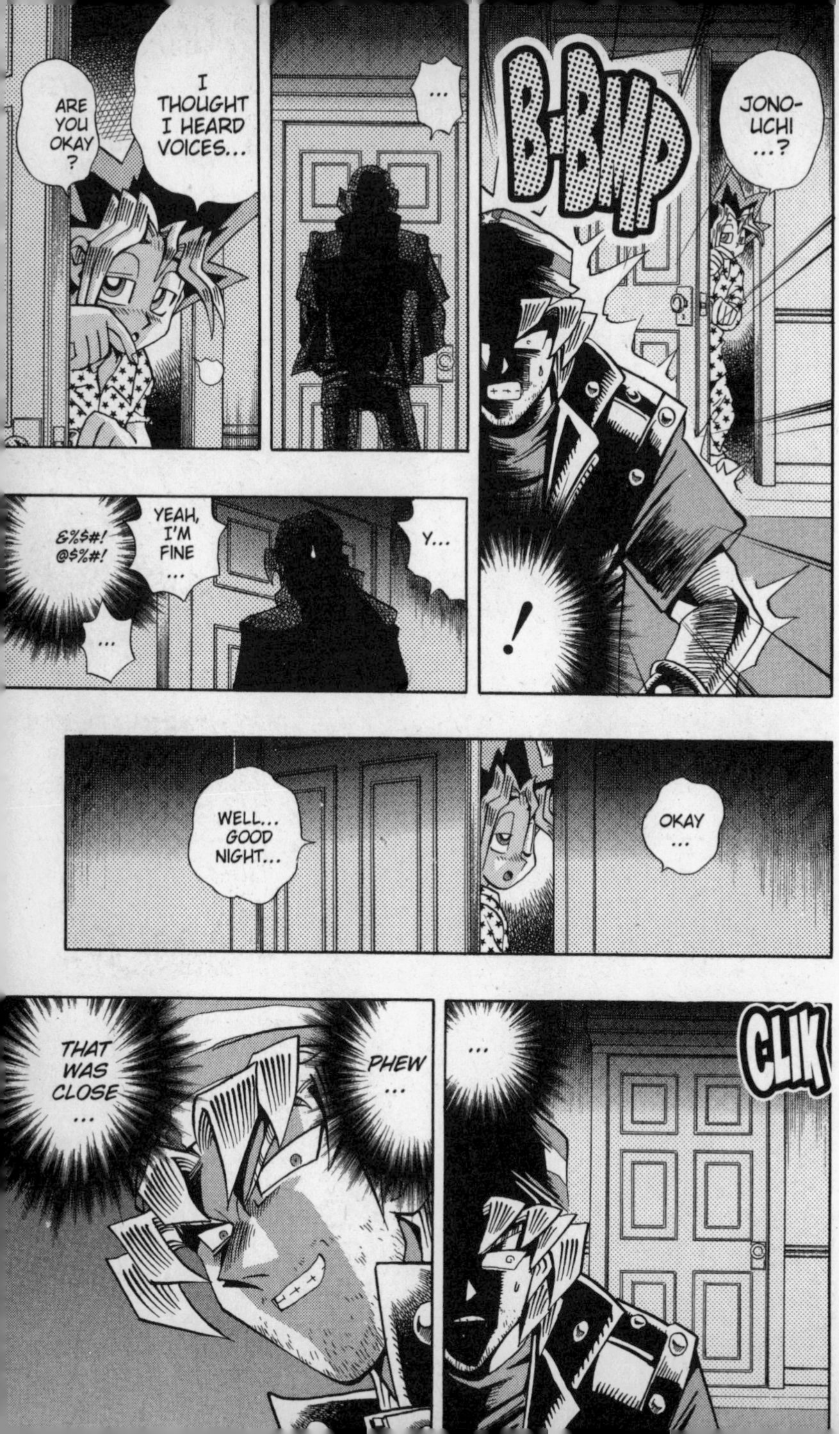
JONO-UCHI ...?
B-BMP
!
...
I THOUGHT I HEARD VOICES...
ARE YOU OKAY ?
Y...
YEAH, I'M FINE ...
&%$#! @$%#!
...
OKAY ...
WELL... GOOD NIGHT...
CLIK
...
PHEW ...
THAT WAS CLOSE ...

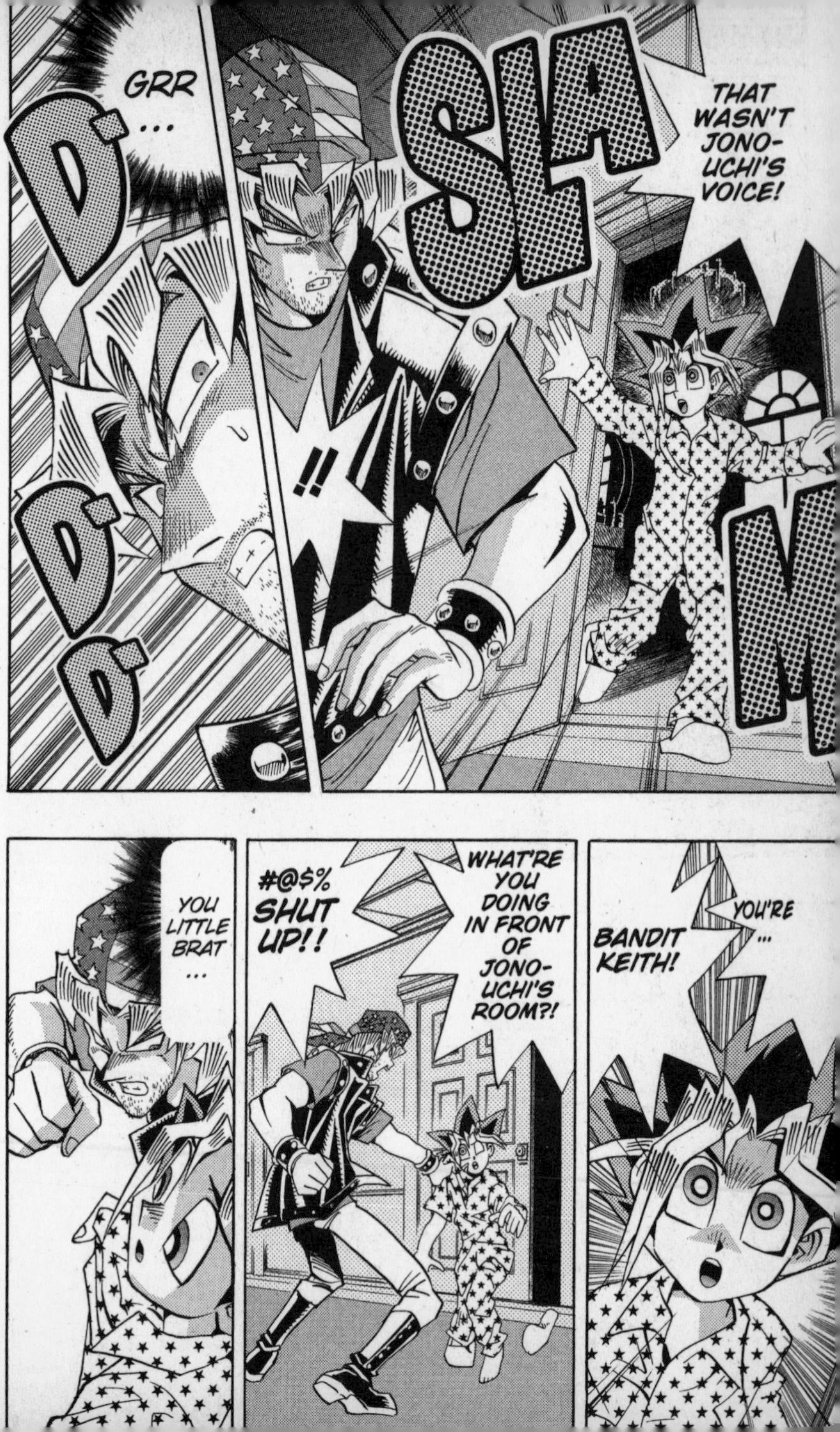
THAT WASN'T JONO-UCHI'S VOICE!
SLAM
!!
GRR ...
D' D' D'
YOU'RE ...
BANDIT KEITH!
WHAT'RE YOU DOING IN FRONT OF JONO-UCHI'S ROOM?!
#@$% SHUT UP!!
YOU LITTLE BRAT ...

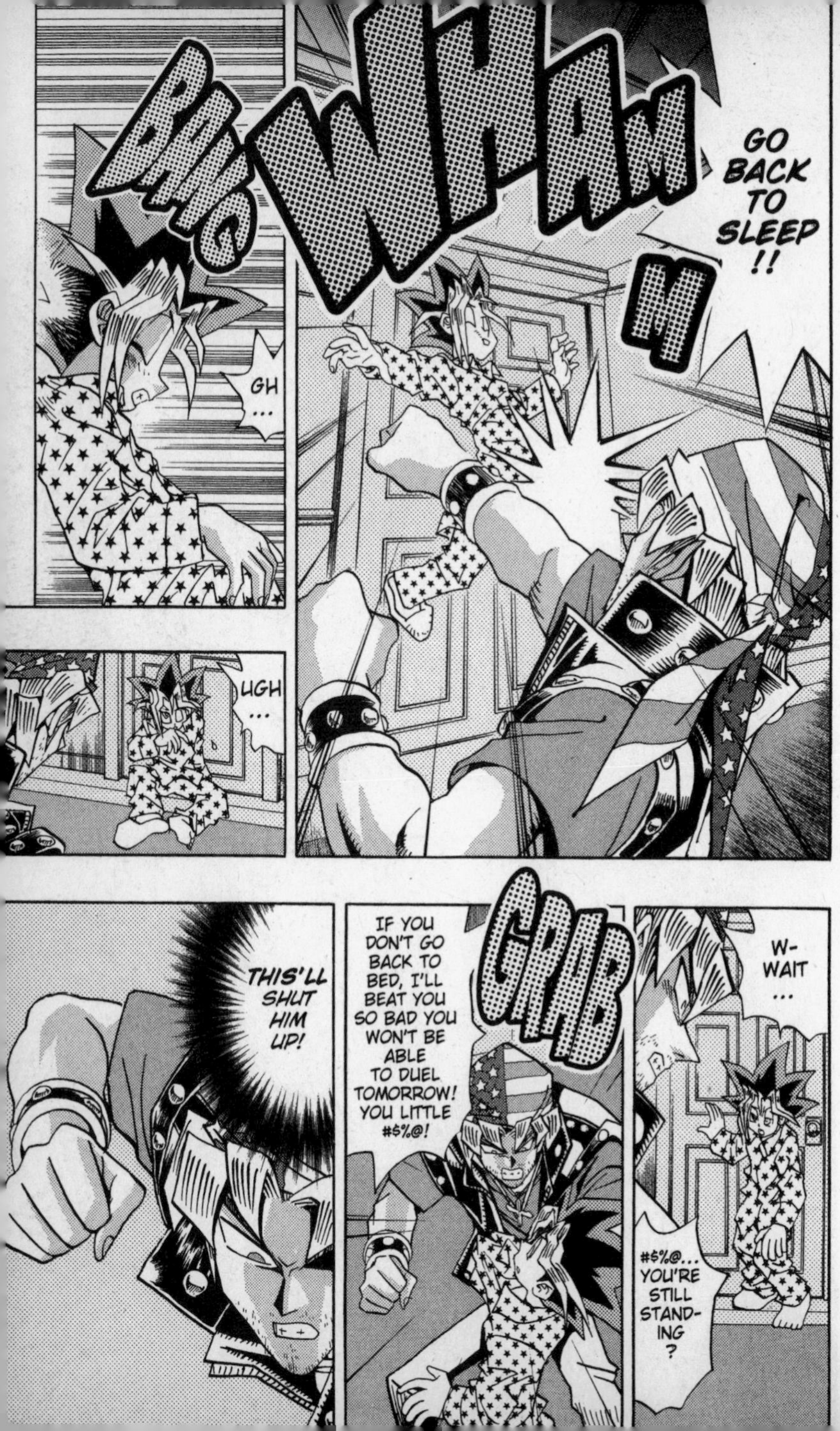
GO BACK TO SLEEP!!
BANG
WHAM
M
GH...
UGH...
W-WAIT...
#$%@... YOU'RE STILL STAND-ING?
GRAB
IF YOU DON'T GO BACK TO BED, I'LL BEAT YOU SO BAD YOU WON'T BE ABLE TO DUEL TOMORROW! YOU LITTLE #$%@!
THIS'LL SHUT HIM UP!

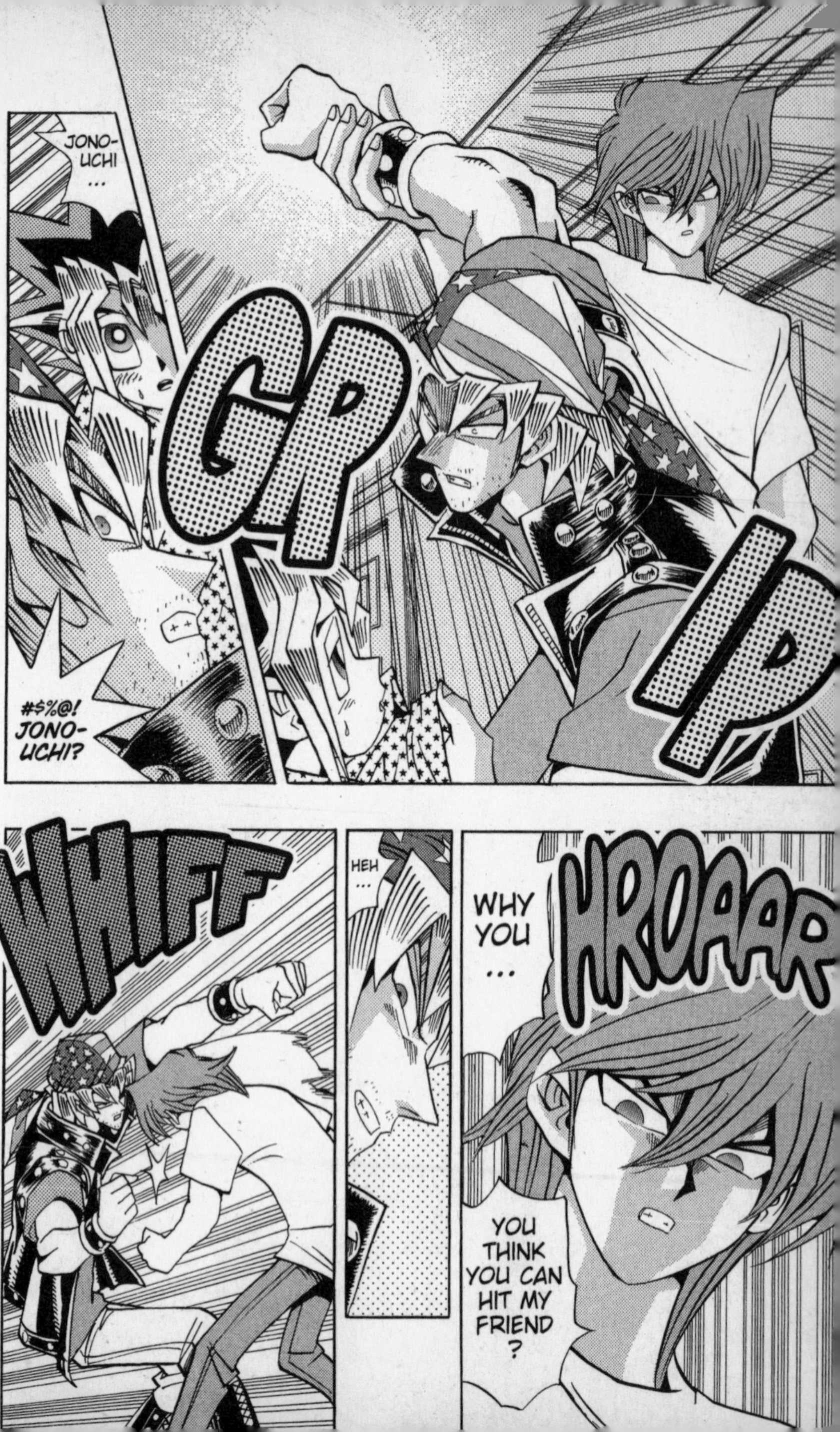
GRIP
JONO-UCHI ...
#$%@! JONO-UCHI?
HROAAR
WHY YOU ...
YOU THINK YOU CAN HIT MY FRIEND ?
HEH ...
WHIFF

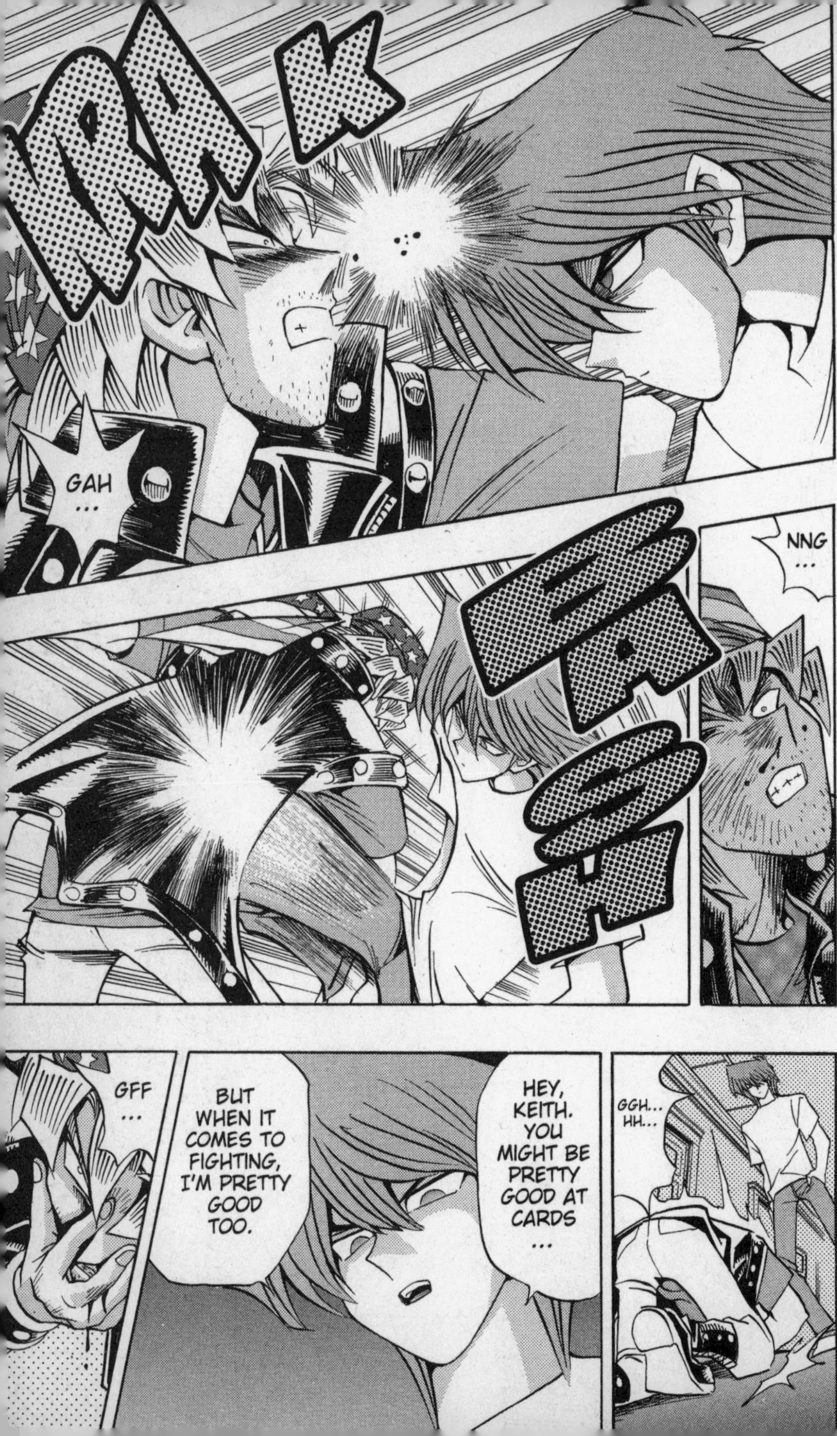
GAH ...
NNG ...
GGH... HH...
HEY, KEITH. YOU MIGHT BE PRETTY GOOD AT CARDS ...
BUT WHEN IT COMES TO FIGHTING, I'M PRETTY GOOD TOO.
GFF ...

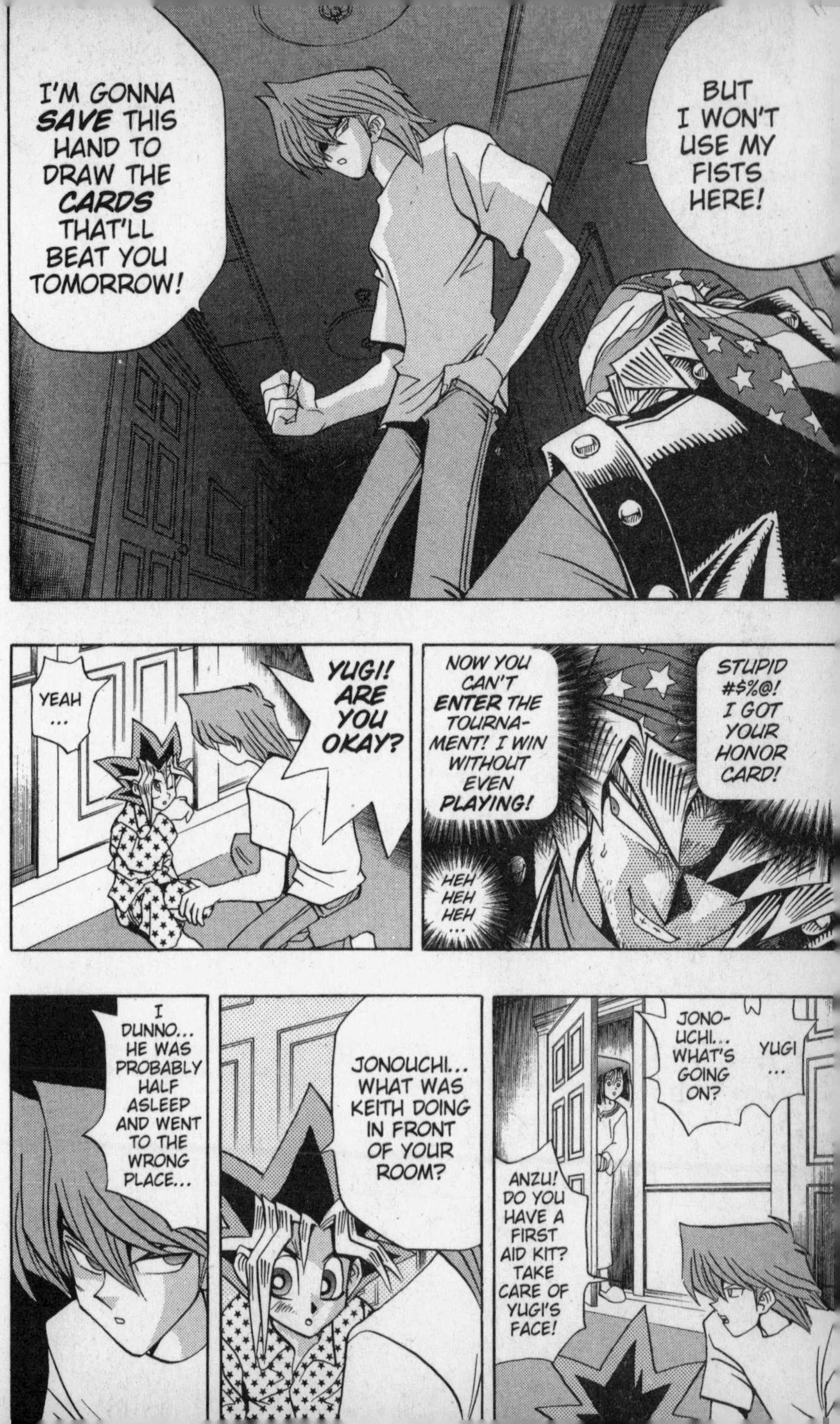
BUT I WON'T USE MY FISTS HERE!
I'M GONNA SAVE THIS HAND TO DRAW THE CARDS THAT'LL BEAT YOU TOMORROW!
STUPID #$%@! I GOT YOUR HONOR CARD!
NOW YOU CAN'T ENTER THE TOURNA-MENT! I WIN WITHOUT EVEN PLAYING!
HEH HEH HEH ...
YUGI! ARE YOU OKAY?
YEAH ...
YUGI ...
JONO-UCHI... WHAT'S GOING ON?
ANZU! DO YOU HAVE A FIRST AID KIT? TAKE CARE OF YUGI'S FACE!
JONOUCHI... WHAT WAS KEITH DOING IN FRONT OF YOUR ROOM?
I DUNNO... HE WAS PROBABLY HALF ASLEEP AND WENT TO THE WRONG PLACE...

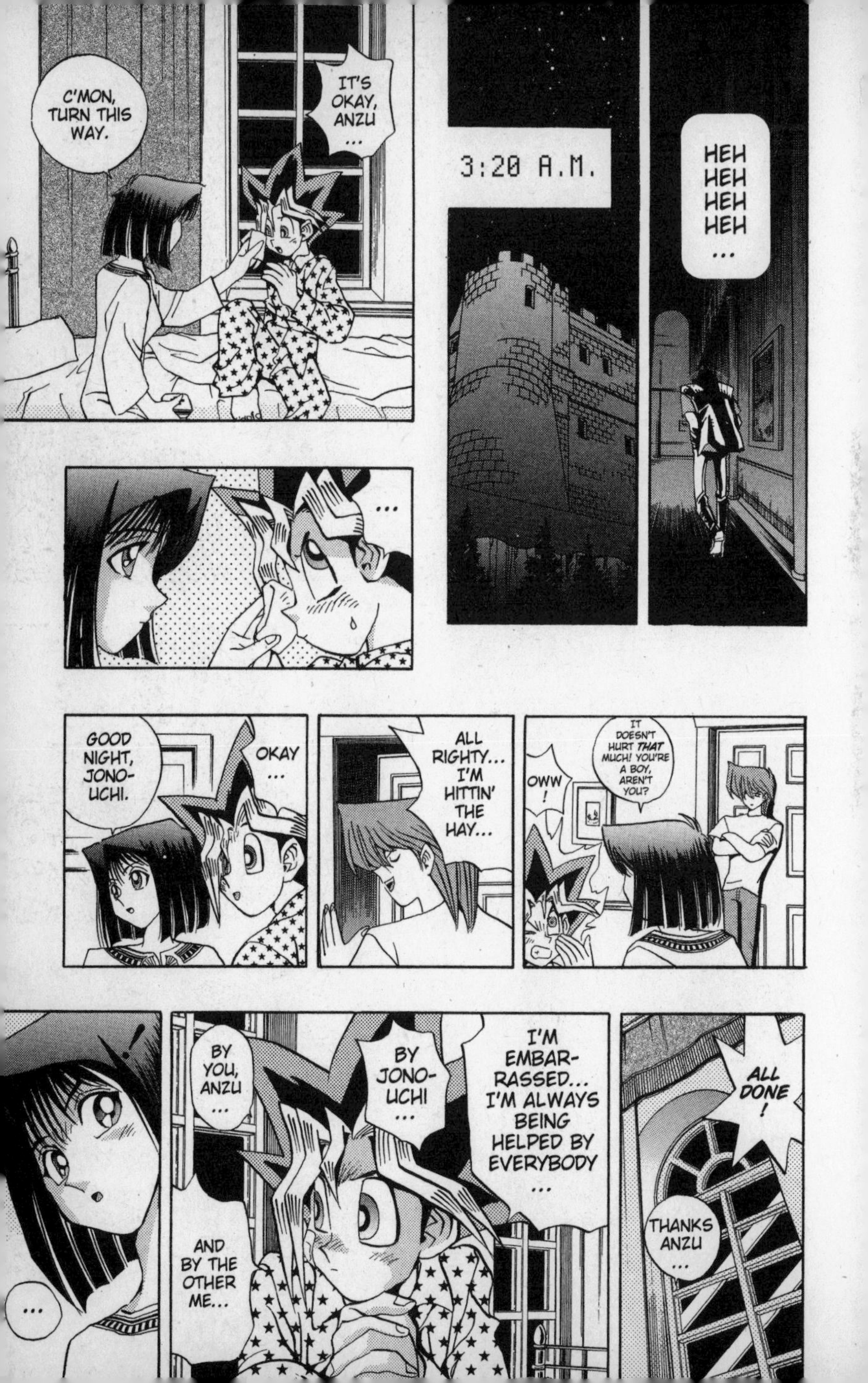
HEH HEH HEH HEH ...
3:20 A.M.
IT'S OKAY, ANZU ...
C'MON, TURN THIS WAY.
...
IT DOESN'T HURT *THAT* MUCH! YOU'RE A BOY, AREN'T YOU?
OWW!
ALL RIGHTY... I'M HITTIN' THE HAY...
OKAY ...
GOOD NIGHT, JONO-UCHI.
ALL DONE!
THANKS ANZU ...
I'M EMBAR-RASSED... I'M ALWAYS BEING HELPED BY EVERYBODY ...
BY JONO-UCHI ...
BY YOU, ANZU ...
AND BY THE OTHER ME...
...

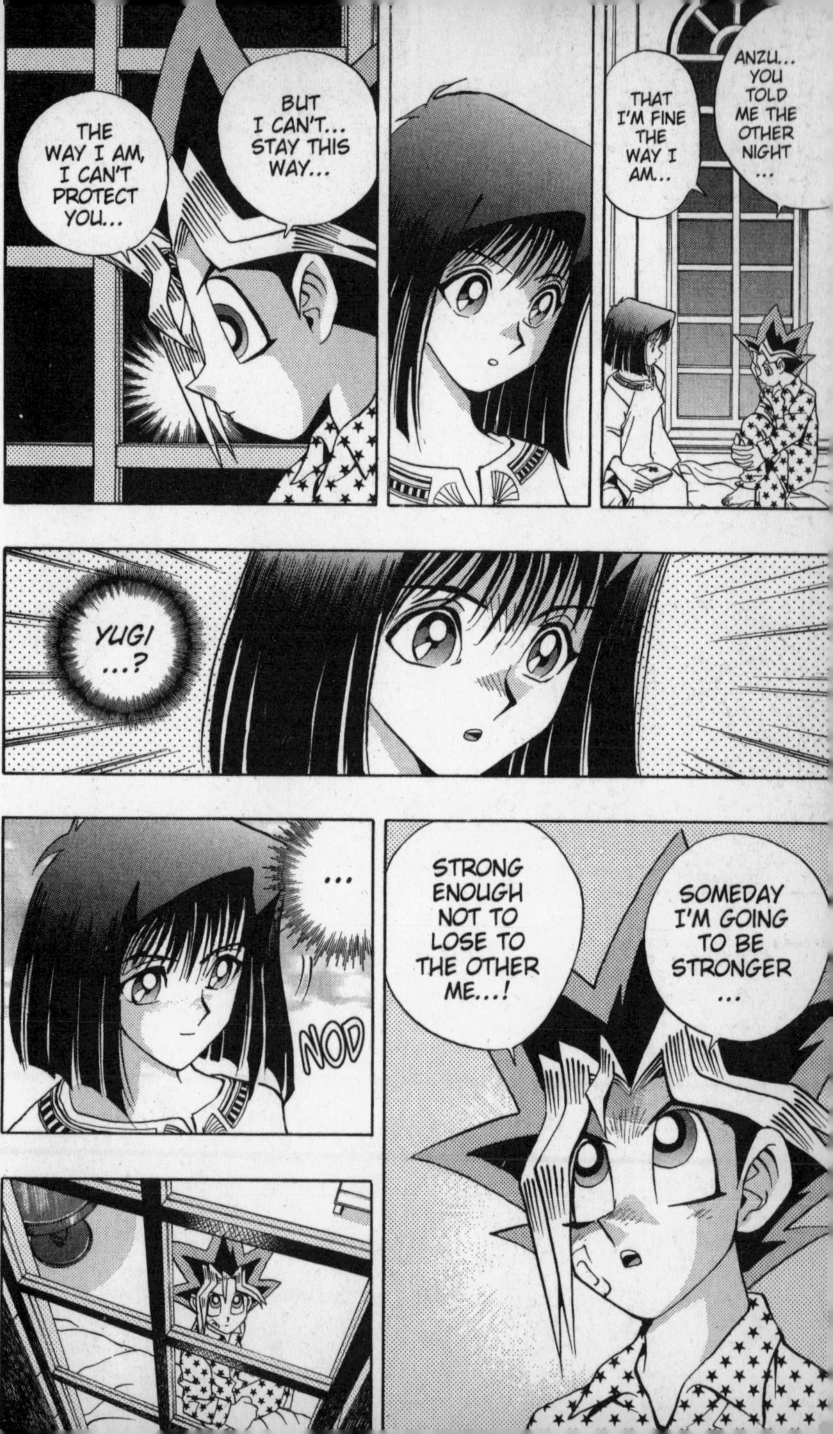
ANZU... YOU TOLD ME THE OTHER NIGHT...
THAT I'M FINE THE WAY I AM...
BUT I CAN'T... STAY THIS WAY...
THE WAY I AM, I CAN'T PROTECT YOU...
YUGI...?
SOMEDAY I'M GOING TO BE STRONGER...
STRONG ENOUGH NOT TO LOSE TO THE OTHER ME...!
...
NOD

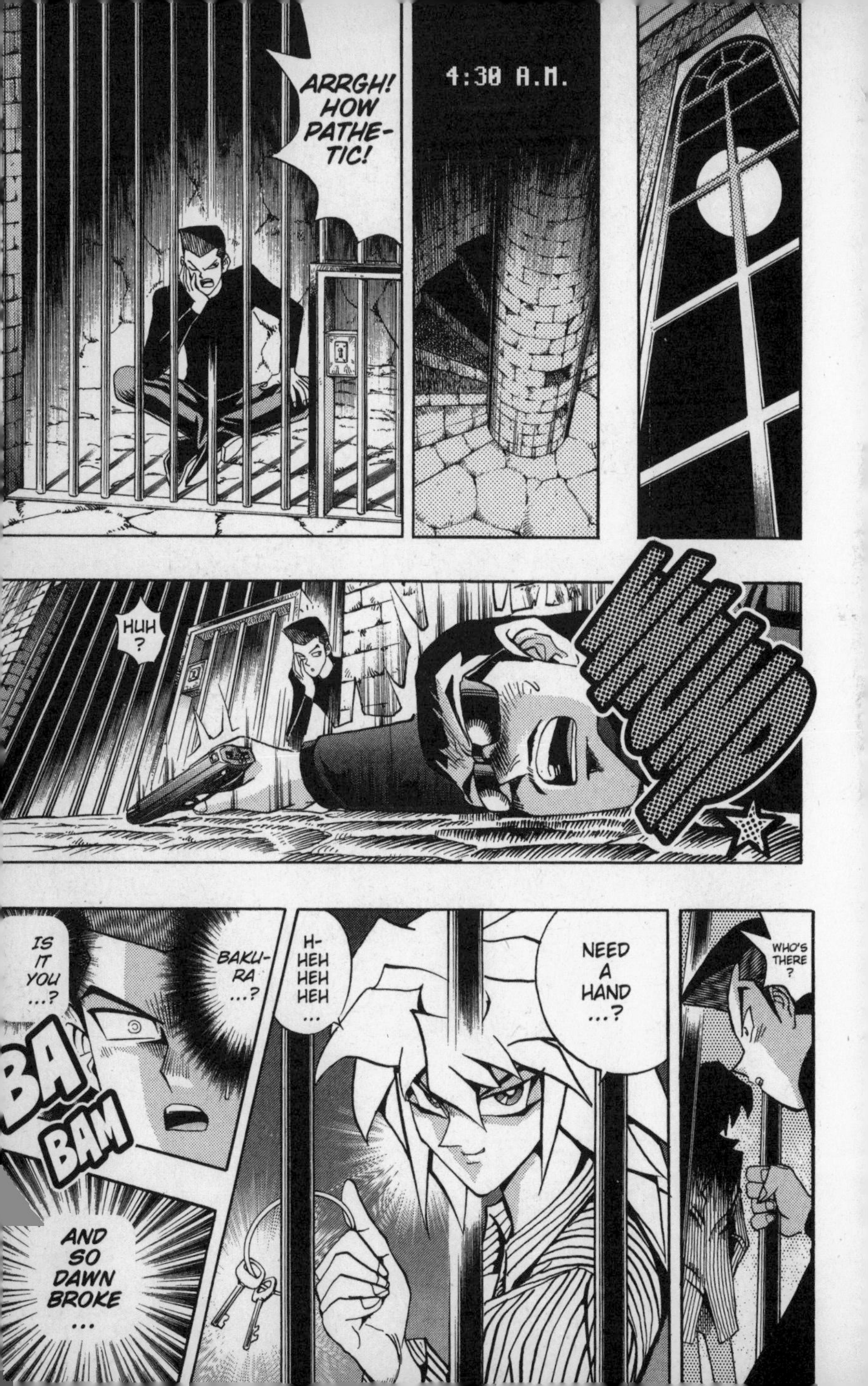
4:30 A.M.
ARRGH! HOW PATHETIC!
WHUMP
HUH?
WHO'S THERE?
NEED A HAND...?
H-HEH HEH HEH...
IS IT YOU...?
BAKURA...?
BA BAM
AND SO DAWN BROKE...

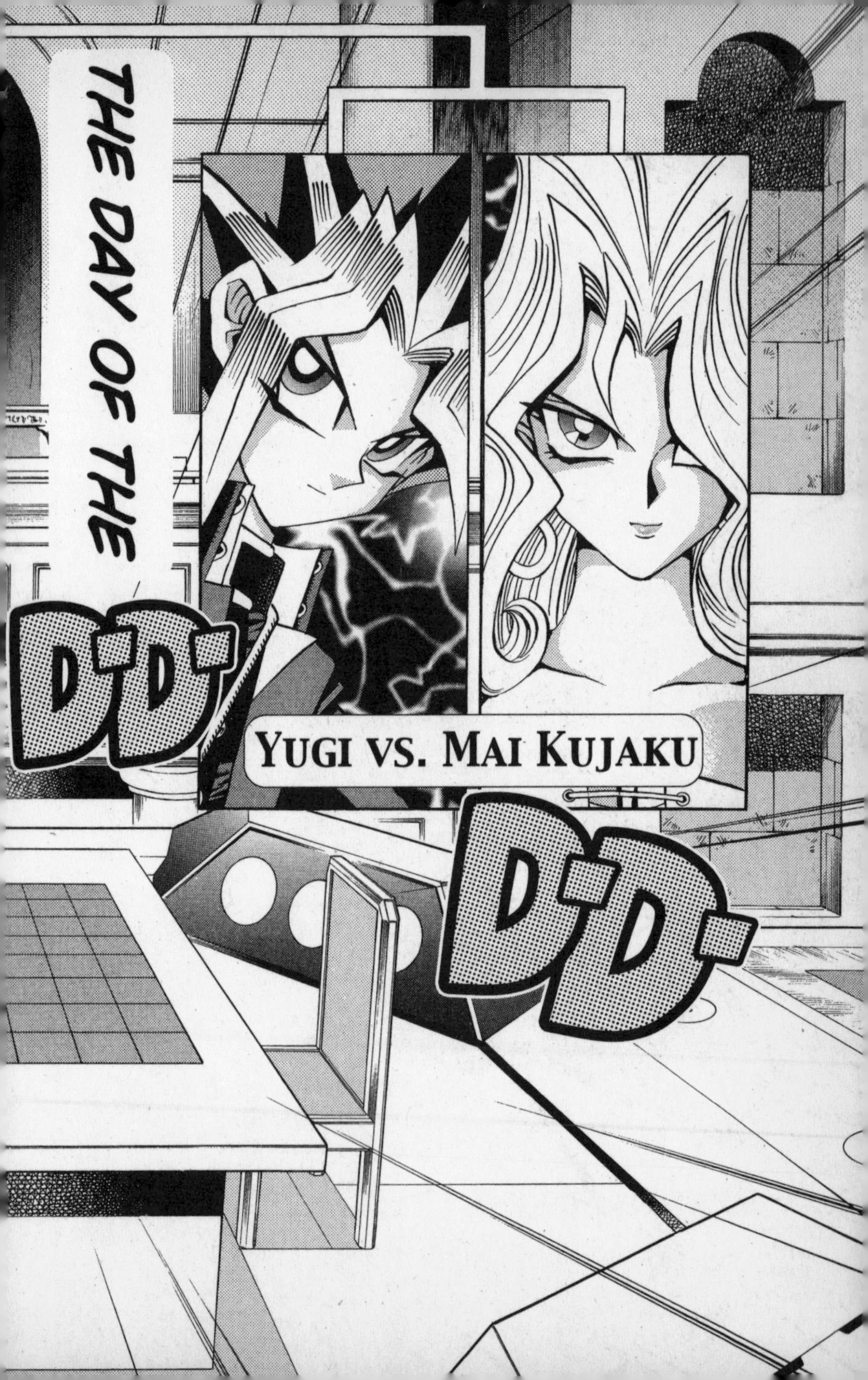
THE DAY OF THE
D·D·D·
YUGI VS. MAI KUJAKU
D·D·D·

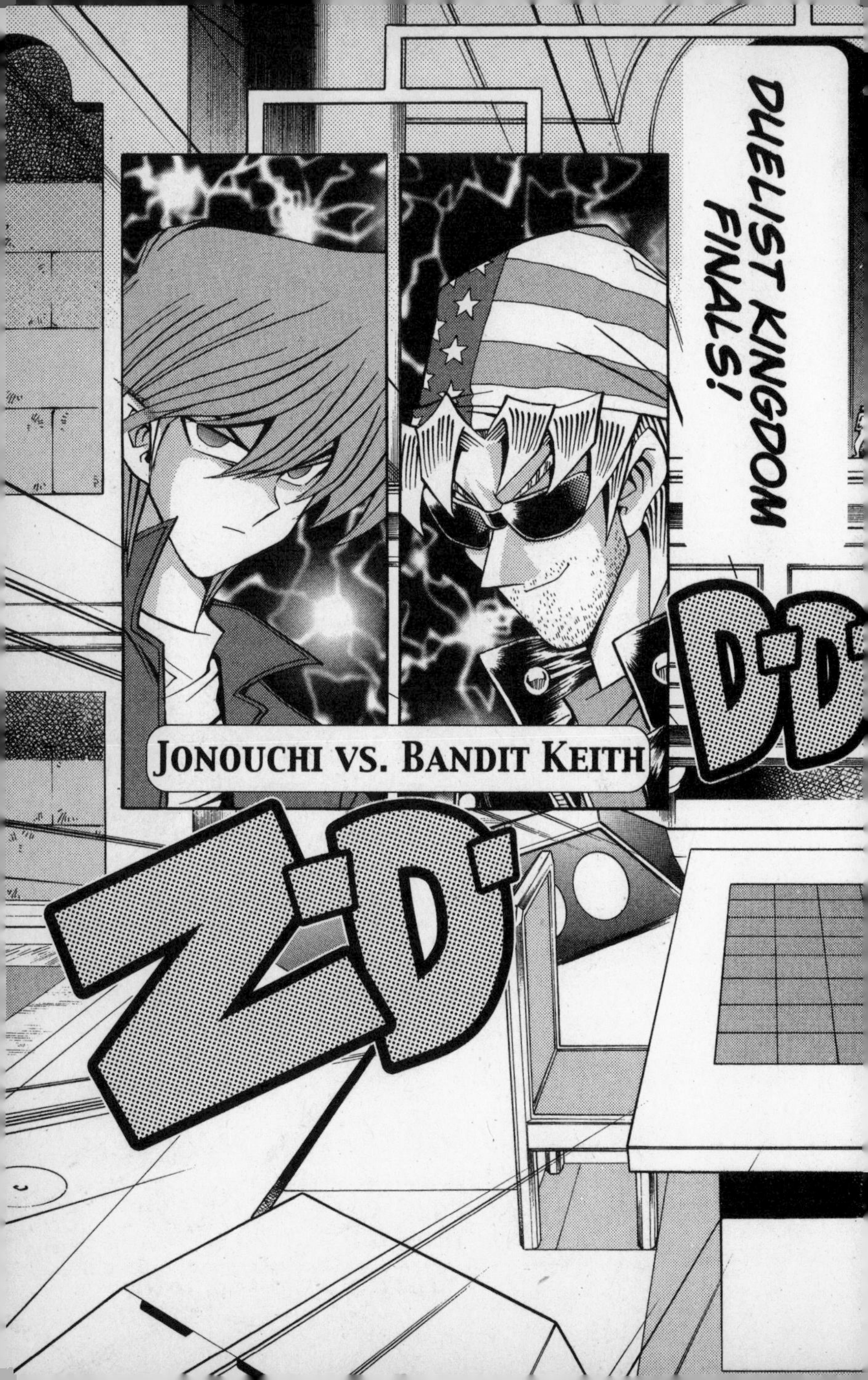
DUELIST KINGDOM FINALS!
JONOUCHI VS. BANDIT KEITH
D'D'
Z'D'

DUEL 55: THE BEWITCHING MAI

SHAAA

IT'S THE FINAL DAY OF THE **DUELIST KINGDOM TOURNAMENT**...THE DAY OF THE **CHAMPIONSHIP FINALS!**

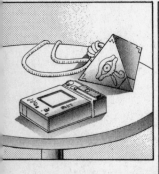

THE MORNING OF THE BATTLE IS FINALLY HERE...

PEEL

OWW...

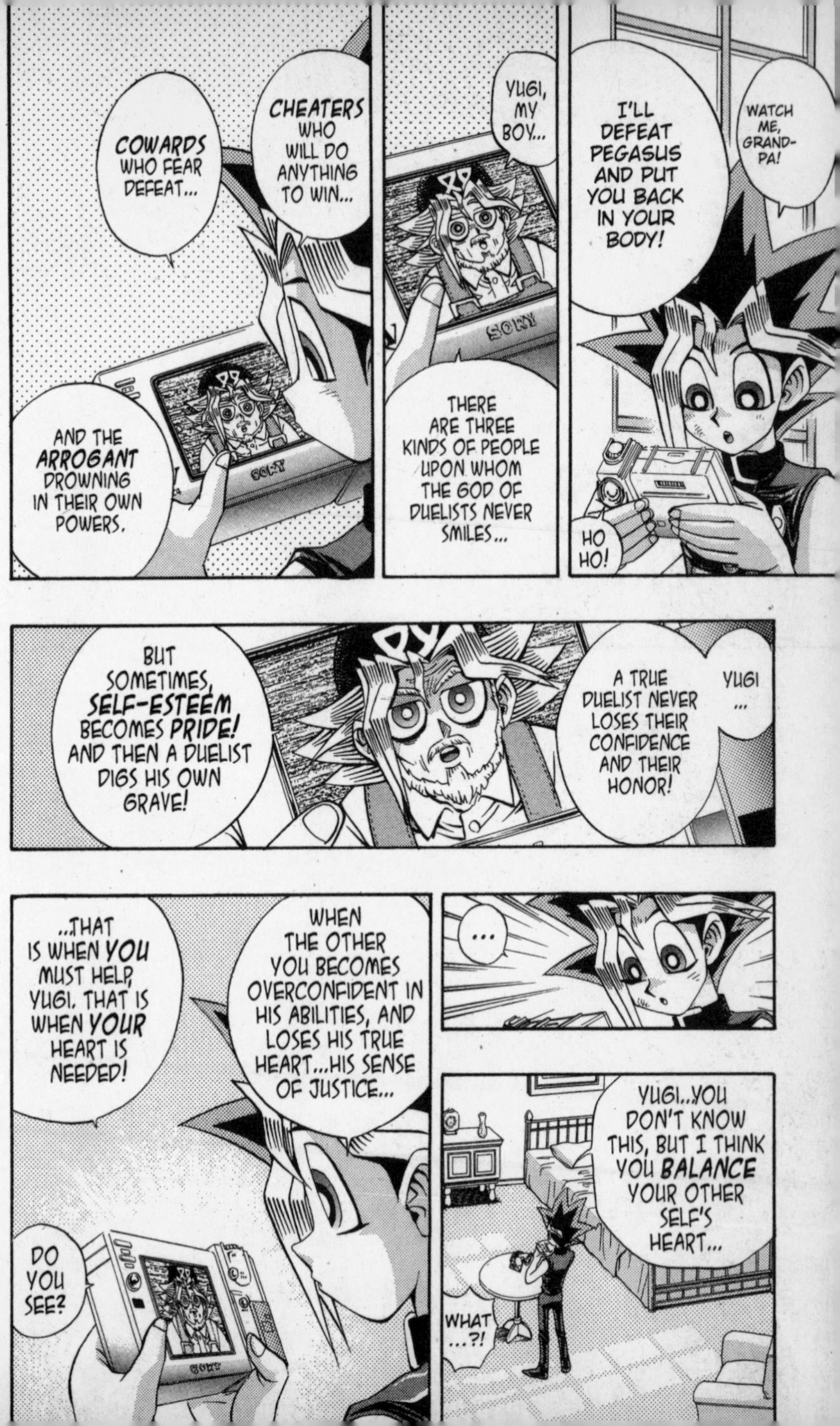
WATCH ME, GRANDPA!
I'LL DEFEAT PEGASUS AND PUT YOU BACK IN YOUR BODY!
HO HO!
YUGI, MY BOY...
THERE ARE THREE KINDS OF PEOPLE UPON WHOM THE GOD OF DUELISTS NEVER SMILES...
CHEATERS WHO WILL DO ANYTHING TO WIN...
COWARDS WHO FEAR DEFEAT...
AND THE ARROGANT DROWNING IN THEIR OWN POWERS.
YUGI...
A TRUE DUELIST NEVER LOSES THEIR CONFIDENCE AND THEIR HONOR!
BUT SOMETIMES, SELF-ESTEEM BECOMES PRIDE! AND THEN A DUELIST DIGS HIS OWN GRAVE!
...
YUGI...YOU DON'T KNOW THIS, BUT I THINK YOU BALANCE YOUR OTHER SELF'S HEART...
WHAT...?!
WHEN THE OTHER YOU BECOMES OVERCONFIDENT IN HIS ABILITIES, AND LOSES HIS TRUE HEART...HIS SENSE OF JUSTICE...
...THAT IS WHEN YOU MUST HELP, YUGI. THAT IS WHEN YOUR HEART IS NEEDED!
DO YOU SEE?

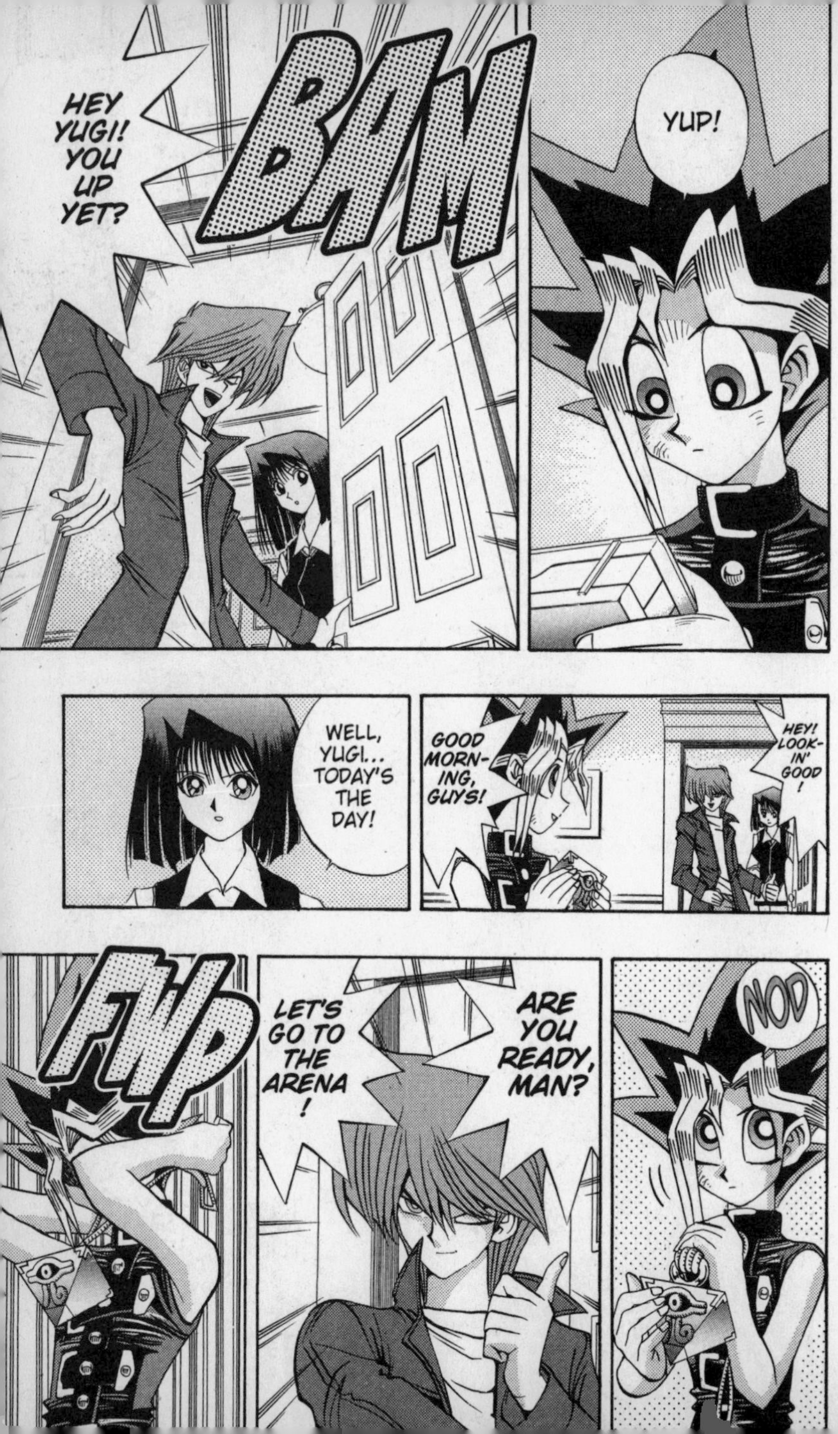
YUP!
BAM
HEY YUGI! YOU UP YET?
HEY! LOOK-IN' GOOD!
GOOD MORN-ING, GUYS!
WELL, YUGI... TODAY'S THE DAY!
NOD
ARE YOU READY, MAN?
LET'S GO TO THE ARENA!
FWP

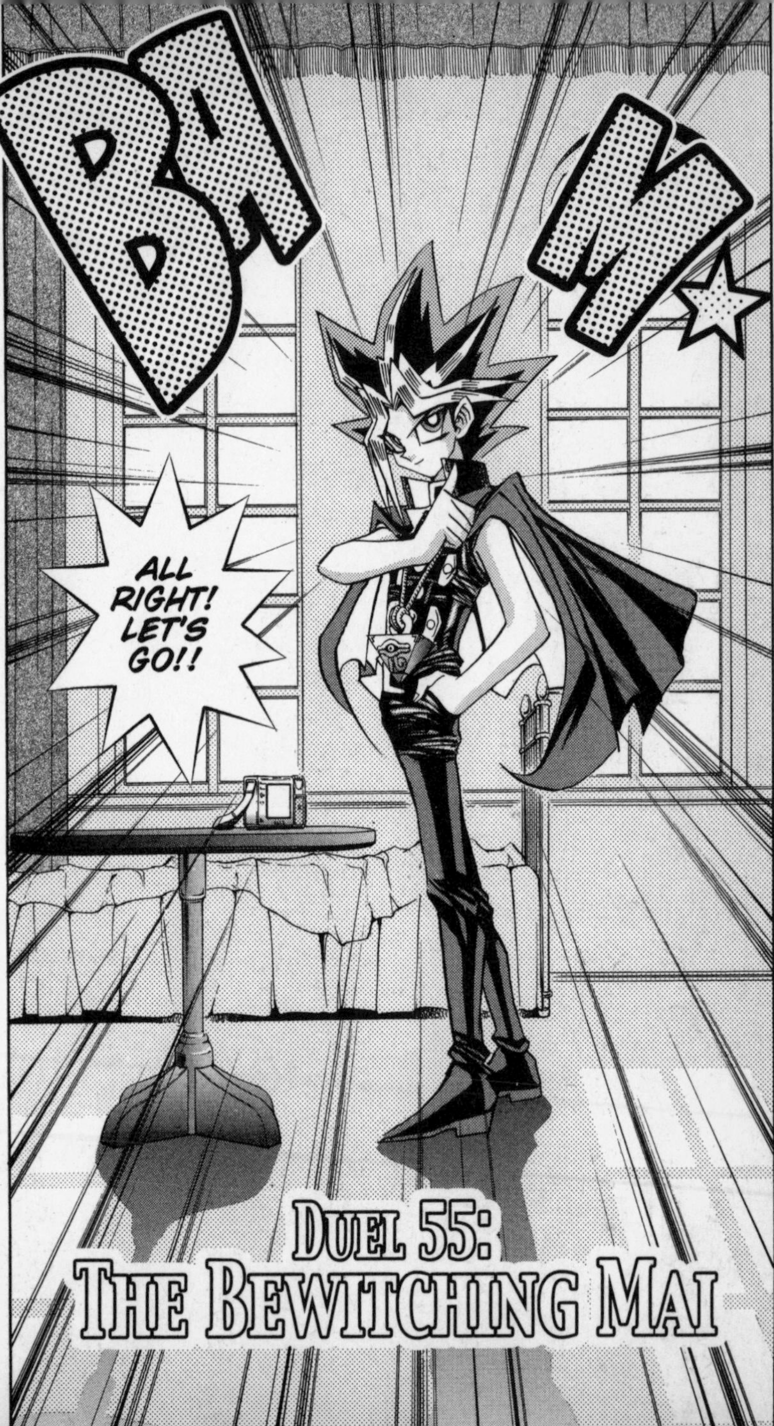
BAM
ALL RIGHT! LET'S GO!!
DUEL 55: THE BEWITCHING MAI

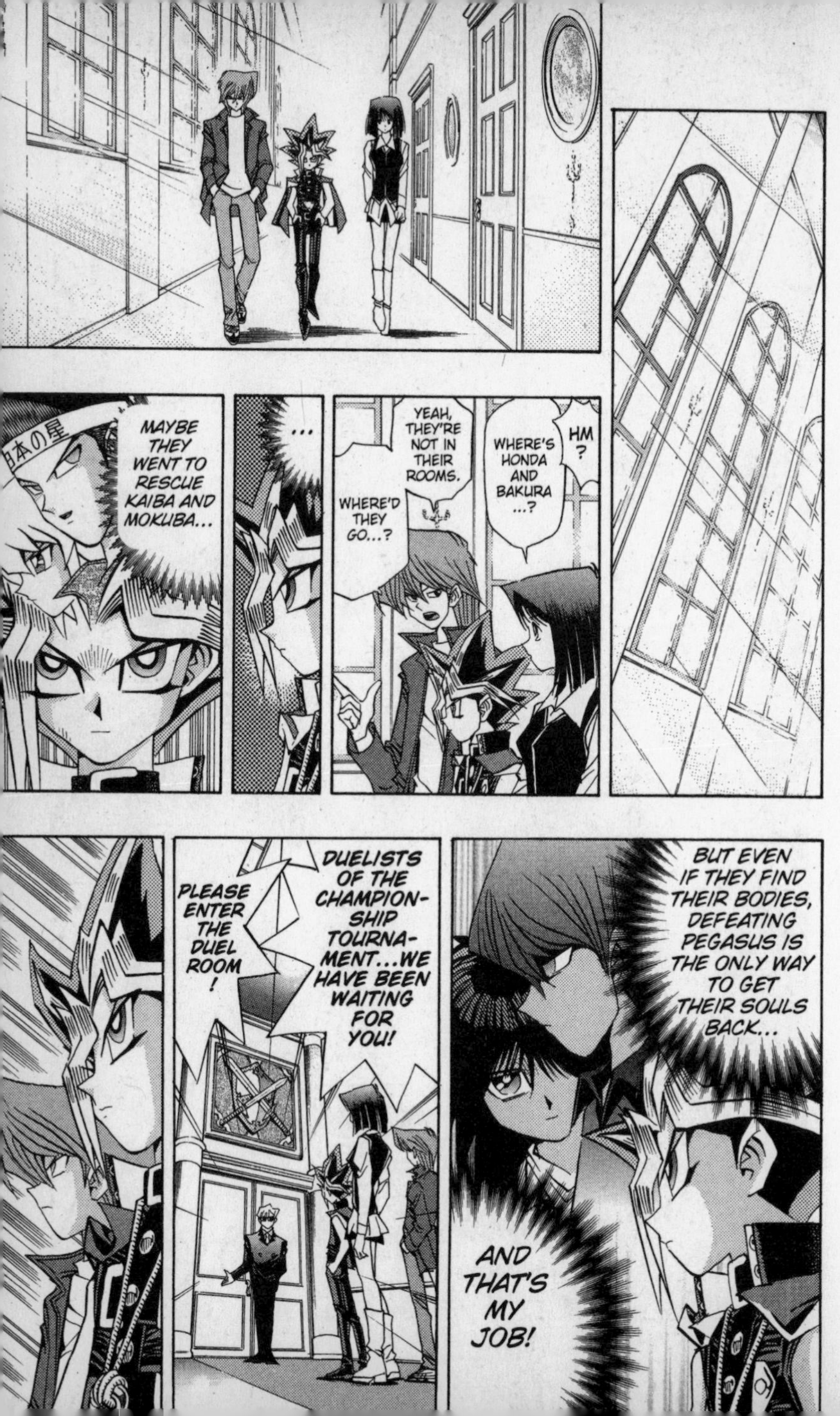
HM ?
WHERE'S HONDA AND BAKURA ...?
YEAH, THEY'RE NOT IN THEIR ROOMS.
WHERE'D THEY GO...?
...
MAYBE THEY WENT TO RESCUE KAIBA AND MOKUBA...
BUT EVEN IF THEY FIND THEIR BODIES, DEFEATING PEGASUS IS THE ONLY WAY TO GET THEIR SOULS BACK...
AND THAT'S MY JOB!
DUELISTS OF THE CHAMPION-SHIP TOURNA-MENT...WE HAVE BEEN WAITING FOR YOU!
PLEASE ENTER THE DUEL ROOM !

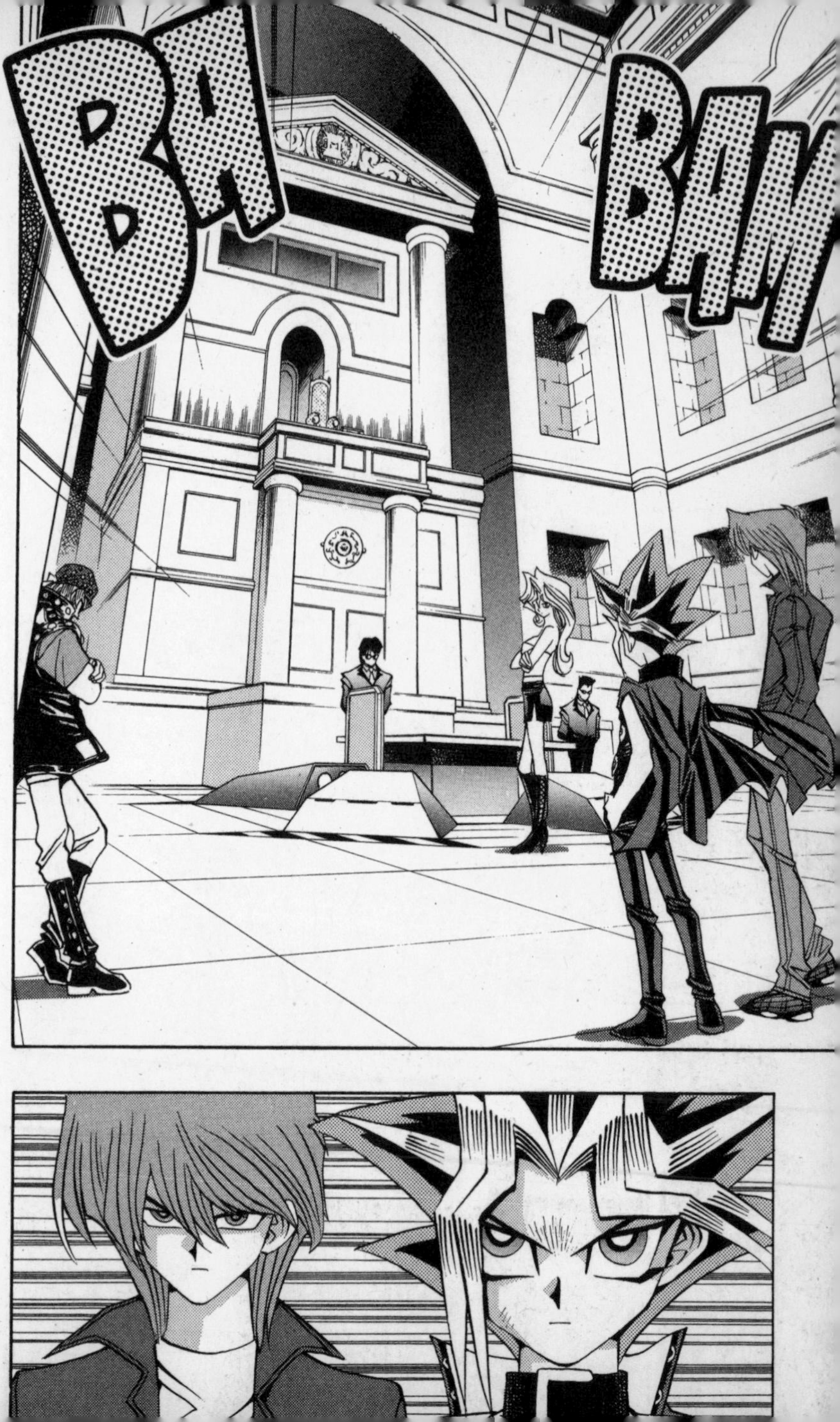
BAM
BA

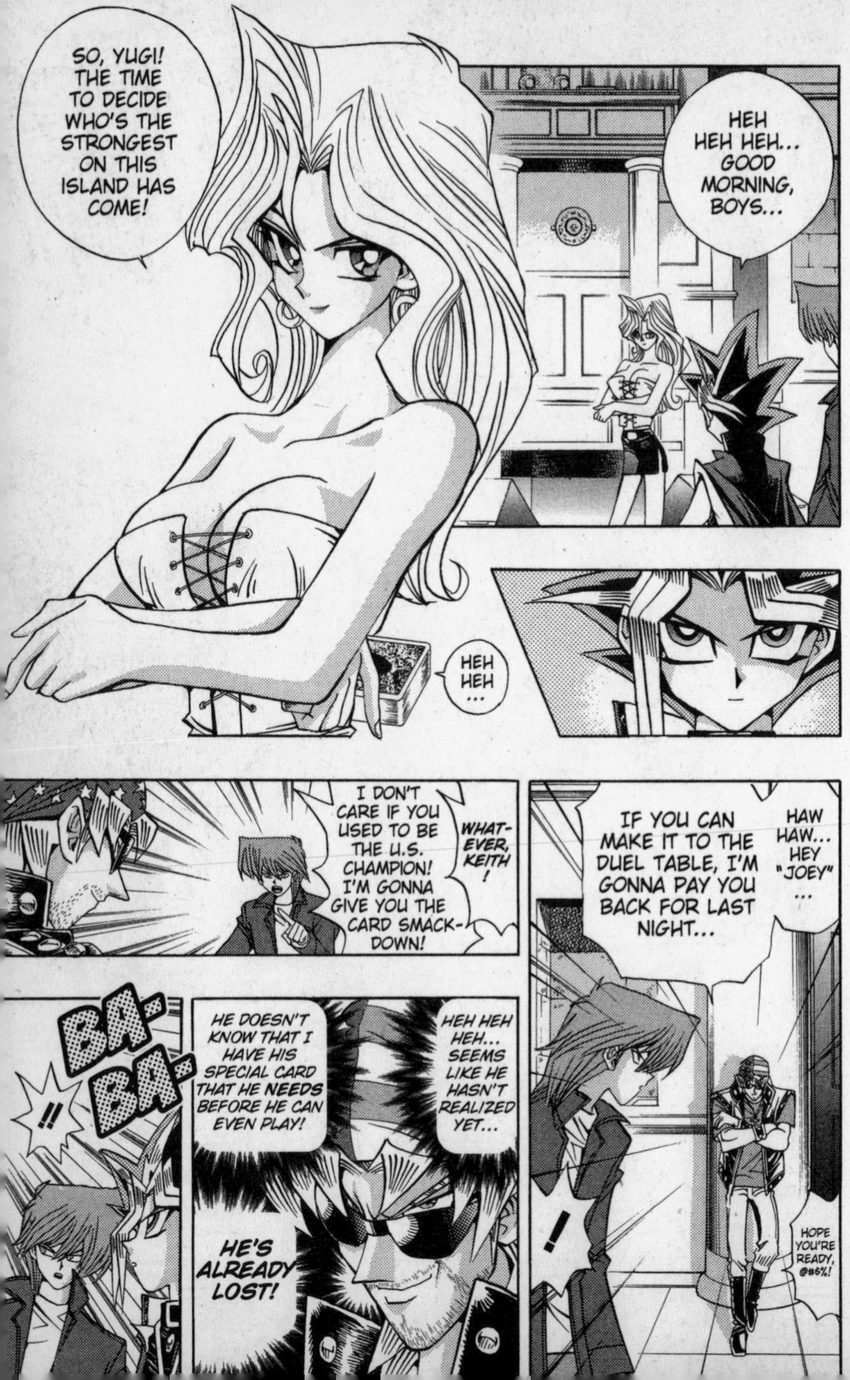
HEH HEH HEH... GOOD MORNING, BOYS...
HEH HEH ...
SO, YUGI! THE TIME TO DECIDE WHO'S THE STRONGEST ON THIS ISLAND HAS COME!
HAW HAW... HEY "JOEY" ...
IF YOU CAN MAKE IT TO THE DUEL TABLE, I'M GONNA PAY YOU BACK FOR LAST NIGHT...
HOPE YOU'RE READY, @#$%!
!
WHAT-EVER, KEITH!
I DON'T CARE IF YOU USED TO BE THE U.S. CHAMPION! I'M GONNA GIVE YOU THE CARD SMACK-DOWN!
HEH HEH HEH... SEEMS LIKE HE HASN'T REALIZED YET...
HE DOESN'T KNOW THAT I HAVE HIS SPECIAL CARD THAT HE NEEDS BEFORE HE CAN EVEN PLAY!
HE'S ALREADY LOST!
BA-BA-
!!

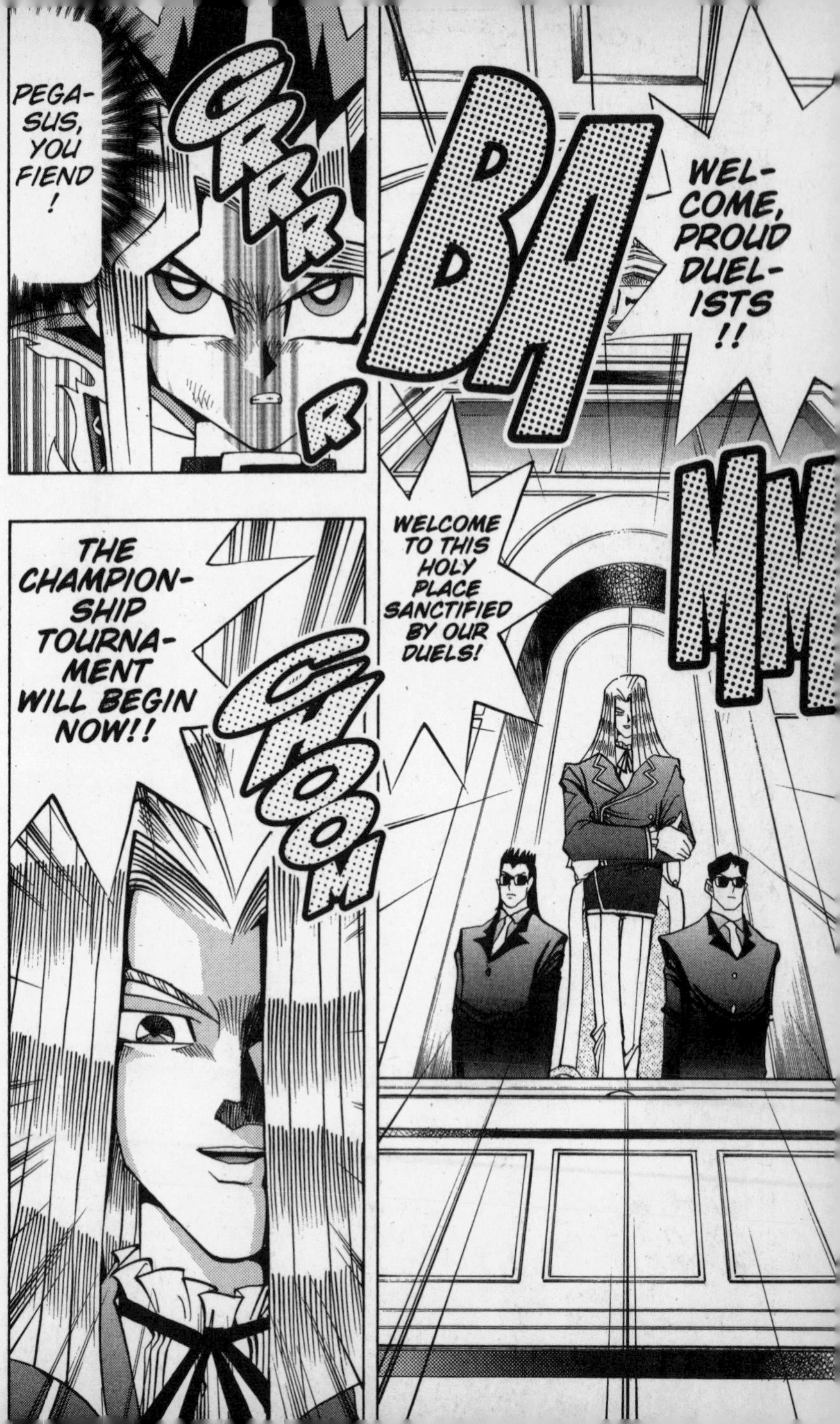
BAMM
WEL-COME, PROUD DUEL-ISTS!!
WELCOME TO THIS HOLY PLACE SANCTIFIED BY OUR DUELS!
PEGA-SUS, YOU FIEND!
GRRRR
THE CHAMPION-SHIP TOURNA-MENT WILL BEGIN NOW!!

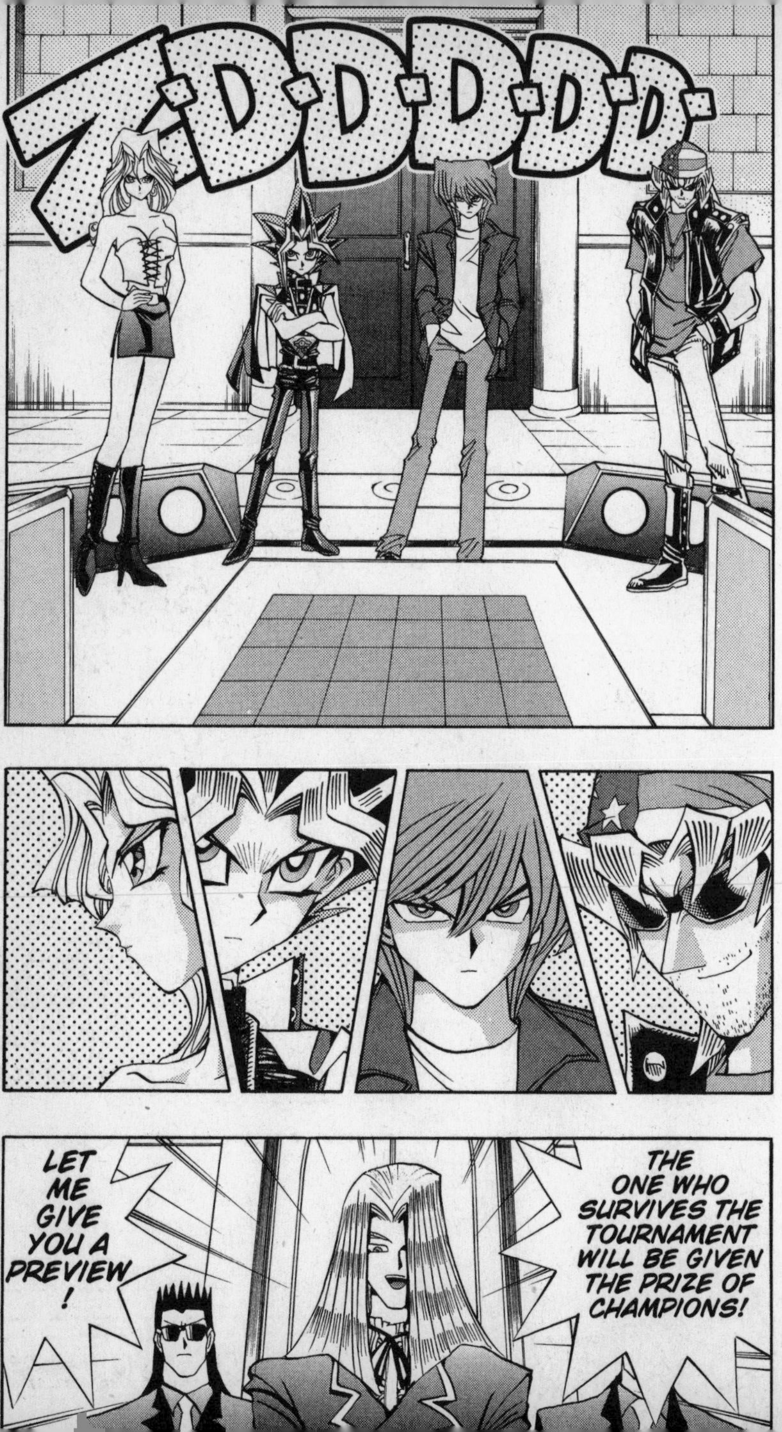
ZDDDDD
THE ONE WHO SURVIVES THE TOURNAMENT WILL BE GIVEN THE PRIZE OF CHAMPIONS!
LET ME GIVE YOU A PREVIEW!

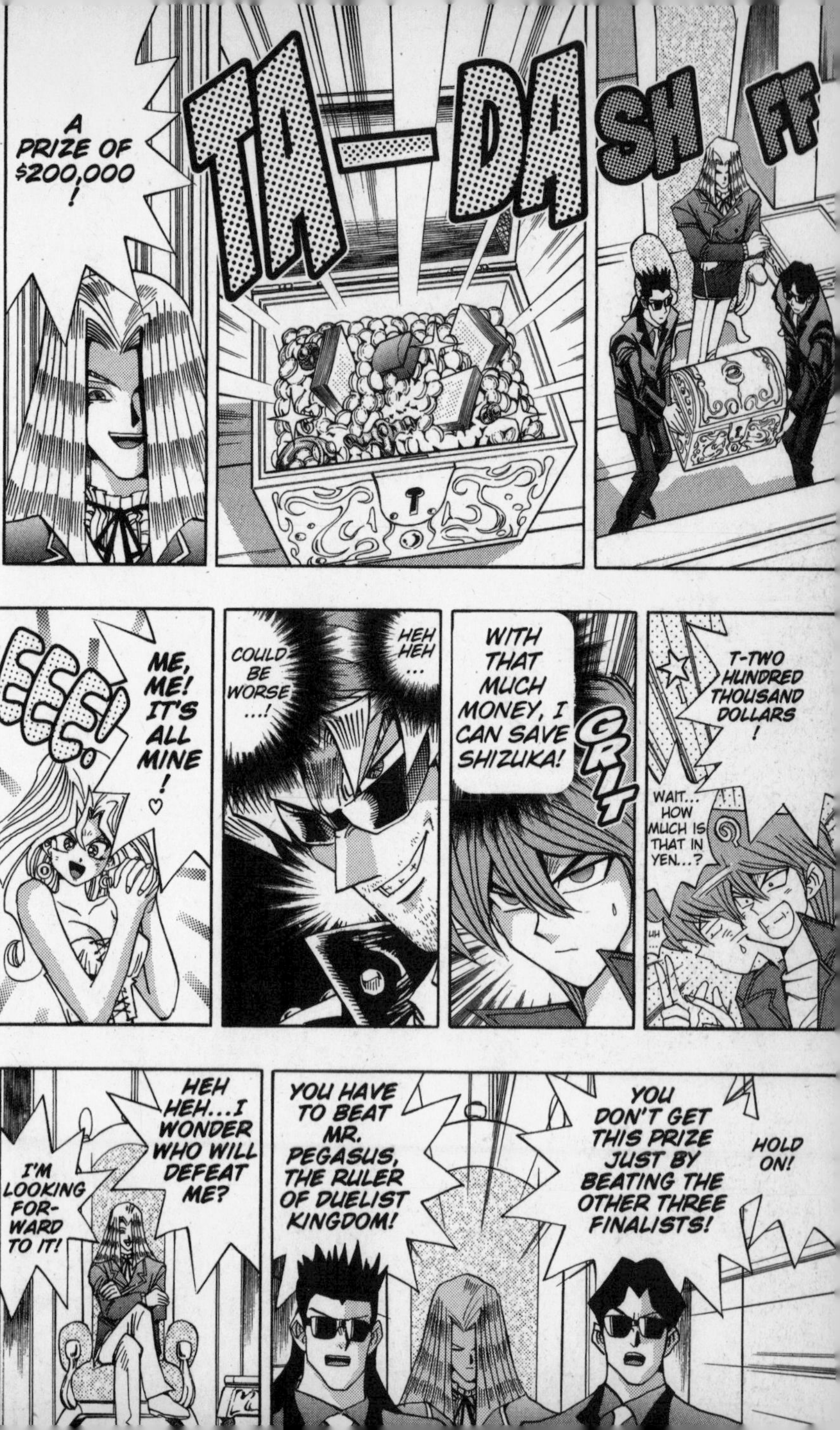
SH FF
TA-DA
A PRIZE OF $200,000!
T-TWO HUNDRED THOUSAND DOLLARS!
WAIT... HOW MUCH IS THAT IN YEN...?
UH...
WITH THAT MUCH MONEY, I CAN SAVE SHIZUKA!
GRIT
HEH HEH...
COULD BE WORSE...!
ME, ME! IT'S ALL MINE! ♡
EEE!
HOLD ON!
YOU DON'T GET THIS PRIZE JUST BY BEATING THE OTHER THREE FINALISTS!
YOU HAVE TO BEAT MR. PEGASUS, THE RULER OF DUELIST KINGDOM!
HEH HEH...I WONDER WHO WILL DEFEAT ME?
I'M LOOKING FOR-WARD TO IT!

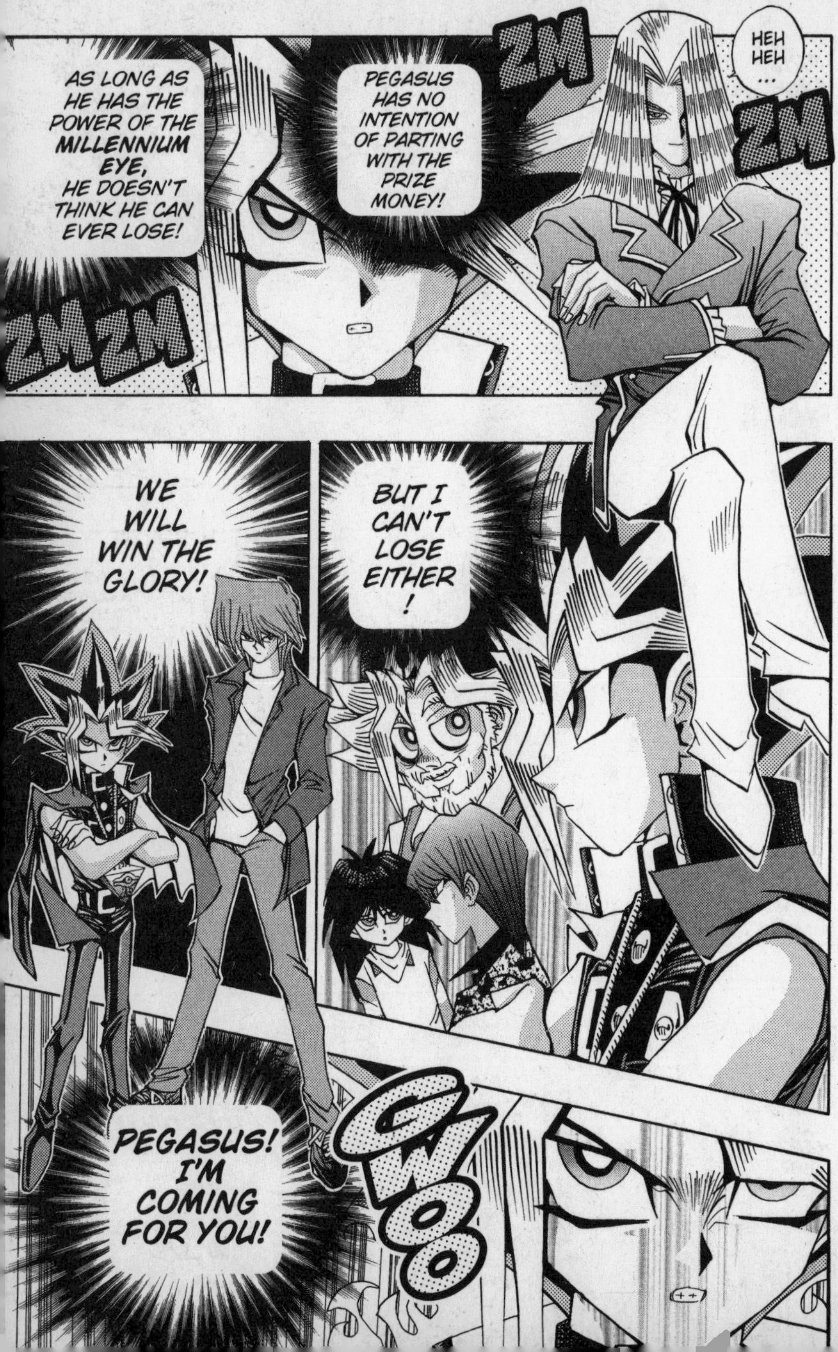
HEH HEH ...
ZM
ZM
ZM
PEGASUS HAS NO INTENTION OF PARTING WITH THE PRIZE MONEY!
AS LONG AS HE HAS THE POWER OF THE MILLENNIUM EYE, HE DOESN'T THINK HE CAN EVER LOSE!
ZM ZM
BUT I CAN'T LOSE EITHER!
WE WILL WIN THE GLORY!
GWOO
PEGASUS! I'M COMING FOR YOU!

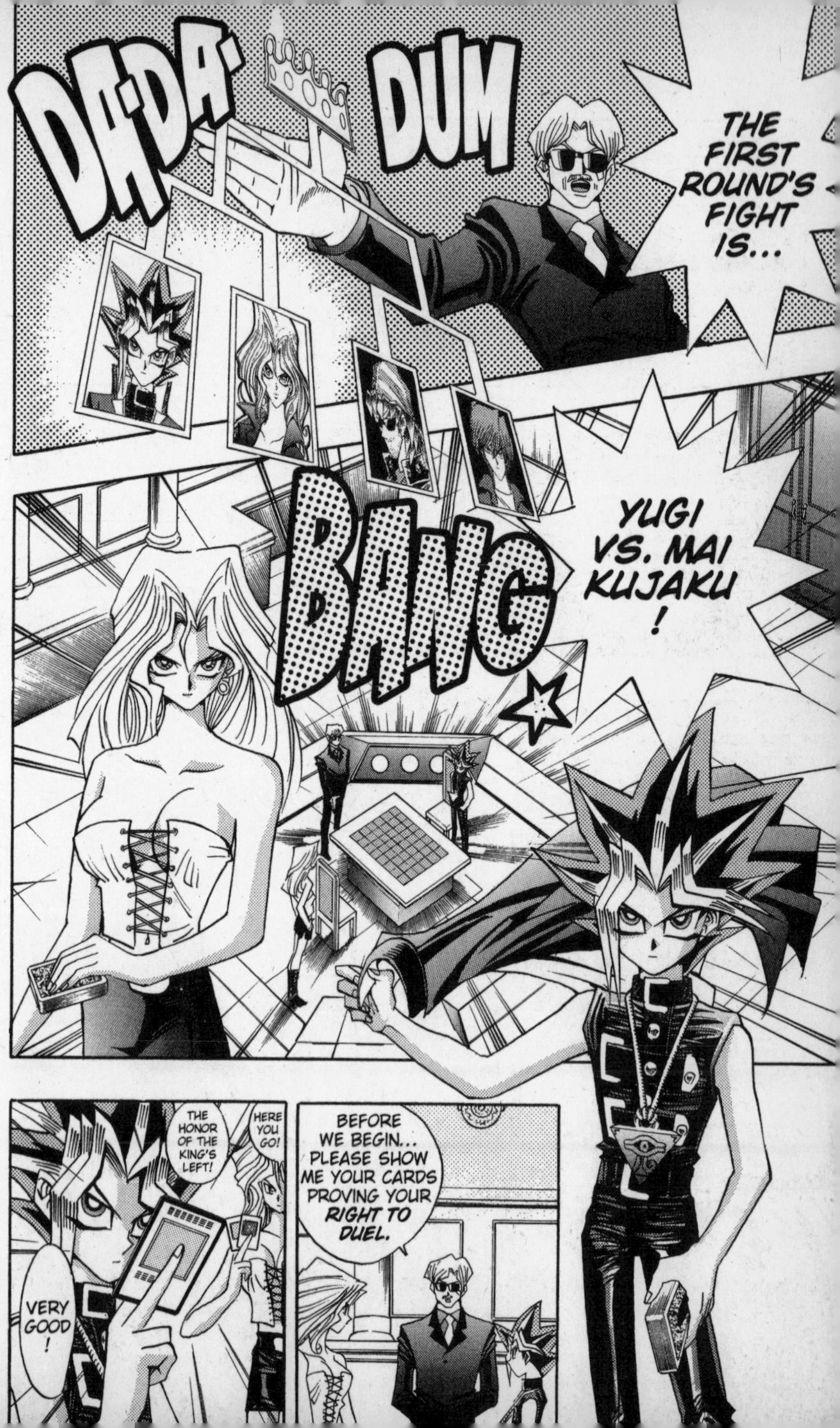
THE FIRST ROUND'S FIGHT IS...
DA-DA-DUM
YUGI VS. MAI KUJAKU!
BANG
BEFORE WE BEGIN... PLEASE SHOW ME YOUR CARDS PROVING YOUR RIGHT TO DUEL.
HERE YOU GO!
THE HONOR OF THE KING'S LEFT!
VERY GOOD!

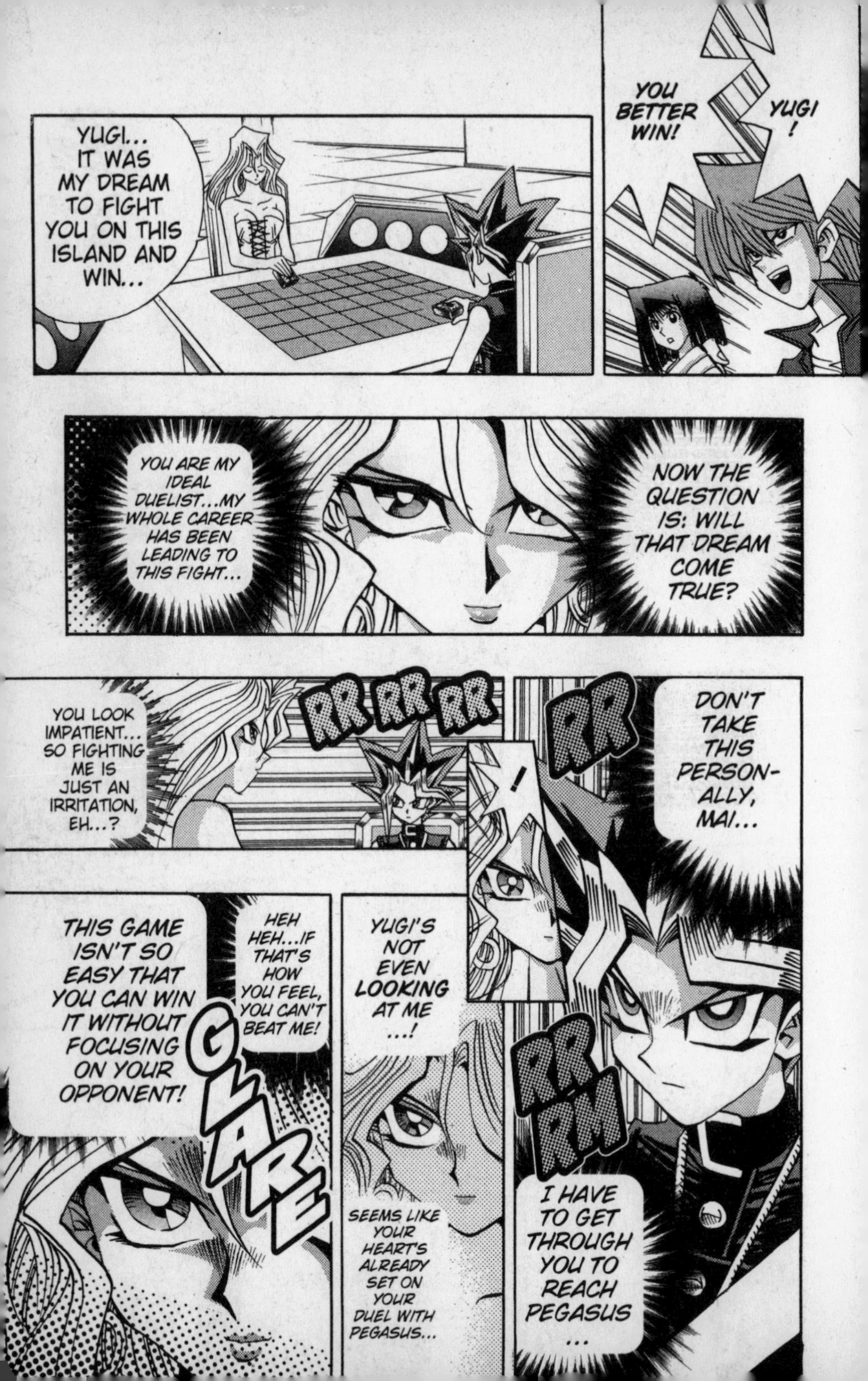
YUGI!
YOU BETTER WIN!
YUGI... IT WAS MY DREAM TO FIGHT YOU ON THIS ISLAND AND WIN...
NOW THE QUESTION IS: WILL THAT DREAM COME TRUE?
YOU ARE MY IDEAL DUELIST...MY WHOLE CAREER HAS BEEN LEADING TO THIS FIGHT...
DON'T TAKE THIS PERSON-ALLY, MAI...
RR
!
RR RM
I HAVE TO GET THROUGH YOU TO REACH PEGASUS...
RR RR RR
YOU LOOK IMPATIENT... SO FIGHTING ME IS JUST AN IRRITATION, EH...?
YUGI'S NOT EVEN LOOKING AT ME...!
SEEMS LIKE YOUR HEART'S ALREADY SET ON YOUR DUEL WITH PEGASUS...
HEH HEH...IF THAT'S HOW YOU FEEL, YOU CAN'T BEAT ME!
THIS GAME ISN'T SO EASY THAT YOU CAN WIN IT WITHOUT FOCUSING ON YOUR OPPONENT!
GLARE

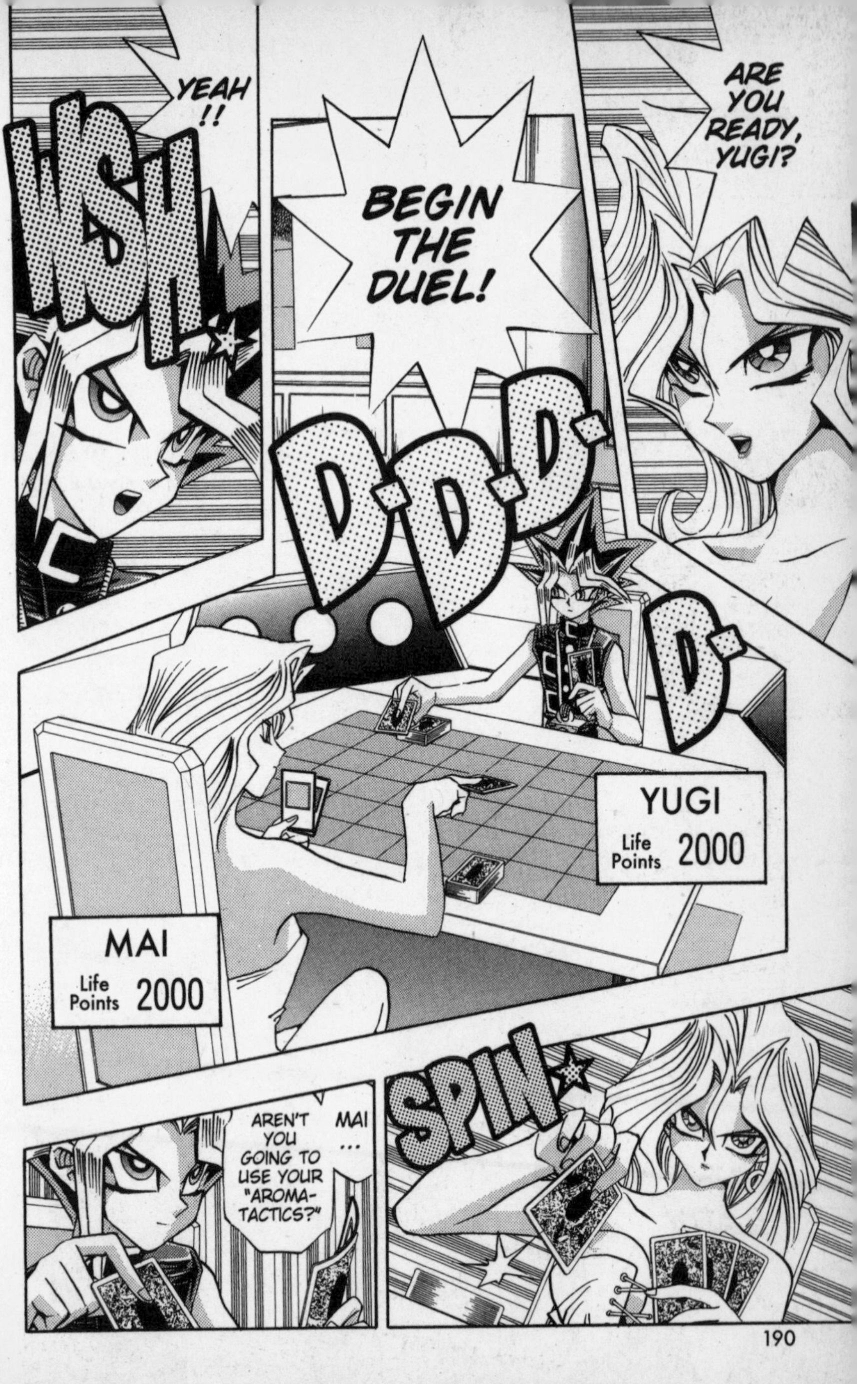
ARE YOU READY, YUGI?
BEGIN THE DUEL!
YEAH!!
WISH
D-D-D-D-
YUGI
Life Points 2000
MAI
Life Points 2000
SPIN
MAI...
AREN'T YOU GOING TO USE YOUR "AROMA-TACTICS?"

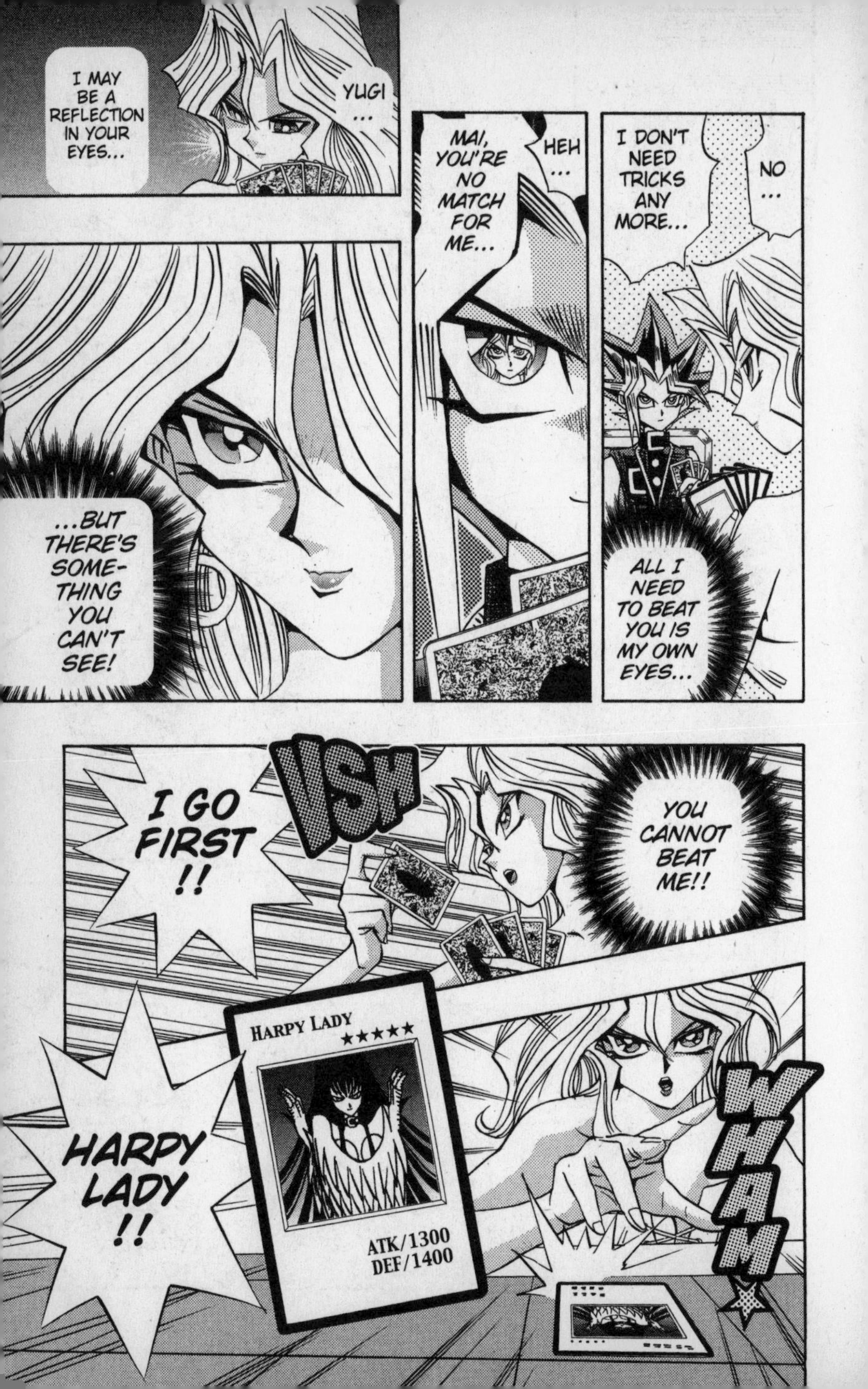
NO...
I DON'T NEED TRICKS ANY MORE...
ALL I NEED TO BEAT YOU IS MY OWN EYES...
HEH...
MAI, YOU'RE NO MATCH FOR ME...
YUGI...
I MAY BE A REFLECTION IN YOUR EYES...
...BUT THERE'S SOMETHING YOU CAN'T SEE!
YOU CANNOT BEAT ME!!
VSH
I GO FIRST!!
WHAM
HARPY LADY ★★★★★
ATK/1300
DEF/1400
HARPY LADY!!

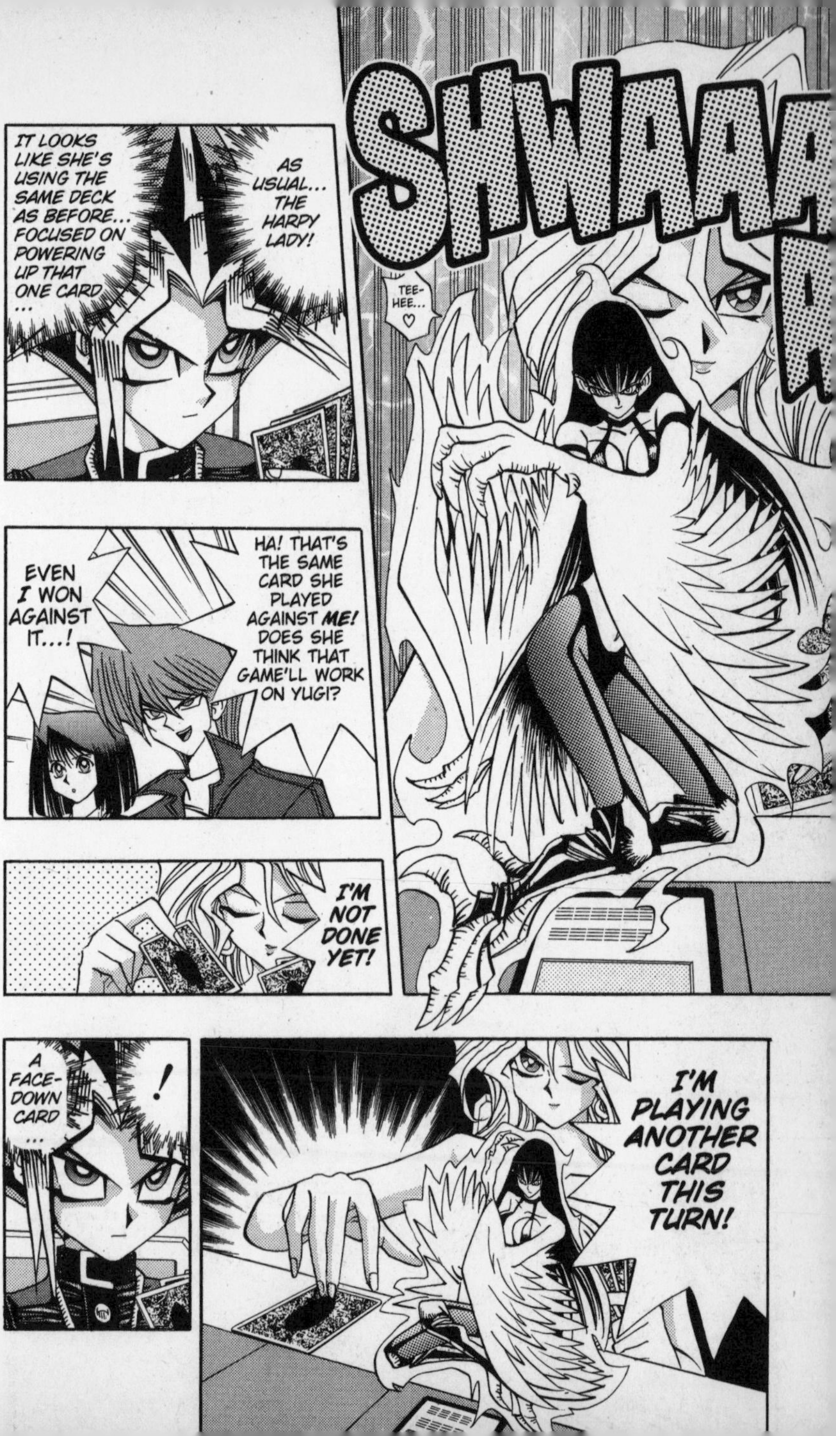
SHWAAA
TEE-HEE... ♡
AS USUAL... THE HARPY LADY!
IT LOOKS LIKE SHE'S USING THE SAME DECK AS BEFORE... FOCUSED ON POWERING UP THAT ONE CARD...
HA! THAT'S THE SAME CARD SHE PLAYED AGAINST ME! DOES SHE THINK THAT GAME'LL WORK ON YUGI?
EVEN I WON AGAINST IT...!
I'M NOT DONE YET!
I'M PLAYING ANOTHER CARD THIS TURN!
!
A FACE-DOWN CARD...

READ THIS WAY

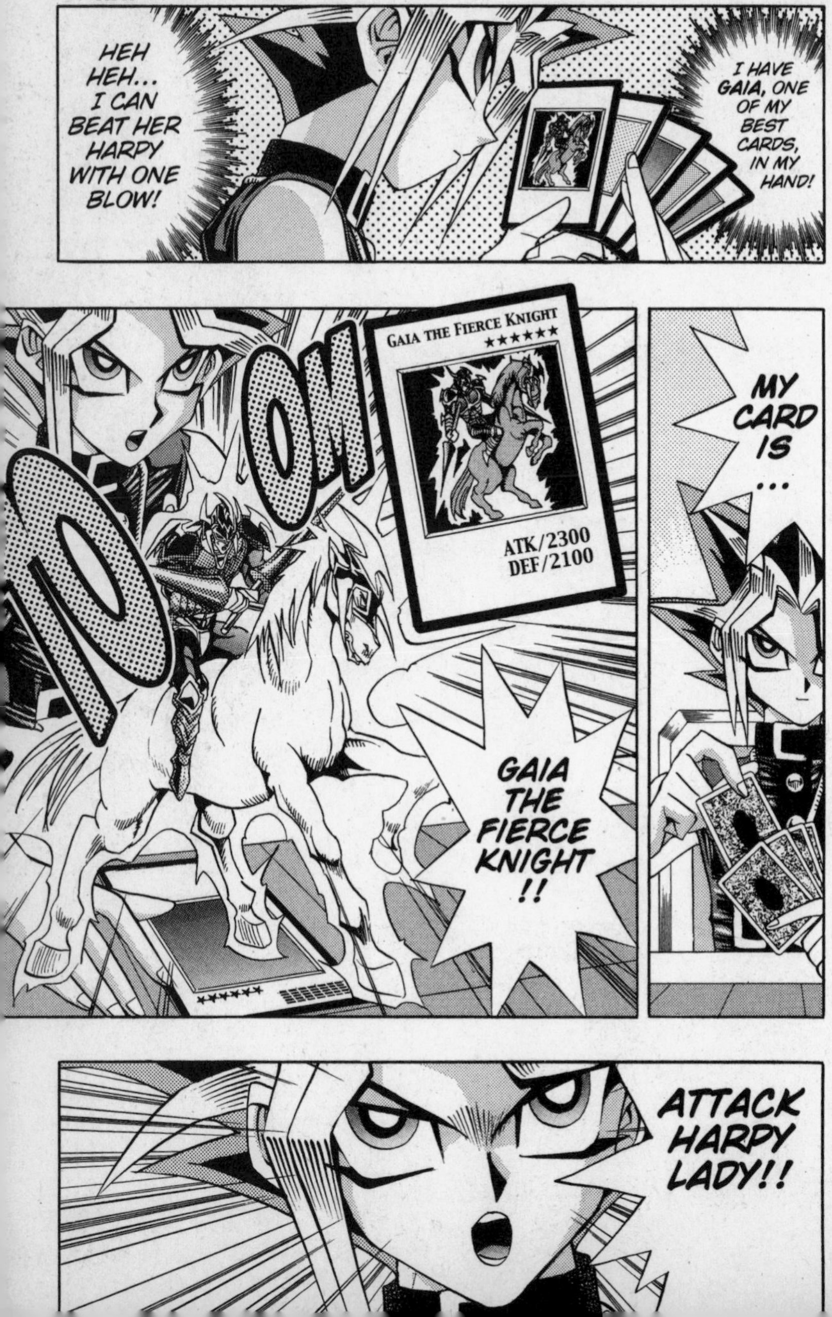
I HAVE GAIA, ONE OF MY BEST CARDS, IN MY HAND!
HEH HEH... I CAN BEAT HER HARPY WITH ONE BLOW!
MY CARD IS ...
GAIA THE FIERCE KNIGHT
ATK/2300
DEF/2100
GAIA THE FIERCE KNIGHT !!
ATTACK HARPY LADY!!

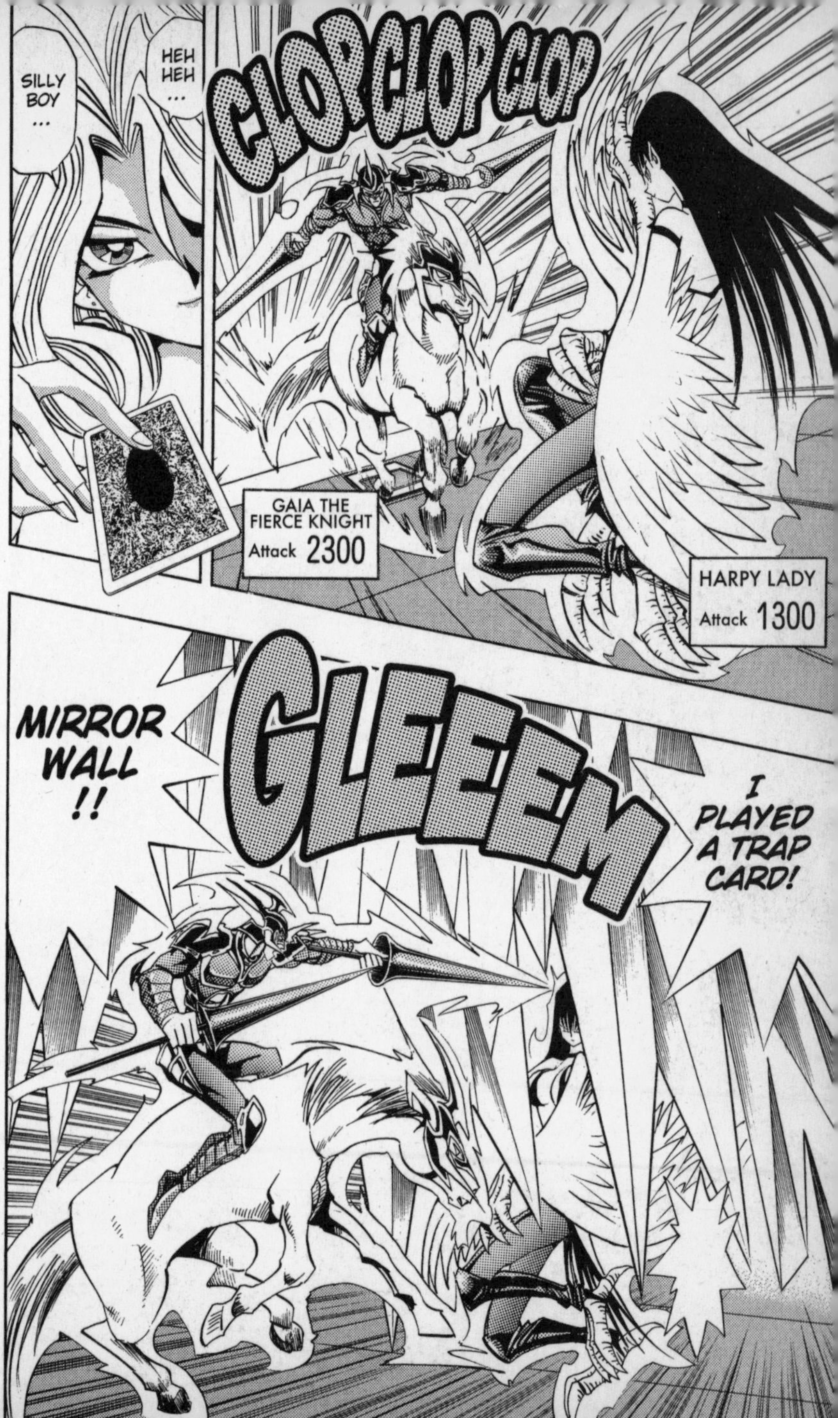
CLOP CLOP CLOP
HARPY LADY
Attack 1300
GAIA THE FIERCE KNIGHT
Attack 2300
HEH HEH ...
SILLY BOY ...
I PLAYED A TRAP CARD!
GLEEEM
MIRROR WALL !!

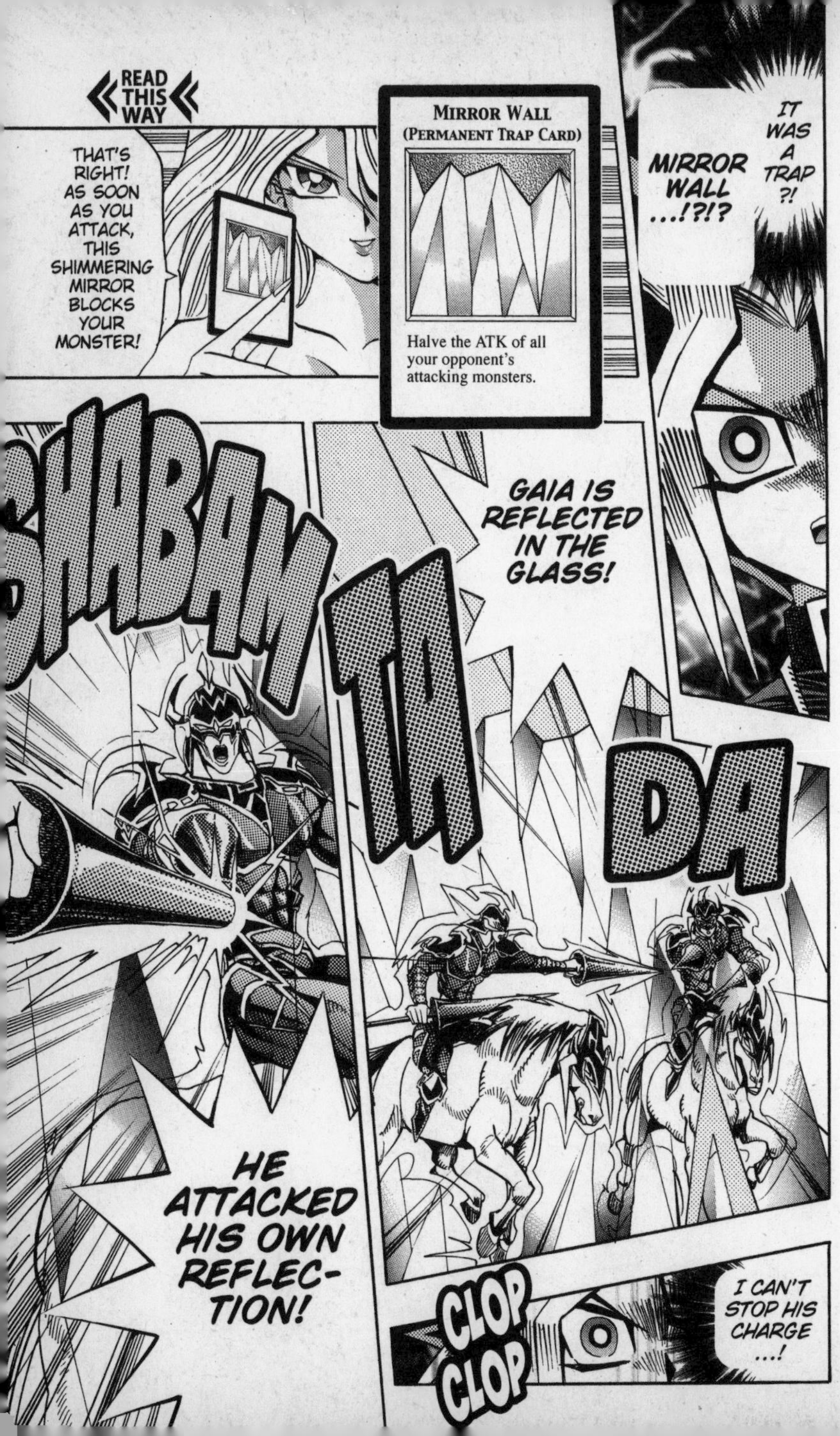
READ THIS WAY
IT WAS A TRAP ?!
MIRROR WALL ...!?!?
THAT'S RIGHT! AS SOON AS YOU ATTACK, THIS SHIMMERING MIRROR BLOCKS YOUR MONSTER!
MIRROR WALL
(PERMANENT TRAP CARD)
Halve the ATK of all your opponent's attacking monsters.
GAIA IS REFLECTED IN THE GLASS!
TA
DA
I CAN'T STOP HIS CHARGE ...!
CLOP CLOP
SHABAM
HE ATTACKED HIS OWN REFLEC-TION!

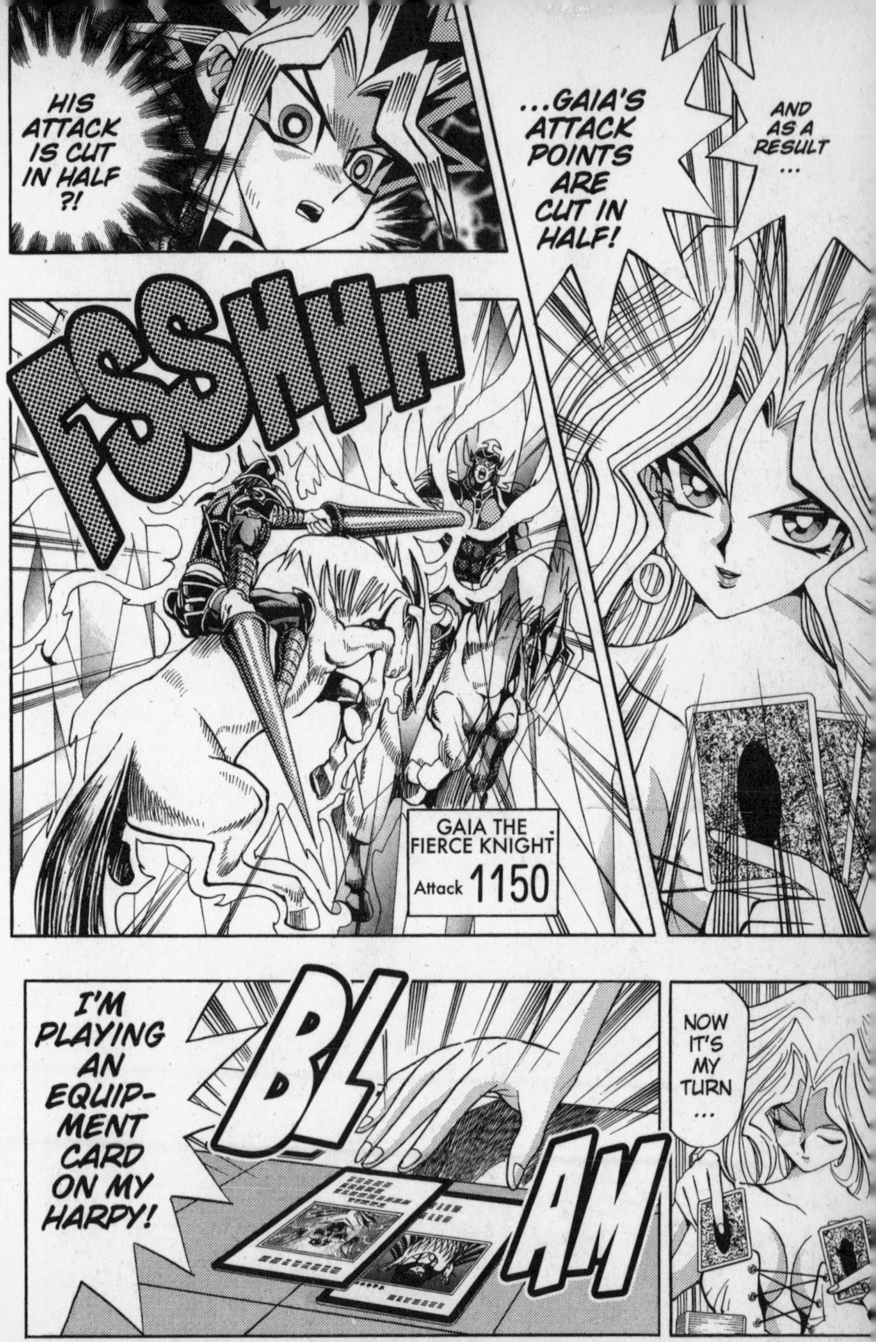
AND AS A RESULT ...
...GAIA'S ATTACK POINTS ARE CUT IN HALF!
HIS ATTACK IS CUT IN HALF ?!
FSSHHH
GAIA THE FIERCE KNIGHT
Attack 1150
NOW IT'S MY TURN ...
I'M PLAYING AN EQUIP-MENT CARD ON MY HARPY!
BLAM

TO BE CONTINUED IN *YU-GI-OH!: DUELIST* VOL. 7!

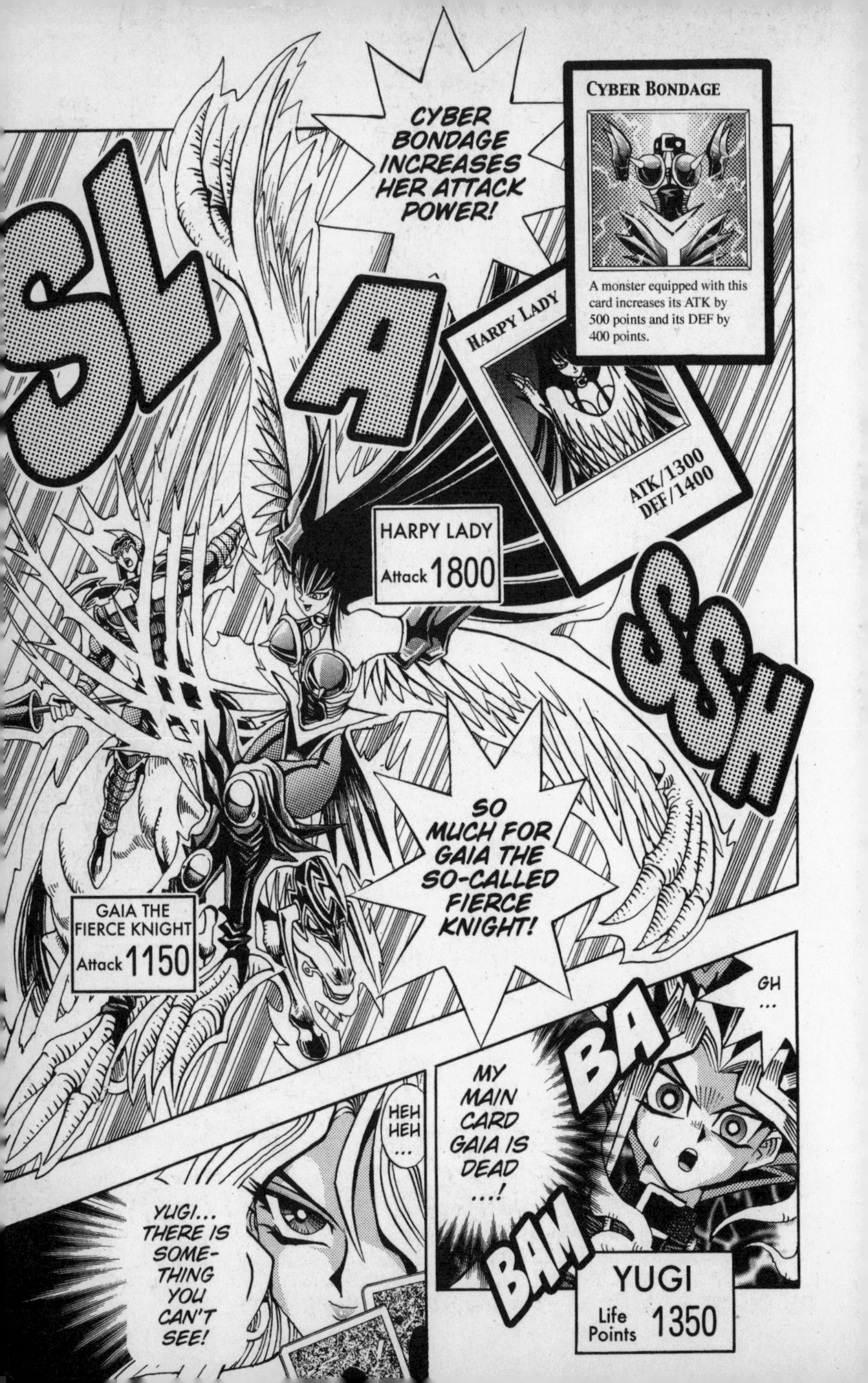
CYBER BONDAGE
A monster equipped with this card increases its ATK by 500 points and its DEF by 400 points.
CYBER BONDAGE INCREASES HER ATTACK POWER!
SL A SSH
HARPY LADY
ATK/1300 DEF/1400
HARPY LADY Attack 1800
SO MUCH FOR GAIA THE SO-CALLED FIERCE KNIGHT!
GAIA THE FIERCE KNIGHT Attack 1150
GH ...
BA
MY MAIN CARD GAIA IS DEAD ...!
BAM
YUGI Life Points 1350
HEH HEH ...
YUGI... THERE IS SOME-THING YOU CAN'T SEE!

MASTER OF THE CARDS

The "Duel Monsters" card game first appeared in volume two of the original **Yu-Gi-Oh!** graphic novel series. but it's in **Yu-Gi-Oh!: Duelist** (originally printed in Japan as volumes 8-31 of **Yu-Gi-Oh!**) that it gets really important. As many fans know, some of the card names are different between the English and Japanese versions. In case you play the game, or you're interested in playing, here's a rundown of some of the cards in this graphic novel. Some cards only appear in the **Yu-Gi-Oh!** video games, not in the actual collectible card game.

FIRST APPEARANCE IN THIS VOLUME	JAPANESE CARD NAME	ENGLISH CARD NAME
p.52	*Tamashii no Rôgoku* (Soul Prison)	Soul Prison (NOTE: Not a real game card)
p.57	*Blue-Eyes White Dragon*	Blue-Eyes White Dragon
p.59	*Toon Alligator*	Toon Alligator
p.60	*Rude Kaiser*	Rude Kaiser
p.61	*Parrot Dragon*	Parrot Dragon

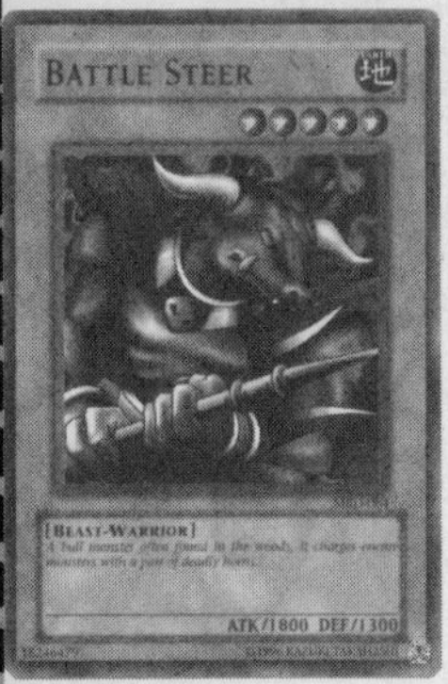
BATTLE STEER
[BEAST-WARRIOR]
ATK/1800 DEF/1300

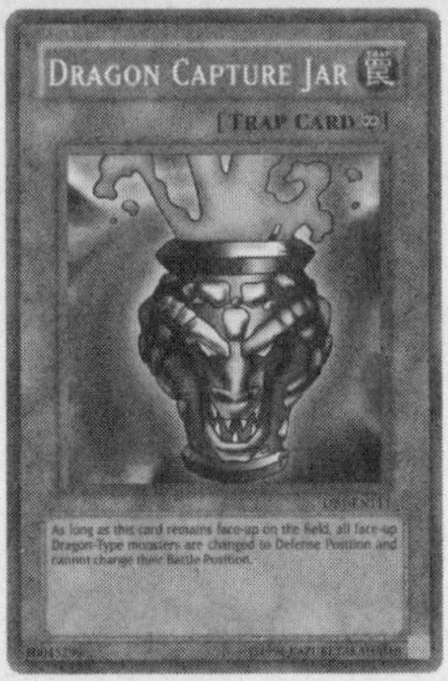
DRAGON CAPTURE JAR
[TRAP CARD]

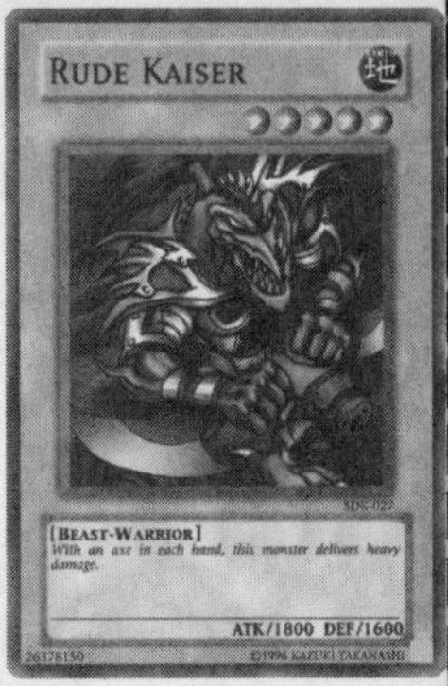
RUDE KAISER
[BEAST-WARRIOR]
With an axe in each hand, this monster delivers heavy damage.
ATK/1800 DEF/1600

FIRST APPEARANCE IN THIS VOLUME	JAPANESE CARD NAME	ENGLISH CARD NAME
p.62	*Saiminjutsu* (Hypnotism)	Mesmeric Control
p.64	*Yogen* (Prophecy)	Prophecy
p.65	*Shi no Deck Hakai* (Deck Destruction of Death) [NOTE: Symbol on card means "death"]	Crush Card
p.71	*Yami Dôkeshi no Saggi* (Saggi the Dark Clown)	Saggi the Dark Clown

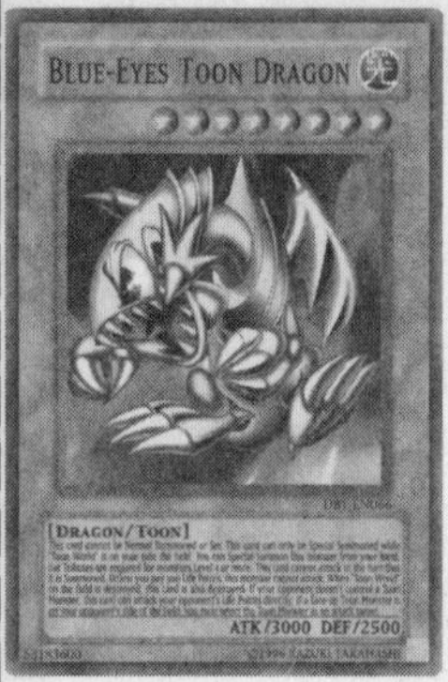
BLUE-EYES TOON DRAGON
[DRAGON/TOON]
ATK/3000 DEF/2500
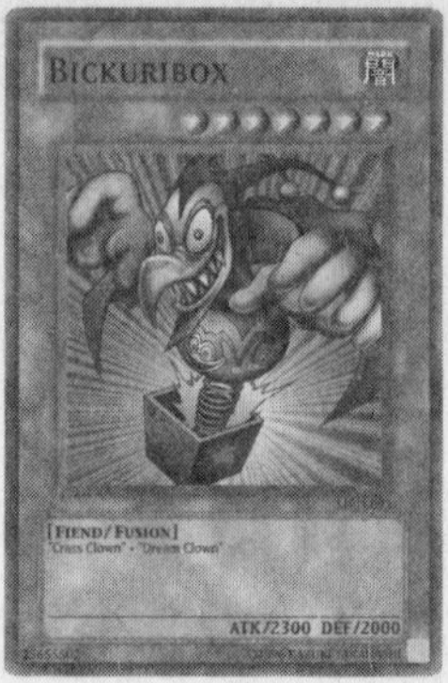
BICKURIBOX
[FIEND/FUSION]
ATK/2300 DEF/2000
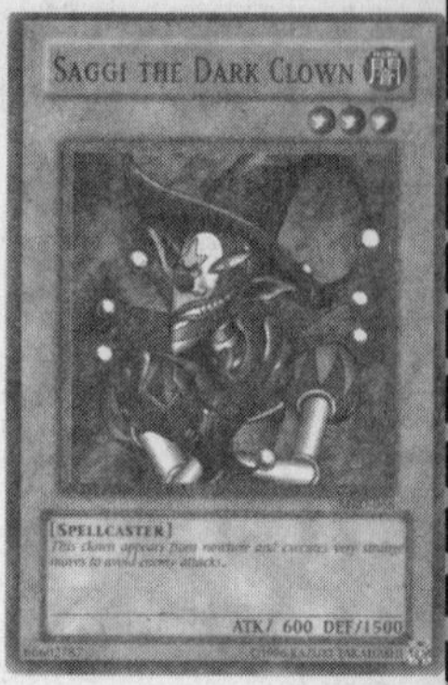
SAGGI THE DARK CLOWN
[SPELLCASTER]
ATK/ 600 DEF/1500

FIRST APPEARANCE IN THIS VOLUME	JAPANESE CARD NAME	ENGLISH CARD NAME
p.72	*Dark Rabbit*	Dark Rabbit
p.74	*Yami Energy* (Dark Energy)	Negative Energy (NOTE: Not a real game card. This card has different art and effects from the game card named "Dark Energy.")
p.77	*Minotaurus*	Battle Ox
p.79	*Toon World*	Toon World
p.83	*Blue-Eyes Toon Dragon*	Blue-Eyes Toon Dragon

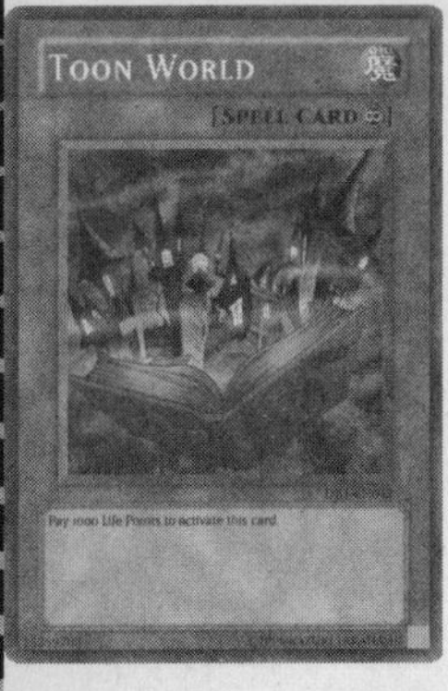
TOON WORLD
[SPELL CARD]
Pay 1000 Life Points to activate this card.

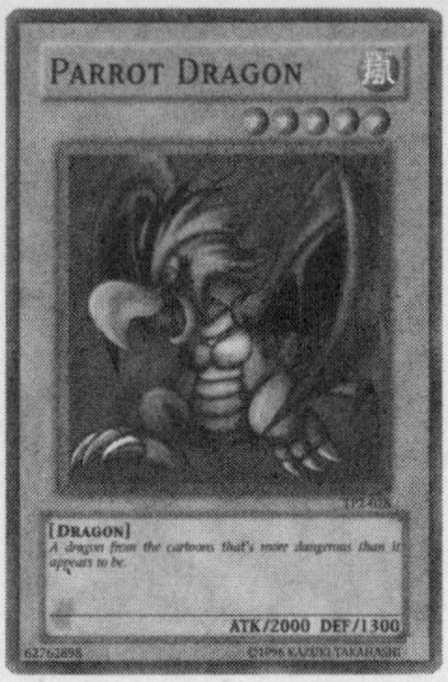
PARROT DRAGON
[DRAGON]
A dragon from the cartoons that's more dangerous than it appears to be.
ATK/2000 DEF/1300

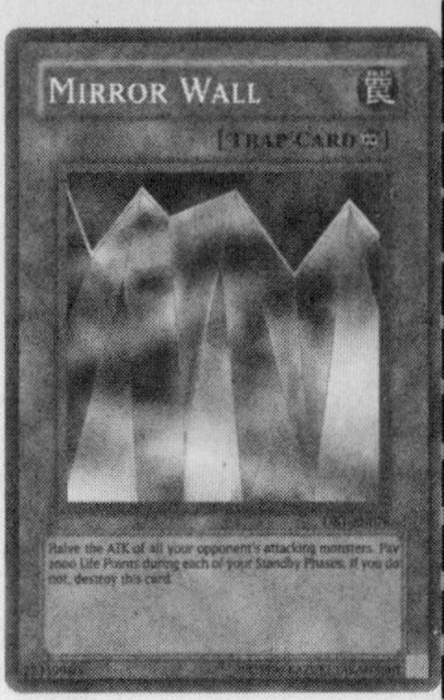
MIRROR WALL
[TRAP CARD]

FIRST APPEARANCE IN THIS VOLUME	JAPANESE CARD NAME	ENGLISH CARD NAME
p.96	*Shine Castle*	Shine Palace
p.98	*Kôgeki no Muryokuka* (Nullification of Attack)	Negate Attack
p.100	*Yami no Jubaku* (Binding Curse/Cursed Chains of Darkness)	Shadow Spell
p.102	*Dragonzoku Fûin no Tsubo* (Dragon Clan Sealing Jar)	Dragon Capture Jar

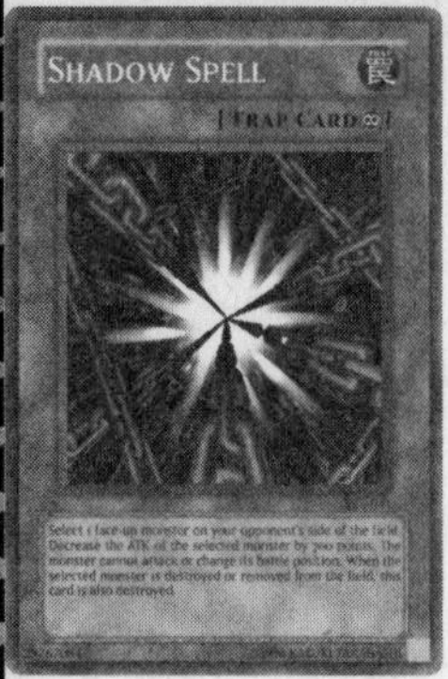
SHADOW SPELL
TRAP CARD
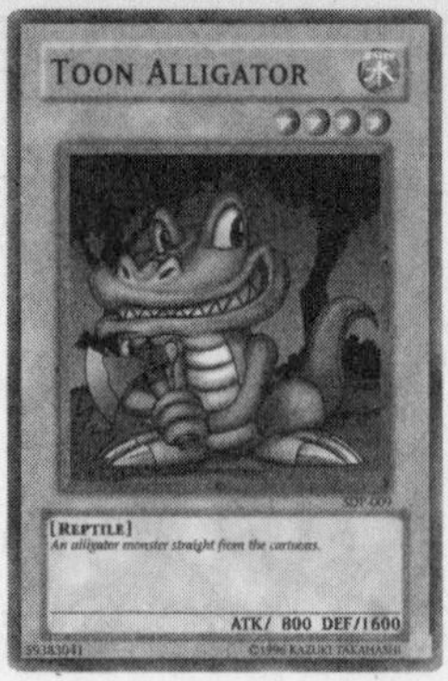
TOON ALLIGATOR
[REPTILE]
An alligator monster straight from the cartoons.
ATK/ 800 DEF/1600
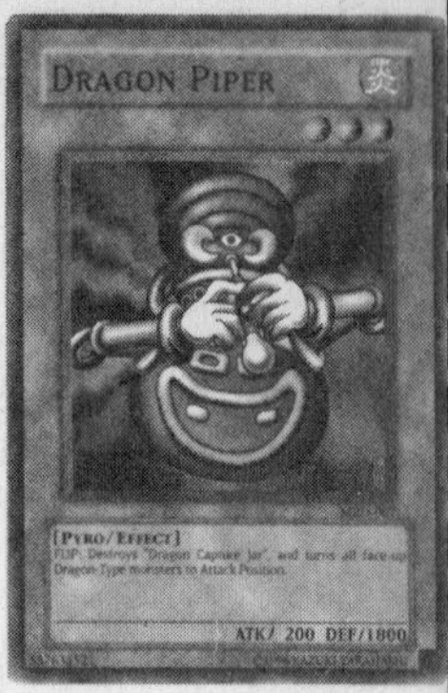
DRAGON PIPER
[PYRO/EFFECT]
ATK/ 200 DEF/1800

FIRST APPEARANCE IN THIS VOLUME	JAPANESE CARD NAME	ENGLISH CARD NAME
p.104	*Fukushû no Swordstalker* (Swordstalker of Vengeance)	Swordstalker
p.105	*Tsubo Majin* (Jar Golem/Djinn)	Dragon Piper
p.108	*Copycat*	Doppelganger (NOTE: Not a real game card)
p.111	*Shisha Sosei* (Resurrection of the Dead)	Monster Reborn
p.112	*Devil Box*	Bickuribox (NOTE: "Bickuribox" is Japanese for "Jack-in-the-Box")

GAIA THE FIERCE KNIGHT

[WARRIOR]
A knight whose horse travels faster than the wind. His battle-charge is a force to be reckoned with.

ATK/2300 DEF/2100

SWORDSTALKER

[WARRIOR]
A monster formed by the vengeful souls of those who passed away in battle.

ATK/2000 DEF/1600

HARPIE LADY

[WINGED BEAST]
This razor-sharp animal with wings is beautiful to watch but deadly in battle.

ATK/1300 DEF/1400

FIRST APPEARANCE IN THIS VOLUME	JAPANESE CARD NAME	ENGLISH CARD NAME
p.191	*Harpie Lady*	Harpy Lady
p.193	*Ankoku Kishi Gaia* (Dark Knight Gaia)	Gaia the Fierce Knight
P.195	*Ginmaku no Mirror Wall* (Mirror Wall of the Silver Screen)	Mirror Wall
p.197	Cyber Bondage	Cyber Bondage (NOTE: Not a real game card. Called "Cyber Shield" in the video games.)

IN THE NEXT VOLUME...

Mai Kujaku has always wanted to fight Yugi, and now she's got her chance! Can Yugi beat her harpies and their pet dragon? Then, Jonouchi fights "Bandit" Keith Howard, America's most unscrupulous gamer, in a battle which pits six-guns and slot machines against Jonouchi's warrior monsters! It's the final rounds before the fight with Pegasus, and only one of four will survive!

COMING AUGUST 2005!

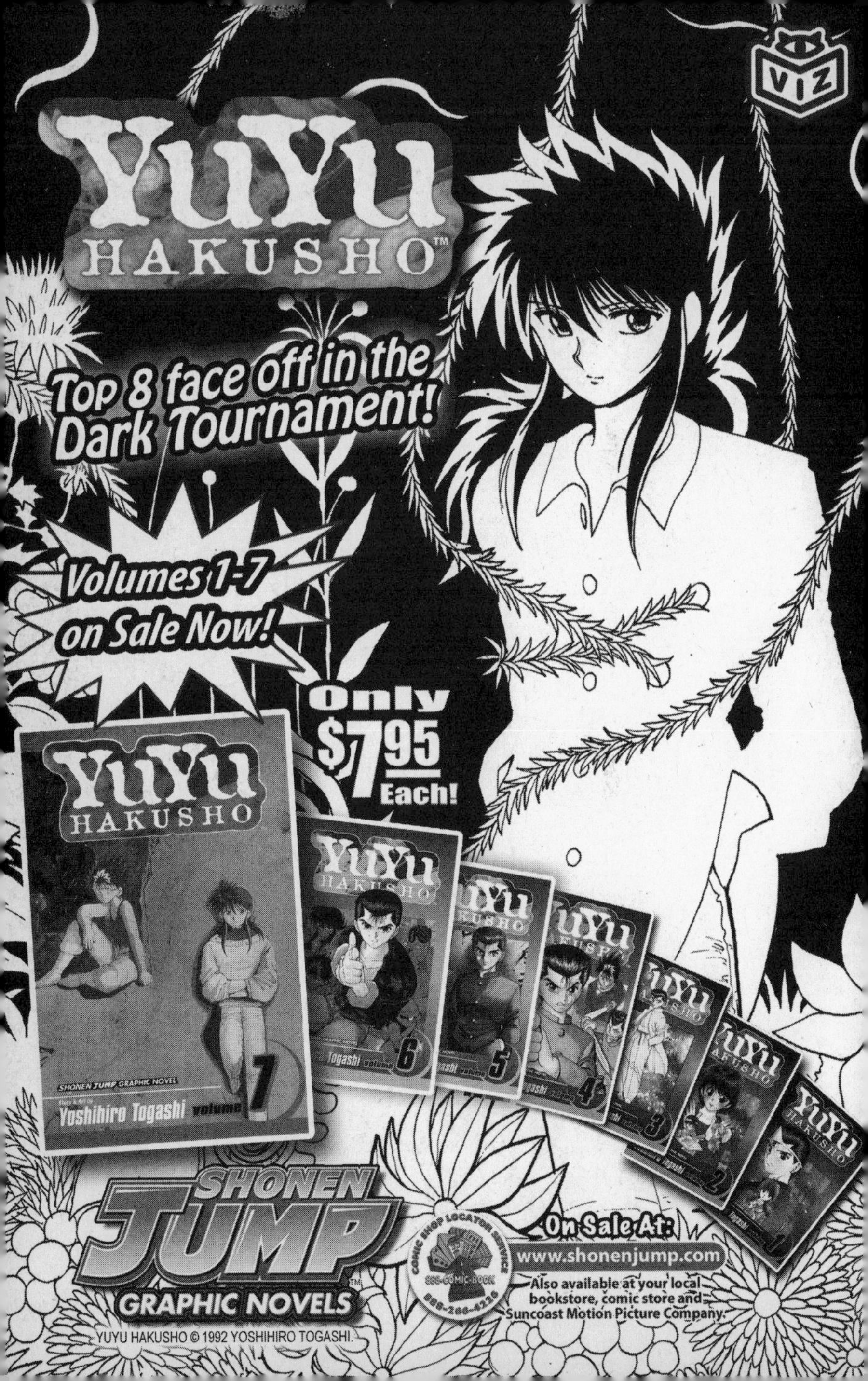

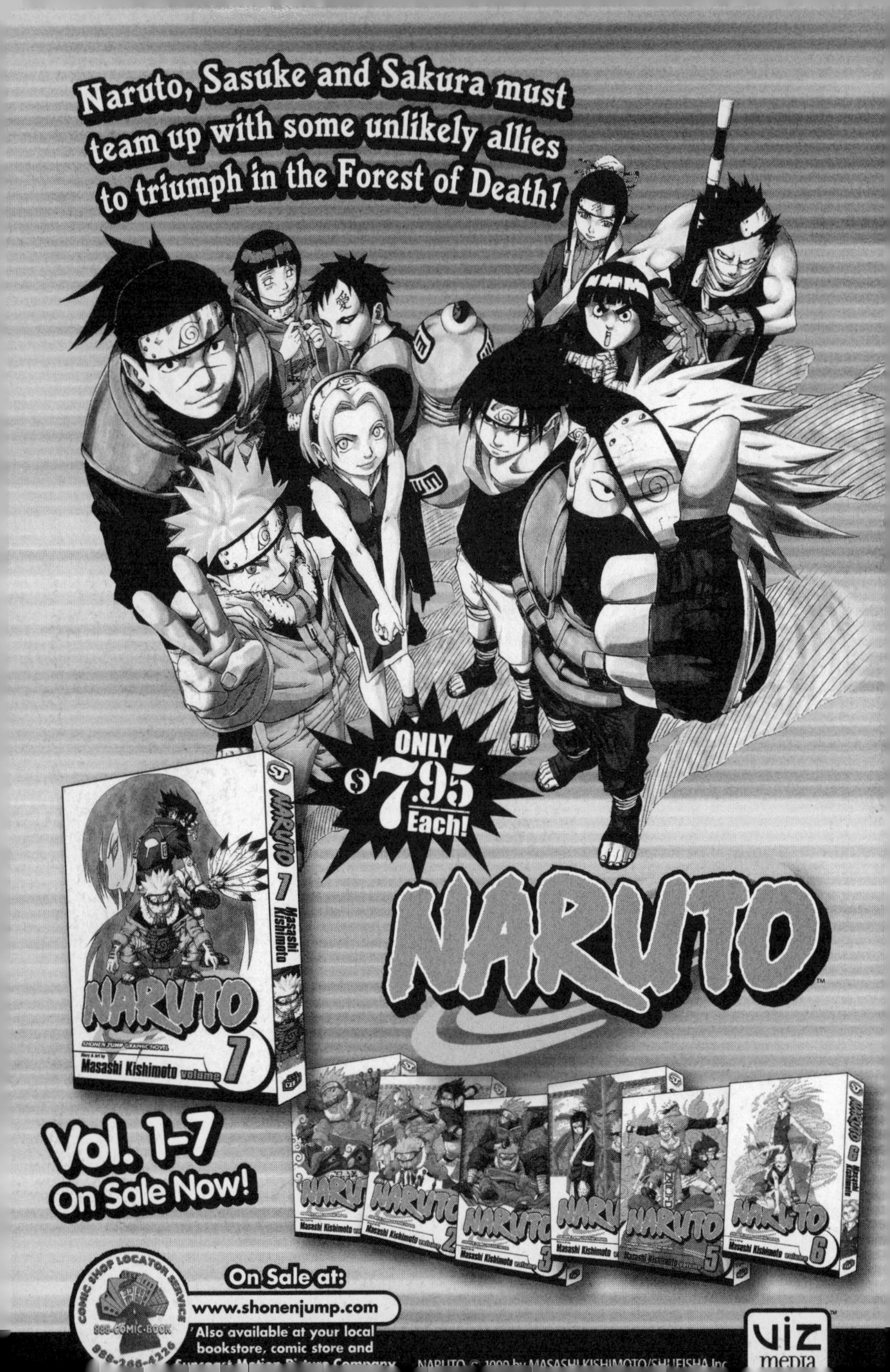

Naruto, Sasuke and Sakura must team up with some unlikely allies to triumph in the Forest of Death!
ONLY $7.95 Each!
NARUTO™
NARUTO 7 Masashi Kishimoto
NARUTO SHONEN JUMP GRAPHIC NOVEL Story & Art by Masashi Kishimoto volume 7
Vol. 1-7 On Sale Now!
COMIC SHOP LOCATOR SERVICE 888-COMIC-BOOK 888-266-4226
On Sale at:
www.shonenjump.com
Also available at your local bookstore, comic store and
NARUTO © 1999 by MASASHI KISHIMOTO/SHUEISHA Inc.
VIZ media™

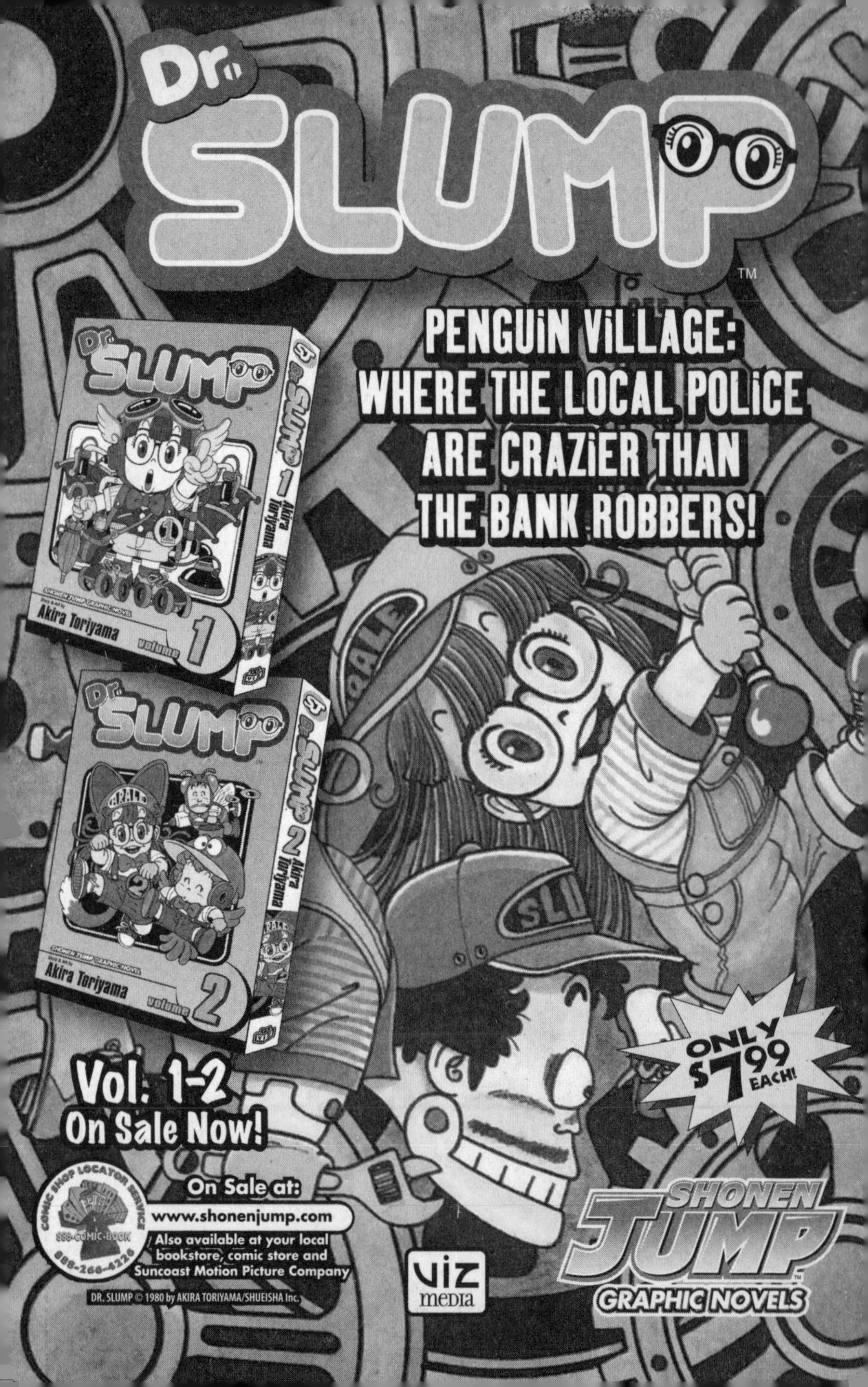

Dr. SLUMP™
PENGUIN VILLAGE:
WHERE THE LOCAL POLICE
ARE CRAZIER THAN
THE BANK ROBBERS!
Dr. SLUMP
Akira Toriyama
volume 1
Dr. SLUMP
Akira Toriyama
volume 2
ONLY $7.99 EACH!
Vol. 1-2
On Sale Now!
On Sale at:
www.shonenjump.com
Also available at your local bookstore, comic store and Suncoast Motion Picture Company
COMIC SHOP LOCATOR SERVICE
888-COMIC-BOOK
888-266-4226
DR. SLUMP © 1980 by AKIRA TORIYAMA/SHUEISHA Inc.
viz media
SHONEN JUMP
GRAPHIC NOVELS

SHONEN JUMP
THE WORLD'S MOST POPULAR MANGA

COMPLETE OUR SURVEY AND LET US KNOW WHAT YOU THINK!

☐ Please do NOT send me information about VIZ and SHONEN JUMP products, news and events, special offers, or other information.

☐ Please do NOT send me information from VIZ's trusted business partners.

Name: ______________________________

Address: ______________________________

City: ________________ **State:** ________ **Zip:** ____________

E-mail: ______________________________

☐ **Male** ☐ **Female** **Date of Birth (mm/dd/yyyy):** ___/___/_____ (**Under 13? Parental consent required**)

1 Do you purchase SHONEN JUMP Magazine?

☐ Yes ☐ No **(if no, skip the next two questions)**

If **YES**, do you subscribe?

☐ Yes ☐ No

If **NO**, how often do you purchase SHONEN JUMP Magazine?

☐ 1-3 issues a year

☐ 4-6 issues a year

☐ more than 7 issues a year

2 Which SHONEN JUMP Graphic Novel did you purchase? (please check one)

☐ Beet the Vandel Buster ☐ Bleach ☐ Dragon Ball

☐ Dragon Ball Z ☐ Dr. Slump ☐ Eyeshield 21

☐ Hikaru no Go ☐ Hunter x Hunter ☐ I"s

☐ Knights of the Zodiac ☐ Legendz ☐ Naruto

☐ One Piece ☐ Rurouni Kenshin ☐ Shaman King

☐ The Prince of Tennis ☐ Ultimate Muscle ☐ Whistle!

☐ Yu-Gi-Oh! ☐ Yu-Gi-Oh!: Duelist ☐ YuYu Hakusho

☐ Other ______________________________

Will you purchase subsequent volumes?

☐ Yes ☐ No

3 How did you learn about this title? (check all that apply)

☐ Favorite title ☐ Advertisement ☐ Article

☐ Gift ☐ Read excerpt in SHONEN JUMP Magazine

☐ Recommendation ☐ Special offer ☐ Through TV animation

☐ Website ☐ Other ______________________________

4 Of the titles that are serialized in SHONEN JUMP Magazine, have you purchased the Graphic Novels?

☐ Yes ☐ No

If **YES**, which ones have you purchased? (check all that apply)

☐ Dragon Ball Z ☐ Hikaru no Go ☐ Naruto ☐ One Piece
☐ Shaman King ☐ Yu-Gi-Oh! ☐ YuYu Hakusho

If **YES**, what were your reasons for purchasing? (please pick up to 3)

☐ A favorite title ☐ A favorite creator/artist ☐ I want to read it in one go
☐ I want to read it over and over again ☐ There are extras that aren't in the magazine
☐ The quality of printing is better than the magazine ☐ Recommendation
☐ Special offer ☐ Other

If **NO**, why did/would you not purchase it?

☐ I'm happy just reading it in the magazine ☐ It's not worth buying the graphic novel
☐ All the manga pages are in black and white unlike the magazine
☐ There are other graphic novels that I prefer ☐ There are too many to collect for each title
☐ It's too small ☐ Other ____________________

5 Of the titles NOT serialized in the Magazine, which ones have you purchased?
(check all that apply)

☐ Beet the Vandel Buster ☐ Bleach ☐ Dragon Ball ☐ Dr. Slump
☐ Eyeshield 21 ☐ Hunter x Hunter ☐ I"s ☐ Knights of the Zodiac
☐ Legendz ☐ The Prince of Tennis ☐ Rurouni Kenshin ☐ Whistle!
☐ Yu-Gi-Oh!: Duelist ☐ None ☐ Other ____________________

If you did purchase any of the above, what were your reasons for purchase?

☐ A favorite title ☐ A favorite creator/artist
☐ Read a preview in SHONEN JUMP Magazine and wanted to read the rest of the story
☐ Recommendation ☐ Other

Will you purchase subsequent volumes?

☐ Yes ☐ No

6 What race/ethnicity do you consider yourself? (please check one)

☐ Asian/Pacific Islander ☐ Black/African American ☐ Hispanic/Latino
☐ Native American/Alaskan Native ☐ White/Caucasian ☐ Other

THANK YOU! Please send the completed form to: VIZ Survey
42 Catharine St.
Poughkeepsie, NY 12601

All information provided will be used for internal purposes only. We promise not to sell or otherwise divulge your information.